1,001
PERFECTLY
LEGAL WAYS

to Get Exactly
What You Want,
When You Want It,

EVERY TIME

1,001 PERFECTLY LEGAL WAYS

to Get Exactly

What You Want,

When You Want It,

EVERY TIME

BY THE EDITORS OF FC&A

FC&A Publishing
103 Clover Green
Peachtree City, GA 30269

Publisher: FC&A Publishing
Editors: Linda M. Sciullo
Production: Carol L. Parrott
Printed and bound by Banta Company

Second printing January 1994

ISBN 0-915099-53-5

FC&A Editorial Staff ——————————————

Editor
Linda M. Sciullo

Layout and Production Editor
Carol L. Parrott

Assistant Editors
Sherryl M. Wade
Cindy B. Eckhart

Principal Writer
Sherryl D. Wade

Contributing Writers

Sallie Satterthwaite
Chris Morris
Viki Brigham
Laura B. Moore
Cindy B. Eckhart
Madeline H. Barrow
Julie Estes

Cherry Powell
Peggy Scribner
Cal Beverly
Jennifer LaBrecque
Janet Halbert
David Houghton

Pleasant words are like a honeycomb, sweetness
to the soul and health to the body.

— Proverbs 16:24

For I will restore health to you, and your wounds
I will heal, says the Lord ...

— Jeremiah 30:17a

Contents

Buying and selling your home...60

You and your car 66

Security and safer living 423

Introduction

Congratulations! You made a great investment in the game of life when you bought this book. You put some money in your pocket, some time in your life and some sanity in your home.

You've given yourself an edge up on your co-workers, on car salesmen, insurance agents, even burglars, and you're privy to the latest health secrets, consumer concerns, tax strategies, pet pointers, travel tips, automotive advice and career-climbing clues. Are we crazy to have put all this information together in one book? Are you crazy to have bought it?

Wouldn't it have made much more sense to have written one book on How To Look Your Best — All You Ever Needed To Know About Which Ties You Should Never Wear, How To Dress Like A Millionaire When You're Not, And How To Get Perspiration Stains Out Of Your Shirts?

Then we could have written a totally separate book on The Complete Guide To Everyday Money Management — How To Keep Your Hospital Bills From Making You Sick, Phone Bills: How To Stay In Touch With Your Friends And Your Wallet, When You Should Never Prepay Your Loan, And How To Invest Profitably In A Mutual Fund.

With all the subjects we cover, we could have published an entire series!

You know that we aren't entirely off our rockers, don't you? You can go to your local library and find shelves and shelves of books filled with legal, financial and personal advice.

But who has time to read them all!?

If there's one thing that any person with a family or a career has in common — it's that TIME is in short supply. You don't have time to read a book on every secret this book holds, from how to finance your child's college years, to how to get a date when you're single, how to buy the best vacuum cleaner or how to be the life of a party.

You need the vital information in one concise, easy-to-read, up-to-date source, and that's what *1,001 Perfectly Legal Ways to Get Exactly What You Want, When You Want It, Every Time* can be for you.

In order to save your valuable time, we've searched through the latest business magazines and newspapers, through the top medical journals, and through those library shelves of financial, self-help, home-handy and career books. We've compiled what we believe to be the best of the useful "how-to" information, and we've left out stuff that isn't specifically designed to help you get ahead.

We're especially interested in helping you win the Money Game. Some chapters are obviously designed to help you make the most of your money — such as "The wise consumer," "Investment strategies," "Money management" and "Tax strategies."

But check out these other sections for more money-saving tips — "Buying and selling a car," "Buying and selling your home," "College strategies," "Credit card concerns," "Estate planning," "Insurance secrets," "Retirement planning" and "Travel smart." A chapter like "Career ladder" will move you up the money ladder, too.

As important as money and jobs are, we realize that people with careers have lives outside of work, too. That's why we included chapters on marriage and family life, social life, pets, recreation and sports, health and food.

These life-after-work chapters should help you have a better relationship with your spouse, keep your kids quiet in church, deal with temper tantrums, help your children with homework, find the best nursing home for your parents, get your cat out of a tree, keep your pet off your furniture, play a mean game of golf, train for a road race, get a date for Saturday night and be a welcome guest at a party.

We just want to help you be a winner — the one who yells Bingo! in the game of chance and Checkmate! on the chessboard of life.

In all seriousness, this book can help you get ahead, because things don't really happen by chance and because life isn't really a game, is it?

Good luck and God bless!
The editors of FC&A Publishing

The wise consumer

Three places to get a great deal on just about anything

Consignment Boutiques. Did you hate hand-me-downs when you were a kid? Then you probably won't like consignment boutiques. If you used to be grateful for what you got, then you'll probably be able to find great bargains on slightly used clothing in a consignment shop.

People bring clothes to these shops that they have outgrown or just no longer wear, and the shop owner gives them a percentage of the profits when the clothes are sold.

Unlike large department stores, these boutiques display clothes that are, for the most part, suitable for the current season only. The clothes are clean, and you won't have to worry about them shrinking or fading, because they have already been washed and dried or dry-cleaned many times before.

Clothes are usually sorted by size, and sometimes by style, so it's very easy for you to look through them and quickly determine if there is anything there for you.

Consignment boutiques are great for special occasions that require you to dress in a way that is not the norm for you. You can find perfectly good clothes at great prices for weddings (you may even find the perfect wedding gown), job interviews, business meetings and travel (both casual and professional).

You can also often find unique jewelry items, purses, shoes and other accessories that you might not ordinarily purchase for yourself. And it's a lot more fun to buy those seldom-worn items when they don't cost you so much.

Owners of consignment shops will sometimes even lower prices further if you ask them to, particularly if the season is near the end. They would rather make a small profit than pack things up and return them to the original owners.

Thrift Stores. You can find a little bit of everything in a thrift store. Items are donated by businesses and individuals, usually through the local Goodwill or Salvation Army, but sometimes directly to the thrift stores.

In a thrift store you can find:

- Clothes for every gender, size and fashion preference. Many will be designer-name brands. Some of the clothes have never even been worn. They still have the original price tags on them.

- Shoes and socks (from dressy to athletic).

- Handbags, wallets, belts, scarves and jewelry.

- Curtains, bedspreads and rugs.

- Pots and pans, dishes, flatware and pressure cookers.

- Irons and ironing boards.

- Televisions and radios.

- Bicycles and exercise equipment.

- Furniture and household appliances.

The treasures to be found at thrift stores are clean and basically in good condition. Some things may need minor repairs, such as a handle on a dresser drawer, a button on a jacket or an off/on switch for a television.

Thrift stores can be a wonderful place to shop if you are:

- Losing weight and need inexpensive clothing as your weight and size are changing.

- Setting up housekeeping for the first time and can't afford new furnishings.

- Having a difficult time buying new clothes for your children's ever-changing sizes. (Some of the children's clothing will be in like-new condition while some may show some signs of wear, but they are still perfect for after-school playtime.)

- Need clothes but don't want to pay high prices.

- Just in the mood to browse and see what you will find!

Garage Sales, Yard Sales and Moving Sales. Watch your local newspapers for these sales and find some terrific bargains. If you miss the newspaper advertisement, you may see several signs at street corners as you drive around doing your weekend chores. But you'd better arrive early, or you'll miss out on the choicest items.

People sell just about everything imaginable when they decide to have a garage sale, especially if they are also planning to move and don't want to take many things with them.

Some garage sales are sponsored by churches, schools and businesses for fund-raising projects.

Most, however, involve one or more families or neighbors who just want to get rid of various belongings, such as:

- Furniture that they will be replacing.
- Appliances.
- Baby clothes and children's clothes.
- Great indoor plants (usually only if someone is moving).
- Household items.
- Lawn mowers and gardening equipment.
- Boats, tents and camping equipment.
- Bicycles, skates and exercise equipment.
- Books, cassette tapes and tape recorders.
- Typewriters.

REFERENCES

Better Homes and Gardens, August 1992.
Changing Times, February 1989.

Shopping tips

If you're not paying attention, saving money on your day-to-day shopping can be a difficult task. Impulse purchases and poor timing can cost you literally hundreds, sometimes thousands, of dollars.

Keeping a level head is the key to keeping a healthy bank account. Think before you buy.

For instance, service contracts on certain products are sometimes unnecessary thanks to that product's warranty. Before committing yourself, find out what repairs are covered.

Off-season shopping is usually the best way to keep your finances in line. Buy your shorts and T-shirts in the dead of winter. Those cold days are also the best time to get your air conditioner fixed, serviced or replaced. If you've got a travel urge, many resorts offer off-season rates.

Buy new car batteries and snow tires in the summer. Need some firewood? July's the best time to buy.

And don't forget those discount stores. Most cities have some sort of outlet for just about every need, including clothing, household goods and groceries. If you play your cards right, you may never have to pay full price again.

REFERENCE

Hints, Tips and Everyday Wisdom edited by Carol Hupping, Cheryl Winters Tetreau and Roger B. Yepsen, Jr., Rodale Press, Emmaus, Pa., 1985.

How to order from mail-order wholesalers

Is it true that you can save 80 percent on carpet, blinds and wallpaper if you order through a mail-order wholesaler? All those ads say you can.

Well, most of the home-decorating mail-order companies aren't including the cost of shipping or installation when they advertise their low prices. But, you can save around 50 percent through mail order firms.

To make sure you don't get burned when ordering sight unseen:

○ Visit local home-decorating stores to check prices. A local store running a good sale may beat the mail-order prices.

○ Many mail-order houses won't send you catalogs or samples. At local stores, find the manufacturer, style and color of the product you want. When you call the mail-order firm, be exact about what you want and how much you need.

○ Only use mail-order firms that accept credit cards, have been in business for five years or more, and guarantee replacement of defective products or a full refund if you're dissatisfied. You usually can't return custom-made blinds unless they are defective, and many companies charge a 10- to 25-percent restocking fee if you return carpet or wallpaper that's not defective.

Prudence McCullough, editor of *The Wholesale-by-Mail Catalog*, recommends some of her favorite mail-order firms:

For carpeting:

Bearden Bros. Carpet & Textiles 800-433-0074

Johnson's Carpets 800-235-1079

For blinds and wallpaper:

Custom Windows & Walls 800-772-1947

American Discount Wall and Window Coverings 800-777-2737

REFERENCE ————————————————————————
Money, January 1993.

How to avoid getting eaten by grocery bills

Keeping a handle on your food costs can be one of the most difficult household tasks.

Family needs and personal cravings can collide, creating weekly bills that run nearly as high as a car payment. Thinking ahead and spending a few extra moments when you're shopping can save you a bundle of money.

○ Plan menus for at least a week in advance.

○ Shop in the middle of the week when the stores are less crowded.

○ Consider the various needs of your family members.

○ Don't buy too much. Purchase only what you need and can conveniently store (leftovers usually get thrown out).

○ Remember, individually packaged goods (such as cereal) cost more than bigger boxes.

○ When an item is on sale, check to see how much the store has lowered the price. Is it really a good deal? Is the sale on the regular size or only on "large" quantities that might be more than you can use? And do you have to meet any qualifications (such as spending a minimum amount) before the sale price applies?

○ Read labels. Remember, the first item listed is the most plentiful. Check to see how much chicken is actually in that chicken noodle soup.

○ Shop the ads. Be willing to drive an extra mile or two if it will save you money. And be willing to shop at more than one store.

○ Never shop when you're hungry. Chances are, you'll wind up with a few more items than you intended to buy.

○ Check your receipt before leaving. Cashiers are human and occasionally make mistakes.

REFERENCE
The Better Business Bureau Guide to Wise Buying, The Benjamin Co., New York, 1980.

Resisting the 'impulse buy' in the grocery store

Why is it so hard to find what you want in a grocery store? Because store planners want you to search down every aisle for the item you need. That way you'll be tempted to buy things that aren't on your list.

These are the same people who moved bakeries to the front of the store so the luscious odor hits you as soon as you walk in the door. Resist temptation! Make a grocery list and stick to it!

REFERENCE
Great American Food Almanac, Harper & Row, Publishers, 1986.

Paper or plastic?

The best answer to the grocery check-out clerk's eternal question, "Paper or plastic?" is: "Neither, I brought my own."

When the brown paper grocery bags are manufactured, a great deal more pollution results than when plastic bags are made. Paper also takes up about seven times as much room in a landfill as plastic.

Paper bags are not biodegradable or recyclable, except by reuse.

So plastic is better? No.

Plastic bags are made of nonrenewable fossil resources, and they are not biodegradable. When dumped at sea, they foul beaches or choke marine life. Carelessly disposed of on land, they blow around and create highly visible litter.

They can be reused or made into more plastic bags, but only in a few locations.

So be kind to the earth and bring your own reusable bag to the grocery store.

REFERENCE
The Fayette Sun, Feb. 14, 1991.

Saving money on drugs

○ Buy generic prescription drugs when possible. Ask your doctor or pharmacist if the generic drug is available, safe and effective. Generics are almost always cheaper than brand-name drugs.

○ When you need over-the-counter drugs, buy store-brands if possible. Some pharmacies and grocery store chains buy over-the-counter drugs in bulk and put their name on it. Read the label, and you may find that the brand-name item and the store-brand item are identical.

○ Purchase single-ingredient over-the-counter drugs instead of combination drugs. Buy a decongestant and an antihistamine separately rather than a cold medication that contains both. It's cheaper, and sometimes you only need one rather than both.

○ Ask your doctor if there is an over-the-counter drug that could work as well as the prescription drug. Occasionally, an over-the-counter drug treats the same symptoms as a prescription drug does.

REFERENCE ───────────────────────────────────
Getting the Most for Your Medical Dollar by Charles B. Inlander and Karla Morales, The People's Medical Society, Pantheon Books, New York, 1991.

How to dress your children on a budget

Children go through new clothes at about the same speed a hot knife will go through butter. Keeping up with growth spurts and roughhousing can put a strain on any parent's pocketbook.

Here are some ways to help cut your expenses:

○ Avoid plastic pants with snaps. They rip off too easily.

○ Buy "neutral" clothing that can be passed on to children of different sexes.

○ Purchase this "neutral" clothing in the boys' department. It's usually more sturdy and less expensive than what you would find in the girls' departments.

○ Buy top quality when shopping for everyday apparel (like underwear) and items that will be passed along.

○ If you're unsure whether a pair of socks will fit, have the child make a fist. Wrap one of the socks around the fist over the knuckles. If the heel and toe don't meet, get another pair.

○ Tube socks are a wise buy. They wear evenly, are easy to put on and "grow" with kids.

○ Buy shoes with laces or Velcro closings. Slip-ons tend to slip off.

○ When buying pajamas, get the two-piece grow-a-size type.

○ Bright T-shirts, especially those with iron-on transfers or embroidery, make wonderful nightgowns.

○ Buy smock-type dresses for girls. Once they're too short, they can be worn as tops over pants.

○ While one-piece snowsuits are easier to put on, two-piece suits can be worn longer.

REFERENCE

Practical Parenting Tips by Vicki Lansky, Meadowbrook Press, New York, 1992.

When clothes go on sale

Storewide clearance! 50-percent off! Columbus Day sale!

Signs like these are beacons for bargain shoppers who'll only buy clothes on sale. Bargain shoppers are usually sharp dressers who get more for their money.

To follow in their footsteps, you need to know when clothes go on sale. Across the United States, stores mark down their stock on a monthly schedule you can predict. Here are the months with their regular sales:

○ January — after-Christmas clearances and preinventory sales, costume jewelry, furs, lingerie, pocket books, shoes

○ February — men's wear, sports clothes and equipment

○ March — children's shoes, baby clothes, ice skates, ski equipment, luggage

○ April — fabrics, hosiery, lingerie, women's shoes

○ May — Mother's Day specials, handbags, housecoats, jewelry, luggage, shoes, sportswear

○ June — Father's Day specials, fabrics, lingerie, sleepwear, hosiery, men's clothing, women's shoes

○ July — bathing suits, children's clothing, handbags, lingerie, sleepwear, luggage, men's shirts, men's shoes, sportswear, summer clothes

○ August — back-to-school specials, bathing suits, cosmetics, furs, men's coats, women's coats

○ September — fabrics, fall fashions

○ October — fall and winter clothing, storewide clearances, lingerie, hosiery, women's coats

○ November — boys' suits and coats, lingerie, men's suits and coats, shoes, winter clothing

○ December — children's clothes, coats, hats, resort and cruise wear, shoes

REFERENCE ————————————————————————————————————
Heloise's Beauty Book, Avon Books, New York, 1985.

Saving money on shoes

Do you buy shoes, wear them until they are embarrassing, then buy a new pair?

If your answer is yes, you can change your wearing habits and give yourself a free pair of shoes.

Shoes last much longer if they get a day's rest between wearings. They need time to air and dry. Buy three pairs of shoes and alternate wearing them, and they will last as long as four pairs when each pair is worn every day. Wearing one pair until they wear out is false economy.

Be careful when economizing on children's shoes. Children shouldn't wear hand-me-down shoes or shoes that are too small. The bones in the feet aren't fully formed until age 20, so the wrong shoes, and even tight socks, can deform a child's feet. Hand-me-downs have already shaped to the first wearer's feet.

REFERENCE ————————————————————————————————————
Consumer Survival Kit adapted by John Dorfman from the television series by Maryland Center for Public Broadcasting, 1975.

Choosing (and keeping) the best cookware

The only hard and fast rule about choosing cookware is that there is no hard and fast rule. The type of cooking you do, the size of your family, your own physical strength and your personal preferences must all be considered.

Here's a list of basic range-top cookware sufficient for a family of two or three:

- ○ Saucepans: at least two, a 2-quart and a 3-quart. Get sturdy, stainless steel with copper or aluminum embedded in the bottom. They should have lids and comfortable plastic handles long enough to support the weight of the pan with one hand.
  (Plastic or wooden handles will stay cooler than metal, but the trade-off is that they should not be placed in a hot oven or dishwasher.) Optional: a nonstick saucepan for cooking oatmeal or sticky sauces that are hard to clean.

- ○ Frying pans: a 10-inch stainless steel skillet that heats evenly, and a 7- to 10-inch omelet or sauté pan with a nonstick coating. The steep sides of the larger skillet hold more and are good for frying or cooking food in liquid. The sloped sides of the omelet pan make it easier to use a spatula.

- ○ Dutch oven: used for baking, braising and for browning meat on top of the stove before placing it in the oven to bake. It should be made of stainless steel or cast iron to hold heat and have metal handles.

- ○ Stockpot: designed to cook food in water by convection. Usually have a relatively narrow bottom, high sides and a lid. Except for being sure it has a thick enough bottom to resist dents, the material is not important.

- ○ Lids: If at all possible, get a lid to go with each pan you buy. Lids are hard to buy separately if you pass them up initially.

A double boiler for delicate sauces or steaming vegetables; a cast-iron skillet for pan broiling; and a large, inexpensive pot to boil pasta or corn-on-the-cob are very useful additions to your cookware.

Following a few simple rules will extend the life and good looks of your cooking utensils:

- ○ Match pan size with burner, and use the lowest possible heat for the food you are cooking.

○ Avoid subjecting pans to sudden extremes of temperature — Don't plunge an overheated pan into cold water or place a pan straight from the freezer onto a hot burner. Such shocks can crack porcelain and warp metal.

○ Besides marring a pan's appearance, scratches will make it difficult to clean. Don't chop or slice in a pan, and use plastic or wooden utensils on nonstick surfaces.

○ Remove from heat and soak pans as soon as they are emptied. By the time dinner is over, most will be easy to clean. Don't use abrasive cleaners on stainless steel.

○ Dishwashers are okay for stainless steel, but their shiny finish will become streaked and dull. Wood and some plastic handles may eventually split when washed repeatedly in a dishwasher.

○ Dry cast iron thoroughly, perhaps over a low heat, and rub a bit of oil into the surface with a paper towel to prevent rust during storage.

REFERENCE

1,001 Helpful Tips, Facts & Hints from Consumer Reports by the editors of *Consumer Reports Books* with Monte Florman, Consumers Union, Mount Vernon, N.Y., 1989.

Choosing the best laundry detergent

Do nonchlorine bleaches really whiten as well as chlorine bleach? No — but they come close if you double the amount the directions recommend.

Not all fabrics or colors can tolerate chlorine bleach, so stick with the all-fabric, powdered, nonchlorine variety for most of your wash. They are more expensive than chlorine bleach, but safer.

There isn't much difference in the cleaning ability of laundry detergents these days.

Those with enzymes are becoming more popular as phosphates are phased out and people use cold water to conserve energy. The best combination of temperatures is warm for washing, cool for rinsing. Except for serious grease, hot water won't do any better than warm, and cold will rinse anything.

A half cup or so of washing soda helps make any detergent more effective. In fact, you can decrease the amount of detergent you use by about a third when you add washing soda.

Add a half cup of vinegar to the rinse water to cut detergent and produce a soft, clean-smelling wash.

REFERENCE ————————————————————————————————————
1,001 Helpful Tips, Facts & Hints from Consumer Reports by the editors of *Consumer Reports Books* with Monte Florman, Consumers Union, Mount Vernon, N.Y., 1989.

How long should your appliances last?

Even toasters and washing machines must die. But for how long should you expect your appliance to perform adequately? If the object breaks down after the following number of years, it's usually best to go ahead, bite the bullet and purchase a new one.

Appliance	Years
Clothes dryer	14
Freezer	15
Range, electric and gas	16
Refrigerator	16
Sewing machine	24
Television, black and white	11
Television, color	7 or 8
Toaster, manual	10
Toaster, automatic	7
Vacuum cleaner, tank	15
Vacuum cleaner, upright	18
Washing machine	11

REFERENCE ————————————————————————————————————
Helpful Hints for Hard Times by Hap Hatton and Laura Torbet, Facts on File Publications, New York, 1983.

Save money and avoid
rip-offs when buying furniture

Decorating a home can be an enjoyable experience. Unfortunately, it's often an expensive one as well.

While you might be able to get a good deal on that old Naugahyde recliner with the spring sticking out of the back, it probably isn't quite what you're looking for. Good, affordable furniture is out there. You've simply got to know the right places to look.

Used or refurbished furniture can be an affordable and attractive alternative for home buyers. You might have to haul it home yourself, and it might not be showroom quality, but the tables and sofas you find at used-furniture shops are sturdy and anything but an eyesore.

But, keep your guard up. While most of these stores are reputable, there's always someone looking to make a quick buck at your expense.

Don't judge quality by price. Read the labels, instead. (You know, the ones that say "Do Not Remove Under Penalty of Law.") If the foam in the material is shredded, flaked or ground, it must be identified as such. You want to look for the words "shredded urethane foam."

Also, wooden furniture should be clearly labeled. If you see a label that only says "walnut color," you're not getting true walnut wood.

Test the furniture yourself. Does it stand properly? Are the joints strong? (If they're simply nailed or glued, then the answer is probably no.) Do the drawers move freely?

If you're buying a couch, is it comfortable? Bounce on it and make note of whether the fabric shifts easily. Check under the cushions, too. Make sure the supporting platform is covered with a tightly woven fabric.

Always bring a ruler or tape measurer with you when shopping for furniture. The most common consumer mistake is buying something, only to find that it won't fit where it was supposed to go.

Also, before you choose a color, take a swatch home with you and compare it to the rest of the room. The light in your house is different from that in the furniture store.

REFERENCES ———————————————————————

Atlanta Business Chronicle, April 9, 1992.

The Better Business Bureau Guide to Wise Buying, The Benjamin Co., New York, 1980.

Buying the best lawn mower

Just because a lawn mower is called a Bolens doesn't mean that Bolens manufactured the whole machine. Most of the parts of the leading lawnmowers like Snapper, John Deere and Bolens are made in foreign countries by the same factories.

If you look inside these mowers, it's almost impossible for the average person to know which is which. So how do you know when you're getting a good machine for your money?

Pay attention to the motor. The brand of the motor is not very important: Briggs-Stratton, Kohler or Tecumseh are common motors used in various lawn mowers. A long-lasting motor will be cast iron or have a cast-iron piston sleeve. If it is not cast-iron, it will be cheaper, but it won't last as long.

The motor should say I/C 11 HP or I/C 8 HP. I/C (or industrial/commercial) means primarily that the motor has cast iron in the engine block where necessary for long life.

If you have to economize, cut down on accessories or convenient designs.

Top reasons for mower breakdowns according to a survey of motor repairmen:

1) Not adding motor oil when necessary. Check your oil regularly, as specified in your owner's manual.

2) Not cleaning the air filter regularly. See owner's manual for instructions.

3) Striking rocks and other objects with the blade.

4) Overheating, caused by clogged cooling fins. Clean the dirt out of the fins on the motor block every spring. Run a wire through every groove between the fins to push out the dirt. Then blow the remaining dirt away with an air compressor or by simple lung power.

REFERENCE
The Low-Maintenance House by Gene Logsdon, Rodale Press, Emmaus, Pa., 1987.

The dirt on vacuum cleaners

Don't be sucked into buying a vacuum cleaner that costs as much as a used car. Vacuum-cleaner salesmen have convinced many people to buy the $1,600 Kirby.

For that price, you could buy 16 Eureka (The Boss Plus model) vacuum cleaners. And guess which one will lift more dirt out of your carpet? The Eureka!

The Kirby is a good vacuum cleaner, but why spend more than $1,000 when $200 or less will buy a vacuum cleaner that performs excellently. Sears, Panasonic, Royal and Hoover also have low-priced models that perform well.

These low-priced cleaners, such as the Panasonic MC-6250, the Eureka Powerline Gold, and the Sears Kenmore 22551 all have excellent suction, are good at deep cleaning and have other conveniences. The Panasonic is lightweight and quiet, too.

The Kenmore, a canister-type vacuum cleaner, has a wide carpet brush, a push-button cord, a handle switch and a height adjustment. The canister variety is more cumbersome than the upright. They are designed to do things uprights can't do well, such as clean upholstery, stairs and around furniture.

You can buy compact canisters that are less cumbersome, but they don't clean very well.

Since vacuuming can be a hazard for people with allergies, a vacuum cleaner that filters dust particles, such as the Nilfisk GS 90, might be helpful. This vacuum cleaner even cleans the air while you vacuum.

REFERENCE ————————————————————————
Consumer Reports, February 1993.

Easy-to-use remote controls

Since we spend hours in front of the TV with remote control in hand, a poorly designed remote can waste us several minutes a day, not to mention the energy we waste in frustration. If you want to purchase a remote that's easy to use, avoid these common flaws:

○ Rows and rows of tiny buttons all shaped the same.

○ Impossible-to-read beige letters on a gray background.

○ Software that makes you punch several buttons or choose from a series of menus to carry out a simple command.

○ Unbalanced and uncomfortable-to-hold remotes.

REFERENCE ——————————————————————
Consumer Reports, March 1993.

Making batteries last longer

Store your batteries in the refrigerator?

Sounds strange, but the cold keeps them fresh, right along with your milk and carrots.

Next time your hardware or grocery store promotes one of those "special buys" on batteries, go ahead and stock up. Stored in a plastic bag (to keep out moisture) in an out-of-the-way corner of the fridge — but not the freezer — batteries will be available when you need them.

However, batteries should be at room temperature before you use them. And if you are using equipment that requires batteries outdoors in freezing weather, keep them in a warm pocket until needed.

How do you know batteries are fresh when you buy them? Buy them from a store that has a high turnover, like a toy store. Pick from the center of the stack — old batteries may have been left at the bottom or recycled to the top for quicker sale.

Take batteries out of equipment you don't use often and store them until you need them. Avoid combining old batteries with new, a practice that can stress the old ones and cause them to leak acid.

REFERENCE ——————————————————————
Reader's Digest Practical Problem Solver, The Reader's Digest Association Inc., Pleasantville, N.Y., 1991.

Prevent a chain saw massacre

It's tempting to buy or rent a chain saw that is too small on the theory that you are less likely to get hurt using it. While caution and a careful reading of safety instructions are your first line of defense against injury, you can also protect yourself by choosing the right chain saw for the job.

○ Avoid gimmicks like self-starters, self-chokes and self-sharpeners. They are just more gadgets to break.

○ The most important piece of safety equipment on a chain saw is a chain brake. You can't help your instinctive reaction to reach forward to break your fall if you slip. But a well-designed guard located just in front of the handle on the body of the saw responds to such motion and activates the brake, stopping chain rotation almost instantly.

REFERENCE ————————————————————————————————
Home Sense by Mike McClintock, Charles Scribner's Sons, New York, 1986.

Saving money on a new computer

It's getting so that not owning a personal computer is almost a social taboo. The technological age is upon us, and if you're not part of it, you're a relic.

Computers aren't exactly cheap. But if you know what you want, you can save yourself hundreds of dollars and still get a top-quality machine.

Most stores offer extended warranties and customer support. Realize, however, that you're paying extra for that luxury.

If you have a fairly firm grasp on how computers work, you might want to consider an alternate purchasing method: mail order. With low overhead (thanks to no showrooms and low rent), companies that do their business out of computer magazines can save you up to 40 percent.

Greater availability is another advantage of buying through mail order. While your local computer "super store" might not carry certain hardware, you can probably find it through the mail.

But remember, mail order customers often have to set up their own machines. Advice before and after the purchase is hard to come by, and service contracts are rare. You also have to wait a bit before you get your machine — at least a day (as opposed to just a few minutes at retail stores).

College bookstores are also a good place to computer shop. In order to entice students into purchasing a system, manufacturers will often offer large discounts on campuses. There's no reason that you shouldn't take advantage of them.

Remember also that it's a buyer's market for computers. Technology is moving at such a staggering pace that what's hot today is considered outdated tomorrow. If you're willing to move a little slower than the rest of the high-tech world, you can save even more.

REFERENCE
Computer Wimp No More by John Bear and David M. Pozerycki, Ten Speed Press, Berkeley, Calif., 1992.

Compact camcorders that don't break

The repair record for all compact camcorders is poor. You should know when you buy the small camcorder that you may well have expenses beyond the purchase price. It's surprising when you consider that most people only use them about six hours a year. The camcorder brand with the worst repair record is the Minolta 8mm. The Sony 8mm needed the least repairs.

REFERENCE
Consumer Reports, March 1993.

When the price is right on cellular phones

These days, the price almost always seems right on a cellular phone. They are even offered as door prizes at office parties and as free gifts if you buy a new home or an appliance.

You've probably figured out that owning the phone comes with plenty of hidden costs. In fact, a few month's phone bills will probably be much more than the up-front price.

Before you buy a cellular phone, ask whether there is an activation fee (it can be hundreds of dollars) and how long you have to commit to service to get the phone at the lowest price (you're usually required to keep the phone and pay for service for one or two years).

Find out which phone company provides the strongest signal in your area. Make sure you buy a phone that connects to the best service.

Otherwise your calls will break up often, and you'll have to redial.

You'll get better reception if you get your car phone properly installed and choose a good antenna. Don't pay car dealers to install the phone. The price will be too high. You can find a good installer at a lower price.

Other features to look for:

○ A heavy-duty battery so you'll have adequate calling power.

○ A phone that allows hands-free operation for use in the car.

REFERENCE ————————————————
The Wall Street Journal, Nov. 14, 1991.

Is shopping ruining your Christmas?

Don't torture yourself over giving gifts at Christmas. Usually while shopping, you see many items that your brother or your aunt could use and would enjoy, but you pass them by looking for something that will light up their life. You are rarely going to find that perfect gift for everybody every year.

To improve this season's gift-swapping experience, try the following:

○ Shift your work hours to shop early in the week and early in the day.

○ Wrap each gift as you get it.

○ Openly discuss gifts with your family and ask for ideas.

○ Consider having a get-together instead of giving gifts.

○ Share one of your own cherished possessions with someone special.

○ Get old family photos reproduced and framed.

○ Contribute to a cause.

○ Go to a mall for a variety of easy gifts.

○ Do something special for someone you don't know.

REFERENCE ————————————————
National Business Association Newsletter, October 1992.

Making Christmas easier with mail order

The generation who grew up using the Sears catalog to make their Christmas wish lists mourn the passing of that great institution. But while the Sears catalog is gone, catalog shopping is stronger than ever. Why shop at home rather than going to a store where you can touch items and try on clothes?

○ It's easier, especially for men who hate trips to the mall.

○ It takes less time.

○ Mail-order companies usually have simple return policies if you aren't satisfied.

○ Catalogs offer a wide variety of unusual items for particular or "hard-to-buy-for" people on your list. If your husband's hobbies are camping and fishing, regular stores may not carry items he needs. Unless you live near an "outdoorsman's" store, your best bet may be catalog shopping.

○ Home shopping gets more attractive when you have children. Children and stores don't always mix well.

REFERENCE
American Demographics, June 1992.

Spotting counterfeit merchandise

If you live in a big city, you've probably been offered the "bargain of a lifetime" at least once. You've seen Gucci bags or Rolex watches at just a fraction of their cost in the store. Bargain? Heck no!

As any undercover police officer will tell you, the amount of fake merchandise on the market is staggering. Be it clothes, handbags or watches, there are a few easy ways to avoid throwing your money away on such items.

○ Know where you shop. Don't go to a place where you don't trust the store or the salespeople.

○ Trust your gut. Why would someone sell you a $100 item for just $15?

If the price cut is over 50 percent, an alarm should go off in your head.

○ Examine labels carefully. Fakes are often fuzzy, off color and may have misspelled words. They also are occasionally the wrong shape or in the wrong place.

○ See how firmly attached the tag is. Designers make money off their name as much as anything else. Real tags will be firmly attached. Fakes might be a bit loose.

○ Quality is important. If something looks cheap or poorly constructed, it probably is.

○ Examine the packaging. Smeared coloring and uneven wrappings (especially on records, toys, watches, etc.) usually signify a fake.

REFERENCE ─────────────────

Secrets From the Underground Shopper by Sue Goldstein, Taylor Publishing Company, Dallas, Texas, 1986.

Avoiding magazine subscription scams

If you're an avid reader of any publication, it's always best to subscribe. Your savings off the newsstand cost are usually tremendous.

Don't let devious salespeople take advantage of you. While there's no reason to automatically assume every door-to-door salesperson is out to rip you off, keep your ears open for a few key phrases that should set off alarms in your head:

○ *"Free."* This is usually followed by a contract for you to sign, which states somewhere in the small print that you will pay for the material. Never sign anything you haven't read closely.

○ *"I'm taking a survey/doing consumer research."* Salesfolk often use these lines to gain entry into your home. Ask for identification.

○ *"You can cancel anytime ..."* Can you? It has to be in the contract.

○ *"You can help me by buying ..."* Appeals to sympathy are usually successful, but they're often lies.

○ *"Only a few cents a week..."* But how often will you pay? More often than not, you pay hefty sums on a monthly basis for several years.

○ *"Save more by bulk subscriptions."* Only order what you want.

○ *"You have been selected ..."* Appeals to the ego are almost as successful as appeals for sympathy.

○ *"Your child needs this publication (these books) for school."* If so, why hasn't the teacher informed you? If the salesperson claims to be a teacher, demand identification.

○ *"This is your final offer at this special price ..."* That is, unless you don't accept, in which case we'll try again in a month or two.

REFERENCE

The Better Business Bureau Guide to Wise Buying, The Benjamin Co., New York, 1980.

Making warranties work for you

Know what the warranty provides before you buy anything.

If possible, all else being equal, choose to buy appliances, tools or electronics from a dealer who will be responsible for warranty work himself.

Most "service" policies for small appliances say, "Do not return to dealer; send directly to manufacturer." But do you really want to repackage a faulty appliance, take it to the post office, ship it to the opposite coast or even out of the country, and wait several weeks to get it back?

Sure, your warranty covers that, but the process will cost you time and aggravation.

File your warranty, manual, receipt and any stickers or tags that came with the purchase in a cabinet or drawer reserved exclusively for that purpose.

Note the date and place of purchase on the warranty and on the instruction or installation manual. (Read the manual even if you're sure you don't need to!)

REFERENCE

Chilton's Guide to Small Appliance Repair and Maintenance, Chilton Book Company, Radnor, Pa., 1986.

Getting your complaints heard (and acted upon)

Got a gripe? You're not alone. Retailers and even the court system are flooded with consumer complaints on a daily basis. If you want to be heard above the masses, it helps to be prepared.

- ○ Know that you're often facing a fight. If you feel you've been conned or ripped off, stand up for your rights. The end result is usually worth it.

- ○ Don't be selfish in your complaints. Stand up for someone else every now and then. The results might end up benefiting you as well.

- ○ Before you close on a deal, know exactly what you're getting. As the cliché goes, an ounce of prevention is worth a pound of cure. A little extra time spent examining a product before the sale can save hours, even days, trying to return it.

- ○ Keep records! Keep records! Keep records! Paperwork always backs you up and makes it a lot easier to get a refund or exchange.

- ○ Start at the bottom of the tree and work up. Take your complaint to the dealer or person who sold you the merchandise first. Then, if things aren't corrected to your satisfaction, start climbing up the chain of command.

- ○ Record your climb up that chain of command. By listing where you've been and who you've talked to, you're more likely to get what you want as you get closer to the top.

- ○ Talk to people, not nameless corporate entities. Find out the name of the person handling your complaint and use it. Recognize that you're talking to a person doing a job, not just a mindless peon.

- ○ Put your complaint in writing. In some cases, it's required, but it's always best to have paper to back your claim. You might even want to send your letter via certified mail to prove that it got where it was supposed to go.

- ○ Make your complaint stand out. Who says written complaints have to be letters? Try a telegram or overnight letter. Certified mail also raises eyebrows.

○ If your complaint requires immediate attention, try a phone call, or better yet, a personal visit.

○ Don't keep your fight quiet. Bring in a state consumer protection agency or the Better Business Bureau. Use the library to find an agency that might help you. (These agencies can also give you good advice before the sale.)

○ If the local television station's news department has a consumer reporter, give her a call. Do the same with local newspapers and radio stations.

○ Begin a consumer protection library. A well-informed consumer is a well-armed one.

○ Find specific consumer complaint agencies. The Bureau of Consumer Protection in Washington, D.C., is always a good place to start.

○ Look to industry groups for help. Peer pressure goes beyond the playground. If a company's competitors and equals take your side, you'll probably win the fight.

○ Arbitration is another good alternative if you can't get results and don't want to go to court.

○ Of course, court is also an option. You might want to take advantage of small claims court, which will save you attorney's fees.

REFERENCE ————————————————————————————
Herb Denenberg's Smart Shopper's Guide by Herb Denenberg, Chilton Book Company, Radnor, Pa., 1980.

For the homeowner

Home improvements that increase resale value

You probably won't recoup half of the money you put into home improvements when you sell your house, but you can improve your chances of getting your money back. Choose indoor, highly visible improvements. They bring better returns than outdoor or out-of-sight improvements.

Putting in central air conditioning and remodeling your kitchen and baths are always good investments. You should also get back most of the cost of new windows and more than 50 percent of the cost of skylights and closet storage systems. Fireplaces, new rooms with windows, improved insulation and roofing will bring you good returns.

If you put in a swimming pool or screened-in porch, landscape your yard or finish your basement, make sure your family enjoys the improvements because they add very little to your resale value. Swimming pools may even be a liability since many buyers don't want to care for a pool.

Most buyers would rather pay a lower price for a home with no improvements than a high price for an improved home. Your home will be particularly hard to resell if the improvements made your home similar to others in the area but more expensive. For instance, you probably won't recoup the costs of adding a third bedroom — an expensive project — when other homes in your area were built with three bedrooms.

REFERENCES

Consumer Survival Kit adapted by John Dorfman from the television series by Maryland Center for Public Broadcasting, 1975.
The Wall Street Journal, June 23, 1992.

How to decrease your taxes with home improvements

Fortunately, home improvements ranging from built-in bookcases to new plumbing pay for themselves in other ways besides resale value. You can add 100 percent of the cost of improvements to the price you paid for your home to get the "adjusted basis" of your home. The "adjusted basis" determines how much tax you will pay on the profits from the sale of your home.

Your profit from the sale of your home is the price the buyer pays for your home minus the adjusted basis. If you keep meticulous records of the cost of your home improvements, you might not even show a profit when you sell your house.

For instance, if you pay to have your lot surveyed as part of installing a fence around your house, you can add the cost of the survey to your basis. If you don't show a profit, you don't have to pay taxes.

If you plan on buying a new, more expensive house within two years of selling your old one, you don't have to pay taxes anyway. If you made $30,000 from the sale of your house, you just subtract that from the adjusted basis of your new house instead of paying taxes on it.

If your new house costs $130,000, your adjusted basis will be $100,000. In the future, if you sell this house for $150,000, the IRS will see your profit as $50,000.

You never have to worry about your profits as long as you can roll them over into new, more expensive houses. (You are only allowed to roll profits over once every two years. Most people don't trade houses like they trade cars, so this restriction shouldn't be a problem.)

Are you worried about what will happen if you need to sell your last house and move into a retirement community or nursing home? What about if you never sell your last home and your children have to sell it after you die? Will they be crushed by the taxes?

Don't worry. Homeowners get to escape tax entirely on up to $125,000 of profit. You only get to do this once so you should save the tax break for when you sell your last house. Your heirs will be able to take the tax break if they sell your home after you die.

You only get to defer your taxes when you buy a house that costs more than or the same as the house you sold. What if you move to a less expensive home?

You may be moving to a less expensive part of the country. Are you stuck with paying a big chunk of your profit on your house sale in taxes?

You can hold down your tax bill or avoid it altogether by keeping track of anything you spend on your new house. If you add on to the house, put in a swimming pool, or renovate the kitchen, you can raise the new home's "price" for rollover purposes. You have to make the improvements within two years after the sale of the first house to be able to roll over your profits.

Spending money from one pocket to save money in another may sound like bad advice. But if you can afford the improvements and you want to make them anyway, saving the money you would have spent in taxes is a welcome bonus.

Consider that a profit of $30,000 in the 28-percent tax bracket will cost you $8,400 in taxes. You can spend that money in home improvements instead of giving it to the government.

When you buy a less expensive home, another factor comes into play — home repairs. The cost of painting, caulking and generally fixing up your home so that it is more attractive to buyers is not tax deductible, no matter what your real estate agent might tell you.

Home repairs or routine maintenance cannot be added to the adjusted basis of your house, either.

However, when you buy a less expensive home and aren't able to roll your profits over, the IRS will let you subtract the cost of sprucing up your old house from the sales price of your home. The fix-up work has to be done during the 90 days before you sign a contract to sell the home.

REFERENCE
Buying & Selling A Home by the staff of *Changing Times* magazine, The Kiplinger Washington Editors Inc., Washington, D.C., 1990.

Making a hassle-free move

There may be nothing more exciting than moving into a new house, but there's little that's more aggravating than dealing with the process of moving. The right timing and a little common sense can make getting yourself and your belongings from Point A to Point B a fairly hassle-free experience.

As far as two months before the move, start planning. Take an inventory of your belongings and get rid of what you don't want to take with you. (Make use of The Salvation Army and garage sales.)

Get a change of address kit from the post office and let magazines, credit cards and close friends know your new address. Most companies take up to eight weeks to change their mailing lists, so it's best to do this early.

Start eating, too! Moving food is more effort than it's worth. Finish off what's in your pantry and shop sparingly. Also, start shopping for a mover about two months before you move. Gather estimates and start weeding out the more expensive companies and movers who don't seem professional.

With one week to go, start packing the fragile items or heirlooms you may want to handle yourself.

Depending on your arrangements with the moving company, you may want to pack out-of-season clothing and books a week ahead, too. While packing, make a list of what items are in what boxes. It will make things a lot easier at your new home.

Begin notifying your utility companies that you're moving and want your services cut off. Follow up your phone call with a letter. Make sure that the utilities in the new house or apartment will be turned on upon your arrival.

When moving day arrives, pack an emergency bag. This should include toothbrushes, toilet paper, aspirin, copies of your packing lists, a flashlight and anything else you think you might need during the move.

Getting a friend or neighbor to watch the children or pets is a good idea. It's guaranteed to cut down on headaches.

Keep a set of keys for both residences on you, and give another set to the foreman. Keep plenty of drinks around as well so you and the movers can avoid dehydration.

Read everything the foreman asks you to sign. While you might be anxious to get to your new home, you want to be certain that you arrive with all your belongings.

REFERENCE ———————————————————————————————————

Helpful Hints for Hard Times by Hap Hatton and Laura Torbet, Facts on File Publications, New York, 1983.

Best time to have a garage sale

It's no secret that cleaning out that closet or attic can bring you more money, but the timing of your garage sale might mean the difference between a few spare dollars and a moderate financial windfall.

Obviously, weekends are the best time to turn your trash into cash. And holding the sale for two days is more lucrative than one. Avoid the three-day, holiday weekends because people often plan vacations around these, cutting down on your crowd.

Late spring is the best time to hold your garage sale. After being cooped up all winter, folks will look for any reason to get out. If you can't arrange it at this time, try late summer.

Starting your sale early in the morning (about 8 a.m. or so) might enhance your take. "Professional" garage sale shoppers often will plan out a map of attack the night before from ads found in the newspaper. If you're open before the other sales, you'll get the serious shoppers before they've had a chance to spend their money.

REFERENCE

The Garage Sale Book by Jeff Groberman and Colin Yardley, Prima Publishing, Rocklin, Calif., 1987.

Painting to hide your house's flaws

Make your house look its best by choosing a color of paint that hides the bad and accents the good. Take a picture of your house and decide what you don't like about it.

Your house may be top heavy, small or short and wide.

If you want your house to look larger, paint the trim, walls and shutters a light color. If you reroof your house, put on a light-color roof.

Paint the upper story a darker shade than the lower story if your house seems tall and skinny. If you have unattractive trim, paint it the same color as the house so it will fade into the background.

Help a squat or awkward house by using a dark color on the roof and the side walls. The house will seem less chunky and short if a dark color outlines the house against the landscape.

REFERENCE

All-New Hints from Heloise: A household guide for the '90s, The Putnam Publishing Group, New York, 1989.

How to stop 'bleeding' when you paint

Crayon marks, cooking grease, asphalt stains from a leaking roof — all these can show through fresh paint, even high-quality latex or oil. The pros call this "bleeding," and cure it with pigmented white shellac (not to be confused with plain old white shellac, which is actually clear).

> - Sand down crayon marks.
> - Wash grease and hand prints with detergent and warm water.
> - Apply a coat of the quick-drying shellac.
> - Repaint.

REFERENCE
Home Sense by Mike McClintock, Charles Scribner's Sons, New York, 1986.

Paint pointers

Here's how to paint a set of stairs without losing the use of them while the paint dries: Paint every other one. You can still walk up and down on the unpainted steps. When the painted ones dry, you can use them while you finish the job.

Head off tedious scraping by keeping the paint off glass when painting window frames. Damp strips of newspaper stick to windows as well as masking tape and can be removed much more easily.

Nail polish remover will wipe away spatters, whether fresh or old and dried on. Newly dried spatters will come off by wiping with a hot vinegar solution.

Hot vinegar will also soften hard paint on brushes. Follow with warm, sudsy water.

Cooking oil or baby oil softens and removes paint from hands and face more pleasantly than harsh turpentine.

Punch a few holes through the groove that runs around the inner rim of a paint can. Paint caught in the groove every time you press excess paint out of your brush will run back into the can and not down the outside. The seal of the lid will not be affected. Those holes will also help prevent spattering when you replace the lid.

REFERENCES

The Household Book of Hints and Tips by Diane Raintree, Jonathan David Publishers Inc., Middle Village, New York, 1979.

Mary Ellen's Best of Helpful Hints by Mary Ellen Pinkham and Pearl Higginbotham, Warner Books Inc., New York, 1980.

When patching your roof will do the trick

Your roof is 20 years old and a couple of leaks have developed. Do you believe the roofer who says he can fix you up with a few new shingles and roof cement, or the one who says it's time to put on a new roof?

Here's how you can make an informed decision yourself. Look at the lifetime of your roof in four stages:

1) Tiny pieces of your roof that look like fine gravel accumulate in gutters and below downspouts.

2) Bare patches of black tar become visible as the roof sheds the tiny pieces.

3) Shingle tabs curl up and become brittle.

4) Curled shingles break off, tar patches wear and nail heads and seams are exposed.

Patching may be a good short-term solution in stages 1 and 2, but by stage 3 and certainly stage 4, the more cost-effective choice is to reroof.

REFERENCE

Home Sense by Mike McClintock, Charles Scribner's Sons, New York, 1986.

How to be your own appliance repairman

To find the problem in any appliance, an electrician will begin by testing components — switches, solenoids, timers, heating elements, thermostats, relays, power cords — with an ohmmeter.

You can buy an ohmmeter yourself for less than $10 in virtually any hardware or automotive department.

Even if you have no intention of doing your own repairs, you can pinpoint the problem and protect yourself from the unethical repairman who tries to sell you unnecessary work or parts.

Use the ohmmeter to check the broken thermostat of your refrigerator or freezer, the water-level switch on your washer, or the heating element of an electric range or a clothes dryer.

The owner's manual that comes with it gives more specific instructions, but briefly put, you simply place the ohmmeter's probes on the appliance part's wires or terminals.

That will answer three vital questions:

> - Does an unbroken circuit exist?
> - What is the resistance to the flow of current?
> - Is a short circuit making the component inoperable?

Make sure the appliance is unplugged so you'll have no danger of electric shock.

REFERENCE
"Popular Mechanics," *The Atlanta Journal/Constitution*, Sept. 18, 1992.

Keep money cooling
its heels in your refrigerator

You can add years to your refrigerator's life and subtract dollars from your energy bill if you can remember these rules.

- Vacuum the dust from the condenser coils at the bottom or the back of the refrigerator once a year.

- Wipe off moisture on bottles and other containers before putting them back in to cool.

- Don't stuff the refrigerator too full.

- Don't put things in the refrigerator that don't need cooling. You think this is obvious, but go look in your refrigerator. That unopened jelly, barbecue sauce and twelve-pack of drinks can go in the pantry.

○ Don't wash most refrigerator's plastic parts in the dishwasher. They will warp.

○ Be sure doors line up with the body of the refrigerator. Overloading deep door shelves may create this problem.

REFERENCE
The Low Maintenance House by Gene Logsdon, Rodale Press, Emmaus, Pa., 1987.

Cutting energy costs

High bills got you down? Almost half of household energy costs go for heating and cooling, but there are a lot of ways to save significantly on those expenditures.

○ Caulk and weather-strip to keep out air leaks.

○ Have an expert check your insulation. Add more if necessary.

○ Keep your heating and air-conditioning equipment well-maintained.

○ Get a clock-operated thermostat that will automatically adjust the temperature when you're not around (or awake).

○ Keep doors and windows near the thermostat closed.

○ Clean and replace filters regularly.

○ To keep things cool, consider using fans. Ceiling fans are fantastic money-savers.

○ Cook at appropriate times. In the winter, it's best to fire up the oven in the afternoon to help warm your home. During the summer, do your major cooking in the morning or late at night.

○ Keep your attic access door closed tight.

REFERENCE
How to Save Money on Just About Everything by William Roberts, Strebor Publications, Laguna Beach, Calif., 1991.

Watching your money drip away: how to save on water

Tired of taking a financial bath every time you get your water bill? There are dozens of ways to cut your costs and help your community conserve water.

○ Deep soak your lawn when you water it (a light watering will evaporate and do little good), and water only during the dry periods of the year.

○ Early morning watering will reduce evaporation. Just before sunrise is the best time.

○ Set your lawn mower blades a notch higher than usual to reduce evaporation.

○ Mulching around trees and shrubs will cut down on evaporation.

○ Watch those drips! Replace washers when needed and fix all leaking pipes and hoses.

○ Wash your car with a bucket of soapy water. Only use the hose for rinsing.

○ Don't let the kids play with the hose or sprinklers.

○ Keep a cover on your swimming pool to avoid evaporation.

○ Don't wash your driveway, sweep it.

○ While waiting for hot water, catch the cold water in a bucket and save it for cooking or watering plants.

○ Avoid unnecessary flushing. Every time you flush that cigarette butt or piece of tissue, you use up to seven gallons of water.

○ Only run the dishwasher when you have a full load. If you wash by hand, don't leave the water running.

○ Keep a bottle of cold drinking water in your refrigerator.

○ Defrost frozen food using the microwave instead of hot water.

REFERENCE ————————————
How to Save Money on Just About Everything by William Roberts, Strebor Publications, Laguna Beach, Calif., 1991.

How to cut your summer electricity bill

Does your summer electricity bill consistently rage out of control? Keep your cool! There are some simple and practical ways to hang onto that cold, hard cash.

○ Draw your shades to block out sunlight. Shade trees, awnings and overhangs can prevent heat buildup as well.

○ Clean or replace your air conditioner filter once a month to improve efficiency.

○ When cooking, cover pots on the stove to minimize steam, which adds to the humidity. Also, open windows when you take a shower to let the steam escape.

○ Remember your high school science classes? Heat rises, so open your attic and second-story windows.

○ Keep those storm windows on the house! They provide a second skin for heat to penetrate and keep temperatures down.

○ Consider installing a whole-house fan.

○ Ceiling fans can be financial lifesavers as well. A fan placed on a low ceiling moving at a mere 2 1/4 miles per hour can make 87 degree air feel like it's 77 degrees. (Higher speed fans don't necessarily mean cooler temperatures.)

REFERENCE ──────────────────────────
Hints, Tips and Everyday Wisdom edited by Carol Hupping, Cheryl Winters Tetreau and Roger B. Yespen, Jr., Rodale Press, Emmaus, Pa., 1985.

Keeping cool (or warm) for 30 percent less

By setting back the thermostat 15 degrees (say, from 68 to 53 degrees) during the eight hours a day no one is home and the eight nighttime hours, you can reduce heating expenses by 30 percent. If your fuel costs average $1,000 a year, that's a $300 savings.

At that rate, a programmable automatic thermostat would pay for itself in less than six months. Then there's the added bonus of having the house warm up before you get out of bed and before you get home in the evening — not to mention the good feeling that you are using 30 percent less Middle Eastern crude.

And if 15 degrees sounds extreme, ten degrees will still help.

REFERENCE ———————————————————————
Home Sense by Mike McClintock, Charles Scribner's Sons, New York, 1986.

Lightening up your lighting costs

To save money and electricity, buy compact fluorescent lights instead of incandescent bulbs.

The amount you pay for electricity runs from five to ten times the cost of the incandescent bulb itself over its lifetime. In the case of two bulbs for $2.50 that's $12.50 to $25 in electricity.

So you think the $12 to $18 for a compact fluorescent is too much? Consider that it will outlast the incandescent and use 90 percent less electricity, reducing pollution and saving you $25 to $40 over its lifetime.

REFERENCE ———————————————————————
The Green Consumer by John Elkington, Julia Hailes, Joel Makower, Penguin Books, New York, 1988.

Why self-cleaning ovens are a smart buy

Can a self-cleaning oven actually cost less to operate?

Yes. The extra insulation built into the walls also acts to contain heat in day-to-day use. U.S. Department of Energy standards-analysis tests show that this feature increases overall efficiency by three percent.

REFERENCE ———————————————————————
Home Sense by Mike McClintock, Charles Scribner's Sons, New York, 1986.

Checking your new home for poison

Make sure your new home won't poison you or your children! Ask about these four substances before you buy a home:

○ *UFFI* (pronounced YU-fee). Urea formaldehyde was a very popular insulation until about 1980. It has been found to cause serious respiratory disease and other medical problems when it is improperly installed. Unfortunately, the use of UFFI is not banned except in Massachusetts. UFFI removal costs more than $20,000.

○ *Asbestos.* This pipe insulator is most likely to be found in houses that are over 40 years old. When asbestos deteriorates, the particles become airborne. The particles can cause lung cancer if they are inhaled. Sometimes encasing asbestos is better than trying to remove it.

○ *Radon.* Radon is a colorless, odorless, radioactive gas that is released naturally wherever uranium is present in the soil. When radon is trapped inside a house, it can be as harmful as smoking four packs of cigarettes a day. You should demand a radon test before you purchase a home. Usually you can solve a radon problem for under $2,500.

○ *Lead Paint.* Children are the victims of lead poisoning. Any house built before 1955 may have lead paint, and a house built before 1940 is very likely to contain lead paint. The use of lead was finally banned in 1970. The removal of lead paint costs at least $6,000.

REFERENCE ————————————————————————
Bob Vila's Guide to Buying Your Dream House by Bob Vila with Carl Oglesby, Little Brown & Co., Boston, 1990.

Snappy snipping

Try using heavy-duty kitchen scissors:

○ To cut fresh-baked pizza into wedges or squares without dragging off the toppings

○ To chop fresh herbs quickly by bunching stems in one hand while snipping as finely as desired with the other

○ For boning poultry and cutting through joints

○ To trim crusts from bread for fancy sandwiches

○ To grip screw-on bottle caps (with the handles) for easy opening

REFERENCE ───
Better Homes and Gardens New Cookbook, Better Homes and Gardens Books, New York, 1974.

Where you should chop your food to keep it clean

If you've been using plastic cutting surfaces to slice your meats and veggies, you might be surprised by this piercing news.

Plastic cutting boards can actually harbor bacteria, allowing them to survive in crevices and multiply.

If you have grown accustomed to your plastic cutting boards, you're not alone. For approximately the past 20 years, sanitation officials have encouraged us to use plastic cutting boards instead of wood, believing that it was easier to remove bacteria from plastic than wood. Even the Department of Agriculture has recommended using plastic cutting boards.

But very little research was conducted to demonstrate plastic's superiority over wood. In fact, one study performed 25 years ago found that cleaning bacteria from wooden cutting boards was just as easy as cleaning bacteria from plastic boards.

Current research indicates that wooden surfaces are actually better at preventing food contamination and illness than plastic.

In a study at the University of Wisconsin, researchers contaminated both plastic and wooden cutting boards with common bacteria that cause food poisoning. In just three minutes, 99.9 percent of the bacteria on the wooden board couldn't be found and were presumed dead.

None of the bacteria placed on the plastic cutting boards died. In fact, when the boards were left overnight at room temperature, the bacteria on the plastic boards multiplied. No live bacteria were retrieved from the wooden boards.

Even if a wooden cutting board was contaminated with a million or more bacteria, it would probably only take about two hours before 99.9 percent of the bacteria disappeared, researchers say. But most of us would probably never be dealing with this many bacteria at once, considering that the number of bacteria that might wash off a chicken would only be about 1,000.

While wooden cutting boards appear to kill bacteria, they don't yield up the dead bodies but, instead, apparently absorb them.

And cleaning your wooden cutting board may be as easy as giving it a good wipe.

However, bacteria that are lodged in knife-cut grooves of plastic cutting boards can survive a hot soap-and-water wash and later contaminate other foods.

All types and ages of wood seem to be effective in fighting off the bacteria, including hard maple, birch, beech, black cherry, basswood, butternut and American black walnut.

Quite often, however, wooden cutting boards come from the factory treated with mineral oil, intended to make the wooden boards more like plastic, which unfortunately it does. Bacteria survive longer on these cutting boards than on untreated wooden cutting boards.

Researchers aren't exactly sure why or how wood works so well against bacteria. But, for now, it seems that any way you slice, dice, chop or carve it — wooden cutting boards are the easiest on your knives and your best barrier against bacteria.

REFERENCE ——————————————————————————————
Science News, Feb. 6, 1993.

14 everyday household cleaners

Before you run out and rent a steam cleaner to get rid of that wine stain on the carpet, check out your kitchen cabinet. Chances are there's something in there that can do the job almost as well.

Vinegar, hair spray, peanut butter: They're all effective, if unusual, household cleaners that could save you bundles of money on chemicals. While not all of these "home remedies" work as well as what the professionals use, they could come in handy if you don't have time to do a major cleaning before the guests arrive.

○ Denture-cleaning tablets can be used to take coffee, tea and juice stains out of teacups.

○ Hair spray, particularly the cheaper brands, will dissolve ink. Be sure to launder the material afterwards, or it will stiffen the fabric.

○ Fingernail-polish remover will dissolve more than fingernail polish. It also removes airplane glue.

○ Cola acts as a mild acid cleaner for toilet bowls and whitewall tires. However, the sugar and caramel coloring occasionally create stain problems of their own.

○ Ashes, combined with fats, form a mild soap that you can use to rub water rings off furniture.

○ Toothpaste can serve as a mild abrasive cleaner, but it can scratch, so use it sparingly.

○ Peanut butter will soften and lubricate hardened stains, like chewing gum.

○ Meat tenderizers will eat up protein stains caused by meat juices, eggs, blood and milk.

○ Salt is quite helpful in absorbing stains such as red wine or Kool-Aid if applied immediately. Brush the area and rinse the salt away when it dries.

○ Alcohol will remove many types of dye stains.

○ Lemon juice is a good mild bleach which helps remove wine and rust stains.

○ Baking soda is one of the two best household remedies. Besides neutralizing acid stains, it absorbs odors and acts as a mild bleach. When mixed with water, it forms a paste and becomes a mild abrasive cleaner.

○ White vinegar is the other champion of budget cleaners. This is the ultimate stain remover and is usually your best first choice.

○ Bars of soap are often overlooked when there's a mess around the house, but they will penetrate stains, making it easier to clean. Don't use soap on fruit stains; it will set them in.

REFERENCE

Don Aslett's Stainbuster's Bible: The Complete Guide to Spot Removal by Don Aslett, The Penguin Group, New York, 1990.

The best cleaner on the block

The super solvent that beats almost any of the products advertised as all-purpose cleaners is brush/roller cleaner. It will clean:

- Pencil and crayon marks from almost anything
- Smudges from stainless steel and chrome
- Engine oil and grease — great for engine parts and your own hands after a tune-up
- Road tar and exhaust grime from trailered vehicles
- Cooking-smoke stains and cigarette film
- "Stickum" left behind by labels or tape
- Paint overspray
- Vinyl and plastic laminate surfaces
- Paint brushes, even those that have been left to harden for years
- Surfaces being prepared for painting — use as a general wipe-down to remove all traces of fingerprints and oil

One important note: Don't confuse brush/roller cleaner with mineral spirits, acetone, paint thinner or turpentine, and don't use it on plastics or fresh paint.

As with anything used for cleaning, it is prudent to test a hidden corner before using where it shows.

REFERENCE

The Sailor's Sketchbook by Bruce Bingham, Seven Seas Press Inc., Newport, R.I., 1983.

Ways to use WD-40 you never thought of

○ Clocks, especially if they have not been kept running, refuse to go most often because small gears become clogged with a buildup of dust and dirt. Try spraying or squirting a small amount of WD-40 into clock works before resorting to expensive repair work. The solvent effect of WD-40 literally washes clock parts free. And if the problem is elsewhere, no harm has been done.

○ To prevent light bulbs from sticking in their sockets because of corrosion, squirt a little WD-40 lubricant on the bases before installing. When the bulb must be changed, even after several years, it will come out easily, preventing possible injury from breakage.

REFERENCE
WD-40 Company, San Diego, Calif.

Saving money on carpet cleaners

You may walk all over it, but don't take your carpet for granted. Ignore certain stains and smells and you'll be stuck with them for life.

There's no need to stock up on expensive chemical cleaners. You can prevent the majority of carpet problems with things you most likely already have around the house.

○ To prevent static buildup (and the resulting shock), mix one part liquid fabric softener with five parts water in a spray bottle. Lightly mist the carpet. When it dries, you won't have to worry about touching metal.

○ Pets, at some point in their lives, are bound to christen your carpet. Don't rush out to the pet store to buy a special cleaner. Vinegar will kill the odor and prevent staining, but only if you get to the spot immediately.
Mix two cups of vinegar with a gallon of cold water and rinse the area with the solution after blotting away the moisture. (If you have a dark carpet, test this mixture on an inconspicuous area first to make sure

it doesn't stain.) You might also try sprinkling cornmeal on the rug. Leave it on for two hours, then vacuum.

○ Regular vacuuming is the surest way to keep your carpets fresh. Run the vacuum at least a couple of times a week to pick up the dirt and loose particles in the rug.

○ If you decide that you absolutely must clean your carpet, pre-treat it by sweeping it first (which will make matted carpet stand up) and then vacuuming. Who knows? You may not need that cleaner after all.

Reference ————————————————————

Hints, Tips and Everyday Wisdom edited by Carol Hupping, Cheryl Winters Tetreau and Roger B. Yepsen, Jr., Rodale Press, Emmaus, Pa., 1985.

Hiring a good chimney sweep

It's a dirty job, but someone's got to do it. And you don't know how.

Their job may not be seen as glamorously as it once was, but chimney sweeps are still a necessary profession. Without proper cleaning, a chimney could be the cause of disease and devastating fires in your home.

To find the right person to clean your flue, shop around. Remember, you get what you pay for, so don't jump at the cheapest price. Ask a few questions first, and make a few mental notes.

○ Is the person you call courteous and thorough on the phone? If so, he is likely to be the same in person.

○ Ask specific questions about what the sweep does. Test his level of knowledge. (Reading a little about the process will help you judge the answers.)

○ Does the sweep guarantee no mess? If not, you might end up paying extra to get the soot out of the rugs.

○ How much insurance does the sweep carry? Good ones have a lot.

○ Ask if he has had any formal training in this profession. If so, where and what did that training consist of?

○ What sort of equipment is used? (Black Magic and August West are two of the top names in the industry.)

REFERENCE ——

Be Your Own Chimney Sweep by Christopher Curtis and Donald Post, Garden Way Publishing, Charlotte, Vt., 1979.

Unclogging a waste disposer

While kitchen garbage disposers are built to handle normal cooking and table scraps, they often balk at cooking utensils and silverware. The overload switch should turn off the unit before the motor burns itself out, but sometimes you will have to free up the flywheel yourself.

Unplug the appliance and put pressure on it with a broomstick handle, not your fingers. If that doesn't work, pull on the object causing the blockage with long-handled pliers.

Better yet, prevent such mishaps by not packing material into the drain before starting it. Let the unit self-feed.

Run cold water at maximum force just before, during and for several seconds after operating the disposer. Besides lubricating the process and flushing the pipes clean, cold water congeals grease so the machine can deal with it.

REFERENCE ——

Home Sense by Mike McClintock, Charles Scribner's Sons, New York, 1986.

Testing your water's hardness

Test your own tap water for hardness before paying for a detailed analysis by a professional. Just add ten drops of liquid detergent to a large glass about two-thirds full of tap water. Cover and shake.

High, foamy suds mean relatively soft water. A low, flat curd means relatively hard water. Compare your results with the softest possible water by performing the same test using distilled or mineral-free water.

Hard water costs more than soft water, an estimated $40 a year in soap and detergent, $60 in plumbing repairs and replacements, $25 in extra fuel, and

$30 in wear and tear on linens and clothes. Very soft water, however, tastes flat.

REFERENCE

Home Sense by Mike McClintock, Charles Scribner's Sons, New York, 1986.

Solving laundry problems

The easiest way to spot a freshman on any given college campus is to look at their socks. Chances are if they're a faded pink, you're looking at a laundry novice.

Washing machines, while designed to clean your clothes, can do more damage than good. Faded and stained clothes can be avoided if you follow this advice.

- Keep jeans (and other cotton clothes) from fading by turning them inside out while washing and drying.

- You can also prevent piling on sweaters and printed T-shirts by reversing them before washing.

- Spot-treat all your clothes immediately when you spill something on them.

- Don't mix chlorine and nonchlorine bleach.

- Check those pockets! Pens and paper can leave stains and lint.

- Close all zippers and fasteners to prevent snagging on other garments.

- Mend rips and secure loose buttons before washing. Otherwise, things could get worse, meaning more work for you in the long run.

- Never add wet clothes to a partially dry load.

- Clean those lint filters before each load.

- Always use the right cycle, water temperature, time and load level.

REFERENCE

Heloise from A to Z, Perigee Books, New York, 1992.

How to throw away
your junk and keep your memories

Take the sting out of getting rid of stuff. Even the most determined anti-packrat sometimes finds her life cluttered with accumulations of souvenirs, out-of-style clothing, books and just plain junk.

Sometimes sentiment makes it hard to part with things. Sometimes you don't want to throw away something that may still have value. And sometimes it's just easier to slam the closet door one more time.

To get to the bottom of your closets, don't try to tackle years of clutter in one cleaning marathon. Concentrate on one room at a time — the attic, the basement, the garage, and don't cheat by simply moving stuff from one room to another.

Label four cardboard boxes as follows:

○ **"Junk"** — everything broken, ugly, faded, outdated and useless goes in here. It goes out on the curb on trash pick-up day.

○ **"Charity"** — things that can be repaired and clothing that is outgrown or just plain wrong. Many charitable organizations will pick up reusable items from clothes to furniture.

○ **"Sort"** — things you use or plan to use. Keep for a month, then sort again. Priorities change.

○ **"Emotional withdrawal"** — things you just can't bear to get rid of. Keep and review again in six months. Eventually the romance will pale, and, if not, resign yourself to keeping it.

REFERENCE
"How to (Finally) Get Your House Clean and Then Keep It That Way" by Dana Jenkins, reviewed in *The Atlanta Journal/Constitution*, 1992.

Cleaning schedules that work for you

No two homes or homeowners will need exactly the same cleaning plan. Take into consideration what is important to you. If cloudy windows drive you up the wall, wash them weekly — you'll feel better for it. For someone else, once a year may be often enough. Having children or pets also generates dirt not experienced by adults who live alone.

Here is a schedule that works well, but it should be adjusted to individual preferences:

○ **Daily** — make beds, wash dishes, sweep kitchen floor, pick up main living areas, hang up clothes, put out newspapers and garbage, and do laundry as needed. Takes about 30 minutes.

○ **Weekly** — vacuum, empty trash cans, change bed linen, clean bathroom and kitchen, dust, clean mirrors, mop floors. You'll need about three hours.

○ **Three times a year** — dust baseboards, move furniture and vacuum under it, clean out drawers and cabinets, clean heating vents, wax floors, turn mattresses, wash mattress pads and blankets, wipe down kitchen appliances and cabinets, clean range hood and oven. Work these chores into your weekly schedule to avoid a two- or three-day marathon.

○ **Annually** — change shelf paper, wash woodwork, windows and walls.

REFERENCE —————————————————————————————————

"How to (Finally) Get Your House Clean and Then Keep It That Way" by Dana Jenkins, reviewed in *The Atlanta Journal/Constitution*, 1992.

Vinegar isn't just for salads

Every household cleaning arsenal should include white vinegar. Buy a large bottle of the cheapest brand and use it lavishly. Not only does it leave a bright finish, it's safe for almost every surface and is environmentally sensitive.

○ Shower heads or spigot aerators get clogged with mineral deposits. Boil for 15 minutes in a solution of white vinegar and water — one-half cup of vinegar in a quart of water, or stronger if the problem is severe. (Don't boil plastic; just soak in hot water and vinegar.)

○ Run a solution of vinegar and water through your coffee maker periodically, just as though you were brewing a pot of coffee; rinse by running clear water through it. Free of mineral deposits and coffee oils, your coffee maker will last longer, and your brew will taste better.

○ Do the same thing with your steam iron, using equal parts of water and vinegar. After steaming for a few minutes, allow iron to stand for an hour. Empty and rinse well with clear water. Remove burned-on spots from the sole of the iron by rubbing with a paste made of salt and heated vinegar.

○ Boil vinegar and water in your tea kettle to remove sediment. For extra thick deposits, add a few marbles. The action of the marbles in the boiling water will help break loose the sediment.

○ Add a few drops of vinegar to the water when poaching eggs. It will help keep the white together, and you'll never notice any flavor.

○ Vinegar and water make the best window-washing solution — for really grungy windows, make the solution as strong as necessary. It also removes soap film from shower tile and glass shower doors.

○ Old decals will come off with gentle scraping, if you soak them well with vinegar first.

○ A cup of white vinegar in the laundry rinse cycle will help dissolve alkalines left from detergent. The clothes will be soft and sweet-smelling, too.

○ Open bowls of vinegar help absorb the odor of cigarette smoke in a room.

○ Hands slick and smelly from contact with bleach? You guessed it: Just a drop of vinegar will cut the bleach instantly.

REFERENCES

Mary Ellen's Best of Helpful Hints by Mary Ellen Pinkham and Pearl Higginbotham, Warner Books Inc., New York, 1980.

The Household Book of Hints and Tips by Diane Raintree, Jonathan David Publishers Inc., Middle Village, N.Y., 1979.

How to clean without damaging

The manufacturers of "soft" cleansers want you to believe their claims that they don't scratch and are safe for fiberglass tubs. Don't believe it.

You may clean a shiny surface dozens of times with a soft cleanser before the damage shows, but abrasion is cumulative. Eventually the surface will turn cloudy and dull.

Stay with liquid cleaners, ammonia or vinegar. If you absolutely must use a cleanser, apply it to the wet cloth or sponge first and rub very lightly.

A mild bleach solution will help remove stains, but never combine chlorine bleach with other cleansers, especially those containing ammonia. The combination produces dangerous gases.

Take off your jewelry or wear rubber gloves when using cleaning solutions to prevent abrasion or chemical damage to soft gems or precious metals.

REFERENCE
1,001 Helpful Tips, Facts & Hints from Consumer Reports by the editors of *Consumer Reports Books* with Monte Florman, Consumers Union, Mount Vernon, N.Y., 1989.

Easy way to keep drains draining

The simplest method to keep drains flowing requires no harsh chemicals or hard work. Just heat about a gallon of water to boiling, pour half down the drain, wait a few minutes, and pour in the rest. Don't risk cracking a porcelain basin — pour directly into the drain.

Done about once a week, you should never have a problem with clogged drains. If despite your efforts a drain becomes clogged, a rubber plunger is the most effective and safest alternative. Corrosive commercial products are dangerous and less effective.

REFERENCE
1,001 Helpful Tips, Facts & Hints from Consumer Reports by the editors of *Consumer Reports Books* with Monte Florman, Consumers Union, Mount Vernon, N.Y., 1989.

When to plant shrubbery

The surest way to get the reputation of a green thumb is to plant trees and flowers that flourish. The time of the year that you stick the plants in the ground can make a big difference as to whether they prosper or wither.

Generally, early fall is the best time to plant. The days are warm and the nights are cool, giving your shrubbery a chance to acclimate itself to both types of weather. By the time winter arrives, the shrubs will have developed the needed root mass to survive.

Early spring is the second best time to plant. The seasonal rains give a tree a chance to develop a root system before the blistering days of summer arrive.

Never, ever plant in the beginning of the hot season. Unless you have a professional helping you, all you'll get for your troubles are headaches and a dead shrub.

REFERENCE

Jerry Baker's Flowering Garden by Jerry Baker, Macmillan Publishing Co., New York, 1989.

How to choose a tree

Not only can a tree provide you with welcome shade on a sunny day, it can also nicely round out a garden. Before you plant one, however, there are a few things you should consider.

○ The size of the tree's root system. A tree will take up a significant amount of space in your garden or backyard. Before committing to one, know how much room you're willing to give up for at least two years.

○ The density of the tree's foliage when it matures. Different flowers and shrubs need different light. Will your tree allow other plants to survive?

○ The tree's height and width when it matures. Be sure your tree won't overshadow the rest of your garden (or your house).

○ The tree's fortitude. A sickly tree will only be an eyesore. You certainly don't want to plant something that will wither at the first cold snap.

Once a tree is planted, it's best to keep it where it is. Moving it can cause severe damage to the root system and will very likely affect all the plants around it which have gotten used to its shade and protection. So, choose carefully.

REFERENCE ———————————————————
Jerry Baker's Flowering Garden by Jerry Baker, Macmillan Publishing Co., New York, 1989.

How to make your houseplants love you

Give your houseplants a dose of TLC by watering them occasionally with the following treats:

- The water in which you boiled eggs — full of minerals
- Aquarium water
- Water in which fish was frozen
- Club soda that has gone flat
- Weak tea — ferns love it
- A very weak solution of ammonia and water — also a fern favorite

REFERENCE ———————————————————
Mary Ellen's Best of Helpful Hints by Mary Ellen Pinkham and Pearl Higginbotham, Warner Books Inc., New York, 1980.

The secrets of composting

Composting is no big secret. It happens in nature every time a leaf falls and turns into loam on the forest floor.

When homeowners compost, they're just hurrying the process a bit.

○ Pick an inconspicuous spot for your compost pile. It can be as simple as just a pile on the ground, or as complicated as a double 4 x 4 x 4 foot enclosure complete with hinged openings. Chicken wire nailed in a circle around some trees will do nicely.

○ Throw some cut branches down for the bottom layer so a bit of air can move under there.

○ From then on, it's whatever you have available: grass clippings, raked-up leaves, any vegetable matter at all, including kitchen wastes (no meat or dairy products — they'll attract pests).

○ Occasionally soak the pile well, or let rainwater collect on and in it. A layer of dirt now and then helps, too.

○ Some people believe in enclosing the compost pile with black plastic to concentrate heat — that's OK, but not required. As the material in the pile breaks down, heat is generated, and that speeds up the process.

○ Turn it now and then, perhaps three times during the summer, to redistribute the materials. Some people turn theirs weekly, others only annually.

○ In about three warm-weather months, longer in the winter, your leaves and grass will turn into rich, crumbling humus, perfect to mulch around shrubs, in flower beds or around young vegetable plants. Worked into the ground, it will condition it and send old nutrients into your plants.

○ Compostable materials account for 18 percent of wastes sent to this country's desperately stressed landfills, where they are buried and never become soil again as nature intended.

○ Your county extension agent can provide all the information you need on building a compost pile.

○ A simple way to compost is to use a composting mower, which shreds clippings fine enough to drop back on the lawn where they can decompose without becoming thatch.

REFERENCES

The Green Consumer by John Elkington, Julia Hailes and Joel Makower, Penguin Books, New York, 1988.

The Recycler's Handbook by The Earthworks Group, Earthworks Press, Berkeley, Calif., 1990.

The Fayette Sun, July 26, 1990.

Say good-bye to grass in the cracks

Salted boiling water will kill grass and weeds that grow between flag-stones or sections of cement walk.

Salt sprinkled in the same places will help prevent grass from growing — but beware it doesn't wash onto lawns or flower beds.

REFERENCE

Mary Ellen's Best of Helpful Hints by Mary Ellen Pinkham and Pearl Higginbotham, Warner Books Inc., New York, 1980.

Don't wear out sandpaper before you use it

To get the most life out of a sheet of sandpaper, rip the sheet into two halves and fold the halves into thirds. By preventing the sandy sides of the paper from rubbing against each other, you won't wear out sandpaper you haven't even used yet. You also get a handy-sized pad, just right for small jobs.

REFERENCE

Boatkeeper edited by Bernard Gladstone and Tom Bottomley, William Morrow and Company Inc., New York, 1984.

Easy way to find a stud

Need to hang a heavy shelf? You can improvise a stud-finder by using a compass. Hold it level and at a right angle to the wall. Pass it slowly across the wall until the presence of a nail makes the compass needle move.

When you are trying to locate studs, it helps to know that 16 inches is the usual distance between centers. Electrical outlets are usually mounted on one side of a stud.

The nails in ceiling moldings or baseboards should also indicate the approximate position of studs.

REFERENCE

Mary Ellen's Best of Helpful Hints by Mary Ellen Pinkham and Pearl Higginbotham, Warner Books Inc., New York, 1980.

How to divide a board equally without a calculator

You can divide a board nine inches wide or less into three equal parts without resorting to math or a calculator.

Place a ruler diagonally across the board with the 1-inch mark at one edge and the 10-inch mark at the other. With a pencil, dot the board at 4 inches and at 7 inches.

Use a T-square to draw your lines. Or make a second set of dots by repeating the process further down the board. The sections will be equal, no matter what the width of the board.

REFERENCE
The Household Book of Hints and Tips by Diane Raintree, Jonathan David Publishers Inc., Middle Village, N.Y., 1979.

Safe way to climb a ladder

Indoors or out, a slipping ladder can cause serious injury. Pieces of inner tube or rubber tire, attached permanently to the feet of your ladder, will help prevent dangerous skidding.

The rough surface of old asphalt shingles will likewise keep a ladder from sliding on smooth floors or grass.

The distance between the foot of your ladder and the wall against which it is leaning should equal one-fourth of the ladder's extended length. A 12-foot ladder, for example, should rest three feet from the base of the wall for greatest stability.

REFERENCE
The Household Book of Hints and Tips by Diane Raintree, Jonathan David Publishers Inc., Middle Village, N.Y., 1979.

Buying and selling your home

Creating a purchase and sale agreement that works for you

Real estate brokers and home sellers often act as though the Purchase and Sale agreement is written in stone — a document that it would be a sin to try to change.

Anything you have to sign should be worded as much to your liking as possible. Protect yourself by making sure certain contingencies, or conditions that have to be met before you will purchase a property, are included in the Purchase and Sale agreement.

The two most important contingencies for the home buyer are the financing contingency and the inspection contingency.

Financing the loan:

○ Be sure the Purchase and Sale agreement states the maximum interest rate and the type of mortgage you are willing to accept. Never accept an agreement that refers to "current market rates and terms."

○ Be sure the agreement states how much time you have to get a lender's unconditional written commitment on a mortgage. You should have plenty of time to obtain a lender's commitment.

○ You are required to make a "good-faith effort" to obtain financing. But you shouldn't be required to apply to several lenders. Specify in the agreement that you are not required to apply to more than one lender or pay more than one application fee.

Inspecting the property:

○ Beware of wording in the agreement that allows you to cancel your purchase only if "serious" structural flaws are discovered. Your inspection contingency clause should simply state that if you are not satisfied with the inspection results, you can cancel the transaction within a certain time period. That period is usually around two weeks, giving you enough time to renegotiate if you still want to buy the house. Longer periods force the seller to keep his house off the market for too long.

○ Don't ask the broker or the seller to recommend a home inspector. Find a bonded home inspector who has been in the business for a while. Get a recommendation from your attorney or from friends who have used inspectors in the past. The inspector must be willing to put his findings in writing.

REFERENCE ───────────────────────────────────
Bob Vila's Guide to Buying Your Dream House by Bob Vila with Carl Oglesby, Little Brown & Co., Boston, 1990.

How to hammer
home deals with real estate brokers

Real estate brokers can make the task of searching for a home so much easier than trying to wade through a sea of classifieds and visiting home after home on your own. Brokers can prequalify you for a loan and let you know how much house you can afford. They can show you a broad range of homes and give you information on various communities and neighborhoods, and they can explain financing alternatives and current interest rates and mortgage products.

But buyers should never expect brokers to:

○ Represent them in any way. Brokers work for sellers. Some states even require brokers to tell you that they don't work for you. You can hire a buyer's broker, although they are unnecessary. You do end up paying the broker's commission because it is reflected in the price of the home you buy.

○ Negotiate a lower purchase price or anything else that would give the buyer an advantage over the seller. Do not depend on the broker's opinion of a property's price. You have to negotiate on your own (or with your lawyer).

○ Tell you where to obtain a mortgage. The broker wants to see the deal go through as quickly as possible, and the lender that processes a loan quickly may not be the lender with the lowest rates or the best terms for you.

○ Tell you about problems a property has before you ask about them specifically. Do ask. Realtors are required to disclose adverse information on properties they represent.

You have no obligation to the broker you choose, so if you come across a "For Sale by Owner" home, you can pursue it even if you've been working with a broker for months. But you should not cooperate with a seller who has listed his home with a broker and then tries to cut the broker out of the deal to avoid paying his fees. If the broker shows you the house, the seller is legally obligated to pay his fees.

If a broker pressures you to buy a property because "it won't be on the market for long," or advises you not to hire an attorney, or pretends to represent you, or doesn't seem completely up front about a property, you should get another broker.

Shop for a good broker by getting referrals from friends and using the classifieds to find brokers that are active in the neighborhoods you are interested in. Interview at least two brokers in order to find out:

○ How long they've been in the business.

○ If the firm is well-established in the markets you are interested in.

○ If the firm has plenty of listings in your price range.

○ How professional the broker seems to be.

○ Can the broker answer basic questions about taxes, schools and city services in the areas you are interested in?

○ Does the broker seem as though he is pushing you to take the houses he has listed, or will he really help you find a home that is best for you?

○ Can the broker work with you in times that are convenient to you?

○ If the broker has "exclusive listings" that can be seen by the buyers working with him before they are advertised more widely.

○ If the broker is a Realtor, a member of the National Association of Realtors. Realtors have access to the Multiple Listing Service offered by their local real-estate board. The MLS is a bulletin board of home sales (usually computerized), and it will provide the most complete listing of homes for sale. (In some areas, the MLS is open to non-Realtors.) Realtors must also subscribe to the Realtor Code of Ethics, which is no guarantee they will treat you fairly, but it is better than nothing.

Disputes with brokers usually center around not getting your deposit back when the home sale does not go through or the broker flat out lying about a property. You can file suit to recover damages, file a complaint with the state licensing body which can impose fines and suspend or revoke the agent's license, or you can complain to the local real-estate board.

Your best bet is to keep your eyes open from the beginning and to make sure you are represented by a lawyer.

REFERENCE

Bob Vila's Guide to Buying Your Dream House by Bob Vila with Carl Oglesby, Little Brown & Co., Boston, 1990.

How not to make enemies when buying a vacation home with friends

A get-away-from-it-all vacation home nestling on the side of a ski slope, looking over a sunny white beach or hidden behind mountaintop trees is a luxury few people can afford on their own. Many people opt for what seems the perfect solution — getting together with friends to buy a vacation house.

Go ahead, buy with friends, but don't make enemies in the process. To keep your friends friendly and your assets intact, set up a general partnership instead of owning as tenants in common.

The partnership agreement you draw up will get misunderstandings out of the way and take care of mishaps before they occur. Make sure you get the following concerns in writing:

○ How ownership will be divided. This will determine who pays how much of the down payment, monthly payments, maintenance and repairs. Decide how to divide profits or losses from rent or sale of the place and how to distribute tax benefits.

○ When each partner gets to use the vacation place.

○ Who will serve as managing partner — responsible for signing checks and paying expenses.

○ What kind of circumstances might need to be voted upon, and what constitutes a deciding vote.

○ When a partner wants to withdraw, how much advance notice will he have to give and how will the buyout price be set.

A partnership may protect the existing mortgage if you need to replace a partner who withdraws with a new partner. The lender might agree that an interest in the partnership is being transferred rather than an interest in the property.

Try to find a lender who will limit the liability of each partner to whatever percentage he owns. Usually, each partner is liable for 100 percent of the loan and can be sued by the lender if there is a default.

REFERENCE ────────────────────────────────
Buying & Selling a Home by the staff of *Changing Times* magazine, The Kiplinger Washington Editors Inc., Washington, D.C., 1990.

When should you refinance your home?

Can't decide whether or not to refinance your home mortgage? Refinancing makes sense when there's a difference of two percentage points between your fixed loan rate and the current rates, as long as you plan to stay in your house for another four to seven years.

If you plan on keeping your house for more than seven years, you will save money by refinancing even if current rates are only one and a half percentage points less than your loan rate.

To figure out how long it will take to break even, divide the total closing costs by the amount of money saved each month by refinancing.

When interest rates are low, consider refinancing for extra money instead of getting a home-equity loan or a second mortgage. If the balance on your mortgage is $80,000, you could refinance for $120,000. You will receive $40,000 in home equity to use for home improvements or other purposes. Just like a home-equity loan, the interest is usually deductible.

REFERENCE

> *Buying & Selling a Home* by the staff of *Changing Times* magazine, The Kiplinger Washington Editors Inc., Washington, D.C., 1990.

Refinancing headaches

Refinancing takes loads of paperwork unless you have an FHA or VA loan. These agencies make refinancing easy for you if you've made your payments on time and aren't increasing the size of your monthly payment.

People with conventional loans have to simply start over with new appraisals, credit checks, title insurance and, possibly, new plot plans and site inspections. Most paperwork is outdated within 120 days.

Make sure your lender requires a survey, an inspection or a new site plan before you pay for one. Every lender is different.

Some states also charge a mortgage tax that's 1.75 percent of your loan. To avoid paying that tax when you refinance, get your old lender to "assign" your mortgage to the new lender.

Don't expect to get your escrow money back from your old lender at the closing table. Some lenders will hold onto the escrow accounts for up to 60 days. When you do get your escrow refund, make sure your lenders didn't overlap when they paid your taxes. You don't want to pay your taxes twice.

Watch out for mortgage-servicing scams, too. It's likely that your lender will sell your mortgage, and you will receive a new coupon book instructing you to make payments to a different lender.

But don't make any payments until you are satisfied that the "new lender" is legitimate. Your original lender should notify you when it sells the loan. Crooks have been known to send a phony notice saying that your loan was sold.

REFERENCE

> *The Wall Street Journal,* March 12, 1993.

You and your car

Keeping tune-ups
from turning into clean-ups

If you know little or nothing about what makes cars work, take these steps to avoid getting gypped by car repair shops:

○ Always ask for a written estimate. The estimate prevents the shop from running up the bill by fixing parts that don't need fixing. The written estimate will hold up in court if the repair shop overcharges you. Call several shops to ask for estimates before you have major work done.

○ Find out what warranty will cover your repairs. Make sure the warranty terms are written out specifically on your copy of the repair order.

○ Never say "Do whatever needs to be done to fix my car," and never sign a blank repair order. If you must leave before you know what needs repairing, provide a number where you can be reached. Have them call before repairs are made. Check over your repair order before you leave and make sure no extras were added.

○ Try to give the mechanic a written list of repairs to be done. You can take the car to a diagnostic clinic or get a friend who knows about cars to take it for a test drive. At least, listen carefully to your car and describe the symptoms to the mechanic. Write the symptoms down and keep a copy for yourself.

○ Ask the shop to give you any parts that they replaced. The shop should agree unless the parts are under warranty and need to be returned to the manufacturer.

○ Steer clear of sales for tune-ups, transmission or brake work. Many shops will try to talk you into unnecessary repairs once they get your car into the shop.

REFERENCE

The Lemon Book by Ralph Nader and Clarence Ditlow, Moyer Bell Ltd., Mount Kisco, N.Y., 1990.

The best auto repair shops

Small, independent garages are the most likely to repair only what is necessary and to charge a fair price. These small shops depend on customers coming back and on their reputation alone, unlike the car dealerships and the "big-name" shops.

The most reliable shops are small shops that pay their mechanics a straight salary instead of following the "flat-rate" manual.

Avoid mass merchandisers. They may be more interested in selling parts than in service, so you may end up buying parts you don't need.

If you go to a franchise such as Midas Muffler, check your local Better Business Bureau for complaints lodged. Another of the franchise's shops nearby may have a cleaner record.

To make sure a mechanic is competent, find out if he has been certified by the National Institute for Automotive Service Excellence.

REFERENCE

The Lemon Book by Ralph Nader and Clarence Ditlow, Moyer Bell Ltd., Mount Kisco, N.Y., 1990.

Highway robbery

You're far from home and the security of your trusted mechanic. You pull into a strange service station, and the attendant has found a problem.

Or has he? Beware of automotive rip-offs like these:

○ A service station attendant, while checking tire pressure, "discovers" a gashed tire you never even suspected. He may be setting you up. Put on your spare and drive home or to a dealer of your choice before replacing the tire.

○ Wires loosened by someone who checks under the hood cause a warning light to come on. He may even create smoke by dropping barbecue sauce on the hot alternator. If there were no warning lights on when you drove in, let the smoke clear and check the wires yourself. If they don't show signs of burning, drive on.

○ A sudden leak in a radiator hose, right there in the service station? Unlikely, unless caused by an unscrupulous attendant with a sharp screwdriver. Carry a spare hose. Or tape the leak with rubber or electrical tape — that should get you to another service station and keep a crook from making a profit.

○ If an attendant spins the fan blade and tells you this means the water pump is failing, don't believe him. The fan of a warm engine should turn freely.

○ You thought your car was riding all right, but the attendant points out an oil "leak" on the shock absorbers and tells you to have them replaced or risk certain calamity. Check them yourself. A real leak will not appear to be fresh; it may even have a coating of dust on it. Bounce that corner of the car, and if it stops bouncing after you stop pushing, you don't have a problem that needs immediate care.

○ Watch closely any time a stranger gets under the hood of your car. It is easy to cut a fan belt when the car owner is inattentive. Carry spare fan belts when driving far from home, so that the most you will have to pay a crooked service station will be for installation.

○ If you didn't actually watch the service station attendant check your oil, and he indicates it is low, ask him to recheck. Watch that he pushes the dip stick all the way in.

○ Make sure no one "forgets" to replace your gas cap when you stop to refuel.

○ When a car is on a lift and the wheels are hanging free, some looseness and wobble is normal. If the service station attendant jerks a front wheel around and tells you the front end is worn, but you feel the car handled normally, drive on. Drive cautiously, if you are concerned, and have it checked — but at a place of your choosing.

○ Don't be suckered into replacing air filters or batteries unnecessarily. Get out of your car and watch the repairman closely to make sure he doesn't disconnect the battery cables.

○ If a shop tries to sell you a new tire or a battery, ask for the owner's name and the shop's address. If the attendant seems hesitant, go to another shop.

Get your car thoroughly checked before you go on a long trip so you can avoid having major repairs performed far from home.

Never give a stranger a big job; have someone you trust check it out. The key is to remain in control of the situation. If you do indeed have a problem, you want to be free to choose where and by whom it is corrected, and not be stampeded by an unscrupulous attendant.

REFERENCES
Listen to Your Car by Ross R. Olney, Walker and Co., New York, 1981.
How to Make Your Car Last Almost Forever by Jack Gillis, Perigee Books, Putnam Publishing Group, New York, 1987.

Saving gas means saving money

Saving money on gas is a nasty Catch-22. Cheaper gas means lower octane. And lower octane means a higher risk of knocking. And knocking decreases engine power, and thus, fuel efficiency.

Check your car's operations manual to determine what octane is the right one for your car.

Test octane levels by driving until the engine is warm. Come to a complete stop, then accelerate hard. If you hear knocking, up the octane. Your goal is to have no knocking with the cheapest possible gas.

Some products — such as gas tank additives and "miracle" spark plugs — claim to increase your car's gas mileage, but view these with extreme caution.

Tests by the Environmental Protection Agency have found little, if any, improvement with these products.

There are other, more basic, ways to improve mileage. This will mean fewer fill-ups and, in the long run, more money for you.

- Check your tire pressure often. Underinflated tires sap a car's mileage potential.

- Keep your engine well-tuned. This can increase fuel efficiency by as much as 10 to 20 percent.

- Turn off your car whenever possible. An idling engine will burn gas while you sit still.

- Avoid jackrabbit starts and brake smoothly. Anticipate what sort of traffic conditions lie ahead.

- Obey the 55 mph speed limit.

REFERENCE ———
The Better Business Bureau Guide to Wise Buying, The Benjamin Co., New York, 1980.

Safest colors for cars

If your car is greenish yellow, your popularity may be in more danger than your life.

Studies have shown that greenish yellow is the safest color for a car. The New York Port Authority says that light-colored, single-toned cars are less likely to be wrecked than darker cars because other drivers can more easily distinguish light cars from their surroundings. White, cream and yellow are safe colors, too. Red and black are the worst.

REFERENCE ———
The Lemon Book by Ralph Nader and Clarence Ditlow, Moyer Bell Ltd., Mount Kisco, N.Y., 1990.

Why be your own mechanic?

Why would anyone want to do any of his own auto maintenance when he can afford to let someone else get greasy? Here's why:

○ Satisfaction and a sense of being in control.

○ Convenience: Your time is worth too much to wait around for an appointment or to be put off. How often have you made arrangements to pick up your car, only to be told, "Couldn't get to it today — come back next week"?

○ Confidence: You know you're not being cheated when you do your own work, you know exactly what was done, and you know the quality of the parts you buy yourself. Not to mention that if trouble strikes while on the road, you may be able to handle it yourself, or at least know when a mechanic's high charges are justified.

REFERENCE ————————————————————————————————————
Do-It-Yourself Car Care by Larry W. Carley, Tab Books, Blue Ridge Summit, Pa., 1987.

Staying ahead of trouble

There's nothing magic about trouble-free driving. A routine of regular maintenance is your single greatest protection against costly and inconvenient automotive downtime. Make it a habit.

Each week, check:

○ Level of oil before first start-up of the day.

○ Level of coolant when car is cold.

○ Tire pressure, also before running.

Once a month, check:

○ Headlights, taillights, turn signals.

○ Level of brake fluid, automatic transmission fluid (with car hot, idling), power steering fluid.

○ Drive belts, radiator and heater hoses.

○ Water level or charge indicator of battery and terminals.

Every six months, or as often as your owner's manual suggests, do the following:

○ Change engine oil and oil filter — this removes chemicals that contaminate and deteriorate the engine.

○ Check muffler and exhaust system.

○ Be sure emergency brake works and check brake lines.

○ Be sure spare tire is inflated.

○ Touch up rust spots or nicks in paint and wax surface.

○ Lubricate hinges, latches, locks and chassis and check wiper blades.

○ Inspect drive shaft U-joints (if yours is rear wheel drive), or the CV-joint boots (in front wheel drives).

○ Check level of differential and/or manual transmission fluid.

○ Check antifreeze for strength and condition.

○ Inspect suspension — loose parts? Leaky shock absorbers?

○ Check shocks by pushing down each corner of car. Motion should stop with one bounce after you stop pushing.

Annually:

○ Check air filter (you should be able to see through it), fuel filter, positive crankshaft ventilation (PCV) filter and wiper blades, and replace if necessary.

○ Check vacuum hoses for airtightness and condition.

○ Rotate tires, unless otherwise advised by your dealer.

Every two years:

○ Replace fluid and filter in automatic transmission.

○ Check ignition timing and ignition components.

○ Repack wheel bearings, unless sealed — in front-wheel drive, repack rear bearings; in rear-wheel drive, repack front bearings.

- Check brake linings.

- Flush and refill radiator and check radiator cap seal. Caution: Radiator fluid is sweet and attractive to animals, birds and children, and it is extremely poisonous.

- Change thermostat.

Every three or four years, these items should be inspected for possible deterioration and replacement:

- Battery, spark plug wires and distributor cap.

- V-belts, and radiator and heater hoses.

- Shock absorbers.

- Exhaust system, including muffler and tail pipe.

- Positive crankshaft ventilation (PCV) valve.

- Disk-brake rotor — check whenever you have brake pads replaced.

Every 25,000 miles or when you hear unusual tapping noises:

- Have valve lifters adjusted correctly, unless they adjust automatically — to ignore this, you almost guarantee yourself an expensive valve job.

Every 40,000 miles:

- Change transmission fluid for a dramatic reduction in the incidence of transmission repair.

REFERENCES ────────────────────────────────────

Do-It-Yourself Car Care by Larry W. Carley, Tab Books, Blue Ridge Summit, Pa., 1987.
How to Make Your Car Last Almost Forever by Jack Gillis, Perigee Books, Putnam Publishing Group, New York, 1987.

Your car diary

Keep a diary for your car. A maintenance and repair history helps you plan ahead for what needs to be done, and also lets you anticipate special sales on items that will need replacement.

Accurate record-keeping pays other dividends such as:

○ Providing a basis for tax deduction claims.

○ Establishing a true picture of what it costs to own and operate a car, essential for good budgeting.

○ Alerting you early to signs of decreasing performance, such as changes in fuel mileage.

○ Documentation of maintenance and performance for resale.

Your owner's manual is an invaluable source of information on proper maintenance scheduling.

REFERENCE ───────────────────────────────────
Lyn St. James's Car Owner's Manual for Women by Lyn St. James, Penguin Books, New York, 1989.

How to jump-start a car

The basic rules for using jumper cables are:

> • Have a set with you.
> • Know how to use them.
> • Take reasonable precautions.

You cannot be electrocuted by a battery. You can, however, cause a battery to explode by making incorrect connections. It's a good idea to wear safety glasses when jump-starting a car.

Here's what you do:

○ Position cars so batteries are as close together as possible, but not touching. Turn off power in both; put them in park and set brakes.

○ The positive posts of each battery are marked "POS" or "+." The negative posts are marked "NEG" or "—." Connect clamps of red cable to the positive posts of each battery, taking care never to touch the metal clamps of the red and black cables together. (Remember: red to red, black to black.)

○ On the car with the good battery, connect the metal clamp of the black cable to the negative post. Connect the other end of the black cable to bare metal on the frame of the "dead" car — this is a grounding connection — and take care to keep cable clear of the fan and fan belt.

(If you have always connected the other end of the black cable to the negative post on the "dead" car, you already know that it will almost always work that way. But it's not the safest way.)

○ Be sure ignition is off in the car with the dead battery. Start the car with the good battery, and rev the engine gently to be sure the battery is charged.

○ Now start the "dead" car. When both engines are running, undo the cables in reverse order: first the black ground connection, then the other end of the black cable and, lastly, the two red cables.

○ Do not shut off the engine with the dead battery until you get help or have reached your destination.

○ And last but not least: Never smoke while working around batteries. They sometimes release highly explosive hydrogen gas.

REFERENCES
Lyn St. James's Car Owner's Manual for Women by Lyn St. James, Penguin Books, New York, 1989.
Do-It-Yourself Car Care by Larry W. Carley, Tab Books, Blue Ridge Summit, Pa., 1987.

Locked out!

The simplest, least expensive, most foolproof way to get into a locked car is with a key. That's not what you want to hear if you've just locked your key in the car.

Consider the alternatives: In many cities, the police will no longer come to the rescue with an entry tool, and calling a locksmith is expensive. It is virtually impossible to open today's car locks with a straightened wire coat hanger. And breaking a window is costly and inconvenient.

Keep with you a record of your car key code, found either in the center of your new car key or on your new car invoice. With proof of ownership, you can get a key made easily by a locksmith or a car dealer.

Easier still: For less than $1, purchase a magnetic key case designed to be hidden, with the spare key inside, somewhere on a metal surface of the car.

So much plastic is used in the construction of today's cars, you may have to search for a metal surface. Try the steel supports inside a bumper.

REFERENCE ─────────────────────────────────
How to Make Your Car Last Almost Forever by Jack Gillis, Perigee Books, Putnam Publishing Group, New York, 1987.

'Drying out' a soaked engine

Drive through a deep puddle during a rainstorm, and your engine may stall because spark plugs or distributor have been soaked by splashing water.

WD-40 sprayed onto the wet parts will get you going again. Intended primarily as a lubricant, WD-40 works by displacing water and lifting it away. And because it is nonconductive, WD-40 will not interfere with electrical systems.

REFERENCE ─────────────────────────────────
WD-40 Company, San Diego, Calif.

Frozen car door locks

A squirt of WD-40 will "defrost" frozen car door locks. WD-40's action is to displace water, and while a truly snow-packed lock may require coaxing with a key, eventually the lubricant will free it from ice.

Better still, treat each lock to a shot of WD-40 when the car is new and dry. In mild climates, such preventive care may ensure smooth locks for the life of the vehicle.

Where winters are severe, the WD-40 treatment should be part of your annual cold-weather readiness program.

REFERENCE ————————————————————————

WD-40 Company, San Diego, Calif.

The basic auto tool kit

Many hardware and auto-parts stores sell basic tools in handy carrying cases. Buy one or put together your own. It should include:

- A couple of regular and Phillips-head screwdrivers in different sizes

- A set of open-end wrenches from 3/8-inch to 3/4-inch sizes (if you own a foreign car, you may need metric wrenches from 10 mm to 17 mm — see your owner's manual)

- A small can of oil or lubricant such as WD-40

- A flashlight that works

- A hand-held tire pressure gauge — those on air pumps at service stations are not always accurate

- A clean, soft rag

- An extra fan belt and jumper cables

REFERENCE ————————————————————————

Lyn St. James's Car Owner's Manual for Women by Lyn St. James, Penguin Books, New York, 1989.

Cracking the tire code

Unfortunately, you can't communicate with a tire dealer by making a circle with your arms and saying you need one "about this big."

How can you learn to speak "tire"? How do you know whether the tires you have are right for your car and the way you use it?

The code is right there on your sidewalls.

Suppose you read "P205/60R15 90H" on the sidewall of your tire. You have safety and performance information, the size, load, inflation pressure, load capability and speed rating right before your eyes.

The "P205" tells you this is a passenger car tire, 205 millimeters in width. The ratio of height to width is "60." The "R" means radial construction, and the "15" is the diameter of the rim it will fit, in inches.

If there is a "B" in place of the "R," it means the tire is bias-belted instead of radial. Diagonal bias gets a "D." In addition, there is information on the type of cord and number of plies in the sidewall and under the tread.

The "90" is a code representing the load index, and indicates the maximum weight a tire can carry at the speed indicated by its speed symbol (the "H"). Most cars range from 75 to 100.

The load index times four is the maximum weight the tires should be expected to carry — including passengers, fuel and the contents of the trunk.

The speed symbol shows the tire's speed capability as determined by tests. The "H" in the example is commonly used to mean 130 mph. Others are "S," which indicates 112 mph; "T," 118; "U," 124; "V," 149; and "Z," more than 149 mph.

Of course, these ratings don't apply if a tire is underinflated, overloaded or worn out.

Now you know.

REFERENCE ────────────────────────────────
The Tire Industry Safety Council, as reported by *The New York Times*, March 1993.

Tire tips

Get a grip — on the road

Your tires may be the most critical part of your car, affecting your comfort, gas mileage, handling and safety.

Buy radials. While nearly all are guaranteed for 40,000 miles, you should be able to get half again that much mileage from a good set of radials — three times the life of typical "bias-ply" tires.

Also, because they run cooler, radials are less likely to fail or blow out, and often improve gas mileage by as much as eight percent.

To rotate or not to rotate

Experts differ as to whether it is necessary to rotate modern tires. Some dealers recommend it strongly; others feel that as long as the car is properly aligned, rotation is not worth the time and cost.

Best advice: Watch closely for signs of wear, and establish a good rapport with a dealer whose advice you respect.

Under pressure

Danger! A tire low on air is a safety hazard because it makes for poor handling and difficult steering. Moreover, low tires decrease gas mileage and tire wear.

At least once a month, check tire pressure with an accurate hand-held gauge. Don't trust the gauges on gas station tire-inflation machines.

Check the pressure in the morning before using the car or the day warms up. As you drive, tires heat up and the air inside expands, causing inaccurate readings. Never let air out of a hot tire just because it seems to be overinflated.

Check tire pressure and add air in the same way. Uncap the valve, and hold the gauge or the air-pump nozzle tightly against the valve so that no air escapes. Replace the valve cap; it keeps dirt out.

Experts advise adding about six pounds to the manufacturer's recommendations, listed inside the glove compartment or on the driver's door. But do not exceed the maximum pressure indicated on the tire's sidewall. An increase in gas mileage and tire life are well worth the slight sacrifice in comfort that you get with a well-inflated tire.

Save your money and your life

While worn-out tires are less likely these days to blow out, they are still a serious threat to your safety and the safety of those who ride with you. Bald tires and a brief rain shower or an emergency stop can be a deadly combination.

Check tire wear regularly, and watch for these patterns:

○ Worn tread on both edges indicates underinflation.

○ Worn tread in the center indicates overinflation.

○ Tread worn on one side indicates poor alignment.

Correct all these problems as soon as possible, and consider rotation to even out tire wear. Keeping tires properly inflated saves lives and money.

REFERENCE ————————————————————————————
Lyn St. James's Car Owner's Manual for Women by Lyn St. James, Penguin Books, New York, 1989.

Protecting your investment: all about cleaning

Keeping your car clean inside and out pays off in pride and pleasure while protecting your investment.

Inside:

○ Abrasive dirt in carpets and upholstery makes a car look shabby before its time. Frequent vacuuming helps keep cars "new."

○ After cleaning vinyl surfaces, apply a vinyl protective spray to keep them soft and new-looking. This is especially important where sunlight falls directly on vinyl. Avoid getting this spray on glass.

○ Saddle soap helps keep leather pliable and free from cracks.

Outside:

○ Remove bird droppings or tree sap right away to prevent them from eating through the paint.

○ Wash regularly. Using as high a hose pressure as possible, try to dislodge most of the dirt first.

○ Use a soft sponge or towel and a mild liquid detergent like those meant for hand-washing dishes or a soap made especially for waxed surfaces. Harsh soaps and detergents cause car paint to lose its residual oils.

○ After washing, rinse well, starting at the top and working down. Then wipe dry to prevent formation of water spots.

○ Avoid washing a car in direct sunlight or when the surface is extremely hot.

○ Wash wheels and tires last, using a stiff brush. Spray water up inside the wheel wells. In cold climates where salt is spread on the road, it is important to flush out deposits of road grime which rust the underbody.

○ Clean windows with any good glass cleaner or a combination of white vinegar and water. "Rain-X" puts a protective coating on your windshield to allow water to drain off quickly. "Rain-X" is especially helpful if wiper blades aren't working perfectly.

Wax? Polish? Rubbing compounds?

There are a lot of car care products on the market. Which does what?

○ Cleaners remove old wax, dirt and stains from the top surface of the paint, but they don't add protection. If you've kept your car clean from the time it was new, you'll probably never need anything stronger than mild detergent.

○ Rubbing or polishing compounds remove stubborn stains, scratches and weathered paint. They should be considered a last resort, however, because the finish will be affected.

○ Polishes usually contain no abrasives or waxes, but they put a shine on the finish by adding oils to it.

○ Waxes are a protective coating for the paint and polish. Use the form you prefer: liquid, paste or hard wax. Waxes protect by helping prevent oxidation, the deterioration of paint caused by exposure to air.

Adding layers on top of layers is counterproductive since each coat removes the one that preceded it. Work in the shade and clean or turn the applicator frequently, waxing small areas at a time.

Apply sparingly, following directions on the container as to the best motion for the product. Let dry thoroughly before buffing with clean towels.

REFERENCE —————————————————————————————

Lyn St. James's Car Owner's Manual for Women by Lyn St. James, Penguin Books, New York, 1989.

Removing road tar from car paint

Asphalt on car surfaces, usually splattered there in hot weather or by fresh road construction, is easily removed by either brush/roller cleaner or WD-40, both available in hardware stores.

The brush/roller cleaner (not to be confused with mineral spirits, paint remover, paint thinner, turpentine or acetone) works best, but because of its flammability, it should be kept in the garage, not in the car. WD-40, on the other hand, works almost as well, and because of its pressure-can container, its safe to carry in the car.

Apply either product to road tar in minimal amounts on a clean cloth, wipe at once, and then wash and rewax the area. Caution should be used if the car is newly painted, but paint which has "hardened" for several weeks should not be harmed if the solvent is removed quickly.

Products sold specifically for asphalt and bug removal are less effective and more expensive than brush/roller cleaner and WD-40.

REFERENCE ————————————————————————
WD-40 Company, San Diego, Calif.

Long-life battery care

Green crystals on the posts and clamps of your auto battery are signs of corrosion. Wet them with water, sprinkle on some household baking soda, wait a few minutes, then wire-brush off. Wash the whole battery with a hose and let dry.

Then spray WD-40 on each post and the area around them to displace water and prevent further corrosion. Respray with WD-40 about every six months.

REFERENCE ————————————————————————
WD-40 Company, San Diego, Calif.

How to find out why your car won't start

To find out why your car battery mysteriously quits working when the vehicle is not being used, do a little detective work with a 12-volt test light or an ohmmeter.

Disconnect the cable from the positive terminal of the battery and attach the test light between the cable and the battery terminal.

Be sure no power is being drawn elsewhere in the car, such as by the dome light. When the test light comes on, you know electricity is being drawn from the battery.

Now begin removing fuses one at a time, checking to see if the test light has gone off each time. If it does go off, you have a good clue about where the drain is taking place.

If it does not go off after all fuses have been tested, try disconnecting the alternator or other electrical devices that do not have fuses.

Once the problem has been identified, it can be repaired or removed if it is a device you can do without, like a cigarette lighter.

REFERENCE ───────────────────────────────────

"Car Talk" by Ray and Tom Magliozzi, syndicated radio show and column, *The Atlanta Journal/Constitution.*

When your car squeals on you

A loud squeal coming from under the hood when you accelerate nearly always means a loose fan belt or drive belt.

As long as the car seems to be performing normally, this is not an urgent problem. Check it soon — you don't want to wait for a belt to break before you change it.

Fan belts are easily changed high-profit items and sometimes service station personnel are tempted to recommend replacing them before it is really necessary.

Trust your own judgment. If you see wear, cracks or pieces missing, buy a new belt (or two, if they are paired, even if one looks much better than the other). A car with a broken fan belt will soon overheat and stop running, especially in city driving.

If the belt doesn't look too worn, ask the mechanic to adjust the tension to relieve the slippage. Properly adjusted, a belt should not flex more than about half an inch when pressed on halfway between the pulleys.

And if tightening doesn't help, have the mechanic apply a belt "dressing" to create extra friction between belt and pulleys, thereby stopping the slippage and squealing sound.

REFERENCE

Listen to Your Car by Ross R. Olney, Walker and Company, New York, 1981.

How to tell what's leaking from your car

The color of the spots on your garage floor or driveway is a good clue to where the fluid came from.

- ○ Green: Leaking radiator coolant. Check hoses and radiator.

- ○ Red: Leaking transmission or power-steering fluid. Look for bad gaskets or seals.

- ○ Brown: Leaking engine oil. Suspect faulty fittings, seals or gaskets.

- ○ Black grease: Rear axles may be leaking.

REFERENCE

Lyn St. James's Car Owner's Manual for Women by Lyn St. James, Penguin Books, New York, 1989.

What's that thump?

Tires cause most thumping sounds cars make. An out-of-round tire, one with a flat spot or even a cold tire may thump, at least for a while.

But the "thump" to worry about is the sudden repeated sound caused by a bulge between the tread and the body of the tire. Even in one of today's tough tires, this could mean a blowout is imminent.

Pull off the road and drive very slowly to a service station or tire store — you're going to have to replace that blistered tire. You may have a lifetime guarantee against such a mishap, so hold onto that tire until you can get back to your dealer to negotiate a possible adjustment.

REFERENCE

Listen to Your Car by Ross R. Olney, Walker and Company, New York, 1981.

Time for a tune-up

How do you know when your car needs a tune-up?

Here's where your record-keeping comes in handy. If your miles-per-gallon average drops by more than 15 percent, chances are you need a tune-up and maybe more.

Some other warning signs:

○ Too fast an idle when car is warm, or a rough idle

○ Stalling and low power

○ Knocking or pinging

○ Rough running, hard starting, hesitation

○ Post-ignition — the engine continues to run with key off

○ Black exhaust smoke

REFERENCES

How to Make Your Car Last Almost Forever by Jack Gillis, Perigee Books, Putnam Publishing Group, New York, 1987.

Listen to Your Car by Ross R. Olney, Walker and Company, New York, 1981.

Some unsuspected highway hazards

○ Slow down and use extra caution in the first few minutes of a rain shower. After a hot, dry spell, a little water mixed with grease and oil, which have collected on the road's surface, makes the pavement slick. A hard rain helps wash the oil and grease away.

○ After a heavy snowfall, it's not enough to clear snow just from the windshield. Make sure headlights and all other lights are fully exposed, and remove snow from all windows and the roof of the car. As it begins to melt, snow on the roof could suddenly slide down the windshield and block your view. If your wipers are on, dragging against heavy snow could break them.

○ Studies show you are twice as likely to be hit from behind if you are driving an older car without a high-mounted third brake light. Auto-parts stores offer these lights at reasonable prices, and installation is not difficult.

REFERENCE

How to Make Your Car Last Almost Forever by Jack Gillis, Perigee Books, The Putnam Publishing Group, New York, 1987.

How to drive in bad weather

Turn on headlights (not parking lights) when you turn on windshield wipers — it's the law in most states.

If you have no choice but to drive through a deep puddle, keep your left foot lightly on the brake pedal to help keep brake linings from getting wet. Go slowly to avoid splashing water on your ignition system.

Once out of the water, pump your brakes a few times to help dry the brake linings.

Hydroplaning

When your tires ride up on a "wedge" of water between them and the road, your car loses contact with the road, and you lose control.

Avoid hydroplaning by taking these simple steps:

- Make sure you have at least an eighth inch of tread depth — bald tires increase your chances of hydroplaning.

- Make sure your tires are properly inflated. Check your owner's manual to be sure.

- Slow down to a steady speed on wet roads, avoiding puddles.

To counteract hydroplaning

- Keep the steering wheel straight.

- Take your foot off the gas.

- Don't try to brake or steer. As the car slows down, it will settle down onto the road's surface again.

Fog

Low beams help you see and be seen. High beams glare back at you.

Turn on windshield wipers, defroster and fan. And roll down the side window — sometimes traffic can be heard before it can be seen.

Although the right edge of the road makes a good guide in fog, beware of slower moving traffic or cars that have pulled over.

Slowing down is important, but driving too slowly or stopping on the shoulder could make you a deadly obstacle in the fog. If you must stop, pull off the road as far as possible, turn on emergency flashers, and occasionally honk your horn so passing cars will know you are there.

Lightning

You are safer in a hard-topped car during an electrical storm than almost anywhere else. (In a convertible or a golf cart, or on a tractor, motorcycle or bike, you become a target for lightning.) If lightning should hit the car, the charge will be conducted to the ground — you will be insulated by the tires.

Never jump out of a car that has power lines lying across it. As with lightning, as long as you remain inside entirely, you are safe. But if charged wires lie across your car and you step out, your foot becomes the ground and your body becomes the conductor.

REFERENCE ————————————————————————————
How to Drive Safely in Bad Weather by Paul Mueller for the Shell Oil Company, Houston, Texas, 1991.

Avoiding a head-on collision

A common mistake made by experienced as well as brand-new drivers all too often results in needless tragedy. Picture this scenario: You are stopped, waiting for oncoming traffic to pass so you can make a left turn. You have your steering wheel turned so that the moment there is an opening, you can jump across.

You are hit from behind by a driver whose attention has wandered for a moment or whose bald tires slid when he locked his brakes. The hit propels you into the other lane in the direction your wheels were turned, and you collide head-on with an oncoming vehicle.

If your wheels were straight and not turned, the worst damage might have been a crushed car rear and perhaps a whiplash injury — unpleasant, but seldom permanent.

Instead: serious injuries in two cars, and possibly death.

REFERENCE

Fayette Sun, Aug. 20, 1992.

Car security

"Don't leave your keys in the ignition" sounds like an obvious reminder, but experts estimate that half the car thieves in the United States take advantage of that careless error.

Keep the ignition key separate from house and office keys. An unscrupulous parking lot attendant could copy your keys while you enjoy the play, track your address from your license plate number and burglarize your home at his convenience. It is virtually impossible to make a car truly secure. Professionals can get into any car in a matter of moments. Don't lock valuables in the trunk or glove box.

Drive with doors locked and windows closed, and constantly observe who is around you. Stay far enough away from other cars so that you can pull out and drive away if you are threatened while stopped at a light.

If rear-ended, keep driving until you can pull off in a busy, well-lighted area. And if disabled, especially at night, pull off the road, lock yourself in and display a white flag (towel, handkerchief) from the driver's window.

When returning to your parked car, carry your key ready for use. Its sharp end can also serve as a weapon, if needed. Check the backseat and the floor behind the front seats for a hiding intruder.

As for car alarms, what did you do last time you heard one go off? Nothing?

Think about it.

REFERENCES

Safe and Alive by Terry Dobson and Judith Shepherd-Chow, J.P. Tarcher Inc., Los Angeles, 1981.

How to Avoid Burglary, Housebreaking and Other Crimes by Ulrich Kaufmann, Crown Publishers Inc., New York, 1967.

Buying and selling a car

How to drive out ahead in a car dealership

Feeling confident, calm and collected in the deliberately confusing world of car salesmen is next to impossible, but you don't have to resort to a no-haggle dealership or a car-buying service when you're ready to buy a new car.

Instead of resigning yourself to paying more than you have to, follow these tips from Remar Sutton's book *Don't Get Taken Every Time: The Insider's Guide to Buying or Leasing Your Next Car or Truck.*

You can learn how to wheel and deal in an automobile dealership — do everything, in fact, but win a popularity contest.

○ First, find out the wholesale value of your present car if you plan to trade it in. Clean your car inside and out, buff the paint, repaint little nicks if you can find the right color, and take your car in for minor repairs. Get blown fuses and worn belts replaced.

Then drive your car to three used-car dealerships and pretend you are interested in selling. Say you will decide where to sell it within the next few days, and you want a definite, firm offer. (You can sell your own car and make the profit yourself. If you decide to sell your own car, go ahead and ask $1,500 more than the wholesale figure. You may only make half that.)

Now don't tell the new car salesman that you know your car's value. Let him make you an offer first. He may make you a better offer, or more likely, you can find out if he's low-balling you.

If the salesman says he'll "allow" you a certain amount of money on your trade-in, he is trying to pull the wool over your eyes. He will charge you more on your new car to make up for the "allowance." Tell him that you want to know what your car appraised for, not what he'll "allow" you.

○ Next, shop for your financing about a week before you shop for your car. Don't be suckered by the dealership financing sources, like

GMAC or Chrysler credit. Your best bets are banks and credit unions. Make sure you get a simple interest loan so you can pay it off early without penalty. Decide how much you want to pay a month and how many months you want to pay, then call a loan officer at several banks and credit unions. Ask:

- What is your APR (annual percentage rate) for new/used car loans for ____ months? The APR tells you exactly how much money you will pay in interest every year.

- What is your charge per month for credit life insurance and credit disability insurance on each thousand dollars? (You don't have to buy credit insurance if you don't want to, and you probably shouldn't buy credit disability insurance if you are young and in good health.)

- Do you have any other loan application charges, such as credit checks?

○ Ignore dealer advertising and car sales. Don't succumb to the promise of easy payment plans and low-down-payment plans. The only advantage to visiting a car dealership during an advertised sale is that the pressure to sell is greater on the car salesmen. You probably won't get a better deal, but negotiating the sale will be easier.

○ The best time to visit a dealership: Thirty minutes before closing time on a rainy night at the end of the month. The salesmen's resistance will be down, and they will need to make a sale to meet their monthly quotas. Even if it has been a good month for the dealership, the sale to you will be an "extra," and you could still get a good deal. Before Christmas is also a good time to negotiate since it's usually a slow time for dealerships.

○ Factory rebates can be a real savings to you, but don't, under any circumstances, let the dealer keep your rebate. Have it mailed directly from the manufacturer to your home. You can negotiate a good deal with the dealer *and* keep your rebate.

○ Want to really get under a car salesman's skin? Be indecisive. You don't really know what car you want or even if you want a car. Even better, don't show any enthusiasm about any car on the lot. If you love a car, frown when you look at it. And most important of all, never, never buy a car the first time you visit a dealership. Prices will drop as soon as you step off the lot to leave.

○ Find out the real cost of a new car by buying the latest edition of *Edmund's Car Prices Buyer's Guide.* Compare the prices in this book to the prices on the manufacturer's sticker on the cars you like at the dealerships. Ignore the dealer's stickers. You don't have to pay for dealer "add-ons" and for "special value packages."
Remember, dealers get kickbacks and refunds from manufacturers, so the dealer would make a profit even if you only paid the amount the sticker says he paid the factory. Paying $150 to $200 over invoice is certainly reasonable.

○ About demos: Don't buy them. Dealers make as big a profit on them as they do on new cars.

○ Buying new trucks or full-sized vans: You won't find a manufacturer's sticker on these vehicles. To determine what the dealer paid, ignore the prices on the dealer's sticker and copy down the model number and the options. Use *Edmund's* truck and van book to figure out what you should pay.

○ What about warranties? New cars come with "free" warranties, so unless you are really paranoid, don't buy the service contracts the dealer will offer you. Almost all manufacturers offer "secret" warranties although neither the dealer nor the manufacturer will volunteer to discuss these with you. If you want to know what secret warranties exist on a particular car, call the Auto Safety Hotline at 1-800-424-9393.

○ Finally, keep your deposit low. Don't pay a lot of money or sign your contract until you are satisfied your car is perfect. Car people need incentive to fix any problems you may have with your car.

REFERENCE
Don't Get Taken Every Time: The Insider's Guide to Buying or Leasing Your Next Car or Truck by Remar Sutton, Penguin Books, New York, 1991.

Avoiding the lemon purchase: a used-car inspection list

Want to get a great deal on a used car but afraid of purchasing a lemon? You don't have to be an expert mechanic to find a good used car. You can decide on your own if a car is worth paying a mechanic to check out for you.

- ○ Wear old clothes, take a notepad and a flashlight when you look over a car.

- ○ Ask to see the car title. Get the name and number of the previous owner. Call the owner and ask what problems he had with the car. Write down the problems for your mechanic to check. Confirm the mileage with the owner.

- ○ Make sure the car hasn't been wrecked badly. Look for ripples in the metal or dull paint. Open and close all doors. (If a door has to be forced, the car has probably been wrecked.) Look for welding seams along the frame or underbody.

- ○ Check for rust. If you see small paint bubbles surrounding the moldings around the bumpers, grill, wheel wells and windows, ask the seller to punch them through firmly with a screwdriver. If the screwdriver goes through the entire piece of metal, the rust is bad and the repairs will be costly. Check the bottoms and insides of the doors for rust.

- ○ Open the trunk. Look for rust and stains that will indicate leaks. Make sure the spare tire is serviceable and matches the other tires. If the other tires are radials, the spare should be a radial.

- ○ Look under the car and in the wheel wells. If the underside has been freshly coated, the seller is trying to hide something from you. There is no reason to undercoat but to hide rust.

- ○ Turn the car on and look at the muffler system. Make sure that fumes aren't escaping at any point along the system. You will have to replace the entire system if there are any holes larger than a pinpoint.

- ○ Check lights, windshield and wiper blades. Have someone use all the lights and the turn signals while you watch. If a light doesn't work, have the bulb replaced, then try again. The problem may be worse than a burned-out bulb.

○ Race the engine and make sure blue smoke doesn't shoot from the exhaust.

○ Look under the hood with the engine off. Belts and hoses should not be cracked and dry, the battery and radiator should not be corroded, and the radiator coolant should not be rusty.

○ Have someone start the engine and push the accelerator down gently. Listen for knocks and funny noises. Let the engine run for five minutes, then move the car. If there is a pool of liquid, you have problems.

○ When the engine is idling, put your foot on the brake and slip the transmission from neutral to reverse and neutral to drive. A loud clunk means the transmission bands need tightening.

○ Hold a dollar bill over the exhaust pipe. If it is sucked towards the pipe, you have serious valve problems. Rub your finger inside the pipe. You shouldn't get oil on your finger.

○ Give the car's interior a good look over. Check for stains or missing parts.

○ Apply strong pressure to the brake pedal for at least thirty seconds. If the pedal keeps going to the floor, you've got a brake leakage.

○ Test drive the car for thirty to forty-five minutes. Make sure the gears shift smoothly, the brakes don't make strange noises, and the steering wheel doesn't jerk and resist when you turn it. Turn the wheel sharply to make sure the car doesn't bounce or sway too much.

○ Check to see if the tires match and are worn evenly.

REFERENCE ————————————————————————————
Don't Get Taken Every Time: The Insider's Guide to Buying or Leasing Your Next Car or Truck by Remar Sutton, 1991.

Rental-fleet cars are up for sale

Automakers are boosting their profits by selling their new cars to daily rental fleets, like Hertz and Avis, and buying them back about six months later. Savvy car shoppers need to know:

The resale value on a car put out by the Big Three — Ford, GM and Chrysler Corp. — just isn't going to be what it used to be. If you like buying new cars and trading them in every year or two, find a car company that doesn't sell to rental fleets — Honda Motor Co., for instance.

If you like leasing your car, you'll also get the best deal from companies that don't depend on fleet sales. The leasing price depends on the projected resale value of the car.

The smartest move is to take advantage of these former rental cars on the market. You can buy your favorite car barely used at a great price.

REFERENCE
The Wall Street Journal, Jan. 6, 1992.

Selling your car at a profit

While you might have countless fond memories of adventures in your car, that's not the sort of thing that can put more money in your pocket when it comes time to sell. For most used car buyers, appearance is everything. Little details could add up to big bucks if you're willing to spend a few hours sprucing up your old car.

- Wash and wax your car carefully.

- Got a few scrapes? Touch up the paint job. Nobody wants a pre-scratched car.

- Make sure your tires are cleaned and inflated properly. Clean tires actually make the car seem newer and really don't take that much effort. Also, make sure your hubcaps match and aren't banged up. (A dented hubcap makes the buyer wonder how carefully you've driven the car.)

- Shampoo, vacuum and deodorize the car's interior.

○ Have all the documentation ready for potential buyers. This includes the title, owner's manual and any service history you might have kept.

○ Steam-clean the engine and top off all fluids.

○ Get rid of all the rattles and creaks. Any lubricant can help you fix that squeaky door.

○ Remove the assorted eyesores, such as bumper stickers, you may have collected over the years.

REFERENCE —————————————————————————

How to Sell a Used Car by Joel Makower, Putnam Publishing Group, New York, 1988.

When to lease a car

Just like when you buy a car, there are good times to lease, too. If you play your cards right, you can drive off with a hefty savings that will continue to add up as long as you hang on to the vehicle.

Visit your dealer at the beginning of the year. The car's price will be lower, and its residual (or lease-end) value will be higher. The longer a car sits on the lot, the older it gets, and the lower its residual value falls.

Older cars don't necessarily mean lower prices. Manufacturers often bump up prices at the turn of the year and in the spring.

The end of the month is also a good time to make an offer. If a salesperson hasn't made his quota, he'll probably be willing to bend over backward to put you in that car. And even if he has met his quota, he'll be willing to deal, if only to increase his take-home pay that month.

REFERENCE —————————————————————————

How to Save Big Money When You Lease a Car by Michael Flinn, Putnam Publishing Group, New York, 1990.

Selling your car through the classified ads

Every Saturday the newspapers are full of them: hundreds, sometimes thousands, of ads trying to lure potential car buyers. There are ways to make yours stand out without lining the paper's pockets with your money and without broadcasting yourself as a novice.

Don't over-abbreviate your ad. Acronyms and abbreviations work up to a point, but use too many and you will leave a sketchy image in the buyer's mind. Remember, most buyers only give your ad a second or so before moving on. If it's difficult to understand, it will probably be skipped.

You do not, however, want to under-abbreviate. It lets the car buyer know you're not skilled at selling vehicles. Savvy buyers may swoop in and take you for a few hundred dollars.

Finally, don't be vague. While too many details clutter an ad, too few won't spark a potential buyer's interest. Be sure to plug the car's advantages — such as air conditioning and an excellent radio.

REFERENCE
How to Sell A Used Car by Joel Makower, Putnam Publishing Group, New York, 1988.

Money management

Easy ways to save money

Don't have enough money, huh? Join the club. With prices seemingly always on the rise, it's as hard as ever to make ends meet. A close examination of your spending habits, however, will probably reveal some wasted funds.

A little self-discipline and belt tightening can go a long way towards improving your financial condition. Not only will you be able to pay your bills, you might be able to put some of that meager paycheck away for a rainy day.

- Set specific, reasonable goals. Know how you want to spend your savings and how much it will cost. Also, set yourself a firm deadline and allow no exceptions.

- Review your finances weekly. This is more than simply balancing your checkbook, it's a thorough examination of where your money is going. Be critical.

- Reduce your largest weekly expenses. More often than not, this is groceries. Look around for good sales and make the extra trip.

- Notice how often you buy unnecessary small items. Video games, that beer after work and that crummy movie you saw can be a bigger financial drain than you thought.

- Avoid buying things that will bring about further expenses.

- Be patient with yourself. A major change in spending habits can be hard to get used to. If necessary, take that savings book out and remember what today's sacrifice will mean.

- Indulge yourself occasionally. Without a little fun every now and then, you'll only get angry and frustrated. Buy yourself a present every week or two.

○ Always take a list when you go shopping. You probably already know how well this works with grocery shopping, but try expanding it to other types of buying.

○ Shop alone. Friends and children might convince you to buy something you don't really need — or want.

○ Avoid sales, unless you had already intended to purchase the item on sale.

○ Get to know a sales clerk and become friends. Once the bond is formed, the clerk may steer you toward bargains. Also, consider leaving some self-addressed postcards so she can let you know about upcoming sales.

○ Look for wholesalers.

○ Consider a buying club. After the initial expense, you can often save 10 percent and more off retail.

○ Rent seldom-used tools and appliances. Why buy a tiller when you'll only use it once or twice?

REFERENCE

Helpful Hints for Hard Times by Hap Hatton and Laura Torbet, Facts on File Publications, New York, 1983.

Prepaying your loan

Don't pay that loan off early, until you find out the facts. You may not save any money on interest at all.

Before you get a loan, you should find out if you will be penalized if you pay the loan off early. Just ask, "Is this a simple interest loan?"

With a simple interest loan, you will save money if you pay more than the minimum each month. The interest you are charged is calculated on the amount of principal outstanding monthly. When you pay more than the minimum payment, you are paying off the principal and reducing the interest you have to pay.

Another type of loan is called the Rule of 78s. You don't necessarily save money if you pay this kind of loan off early.

The Rule of 78s is also called the Sum of the Digits method. The numbers 1 through 12 total 78 when added together. In the first month of the loan you pay 12/78 of the total interest. In the second month, 11/78; the third month 10/78, etc. At the end of 12 months, you have paid 78/78, or 100 percent, of the interest.

You pay most of your interest in the first months of the loan, and this means you may not save money if you pay off early.

If you pay off a 12-month Rule of 78s loan in six months, you will have already paid 57/78 of the interest (12+11+10+9+8+7=57). You only save about 27 percent of the interest, instead of the 50 percent you would expect.

Lenders are required to tell you how the interest is calculated, so if you think you might be able to pay off the loan early, stay away from the Rule of 78s.

REFERENCE
Credit Union News, Fall 1992.

Simplest way to lower your phone bill

When is the least expensive time to make a phone call? Most people aren't sure.

Long-distance tolls are about 25 percent cheaper between 5 p.m. and 11 p.m. weekdays and Sunday and, in some states, between 12 noon and 1 p.m. on weekdays. Rates are about 50 percent cheaper on weekdays from 11 p.m. to 8 a.m., on Sundays before 5 p.m. and anytime on Saturdays.

REFERENCE
Telephone companies.

Keeping down the hospital bill

Hospital bills can be shocking — $10 for a couple of aspirin, $100 for a test you don't even remember having done, $75 for the time the doctor came in and asked you how you were feeling ... the list goes on.

Since most of the money you spend on health care is spent at the hospital, you can and should work to lower your hospital bills. How can you do that?

- First, when you need to have surgery or other nonemergency hospital care, check prices at various hospitals. Room rates differ, and some hospitals offer inexpensive rooms with three or four beds. For-profit hospitals are generally more expensive than others. Try to find a hospital that has performed the procedure you need at least 200 times. You're less likely to suffer complications there.

- See if your simple surgery or test can be done on an outpatient basis.

- Refuse tests the hospital requires before admitting you if they have nothing to do with your illness or your surgery.

- Find out if your doctor charges hospital admitting fees or release fees. You can refuse to pay these fees because no service has been done for you.

- Enter the hospital on Monday rather than on the weekend. Weekend rates are high, and you often receive little or no medical care on the weekend. The same goes for holidays.

- Consider bringing your own food instead of eating the expensive hospital meals.

- Bring your own drugs, even prescription drugs, and painkillers, like aspirin or acetaminophen. Ask your doctor what you'll need.

- If a doctor you don't know enters your room, find out why she's there. Refuse to accept services you don't think you need. You'll certainly pay for them later.

- Before delivering a baby at a hospital, find out if they allow "rooming in" (keeping the baby in the room with you) and if they let you leave the hospital early. Some hospitals will let you go after 24 hours, others after three days. Longer hospital stays will expose your baby to more infections anyway.

- Unless you expect complications, use a nurse-midwife or your family practitioner instead of an obstetrician.

○ Avoid Caesarean-section deliveries whenever possible. They are major surgery, risky, expensive and not always necessary.

○ Make a living will if you'd like to limit your medical care when you're terminally ill.

Once you receive your bill, check it for errors. Strange things have been known to show up on hospital bills.

Make sure your bill lists:

○ the right kind of room (semiprivate or private).

○ the right number of days you stayed. If you left before checkout time, check to see that you weren't billed for an extra day.

○ the correct type of treatment and the right number of hours of treatment by therapists or in specialized units.

○ only tests, X-rays, supplies, medications, therapy, injections, etc., that you received. Were you charged for an entire prescription although you only took the drug once or twice?

○ no thermometers, bedpans, humidifiers or personal items you weren't allowed to take home.

○ no blood transfusions if a donor or a blood bank replaced the blood.

○ no extra nursery care if you were able to keep your baby in your room.

○ no visits from your doctor that didn't occur.

REFERENCE

Getting the Most for your Medical Dollar by Charles B. Inlander and Karla Morales, The People's Medical Society, Pantheon Books, New York, 1991.

What price are you paying for your 'free' checking?

If you are leaving a minimum balance in your checking account in order to get free checking privileges, it may be costing you money. That money invested elsewhere could be earning at least 5 percent in interest. Calculate whether or not losing that 5 percent is worth the services the bank is giving you.

Also, banks usually charge a monthly service fee if you allow your balance to drop below the minimum. You end up paying for your checking anyway.

Remember, you only need to keep enough in a checking account to cover your monthly expenses.

REFERENCE ————————————————————————————————————
Terry Savage talks money: the common-sense guide to money matters by Terry Savage, Dearborn Financial Publishing Inc., Chicago, 1990.

Outlandish bank fees to avoid

Banks are getting creative in thinking of ways to nickel and dime you out of your savings. But don't hand over your piggy bank — you shouldn't pay those ridiculous bank charges!

If your bank comes up with any of these small fees, either refuse to pay (many banks will waive fees for customers who ask) or switch banks:

- A fee for making a deposit. One bank charges 35 cents for each deposit if your average daily balance drops below $2,000.

- A charge for withdrawing money if you use a blank counter slip rather than a preprinted one.

- Fees up to $2 for getting cash from another bank's automated teller machine.

- Over $15 for a bounced check.

- Monthly checking fees in the $10 range for customers with average daily balances under $3,000.

REFERENCE ————————————————————————————————————
Money, February 1993.

Catching credit report errors

Check your credit report before you apply to refinance your mortgage or take out a loan. You will gain valuable time by correcting any errors you find early.

You can either send requests to the three major credit bureaus — Equifax, Trans Union and TRW — or contact Credco Inc. at 1-800-637-2422.

Credco Inc. sells an easy-to-read report with all of your credit history combined. The report costs $24, about the same as ordering reports from the credit bureaus. TRW gives consumers one free report a year, but Equifax charges $8 and Trans Union charges $15. (California, Louisiana, Maine, Maryland and Vermont do not allow the credit bureaus to charge this much.)

The Credco report includes a form you can send to the three credit bureaus to dispute errors.

REFERENCE ——————————————————————
Kiplinger's Personal Finance Magazine, November 1992.

When you can get a credit report for free

You can get a copy of your credit report for free in three instances:

○ A collection agency notifies you that an unpaid debt is going on your credit report.

○ You are denied employment because your credit is poor.

○ Your credit or insurance rates are increased because of your credit report.

All you have to do is request a copy of the report within 30 days of receiving notice of your poor credit, and the agency will send you one for free.

REFERENCE ——————————————————————
Debtors' Rights, A Legal Self Help Guide by Gudrun M. Nickel, Sphinx Publishing, Clearwater, Fla., 1992.

What you can hide from the credit bureau

Remember, your old report card didn't tell every time you pushed Billy down on the playground, and your credit report won't tell everything about you either. It's not true that a mark goes against you every time you bounce a check.

Items that don't show up on credit reports:

> - bounced checks
> - late utility bill payments
> - late telephone bill payments
> - book or record club memberships
> - newspaper or magazine subscriptions

If you do have bad marks on your credit report, you can write a hundred-word letter that will be sent to everyone who wants to see your credit history. You may have a good reason for not paying your bills, and writing a letter at least shows that you care about your credit status.

REFERENCE
The Business of Living by Stephen M. Pollan and Mark Levine, Simon & Schuster, New York, 1991.

Stopping automatic payments

Have you authorized your mortgage company, insurance company or mutual fund manager to make automatic deductions from your bank account every month? At some point, you may want or need to stop the electronic transfer of your funds.

Some people have had trouble stopping payments because their bank said that it couldn't block payments without authorization from the company who was receiving their money. But don't believe your bank if it tries this tactic on you.

Under a Federal Reserve regulation, the bank is required to stop electronic transfers as soon as you tell it to do so. The bank can ask you for proof that you informed your insurer or your mortgage company that it can no longer make automatic deductions from your account. But you're the one who says when your money can be transferred, not the companies you pay.

REFERENCE
Consumer Reports, March 1993.

Cellular phone thieves —
do they have your number?

Own a cellular phone? You may be paying the phone bills, but you may not be the only one making calls.

Make sure you check your phone bill closely every month because cellular phones are computer hackers' dreams come true. Hackers can tap your phone line by cloning your mobile identification number and your electronic serial number.

The crooks can pluck these numbers from the airwaves with a small device that can be plugged into a vehicle's cigarette lighter receptacle. They then alter computer chips to match your phone-identification numbers and fit the chips into cellular phones. They usually sell the phones to drug dealers.

If your number is cloned, you could end up with a whopping phone bill for thousands of dollars. You will probably see calls to Columbia, Bolivia and other drug-exporting countries on your bill.

If you notify the cellular company, you will not be held responsible for these charges, but you may be forced to change your cellular phone number.

REFERENCE
Forbes, Dec. 21, 1992.

Record-keeping for hoarders and neat-freaks

The hoarders have monthly credit card statements from 1990 in their files while the neat-freaks throw away the statement before they get their canceled check paying the bill.

How long you should keep records is a mystery to most of us. As a general guide:

○ If a record can be easily replaced and you won't need it at tax time, toss it. If you use records for taxes, keep them for six years — that's as long as the IRS can ask for documentation for a claim, unless they suspect you of fraud.

○ For tax purposes, don't keep both a canceled check and a receipt for the same item. Keep just the check, except when you buy medicines at a drug store. Then you'll need the receipt, too.

○ Keep your credit card statement only until you receive the canceled check showing you've paid.

○ Keep monthly bank statements and investment statements until you receive your year-end summary, then throw them away. Keep investment statements that show a trade or dividend reinvestment.

○ Keep your pay stubs until you receive your year-end 1099 form showing your total salary and tax payments. Keep 1099 forms for six years.

○ Keep records of home improvements as long as you own your house so you can decrease your tax when you sell. Only keep home maintenance records to prove that you've kept the home in good condition when you sell. Keep house deeds as long as you own the home.

○ Keep receipts for major purchases as long as you own the item.

○ Throw away old insurance policies and ID cards that are no longer in effect.

○ Records to keep for six years: accident reports, alimony payment records, brokerage fund transaction reports, charitable-contribution receipts, Keogh statements, loan records, medical bills, nondeductible IRA records, partnership returns, property tax records and tax returns.

○ Records to keep for life: birth certificates, death certificates, divorce decrees, military papers, naturalization papers, trust agreements, vaccination records, wills and X-ray films.

○ Records to keep as long as they are valid: alimony agreements, certificates of deposit, custody agreements, negotiable instruments, partnership agreements, powers of attorney and prenuptial agreements.

REFERENCE ——————————————————————————————

The Business of Living by Stephen M. Pollan and Mark Levine, Simon & Schuster, New York, 1991.

Bankruptcy's no bonanza

In the 1980s it became almost fashionable to declare Chapter 13 personal bankruptcy. Doing so was less a sign of personal failure than a status symbol. Unfortunately, the flood of filings have left an almost romantic vision of what bankruptcy is all about.

If you're considering Chapter 13, know exactly what you're getting into.

- All of your listed, nonexempt debts will be discharged, but all of your nonexempt belongings are sold, with the money given to your creditors.

- Some debts, like overdue rent, are not exempt and you're still responsible for them. Also, say good-bye to things like your boat and summer beach home.

- You will not be permitted to file bankruptcy again for six years. So if a major bill arises in that time, you're stuck with it.

- Any friend or family members who co-signed loans for you are left exposed. Creditors can go after them for the money you can't pay.

- Your filing will be a black mark on your credit rating and financial records for 14 years.

- You start over, basically from scratch. You retain the tools of your trade, your clothes, perhaps a small amount of savings, your car, certain personal belongings and, if you're lucky, your house.

- Bankruptcy does not excuse you from paying alimony, child support, student loans, debts you forgot to list on your filing or any loans you got by lying about your finances.

REFERENCE
Helpful Hints for Hard Times by Hap Hatton and Laura Torbet, Facts on File Publications, New York, 1983.

Is your money safe?
Financial-planning fraud on the rise

"Sure, give me your money and I'll double it, no, triple it, in two years. And

I've got some swamp land in Florida I can sell you, too."

If you've handed your money over to a financial planner, you probably have nightmares that start something like this. For some people, these nightmares have come true.

You may need the services of a financial planner to make the most of your money, especially when you receive all your benefits and savings at retirement. But be aware of the incompetence, conflicts of interest and outright fraud that exist in the financial planning industry.

○ Interview at least three financial planners before you sign a contract or make any investments. Ask these questions:

- What is your educational and professional background? It's easier to qualify as a financial planner in some states than to get a driver's license. Usually, planners are not legally required to have any training or experience.

- May I review a copy of Part II of your Form ADV? This is the form investment advisors/financial planners must use to register with the Securities and Exchange Commission (SEC) and the state. They are required to show it to you if you ask. In the form, you will find information on their experience, their investment strategies and any potential conflicts of interest they may have.

- Will you give me the names and phone numbers of three of your clients? Call these people and make sure they are satisfied and have been receiving adequate returns.

- Can you show me three examples of investment plans and follow-up reports you have drawn for other clients?

- Has your track record been calculated according to the new performance standards of the Association for Investment Management and Research? (This association is a trade group of 23,000 money managers and stock analysts based in Charlottesville, Va. Its standards technically apply only to its members. Money managers must provide performance figures for all fee-paying accounts, not just the successful ones. They must furnish separate results for each of their investment styles and deduct wrap fees when calculating returns.)

○ Check your planner's record with your state securities commission and the SEC. Find out if your planner is licensed, if any complaints against him have been filed, and if the planner has a disciplinary record. The SEC can be reached at 202-272-7450.

○ Stay away from investments you don't understand. Stick to simple ones such as stocks, bonds and mutual funds. Only try limited partnerships and CMOs if you are a financial whiz.

○ Watch out for conflicts of interest. Find out what products the financial planner receives commissions on, and make sure they don't push these products on you. Limited partnerships often carry high commissions, for example. Ask the planner if she sells products or services other than providing investment advice. This may alert you to possible conflicts of interest.

○ Get all information in writing. If a planner recommends an investment, get a prospectus, audited financial statements and a signed statement of advice from the planner.

REFERENCE
Money, November 1992 and February 1993.

Where to go for free financial advice

There's no such thing as a free lunch, the financial experts say. But as they speak, they are handing out plenty of free advice.

Free (or practically so) books, brochures and pamphlets abound to help you learn how to handle your financial affairs.

Most industry-sponsored pamphlets are little more than sales brochures, but you can get free materials that are accurate and unbiased.

The federal government puts out about 50 free personal-finance brochures. To find out what is available, write to the Consumer Information Center, Pueblo, Colo. 81002.

Include a self-addressed, stamped envelope when you request any free publication.

Here are some of the best of the free publications grouped under various aspects of personal finance:

Banking and credit:

○ *Consumer Credit Handbook* (Consumer Information Center, Pueblo, Colo. 81002, Item No. 441Y; 50 cents). How to fix errors on your credit report and what you can do if you are turned down for a credit card.

○ *The Consumer's Almanac* (American Financial Services Association, Consumer Credit Education Foundation, 919 18th St. N.W., Suite 300, Washington, D.C. 20006; $2). Worksheets to help you keep track of monthly expenses, and more. Also published by this association: *What You Should Know Before Declaring Bankruptcy.*

○ *How to Get Safety Information From Your Financial Institution* (Weiss Research, 2200 N. Florida Mango Road, West Palm Beach, Fla. 33409; $2). Questions to ask your bank broker or insurer to determine how much risk they are taking with your money.

○ *Managing Family Debt* and *Getting Out of Debt* (Bankcard Holders of America, 560 Herndon Parkway, Suite 120, Herndon, Va. 22070; 703-481-1110; $1 each). Budgeting strategies and credit card advice.

Financial planning:

○ *Estate Planning: A Guide for the Days After a Loved One Dies* (Aetna Public Service Library — RWAK, 151 Farmington Ave., Hartford, Conn. 06156; 203-273-2843)

○ *Money Matters* (AARP-Fulfillment, 60 E St. N.W., Washington, D.C. 20049). Choosing a tax preparer, lawyer, financial planner and real estate broker.

○ *Selecting a Qualified Financial Planning Professional* (The Institute of Certified Financial Planners, 7600 E. Eastman Ave., Suite 301, Denver, Colo. 80231; 1-800-282-7526).

Fraud:

○ *Avoiding Travel Problems* (The American Society of Travel Agents,

The Fulfillment Center, 1101 King St., Alexandria, Va. 22314).

○ *Investment Swindles: How They Work and How to Avoid Them* (National Futures Association, 200 W. Madison St., Suite 1600, Chicago, Ill. 60606; 1-800-621-3570).

○ *Phone Fraud, We All Pay* (The National Association of Consumer Agency Administrators, 1010 Vermont Ave. N.W., Suite 514, Washington, D.C. 20005; 202-347-7395). How to guard against rip-offs such as calling-card abuse and phony third-party charges.

Insurance:

○ *A Personal Property Inventory* (Aetna Public Service Library — RWAK, 151 Farmington Ave., Hartford, Conn. 06156; 203-273-2843). Forms that help you list and describe your valuables to make filing insurance claims easier.

○ *Here Today, Gone Tomorrow* (The Insurance Information Institute, 110 William St., New York, N.Y. 10038; 212-669-9218). A glossary of basic insurance terms and points to remember when buying renter's insurance. Also published by the Institute: *Auto Insurance Basics*, *Tenants' Insurance Basics* and *How to File an Insurance Claim*.

○ *Shaping Your Financial Fitness* (The National Association of Life Underwriters, 1922 F St. N.W., Washington, D.C. 20006). Explanation of annuities, Medigap insurance and other insurance products that are hard to understand.

○ *The Consumer's Guide to Health Insurance* (Health Insurance Association of America, P.O. Box 41455, Washington, D.C. 20018). The basics of private health coverage.

Investing:

○ *A Common Sense Guide to Taking Charge of Your Money* (Fidelity Investments; 1-800-544-4774). How to handle a lump-sum pension distribution.

○ *Investors' Bill of Rights* (National Futures Association, 200 W. Madison St., Suite 1600, Chicago, Ill. 60606; 1-800-621-3570). What a broker must disclose to you before selling you an investment, and other useful facts.

○ *Nine Tax Tips for Mutual Fund Investors* (GIT Investment Funds, 1655 Fort Myer Drive, Suite 1000, Arlington, Va. 22209; 1-800-336-3063).

Mortgages:

○ *Home Buyer's Vocabulary* (Consumer Information Center, Pueblo, Colo. 81002, Item No. 121Y; $1). Information on mortgage jargon such as escrow, earnest money and points.

○ *How to Shop for a Loan* and *How to Shop for a Home* (Great Western Financial; 1-800-492-7587).

○ *Refinance Kit* (HSH Associates, Attn: RESI, 1200 Route 23, Butler, N.J. 07405; $3). How to calculate the cost of various mortgage refinancing deals.

○ *Your Money & Your Home* (Countrywide; 1-800-669-6064). How to take out a mortgage, from application to appraisal to closing.

Retirement:

○ *A Single Person's Guide to Retirement Planning* (AARP-Fulfillment, 60 E St. N.W., Washington, D.C. 20049). Financial guidance on investing, insurance, etc., and tips on nutrition, relationships and housing.

○ *Can You Afford to Retire?* (Life Insurance Marketing and Research Association, P.O. Box 208, Hartford, Conn. 06141; 1-800-235-4672; $1.50). Sources of retirement income, plus worksheets to calculate your current and future net worth. There is a $10 minimum order, so get friends to order with you.

REFERENCE ————————————————————————

Money, November 1992.

Credit card concerns

Give yourself a little credit

They're awfully handy at times, but credit cards are one of the surest and quickest ways to run up a hefty debt. Add in the service charges and interest accrued on your revolving debt and that nice dinner on the town can cost a lot more than you originally thought it would. You can save yourself money when it comes to credit cards. You just need to use a little common sense.

- Use a maximum of two cards — one with no annual fee, which you pay off in full each month, and another with a "low interest rate" which you pay in installments.

- Consolidate all your business and travel expenses onto one card.

- Always read the fine print that comes with your credit card. If you don't understand something, ask!

- Deal only with an institution you recognize. Don't pay money up front to apply for a charge card. And never call a 900 number to apply.

- If you lose your credit card, notify the card company immediately. That way you won't have to pay if someone makes charges on your card. If you wait until after charges are made to notify the company, you have to pay the first $50 charged.

REFERENCE ——————————————————————————————
How to Save Money on Just About Everything by William Roberts, Strebor Publications, Laguna Beach, Calif., 1991.

"So that's why my bill is so high!": Credit card facts you need to know

If you are an average American consumer, you carry nine credit cards in your wallet and keep an average balance of $2,000 on your bank credit cards. But many cardholders don't know these facts:

○ If you've been enjoying a credit card with no annual fee and the card company decides to impose one, call to tell them you will cancel the card unless they waive the fee. Most card companies will waive the fee rather than lose a customer.

○ If you want to cancel a credit card, don't just stop using the card. That leaves you with an open line of credit on your credit history and a potential victim of credit card fraud. Instead, mark "cancel account" on a bill showing a zero balance, cut your card in half, and send it back to your credit card company.

○ Your interest-free grace period on purchases is usually forfeited if you carry a balance. So, the credit-card company starts charging you interest on purchases right away if you have an outstanding balance on your account.

○ Most banks charge interest from the date a purchase was made rather than from the date the charge was posted.

○ When you don't pay your balance in full, many credit card companies charge interest based on the average daily balance from the previous month, instead of charging interest simply on the balance still owed. In other words, if you charge $1,200 one month and you pay $1,000, you will be charged interest on the average daily balance of the $1,200 in charges, not just on the $200 you still owe.

○ The Annual Percentage Rate (APR) most banks show on their credit cards is misleading. They state the APR as a simple interest rate while it is actually compounded. If you don't pay in full every month, you pay interest on your purchases and interest on the interest. If your card has an 18.5-percent APR, you actually pay around 20.15 or more in interest.

○ If you only make the minimum payment on a $2,000 credit card bill, you will pay off the bill in 33 years and pay over $7,000 in interest.

REFERENCE ———————————————————————————
Nolo News, Winter 1992.

What credit card companies don't want to know

Beware of crooked credit card companies! Credit card companies can cheat you by sending you a bill without giving you credit for payments. They can purposely send your bill late so you'll have to pay interest. Even when credit card companies don't break the law, they are gouging you by charging exorbitant interest rates and high annual fees. You don't have to be a credit card sucker.

Choosing and using a card:

○ Choose a card with low or no annual fees. There are plenty of them, and they are just as good as the cards with high annual fees. Especially avoid the gold or prestige cards. The advantages you get aren't worth the cost of the card.

○ Be a free rider. That's what card companies call people who use their card and pay it off every month, never paying a cent of interest.

○ Choose a card with at least a 25-day grace period. You should have a long period after you make a purchase during which you are charged no interest.

○ Do not have your credit card at any financial establishment where you have other accounts. The card company could grab your money without telling you.

○ Don't use your card for cash advances except in major emergencies. Credit card companies charge high fees for cash advances and usually waive the interest-free grace period when you receive a cash advance. You end up paying interest not only on your cash advance, but on all the other purchases you made during that period. If you insist on getting cash advances, find one low-interest card with no cash advance fee and use it only for this purpose.

○ Never use a "cash advance check." It looks like a regular check, but you pay a ridiculous amount in interest and you lose your credit card legal rights.

Correcting billing errors:

Card companies are required by law to look into and correct billing errors, and billing errors are just about anything that looks wrong to you on your credit card statement.

Some examples of billing errors are:

○ You received your statement late.

○ The statement lists goods or services that were not accepted by you. (For example, you returned the goods, the product was defective, you refused a service, or you stopped payment because the service wasn't satisfactory.)

○ The statement lists a purchase you don't remember making.

If you spot a billing error, send the credit card company a letter saying that there is a billing error on your account.

Don't pay the disputed amount until the card company proves to you that the bill it sent you was right. If the company ignores your letter or doesn't get back to you for 30 days, you never have to pay the amount you said was a billing error (as long as it's under $50).

Always dispute an entire amount charged to your account rather than a partial charge. For instance, you may have bought several items of clothing from a store and then returned one shirt because it had a hole in it. The return doesn't show up on your account. When you write to the credit card company, dispute the entire clothing store charge, not just the $14.95 you paid for the shirt. That way, you'll be "playing it safe," in case you need to stop payment on some unexpected charge.

If the credit card company tells you they are right and you are wrong, write another letter and still don't pay the amount. If the credit card company reports you to a credit bureau, it must also report that there is a dispute and give you the name and address of the credit bureau. You can sue the credit card company and take them to small claims court, but usually the threat to do so is enough.

You can get copies of your charge slips from the credit card company for free if you tell them you are investigating a billing error. It is illegal for them to charge you. You have to ask for them within 60 days of receiving your erroneous bill.

Stopping payment on your credit card:

If you paid more than $50 for a service or product in your home state or within 100 miles of your home and you were ripped off, all you have to do is write a letter to the merchant telling him that you are unhappy with his services and demand a refund.

Then write a letter to the credit card company saying that the amount is a billing error, explaining that the service was not done or the product is defective. Say that you have made a good-faith effort to settle the dispute with the merchant.

Demand a "charge back" to the merchant. The credit card company should charge the disputed amount back to the merchant's bank.

You can get your money back if you are unhappy with a service even months after you paid the bill. As long as you complain before you pay, you can tell the credit card company you want your money back years after the purchase, and you should get it.

Calling the credit card cops:

Many government agencies enforce credit card laws. Threatening in writing to report a credit card company to the correct agency is very effective. To find out which government agency regulates your credit card company, call the Consumer Complaint Office of the Federal Deposit Insurance Corp. in Washington, D.C., at 1-800-424-5488.

How to complain to the card company:

- Be nice. Nastiness gets you nowhere.
- Do not start at the top. Move up the line.
- Use the line "I have a problem, and I need your help."
- Make someone else the bad guy, not the person you are corresponding with.
- Be brief.
- Type your complaint.

○ Never send originals of your documents.

REFERENCE ————————————————————————————————

Credit Card Secrets — That You Will Surely Profit From by Howard Strong, The Boswell Corp., Beverly Hills, Calif., 1989.

Protecting your number from credit card crooks

Do you realize what you throw away every day? If someone sifted through your trash, would they find —

○ Any pre-approved credit card applications? You probably get pre-approved applications in your mail several times a month. If you don't tear them up before you throw them away, crooks who sift the trash can send them in and get a card in your name. All they have to do is forge your signature and put a "new" address. You may never know you have a problem until you get turned down for credit because "you haven't paid your credit card bills."

○ Old credit-card statements or shopping bags with old charge slips left inside? It's true that the most you'll be held responsible for on your credit card is $50 worth of unauthorized charges. And if someone used your card number but not your card to make a transaction, you won't have to pay for any of it. But you could be in for months of hassles with a credit card company.

Don't make it easy for crooks to get your number — credit card, social security, phone card, etc. Take some simple precautions to protect yourself, such as shredding canceled checks, pay stubs, airline and train ticket stubs, travel itineraries or any document that might contain your credit card or social security number before you throw it away. A public trash can at an airport or a mall is an even easier target for crooks than your home garbage.

Other protective measures:

○ When you shop, refuse to write your address and phone number on credit card receipts and your credit card number on checks. You can tell the shop clerk that these practices are against the card issuers' regulations and are illegal in some states.

○ Consider applying to change your driver's license number if it's the same as your Social Security number. Merchants often insist that you write your driver's license number on checks, and a crook with all that information can apply for a credit card in your name. If you live in a state that won't let you change your number, don't let clerks write it on checks.

○ If your credit card statement doesn't arrive when it should, notify the credit card company right away. In the past, crooks have stolen statements from peoples' mailboxes and used the information to make purchases.

○ When renting a car, don't leave your rental agreement in the car after you turn it in. Also ask for carbons of car rental agreements and shred them yourself.

○ Don't use an obvious number for your calling card number — like birth date, work extension or consecutive numbers.

○ When using your calling card, cover the phone with your body, even if you don't see anyone nearby. Crooks use video cameras and binoculars to see the card number and to record what you punch in.

If someone does use your credit card number, write to the card issuer and tell them an "unauthorized charge" was made. Don't call it a "billing error." There's a difference. A billing error, for instance, has to be reported within 60 days. There's no time limit on unauthorized charges.

REFERENCE
The Wall Street Journal, July 17, 1992.

Trading in for a debit card

Whether you present a debit card or a credit card to a merchant makes no difference whatever to him. The cards look alike and are handled in the same way.

The difference to you, however, is significant, and you may find it well worth your while to consider trading in one of your credit cards for a debit card.

A debit card works almost like your checkbook: Payment is drawn automatically from your account at the time of the transaction. Your checking account statement includes a list of the month's transactions, but, like check transactions, they are already paid. And because you don't have a bill to pay each month, the debit system is ideal for people who travel for long periods of time.

There are two kinds of debit cards. "On-line debit cards" are similar to your ATM card, require a Personal Identification Number (PIN), and draft money from your account instantly. "Off-line debit cards" do not need a PIN and usually take two to three days to clear a charge.

Some banks charge a $10 to $15 annual fee for off-line cards but not for on-line cards. Some charge for neither.

You may pay 25 cents to $1.50 per transaction, however, for on-line cards you can use at an automatic teller machine, depending on whose machine you use.

There are, of course, advantages and disadvantages to both.

The advantages:

- There are no high interest rates because you can't carry over charges from one month to the next.

- Some banks charge no annual fee on debit cards. With all-electronic handling, their costs are less, and they make their money on the fee charged to the merchant.

- You can leave your checkbook at home, reducing the chance of its being lost or stolen.

- Even supermarkets are accepting credit and debit cards these days, substantially speeding up payment at the cash register.

- Checks are seldom accepted out of town, but credit and debit cards are welcomed, even internationally.

The disadvantages:

- You must keep track of your expenditures and remember to deduct them from your checkbook balance.

○ Forget the "float" you're used to with checks (two to three days) and credit cards (as much as a month until the end of the billing cycle).

○ Some banks charge an annual fee.

○ It's next to impossible to stop payment on an on-line debit transaction.

○ There's the possibility of theft. Never write your PIN on an on-line debit card.

REFERENCE
"*Smart Banking*" by Robert Heady, *The Atlanta Journal/Constitution*, April 12, 1993.

Insurance secrets

Insure yourself against these insurance traps

Unless you want your goldfish to be well-provided-for when you die, don't buy life insurance when you are single with no dependents. Close your ears to the pleas of your insurance agent: He wants you to believe you need it.

Insurance agents have convinced a lot of people. Thirty percent of all life insurance policies are owned by single people without dependents. If you list your parents as beneficiaries and they are not dependent on you, you are wasting your money. Buying life insurance on your children is a waste of money, too. The only purpose insurance should have is to protect you from the loss of income or financial assets.

Insurance salesmen may tell you that buying insurance on a child will guarantee their insurability later. Or, he may try to sell it as a method of financing college. Both are terrible reasons to buy insurance on a child. There are many ways to build a college fund, and life insurance is one of the least efficient.

Buy less life insurance when you get older, not more. An insurance salesman may try to convince you that you need more insurance as you grow older. You tend to have fewer responsibilities as you grow older and more of your income comes from non-job-related sources, especially when you retire.

REFERENCE —————————————————————————————————
More Wealth Without Risk by Charles J. Givens, Simon & Schuster, New York, 1991.

Why your insurance agent doesn't work for you

Here's a great idea: Pay your life insurance agent an hourly fee and let him give you whatever commission he receives as a rebate. That way you will know he has no reason not to sell you the best plan. Forget it. It's illegal. Because of anti-rebate laws in every state except California and Florida, your life insurance agent can't work for you.

Why is this such bad news? If an agent makes a lot of commission on one policy, he will push you to take that policy instead of one that might be better and cheaper for you. Most insurance companies even offer several policies that are exactly the same except for the amount of commission the agent receives.

Ask your agent questions like: "How much will you earn if you sell me this policy?" and "Do you have any policies that pay you only a 50-percent commission?"

If you choose to get whole life insurance instead of term life insurance, buying a "low-load" life insurance policy can be the smartest move. You buy straight from the company or through fee-for-service advisors, paying little or no commission. Doing your own research is harder than going through an agent, but worth it.

The advantages:

○ Saves money. The policy will be less expensive.

○ Higher returns. Since your first year's premiums aren't going to pay the agent's commission, the money goes to work for you.

○ Changing your mind. You can get your money out in a few years without hurting yourself. With a commission policy, your cash value is less than your investment for several years.

○ Stability. Without commission, the company's expenses are lower, so they don't have to practice risky investments to get adequate returns on your money.

○ Best policy for you. Advisors not affected by commission are more likely to be impartial when recommending policies.

Some prominent low-load insurance companies are:

Ameritas	1-800-552-3553
USAA	1-800-531-8000
Lincoln Benefit	1-800-525-9287
Fee for Service	1-800-874-5662

REFERENCE

Consumers' Research Magazine, October 1992.

Don't throw your money
into the whole-life hole: buy term insurance

There is no comparison between term insurance and whole life insurance. Whole life insurance is overpriced by up to 600 percent. Some people choose whole life because the premiums don't go up as you age, but level premiums mean only one thing: You are grossly overpaying for your insurance when you are young.

All the added benefits that insurance salesmen tell you you'll receive with a whole life policy are not really benefits at all. They say you'll earn interest on your policy, but the average interest is around 1 percent, and even that is added to your cash value instead of given to you.

When you die, your survivors won't receive your cash value (what you've actually paid to the insurance company). They will only receive the death benefit. So if you've paid in $30,000, your survivors won't receive your death benefit plus $30,000, unless you have a special policy that is even more grossly overpriced. Another myth about whole life insurance is that it has a special tax status.

Life insurance is not a tax shelter. If your insurance salesman tells you that you can borrow money from your insurance policy tax-free, tell him that you can borrow money from anywhere tax free — there are no income taxes on borrowed money.

You can save 70 percent to 80 percent of your insurance costs if you choose an annually renewable term insurance policy. Your policy lasts for one year, and you receive a renewal notice at the end of the year. Your premium will go up a few dollars every year. As long as you pay your premium, you are guaranteed that you will be allowed to renew your insurance policy.

Another money-saving strategy: Switch insurance companies every four or five years to get the lowest rates they offer. Insurance companies will often offer the first four or five years of a term policy at discount rates to woo you to the company, then begin to increase your premiums significantly. If you change companies every five years or so, you can take advantage of the lower rates offered to new customers.

Insurance companies often vary dramatically in the rates they charge to people of a certain age. Company E may have the best rates for 30-year-olds, while company B has the best 40-year-old rates. You can start this money-saving technique by picking the company with the lowest initial rate for your age.

REFERENCE
More Wealth Without Risk by Charles J. Givens, Simon & Schuster, New York, 1991.

How to buy two insurance policies for the price of one (almost)

Business partners or two-income couples with no children might benefit from a new product offered by the insurance industry. It's called "first-to-die" life insurance.

The policy covers two or more people and pays off when the first one dies. Since there is only one death benefit, it is cheaper than buying two individual life insurance policies.

Of course, the "first-to-die" plan leaves the survivor with no insurance, so a couple with children would not want to choose this option. If a couple has no children, the survivor after the first death might need some help paying off the mortgage, but the second-to-die may not need any insurance. Remember, you don't need insurance if you have no dependents.

While you are not getting more for your money with this plan (it is cheaper because it pays out less), "first-to-die" may be the best and most cost-efficient plan for you.

REFERENCE
Forbes, Oct. 26, 1992.

How to get the best risk rating

One life insurance company's poor risk is not necessarily another's. If you have health problems or work in a dangerous job, don't assume that every company will put you in the "poor risk" category. Shop around for the insurance company which will give you the best rating and the best price.

If you think you have been rated unfairly, ask the company what additional tests or information might help to change your rating.

An error in your Medical Information Bureau (MIB) file might cause you to get a poor rating. If a company rates you for something in your history that seems wrong, you can call 617-426-3660 to check your MIB file.

Don't put off buying insurance until you lose weight or quit smoking. Most insurance companies will rerate you after a year of improved health.

America's best life insurance companies

Allstate

Connecticut General Life

Hartford Life

John Hancock Mutual

Manufacturers Life

Massachusetts Mutual

New York Life

Northwestern Mutual

Principal Mutual

Prudential

State Farm

Sun Life Assurance

Teachers Insurance and Annuity

Variable Annuity Life

REFERENCE
Kiplinger's Personal Finance Magazine, September 1992.

How much house insurance you need

You should look at the market value of your house to figure out how big a homeowners policy you should buy, right? Wrong.

The "replacement value" of your house should determine how much insurance you need. Replacement value is how much it would cost you to rebuild your house if it burned down or was destroyed, and it's usually not the same as the market value.

You'll never have to replace the land your house is on, so you don't have to insure it. If property values are high where you live, your house's replacement value is probably less than the market value.

If your house is very old, the replacement value may be much more than the market value.

You'll need to have an appraisal done on your house to find out its replacement value. You may be able to get one free through your mortgage lender or your insurance agent.

The insurance policy you buy should be for at least 80 percent of the total replacement value of your house. That's how much you have to buy to get the full replacement value of any property that is stolen or damaged. (The insurance company considers 80 percent to be full replacement value because they're willing to take a bet that your house will never be totally destroyed.)

Maybe you're willing to bet that nothing will ever damage more than half of your house. You might want to buy an insurance policy that covers only 40 percent of your total replacement value (half of the 80 percent the insurance company requires to give you full replacement value).

Bad idea.

Why?

If your television, VCR and stereo are stolen or if your hot water heater leaks and floods the house while you're on vacation, you'll regret your insurance decision.

Instead of getting the full replacement value for your electronics equipment or for your carpet and hardwood floor, you get the greater of fifty percent of the total loss, or the actual cash value of your loss (replacement value minus depreciation for its age).

Depending on how old your carpet or your equipment is, you could be left collecting almost nothing!

Review your homeowners insurance policy every year to be sure you are keeping up with inflation. If you make changes or improvements in your house, your policy should reflect that, too.

REFERENCE

How to Get Your Money's Worth in Home and Auto Insurance by Barbara Taylor, McGraw-Hill Inc., New York, 1991.

What your homeowners insurance covers

Does your homeowners policy cover what you think it does? If your kids knock a softball through your window will your insurance pay to replace it? Probably not. But if they crack your neighbor's window, you're covered.

Every homeowners policy is different and can be custom-designed to meet your needs, but here's the standard coverage:

- Your home (of course) and any other structures on your property. Usually detached garages, toolsheds or gazebos are covered for up to 10 percent of the amount of coverage on your house. (If your house is covered for $100,000, your gazebo is covered for up to $10,000.)

- Your yard — trees and plants — for up to 5 percent of the coverage on your house. Trees and plants are protected against anything except wind damage. The insurance companies can't afford to remove and replace every tree that falls. But if the tree falls on your house, the policy pays to have the house repaired and the tree removed from the house.

- Personal belongings for up to 50 percent of the amount of the coverage on your house.

- Losses of personal property away from home, like suitcases and clothes while traveling. In some parts of the country, like New York City, a high-crime area, off-premises coverage is extra.

- Credit cards and ATM cards, up to $500 for an unauthorized use of your card. (The truth is, you'll never have to pay more than $50 in unauthorized credit card charges — it's the law.)

- Loss of use of your home — hotel stays and living expenses while you're waiting for your home to be rebuilt after a fire or other disaster. Many policies provide up to 20 percent of the amount of the coverage on your home (that's $20,000 if your home is insured for $100,000).

- Liability to others — covers you against lawsuits for bodily injury and property damage that you, your family members or your pets cause to other people. If your dog chews through the leg of your antique table, you're not covered, but if he chews through your neighbor's table leg, you're covered.

What homeowners policies don't cover:

○ Damage by floods and earthquakes.

○ Home business risks. If you run a business out of your home, you probably need additional coverage. A standard policy pays little for damage to business equipment and won't cover you for lawsuits that stem from your business activities.

○ Theft and damage related to burglaries if you live in a high-crime area.

REFERENCE ─────────────────────────────────

How to Get Your Money's Worth in Home and Auto Insurance by Barbara Taylor, McGraw-Hill Inc., New York, 1991.

Why you should never buy mortgage insurance

Don't fall prey to an insurance industry gimmick — mortgage insurance. Mortgage insurance is a gimmick because it's overpriced, and you don't need it.

The insurance salesman will try to convince you that you have to have it, but you don't. It is designed to pay off your mortgage when you die, but it protects the mortgage company much more than it protects you.

Instead of buying mortgage insurance, which will cost you about $600 per year for a $100,000 house, buy a $100,000 term life insurance policy. Or simply add $100,000 worth of coverage to the term policy you already have.

A $100,000 term policy for a nonsmoking, 40-year-old male should cost under $200. You might even be able to find a policy for $100 per $100,000 worth of insurance.

The disadvantage: Term life insurance premiums will go up as you get older while mortgage insurance premiums will stay the same.

But, as you pay off your mortgage, you can purchase less and less term insurance. With mortgage insurance, as you pay off your mortgage, you don't pay less in premiums and your survivors only receive how much you still owe on your mortgage.

Also, the average mortgage only lasts seven years — most people either sell or refinance in that time. So, premiums that don't go up aren't that significant anyway.

(There are mortgage insurance policies with premiums that increase as you age and coverage that falls with your balance, but they still cost about three times what the same coverage from a term life policy would cost.)

The final drawback to mortgage insurance is that most policies actually pay off the mortgage when you die, while term insurance policies will hand a check to your survivors to be used as they think best. If you leave behind a pile of medical bills, your house payment may not be the most pressing cost facing your survivors.

REFERENCE ─────────────────────────
1,001 Home Ideas, May 1991.

Canceling mortgage insurance you no longer need

Your mortgage company will never tell you, but you don't have to pay mortgage insurance forever.

If you made a down payment of less than 20 percent, you are probably still paying mortgage insurance every month. Once the balance on your loan equals about 80 percent of the value of your house, you can cancel your mortgage insurance.

Ask your lender at what loan-to-value ratio it will agree to release you from paying premiums. If you have been in your house several years and the homes in your area have held their value, you have probably reached the balance you need.

REFERENCE ─────────────────────────
The Wall Street Journal, Nov. 20, 1992.

Four steps to cheaper automobile insurance

○ **Step one**: Buy only the coverage you need. When you buy an automobile insurance policy, you're really purchasing a package of six different coverages. The state you live in requires you to purchase some of these coverages, and the rest you may or may not need.

The state usually requires a certain amount of bodily injury liability insurance, property damage liability insurance and uninsured motorist coverage. Some states require personal injury protection, or no-fault, insurance.

Collision insurance and comprehensive insurance are usually offered in the insurance package, but they're not required by the state. They cover damage to your car, rather than damage to people and other people's property. You may not want comprehensive, or collision, for an old car that's worth about $2,000.

○ **Step two**: Get the highest deductible you can afford, afford to lose unexpectedly, that is. You could save up to 30 percent on your premiums if you take a $500 deductible on your collision coverage instead of a $250 deductible. A $1,000 deductible would save even more.

○ **Step three**: Shop around for the best deal. Get price quotes from at least three insurance companies. Prices can vary dramatically from insurer to insurer.

New York did a cost comparison survey a few years ago to see how much a 35-year-old male driver would pay annually in premiums for the minimum auto insurance required by the state. They checked with 20 insurers and got a price range of $362 to $655!

○ **Step four**: Ask the insurance company what discounts you qualify for. Some discounts available are:

— Good driver. Drivers with no accidents or violations on their records can get a discount from most insurers.

— Mature driver. Drivers at least 50 or 55 years old can get discounts of 10 to 20 percent, depending on how much they drive every year.

— Carpool driver. Carpoolers may get 10 to 20 percent premium discounts.

— Multicar household. Put all the family cars on one policy and you might get a 15 to 20 percent discount.

— Multipolicy discount. If you get your homeowner's and automobile insurance through the same company, you may get a discount.

— Antitheft device. Install an alarm, an ignition-shutoff system or a wheel-locking device, and you may receive a 5 to 15 percent discount.

— Automatic seat belts and air bags. Some insurers give discounts of up to 30 percent for cars with automatic seat belts and air bags.

— Nonsmoking driver. Don't smoke? You may receive better rates on liability, no-fault and collision insurance. (It's difficult and dangerous to light a cigarette while driving.)

Make sure you ask each insurance company you call for available discounts. Some companies will offer more discounts than others, and many won't offer any at all unless you ask for them.

REFERENCE
How to Get Your Money's Worth in Home and Auto Insurance by Barbara Taylor, McGraw-Hill Inc., New York, 1991.

Rental-car insurance rip-off

Travelers who have to rent cars when they reach their destination should be aware of one of the biggest rental-car rip-offs: the collision damage waiver (CDW). You do not have to purchase CDW. In fact, more than 20 states require that renters be told that the coverage is optional. Illinois and New York even ban the sale of CDW.

CDW is basically worthless because it either duplicates your own insurance coverage or the rental car company will find a way to deny your claim. The company can claim that you breached the rental contract, especially if you violate a traffic law or you let someone else drive the car. In other words, if you wrecked the rental car while speeding or running a red light, you probably won't be covered anyway.

To make sure you aren't taken in by the rental car company, you need to call your car insurance broker and check your credit card for coverage.

Your car insurance broker can tell you whether your present policy will pay if your rental car is stolen or damaged and how much it will pay. If your coverage seems inadequate, you can buy a rider that will cover your rental car.

Most company credit cards and gold credit cards cover damage to rental cars. The coverage usually takes over where your regular car insurance leaves off.

Credit card companies can reject your claim if they can prove you broke the rental agreement, but so can rental car companies. You will come out ahead if you rely on your credit card CDW coverage instead of buying CDW from the rental car company.

REFERENCE ——————————————————————————
Nolo News, Winter 1992.

What your health insurance company doesn't want to know

"Why can't they write these things in plain and simple language?" you grumble as you try to read your health insurance policy for the tenth time. "I have a better chance of understanding the proposed amendments to the Constitution on my voting ballot."

Would it surprise you to learn that your deepest suspicions are correct? That complex, confusing language in your insurance policy was put there to give insurance companies an out when you file a claim they don't want to pay.

The company can point to some confusing small print informing you that you weren't covered for that after all.

But, you aren't at the mercy of your insurance company. Since you have little choice about buying insurance, the courts have passed many rules to make it more difficult for insurance companies to deny your claims. If you know these rules, you can fight back even without the help of a lawyer if a claim you file is denied.

> ○ **The courts have ruled that where insurance policy language is unclear, the language will be construed against the insurance company.** That means that if the language can mean two different

things, what you think it means will prevail. You don't have to take the insurance company's word for what a phrase in your policy means. Don't feel that you have to be an expert to stand up to your insurance company, either. The policy has to make sense to an ordinary policyholder.

○ **The reasonable expectations of the policyholder will govern the meaning of policy language.** This means that you get the coverage you thought you were getting as long as your expectations were reasonable. You get it even though some little fine print in the back of the policy tells you otherwise.

○ **Exclusions in any insurance policy must be phrased in plain, clear and conspicuous language. The burden is on the insurance company to prove that the exclusion applies and that it is clear and understandable.** Usually, when an insurance company denies your claim, it points to some little clause or phrase called an "exclusion." The exclusions usually appear on the last pages of your policy, and they take away most of the coverage the first pages gave you. These exclusions are often impossible to understand. This is another rule to fall back on if you don't understand why your claim was denied.

○ **Failure to properly fill out insurance forms or get them in to the company on time is of no consequence to an otherwise valid claim, unless the insurance company can show it has been harmed by this failure.** Most insurance companies have time limits on how long you can wait to file a claim, and they may have certain procedures you need to follow to fill out a claim.
You certainly should try to follow their requirements, but the company cannot deny your claim just because you file late or you forget to sign your name with your middle initial. The company has to prove that they weren't able to handle or investigate your claim because of your mistake. Even if you send a form in months late, an insurance company would not normally have problems paying your claim.

○ **If your claim is denied, insist on a written explanation. Most**

states require insurance companies to provide a written explanation. With a written explanation in hand, you can reread your insurance policy to determine if the company had a legitimate reason to deny your claim.

○ **In a group policy, the booklet you receive outlining your coverage may govern over the fine print in the master insurance policy.** You may have insurance through your job or through a club or association you belong to. If so, you probably received a booklet describing your insurance while your company's business manager keeps the master policy.

If your booklet indicates to you that you are covered for a procedure, and the insurance company has to point to the master policy to show you that you are not, you have grounds to refute the denial of your claim.

If you have trouble getting your claims paid on your own, you do have two places to turn:

○ **The agent who sold you the insurance policy or your group policy administrator.** Your insurance agent has a duty to obtain the correct coverage for you and to protect your interest. He will often contact the claims department on your behalf. For group policyholders, the insurance company usually appoints an administrator to handle claims filed by your group.

○ **The State Department of Insurance.** In most states, the State Department of Insurance will help with consumer disputes. They will generally contact the insurance company to see if they can settle the dispute for you.

Keep copies of letters you send to the insurance company and, when you call, always ask for the name of the person you are speaking with. Keep your phone bills to prove you called.

Exercising your rights may just be a matter of informing your insurance company by letter or by mail that you know what your rights are.

REFERENCE ————————————————————————

Payment Refused by William M. Shernoff, Richardson & Steirman Inc., New York, 1986.

About Medicare and
Medicare-participating doctors

If you are 65 or older, are permanently and totally disabled or have end-stage renal disease, you are eligible for Medicare. You have paid for this benefit through the Social Security taxes withheld from your paycheck. If you think you are eligible for Medicare, apply at your local Social Security office.

Medicare has two parts. When you enroll in Medicare, you're automatically covered under Part A, the hospital insurance. It provides some coverage for hospital care, post-hospital skilled-nursing care, home health care and hospice services. The only hospital care you have to pay for is the Medicare deductible.

You are not automatically enrolled in Part B, the medical insurance. If you opt for this section, you get some coverage for doctors' and therapists' fees, outpatient services, laboratory fees, home health care and medical equipment.

Even if you're covered by an employer-provided retiree health plan, purchase the Part B of Medicare during your individual enrollment period. Your employer will appreciate the federal money and will be more likely to keep your benefits going.

Your enrollment period is from three months before your 65th birthday to three months after. You can enroll during the general enrollment period (January 1 to March 31), but you pay an additional 10-percent premium every year you wait.

The biggest gaps in Medicare insurance are in Part B. Doctors don't have to limit their fees to what Medicare has agreed to pay.

When you choose a new physician, try to choose one who has accepted "Medicare assignment." That means that the doctor has agreed to charge only what Medicare has decided is appropriate for the service the doctor provides. Medicare will still only pay 80 percent of the doctor's fees, but at least the doctor is limited in what he can charge you.

To find a Medicare-participating physician, consult the free booklet *Directory of Participating Doctors in Your Area.* You can get the booklet from the Medicare carrier for your state or from your local Social Security office.

If a doctor does not participate in Medicare, he is still limited in how much he can charge you. To find out the maximum allowable actual charge (MAAC) for a doctor's service, call your Medicare carrier and give them your doctor's name and address, the description of the medical service needed, and the Medicare code number for the service. You can get the code number from your doctor.

For a chart of the exact coverage Medicare provides, check *Your Medicare Handbook.* After looking over the chart, you may decide you need an insurance policy that will supplement your Medicare coverage.

REFERENCE
Getting the Most for your Medical Dollar by Charles B. Inlander and Karla Morales, The People's Medical Society, Pantheon Books, New York, 1991.

Supplementing your Medicare insurance

Those tie-in-the-back, show-it-all hospital gowns provide more coverage for you when you're in the hospital than your Medicare policy does.

Medicare does cover most of the services you receive from hospitals and doctors, but what they mean by cover and what you think they mean may be two different things entirely.

If you can afford it, you need to purchase an insurance policy that is specially designed to supplement your Medicare insurance. These policies are often called medigap policies.

One option many people have for supplemental insurance is retiree health insurance provided by their employer. These are usually the best plans for your money.

If you're not covered by an employer plan, your choices for supplemental insurance are a service benefit policy and an indemnity benefit policy. The indemnity benefit policies give you a fixed amount of coverage per day or per service. These policies are better than the service benefit policies.

A service benefit policy pays the difference between the amount charged for a medical service and what Medicare pays for the service. But if Medicare doesn't cover a service at all, the service benefit policy usually doesn't either. With a service benefit policy, you still have gaps in your coverage.

Some dos and don'ts when purchasing a supplemental indemnity benefit policy:

○ Don't purchase disease-specific insurance (like cancer insurance) or limited-purpose insurance (like accident insurance). Usually these policies just duplicate ones you already have.

○ Don't buy policies that exclude pre-existing conditions, if possible. If you have to, the exclusion should be limited to six months. (Federal law says that a policy that excludes pre-existing conditions for more than six months cannot be called a Medicare supplement.)

○ Don't buy a policy with a limit on annual payments or a lifetime limit, unless the limits are very high.

○ Don't purchase policies that you can't renew or that are hard to renew.

○ Don't fall for an insurance salesman's claim that a policy will pay for reductions in Medicare payments due to the Gramm-Rudman-Hollings balanced budget law. Medicare already provides for this.

○ Do make sure the insurance company is licensed in your state and check its rating in *Best's Insurance Reports — Life/Health.* This book should be available in your local library.

○ Do look to see if the policy covers doctor's fees even if they are over the amount Medicare has approved for doctor's services. If the policy will only cover the 20-percent copayment that Medicare approves, you may be left with some huge doctor's bills.

○ Do ask the insurance salesman what the average out-of-pocket expense is for policy-holders.

○ Do try to choose a policy with a "stop-loss provision." Once you've paid a certain amount of money out-of-pocket, the stop-loss provision will keep you from having to pay any more.

Remember, state law gives you the right to buy a policy and cancel it within a certain period of time if you decide it's not what you want.

REFERENCE ─────────────────────────────────────

Getting the Most for your Medical Dollar by Charles B. Inlander and Karla Morales, The People's Medical Society, Pantheon Books, New York, 1991.

How to increase Medicaid eligibility

If you need help paying for your spouse's or a parent's nursing home costs, you can try to increase their eligibility for Medicaid. Unfortunately, anything your spouse or parent gives away 30 months prior to applying for Medicaid counts as an asset in determining their eligibility.

But there are a few exceptions to the 30-month rule that apply in many states:

○ Your parents' home will not be considered an asset as long as one parent or a dependent relative is living in it.

○ You and your spouse can evenly divide a jointly owned asset, such as a bank account or stock. The half you take for yourself will not be counted as an asset of your spouse when determining eligibility.

○ If a spouse or another co-owner takes money out of a bank account, in some states that money will not count as an asset.

○ Your parents can get rid of assets by paying you or other relatives for providing care and assistance. As long as you draw up a written contract, you can get around the 30-day rule this way.

The rules in every state vary, so check with an expert on your state's Medicaid rules before you reorganize assets.

REFERENCE
Finances after 50: financial planning for the rest of your life by Dorlene V. Shane, Harper & Row, New York, 1989.

What is your claim worth?

Ouch!

You tripped on the stairs at your favorite department store and broke your hip. Your car was hit from the rear while you sat at a red light, bruising your ribs and cracking your wrist.

How much will you receive from the insurance company when you file your personal injury claim? Impossible to know? Yes, but with this knowledge you can make a pretty good guess:

Insurance companies use a formula to determine how much you should be paid for your accident injuries. They start with your total medical expenses related to the injury (these are called "medical special damages"). They then multiply that amount by 1.5 to 5, depending on how serious your injury is.

The "multiplier" is higher when your injury is very painful, when the medical treatment lasts a long time, when your injury is obvious or easy to see, or when you have a long recovery period.

The multiplier also depends on the type of medical treatment you receive. Treatment by a physician will have the most weight, while massage therapy and chiropractic treatment will make the multiplier lower.

Finally, the insurance company will determine fault. If you are hit from the rear in your car through no fault of your own, you will receive 100 percent of the figure you came up with using the damages formula. If you are 25 percent at fault, the insurance company will give you 75 percent of your damages-formula figure. Often, you will have a pretty good idea of how much you were at fault in an accident.

However, you have the most influence over the "fault" part of the formula. If your eyesight is poor or your walk is unsteady, you may be too willing to blame yourself for a fall. Instead, give the insurance company plenty of reasons to award you money for your injury.

For instance, if you fell down the stairs at a department store, go back to the store with a friend armed with a camera and measuring tape. You may find that the stairs are uneven, the white carpet makes the edges blurry and lights shine in your eyes when you step on the stairs.

Next, check out the county's building code at your public library. The stairs in the department store may not comply with the code. For example, a handrail is probably required for stairs of a certain length or width.

List the facts you gather, especially violations of the building code, when you send your claim to the store's insurance company.

Remember, stores have to be safe for elderly shoppers or shoppers whose eyesight isn't the best. Your settlement can be dramatically affected if you do your homework.

REFERENCE ————————————————————————————————
Nolo News, Winter 1992.

Cash vs. coverage:
Which one should you take?

Everyone needs health insurance ... so you wouldn't get off your employer's insurance plan for love or money ... or would you?

Many employers these days are asking employees to opt out of the company's medical plan in exchange for extra cash. It's easy to see why. One company got eight percent of its employees to opt out of its insurance plan and saved more than $500,000 the first year.

If you think that you can get on your spouse's plan for less money than your company is offering you to opt out, you might jump at the chance. But look before you leap.

Say you are a woman who chooses to join your husband's insurance plan. What if he loses his job or switches jobs to a company that discourages family coverage? Many companies are charging from $50 to $100 a month extra to cover spouses who have coverage available elsewhere.

You will probably be allowed to get back on your company's plan if you lose your outside coverage (note the "probably"), but if your health has deteriorated or you have a pre-existing condition such as pregnancy, you are out of luck.

First, you should never take money instead of health insurance coverage if you don't have coverage available elsewhere. Second, if you could get on your spouse's plan, look over the summary plan description of both plans before you make a decision. Most of all, make sure your company will take you back once you opt out of the insurance plan.

REFERENCE
The Wall Street Journal, Nov. 20, 1992.

Is this HMO for you?

Has your employer offered you the option of joining a Health Maintenance Organization instead of sticking with your traditional insurance plan? You may be trying to weigh how much you like your family doctor against some of the benefits of the HMO — no claims to be filed, no high-priced deductibles or copayments, etc.

Studies have shown that HMOs offer quality medical care, but to decide if the HMO your employer offers is the best option for you, ask these questions:

○ What type of HMO is it — a multispecialty clinic or an office-based HMO? A multispecialty clinic houses your primary physician, specialists for you to consult, a laboratory where your tests are done and a pharmacy to provide your drugs. You may like this convenience, or you might rather have the more personal, private feel of an office-based HMO.

○ Has the HMO been in business for at least two or three years? Many HMOs aren't doing well financially, so make sure the one you choose is stable.

○ What is the atmosphere of the clinic? Is it clean and up-to-date? Is the staff courteous and professional? Are there too many people sitting in the waiting room? Are the physicians sticking to the appointment schedules?

○ How long does it take you to get to the HMO's primary care facility and the hospital? The family physician you have now may be only five minutes away. Travel distance becomes more important when you or a family member is sick.

○ How long does it take to make an appointment and see a doctor? If you're sick, can you see a doctor in one or two days or does it take a week or two? Can you see a doctor right away if you have an urgent problem?

○ What's the procedure for receiving emergency care? If you can't use the HMO's emergency center or the emergency room at their affiliated hospital, what do you have to do to make sure the HMO will pay the bill? Approval from your primary physician is usually required ahead of time, but what if you can't get in touch with him?

○ Is your primary care physician compatible with you? The HMO may let you interview prospective physicians before you join if you insist on it. Ask how the HMO controls quality of care and how accessible the physician is. The HMO should let you select a different doctor if you're not satisfied with the one you choose.

○ What hospitals and specialists does the HMO use? Does the hospital used by your primary care physician have a good reputation for quality and service? Does the HMO physician list cover all the major specialties?

With all of this information in hand, you should be able to decide if the HMO offers the quality medical care you need.

REFERENCE
Getting the Most for your Medical Dollar by Charles B. Inlander and Karla Morales, The People's Medical Society, Pantheon Books, New York, 1991.

Getting the most out of employee benefits

Most employees are getting 20 percent fewer benefits now than they had in the '80s, but they have to make twice as many benefit choices. Here are some guidelines to help you wade through all the options you are offered:

○ If available, set up a **dependent care account.** Working couples and single parents can contribute up to $5,000 a year to pay for baby-sitting, day camp, pre-school and after-school costs for children under age 13, or to pay for the care of dependent parents. Your contributions to the account are exempt from Social Security tax and federal and state income tax (except in New Jersey and Pennsylvania). Using this account, you can save hundreds more dollars in taxes than you could using the dependent care tax credit.

○ Choose to set up a **medical reimbursement account.** With these accounts, you can save pretax dollars to pay for medical and dental expenses, physical exams and eye care. You can usually save up to $2,000 to pay for deductibles and other things not covered by your health insurance. You do have to use everything you contribute or you lose it.

○ Participate in the **401(k) plan**. These are the best savings plans around. And, remember, most plans let you borrow against the money you've saved in the plan without incurring a tax liability.

○ Choose your **health plan**. You may be given a choice between a traditional fee-for-service plan and a health maintenance organization (HMO). If choosing your own doctor is important to you, go with the traditional plan. Otherwise, consider that HMOs have no deductibles, little paperwork and small payments per visit.

○ Think about choosing the **optional hospitalization coverage.** Many insurance plans only pay 80 percent of hospital costs. Often, you can buy coverage for the extra 20 percent for only a few dollars a week. The money is deducted before taxes, so you really only pay about 70 cents of every dollar in premiums.

○ Steer clear of the **extra life insurance** option. If you need extra life insurance for children or other dependents, only get it through your company if you are uninsurable elsewhere. Otherwise, you can probably get cheaper term life insurance from an outside provider.

REFERENCE ———————————————————————————————
Kiplinger's Personal Finance Magazine, November 1992.

College strategies

Getting a college loan when you're not poor

Are you caught in the middle on college costs? Low-income families can get loans for their children, and the rich don't need them. That leaves you, heading for broke, although you make $40,000 to $100,000 a year.

But don't despair. Here are some loans available to middle-income parents:

○ *Home-equity loans.* You can borrow up to 80 percent of home equity, which is the appraised market value of your home minus the unpaid debt. If you itemize deductions, the interest on the loan is deductible.

○ *Government loans.* Most government loans are for poor families, but there are some that the middle-incomers can apply for. Consider one called PLUS, or Parent Loan for Undergraduate Students. You can borrow the cost of tuition minus other grants received. The interest on the loan is the going rate on a one-year Treasury bill plus 3.25 percentage points. The application fee is 3 percent.

○ *Special loans.* Many major banks offer education loans, sponsored by groups such as Nellie Mae Inc. and the Education Resources Institute. The maximum a parent can borrow is usually $20,000 per year for each child, and you have from 15 to 20 years to pay off these loans. Application fees are around 5 percent, and interest rates are based on the prime rate or a short-term Treasury bill rate, plus 2 to 4.5 percent.

○ *Retirement-plan loans.* This possibility involves borrowing from your profit-sharing plan or 401(k) plan. Many companies will allow you to borrow up to 50 percent of the amount vested or $50,000, whichever is less. Typically, the interest rates are good (the prime rate plus 1.3 percentage points), but you usually have to repay within five years. If you don't repay or if you leave the company without repaying, the outstanding balance becomes taxable.

○ **Life-insurance loans.** You can borrow much of the cash value of your life insurance policy at an interest rate slightly higher than what your money earns in the policy. The interest compounds and is subtracted from your policy's cash value. If you don't pay the loan back, the amount of the loan will reduce the death benefit.

REFERENCE
The Wall Street Journal, Dec. 3, 1991.

New college financial-aid rules

Government is paying attention to the plight of the middle-income family. Take advantage of the new amendments to federal higher-education laws that will help send the kids to college.

○ Now it is easier to apply for financial aid. Each family will have only one form to fill out, and most families that earn less than $50,000 a year will need to provide only income information. (For private aid, schools may require more forms.)

○ More families are eligible for the government loans called Pell grants. The family income limit is $42,000, up from $35,000.

○ Loan limits for all programs, including Stafford, Perkins, SLS and PLUS, have risen. Parents, regardless of income, can borrow up to the full year's tuition plus expenses for their child.

○ Home or farm equity is no longer included when judging your financial need.

REFERENCE
Kiplinger's Personal Finance Magazine, September 1992.

Making college affordable

If you know you won't be able to save enough to finance four years in the

Ivy Leagues and the thought of lots of debt gives you the willies, consider these options:

- ◯ Send your child to a local college for the first two years. Some colleges even have lower admission standards for students who have some college years under their belt. A local college can be less expensive, and your child can live at home to save on room and board. First, make sure your dream school will accept transfer students. And next, check to see what courses the school will accept for credit before you waste money on classes that won't transfer.

- ◯ Encourage your child to take advanced placement courses in high school. They can get college credit for them by passing "AP" exams and could save you a semester's tuition.

- ◯ Contact your alma mater. Many colleges will provide a special deal for the children of alumni.

- ◯ Send all your kids to the same school. Some colleges will cut tuition as much as 50 percent when a sibling attends the school.

- ◯ The hallowed halls of academia beckon: Become a professor. Faculty offspring usually receive tuition cuts of 50 percent to 100 percent. Other university employees can often get tuition cuts for their children, too.

- ◯ Take advantage of colleges' various payment plans. For instance, you can split your tuition payments up, or you can pay for two years at once to protect yourself against tuition hikes.

High school children can help out by working part time and during the summer. But remember the Catch-22: If they save too much, they may not be as eligible for financial aid.

A better option is the co-op program many colleges offer. Students can go to school one semester and do career-related work the next. Students make money, gain experience and get their foot in the door of major companies.

REFERENCE ——————————————————————————————
Fortune, 1993 Investor's Guide.

Learn the best ways to build education savings

These days, you have to start saving for your kid's education before he's even a twinkle in your eye. If you'd rather save now than borrow later, follow these steps:

- ○ Put a hefty percentage of your money into growth-oriented stocks and mutual funds when your child is young. Stocks generally outperform all other financial investments over time. Several of the big fund groups, such as Vanguard Group and Fidelity Investments, will lower their investment minimum if you are saving for education and will set up a "custodial account."

- ○ When your child's teen-age years approach, you should start shifting your savings out of stocks into more stable investments, like intermediate-term bonds and other fixed income securities. Now if the stock market crashes when your child is 17, you're safe. You might try to buy securities whose maturity dates match the date you'll need to cash them in. That way you don't have to worry about cashing in a bond when it's selling below par.

- ○ You can set up a savings account in your child's name. This is tempting because the interest is taxed at a much lower rate. But be warned! Saving in your child's name can kill her eligibility for financial aid. Children are expected to contribute much more of their savings to college than parents are. Also, your child can legally do anything she wants with the money at age 18 or 21 (depending on the state), including not go to college.

REFERENCE ————————————————————————
Fortune, 1993 Investor's Guide.

Economic update for college kids: Don't start out behind

Full-time workers weren't the only ones to be hit hard by the recession of the early 1990s. It's put added strains on college students, too.

Many more students are taking part-time jobs to help with expenses, working an average of 20 hours a week. But these same students are accumulating debt instead of savings.

About 80 percent of college graduates in the New England states have debts besides their student loans. Over one-quarter pay between $251 and $500 in car, credit card and other loan payments every month. Ten percent pay over $1,000 per month in noneducation debt.

Add this to the fact that 60 percent of college graduates leave college owing a bundle in student loans, and you've got a scary economic future for college grads. In 1990, graduates in the New England states had an average student loan debt of $8,200.

Make sure your kids know what to expect on the economic horizon. High-paying jobs that will take care of loads of debt may not be looming there. Only three percent of college undergraduates expect to earn more than $35,000 in their first jobs.

Most students are aware that the job market is more competitive than ever these days. Almost half of all college students begin their job search six months before graduation, and more students have decided to pursue advanced degrees.

College students must learn to set a budget and plan on ways to pay off their student loans as soon as possible.

REFERENCE ————————————————
American Demographics, June 1992.

The parent network

You can send something to your college kid that's a lot more valuable than an allowance — a job lead. One of the best ways to support your child, and your child's college, is to alert the school to job openings at your employer.

You may not want to recommend your child for every position that comes open at your employer, but if you send in job leads and encourage other parents to do the same, you will create a job network for your child. Arrange to fax or mail job openings to the college's career development center, and the career counselors will contact qualified students.

If the college hasn't considered parents as a resource for jobs, you may be the spark that spurs them to send letters to other parents asking for their participation in a "parent network."

REFERENCE ────────────────────────────────

The Wall Street Journal, Feb. 22, 1993.

The scholarship-search fraud

A warning to high-school students searching for college scholarships and to hopeful entrepreneurs searching for an easy business to start: Stay away from services that use computerized databases to match prospective students to scholarships.

It seems like a good investment to pay $50 or $100 to a service that will find scholarship information for your child. But some of the information you buy will be outdated or inappropriate or just plain false. Scholarship information is available at public libraries and high-school counselors' offices for free, if you are willing to spend time digging it up.

Even more entrepreneurs are getting ripped off than students. Entrepreneurs, hoping to profit from escalating college costs, are buying licenses to operate student-scholarship matching services from small parent companies.

Licenses usually cost under $500, and that's about as cheap as you'll ever start a business.

But don't be tempted. You probably won't earn as much as the parent companies say you will. Many companies have been sued or are being watched by the Federal Trade Commission for misleading licensees.

One company, Academic Guidance Services, told prospective licensees that it would limit the number of licensees to 200 nationwide. When the Federal Trade Commission sued AGS, they had handed out 17,000 licenses.

The companies also charge the entrepreneurs ridiculous fees for mailing lists and promotional materials.

Whether you are looking for a scholarship or looking to make money, this is one time you should do it the hard way.

REFERENCE ────────────────────────────────
The Wall Street Journal, Nov. 6, 1992.

Testing, testing: which test to take

The two main tests used in the college admissions process are the ACT assessment program and the Scholastic Aptitude Test (SAT). Most colleges will accept either test, and many college admissions offices will advise you to take both.

The test used the most in college admissions varies depending on your home state. For instance, the SAT is more widely used in Georgia while the ACT is preferred in Tennessee. The SAT has traditionally been more popular, but the ACT is gaining ground, especially with the Ivy League colleges.

The ACT consists of four academic tests taken during standard time periods plus a student profile section and an interest inventory. The English, mathematics, reading and scientific reasoning tests assess students' educational development and readiness to master college course work.

For all four tests, the minimum standard score is 1 and the maximum standard score is 36. The composite score is the average of the four standard scores, also in a 1 to 36 range.

In 1990, the mean composite score for college-bound graduating seniors who took the test was 20.6.

The profile section asks the student about admission and enrollment plans, academic and extracurricular achievements, as well as biographical information and grades in the four test areas. The interest inventory section of the ACT is designed to measure the student's six major interest areas.

The Scholastic Aptitude Test is intended to show a student's aptitude for college work and is not dependent on mastery of any particular academic discipline.

The test has two parts, verbal and math. The verbal section consists of multiple choice questions designed to test the student's reading comprehension and vocabulary. The math section shows the student's ability to solve problems involving arithmetical reasoning, algebra and geometry.

Each section has a scoring range of 200 to 800 or 400 to 1600 overall. The national average score for 1990 graduating seniors was: verbals — 424 and math — 476.

The SAT also has a short section asking students about their college plans. The College Board compiles this information, and many colleges use it for mailings to prospective students. If you indicate that you're interested in a small, private, four-year college in a big city, colleges that fit that description will send you information.

REFERENCE ————————————————————————

Peterson's Guide to Four-Year Colleges 1992, Peterson's Guides Inc., Princeton, N.J., 1991.

The maze of college admissions

If you thumbed through a stack of college brochures recently, you probably got the idea that all colleges are looking for the same four or five students — those healthy, clean-cut, laughing youths that grace the glossy covers of most college brochures.

That really isn't true, but colleges do want students who will enjoy the lifestyle the college offers and will want to stay the entire four years. To find out what type of person a particular school is looking for, look to alumni and ask yourself if these people project the type of image you wish to project.

Once you've figured out the type of student the school has chosen in the past, try to find out why these particular people were admitted. You will probably discover that there will be a strong correlation between the school's best-known departments and the students.

Say you've settled on Northwestern University. You know the school has a strong journalism department and a weak football team, and so you might want to sell yourself as an aspiring journalist who was starting quarterback for Smalltown High.

The trick is to package and sell your unique talents to the school that is looking for those particular talents.

Once you've narrowed the choice down to three or four potential schools, study the brochures and begin getting your paperwork together.

The highest hurdle for most applicants is the essays you must write. Often, the essay topics will give valuable clues about the feasibility of applying to a particular school. For instance, if the essay topics all revolve around books or poems, and you are a math and science person who is still wondering why Milton's *Paradise Lost* didn't mention the Big Bang Theory, you might want to rethink that school.

Be sure when you are filling out the application to follow directions. If the application says to submit typed essays, type them. Some schools receive so many applications that they automatically discard those where the applicant did not follow directions.

To guard against this, have a high school guidance counselor or your parents look over your application. In addition, make a list of all the parts of the application — transcripts, essays, payments, and so forth — so you can check each when it has been accomplished.

Be sure to write thank-you notes to those people who took the time to write references for you. Also, write thank-you notes to any alumni who spoke with you, to the admissions counselor who interviewed you, and to anyone else who was helpful during the admissions process.

REFERENCE
U.S. News and World Report, America's Best Colleges, Washington, D.C., 1992.

How to choose a college

People choose colleges for a variety of practical and not-so-practical reasons. The following questions might help you focus on a range of colleges:

- Where do you want to spend the next four years? Do you prefer a rural environment? Small to medium-sized town? Large city?

- Do you want a residential college experience? Or, would you be happier living off campus?

- Do you want to live close to home or as far away as you can get?

- Are climate and section of the country important to you?

- If you had to label yourself, would you say you're liberal? Conservative? Libertarian? Preppie? Nerd? Misplaced hippie? Skinhead?

- Do you enjoy spectator sports? Greek life? Campus politics?

- Do you thrive on small classes and lots of personal attention from teachers or large classes with no personal attention?

○ Do you do better on essay tests and papers than multiple choice tests and few or no papers? Does the word "curve" fill you with glee or dread?

○ Would you be comfortable in a single-sex college? Or a religiously oriented college?

○ Would a wide diversity of students, lifestyles and values challenge or bother you?

REFERENCE ————————————————————————————

Peterson's Guide to Four-Year Colleges 1992, Peterson's Guides Inc., Princeton, N.J., 1991.

Toughest and easiest college admission policies

Like competition? There are colleges designed especially for you.

The colleges and universities reporting the most stringent admissions policies say that on average, they accept fewer than 30 percent of their applicants.

Seventy-five percent of the entering freshmen in 1991 were in the top 10 percent of their high school classes and scored more than 1250 on the SAT or more than 29 on the ACT.

Peterson's Guide to Four-Year Colleges, updated every year, lists the top colleges and their admissions requirements. Some of these big-name universities are Bryn Mawr, Cornell University, Dartmouth College, Duke University, Harvard University, Massachusetts Institute of Technology, Rice University and the U.S. Air Force Academy.

But there's a flip side to the college coin. No matter how bad your high school grades or how low your ACTs and SATs, there are many colleges and universities across the country that will accept you.

Peterson's Guide also lists these "noncompetitive" schools. That means virtually all applicants are accepted. Many Bible colleges are noncompetitive, along with a few state schools and many two-year community colleges.

REFERENCE ————————————————————————————

Peterson's Guide to Four-Year Colleges 1992, Peterson's Guides Inc., Princeton, N.J., 1991.

Best college buys

Want a name-brand college or university at Kmart prices?

Try Trenton State College in New Jersey; Berea College in Kentucky; Northeast Missouri State University in Kirksville, Missouri; or the University of Alaska at Fairbanks.

In order, the tuition charges for the school year are: $4,400, free, $3,504 and $3,900. Those figures include out-of-state tuition but not room and board, books or personal spending money.

Top-ranked liberal arts colleges at bargain basement prices include St. Mary's College of Maryland in St. Mary's City, Maryland; Spelman and Morehouse colleges in Atlanta; College of the Ozarks in Branson, Missouri; and Texas A&M at Galveston, Texas.

REFERENCE
   U.S. News and World Report, America's Best Colleges, Washington, D.C., 1992.

10 steps on the road to Ivy

If your dreams include a son or daughter at an Ivy League school, the time to begin preparation is shortly after the child's birth. Although enrolling your child at a fancy nursery school and prep school can help, it's not always possible when you're saving your money to pay for Ivy League tuition.

You'll pay well over $100,000 for a four-year stint at the Ivy League schools: Brown University, Columbia University, Cornell University, Dartmouth College, Harvard University, Princeton University, University of Pennsylvania and Yale University.

You can enhance an average education yourself by preparing your child at home. Here are 10 things you can do to ready your child for Ivy League competition:

- If you must have a television set, monitor it very closely, allowing no more than one hour a day.

- Read to your child and to yourself daily. When the child becomes old enough, insist that he read something daily, and then discuss what he has read with him.

○ Talk about ideas frequently. Explore ideas with your child through field trips, more books and projects.

○ Never shame or scold a child for his ideas. Listen carefully and point out other ways of looking at the same issue, but always treat his ideas and opinions with respect.

○ Insist on high grades. Achieve them with firm discipline and assistance. Be enthusiastic and knowledgeable about your child's school.

○ Make constant learning a part of your home life. Play word games so that learning new vocabulary is a normal, fun part of life.

○ Talk frequently about various colleges and visit them if possible.

○ Make friends with Ivy League alumni and invite them to your home often so that your child will see what sort of person goes to the top schools.

○ Help your child develop a strong body and healthy habits by encouraging him to participate in some sort of sports activity. This will assist his mental efforts, as well as boost his self-esteem.

○ Genuinely commend your child's efforts and his achievements. Don't pressure him with how much better he could have done or how much more you expect out of him next year. Glorying in the achievements of the present will provide the necessary inspiration for the future.

REFERENCE —————————————————————————
U.S. News and World Report, America's Best Colleges, Washington, D.C., 1992.

The payoff

If you don't have an answer when your child stares at his homework and says, "I don't see how this is going to help me in real life," here's one: Every additional year you go to school, you increase the wages you will earn by an average of 16 percent.

REFERENCE —————————————————————————
National Bureau of Economic Research.

But if you can't make it through school ...

Don't despair. If your child does drop out of high school or refuses to go to college, he probably won't starve. Eight of the 10 occupations that will grow the most over the next 15 years require a high school education or less.

The Bureau of Labor Statistics predicts that the United States will need an extra 2.6 million cashiers, janitors/maids, retail salespeople, and waiters/waitresses over the next 15 years. We'll only need 1.2 million additional lawyers, doctors, engineers and writers/artists/entertainers.

REFERENCE
Bureau of Labor Statistics.

⧈ Investment strategies

The easy way to become
a millionaire: mutual fund magic

Want to be a millionaire by the time you retire? It's really easy. If you are 25, put away $30 a month in a mutual fund. Thirty-year-olds will need $70 a month.

If you are 35 and just getting started, stash $150 a month in a mutual fund. A 40-year-old needs to sock away $300 a month to retire a millionaire in 25 years.

It sounds too good to be true, especially for the youngsters, but it's a fact. Mutual funds will earn a 15-percent return every year if managed properly. Plus, you can invest in a fund without being an investment expert or knowing much about stocks.

You pay a small fee for a professional to pool your money with other people's and spread all the cash out over a variety of investments.

Another plus: Mutual funds are not risky investments. Charles Givens, the famous writer of *Wealth Without Risk,* recommends mutual funds as one of the best ways to "develop a personal fortune without going out on a limb."

Mutual funds are safe because they are diversified — that means they own many stocks or bonds or other investments instead of just one. If one stock or investment vehicle the fund holds does poorly, there are plenty of others in the fund doing well.

There are three types of mutual funds — bond funds, stock funds and money market funds. A mutual fund that invests mostly in stocks is called a stock mutual fund.

Bond mutual funds invest primarily in bonds — loans to a corporation or a government agency that pay guaranteed interest rates like CDs but go up and down in value.

Mutual funds are called money market funds when they invest in short-term, very safe instruments that bear interest. (Note: Money market funds are not the same thing as money market bank accounts. The banks are just trying to confuse you by using the same name.)

Two simple steps to managing your money in a mutual fund account

1) First, find out the prime rate — the interest rate banks charge to their most favored customers. The prime rate is easy to follow because it moves very slowly and any change will make front-page headlines.

2) Next, use the prime rate to decide which mutual fund to put your money in. Remember the three types of mutual funds? You only want to invest in one of these three types at a time. If the prime rate is above 9 1/2 percent and on a downward trend, pick a bond fund. If the prime rate is below 9 1/2 percent, pick a stock fund. If it is above 9 1/2 percent and rising, pick a money market fund.

If you choose a stock fund because the prime rate is below 9 1/2 percent, and the prime rate rises above this level and seems to be on an upward trend, you should switch your money to a money market fund.

How to pick a mutual fund

The choice of funds seems bewildering, but don't panic. You can narrow down the list quickly armed with some qualifications:

○ Choose a fund that is part of a family of funds with at least one stock fund, one bond fund and one money market fund. Once you get in a family of funds, it will be very convenient to switch from one fund to another when the prime rate changes.
Libraries, newspapers, business magazines and books, such as Charles Givens' *Wealth Without Risk,* list mutual fund families with their addresses and toll-free phone numbers and show the funds' past performance.

○ Choose only a no-load or a low-load fund. A load is a sales commission. If you think you are getting a better fund when you pay a commission, think again. No-load funds perform as well or better than high-load funds.
To get a list of the names, toll-free phone numbers and objectives of

150 no-load funds, you can write to The 100% No-Load Mutual Fund Council, 1501 Broadway, Suite 1809 New York, N.Y. 10036, 212-768-2477. The cost of their publication is $3.

○ Choose a fund you can afford. You have to be able to make the fund's minimum-required initial deposit. Many funds require an initial investment of $1,000, but a few have no initial-investment requirements, such as the Twentieth Century family of funds.

○ Choose a fund with more than $25 million and less than $3 billion in assets. Tiny funds probably cannot afford the best fund managers. The big funds lose their flexibility.

○ Stay away from the "specialty stock mutual funds" unless you are a knowledgeable investor who can handle extra risk. These are the sector funds, precious metal funds, industry funds, etc. Balanced funds and closed-end funds are also poor performers. You will probably do the best in regular growth and, especially, aggressive growth stock funds.

○ Pick a regular money market fund instead of the "tax-exempt" or "insured" varieties. If the top tax bracket ever hits 45 percent again, the tax-exempt fund will make sense.

How to evaluate a fund's performance

To evaluate how well a fund did in the past, don't necessarily look at 5-year or 10-year performance records.

If you're smart, you will be switching between the three types of funds when the prime rate changes, so you are only interested in the fund's performance in the interest-rate environment you will use it in. (See the history of the prime rate chart below.)

For instance, late 1985 and 1986 were years of low interest rates. You would have invested in stock mutual funds at that time. So only check the performance of stock mutual funds for 1985 and 1986. It doesn't matter how bond funds and money market funds did in these years. You wouldn't have had your money in those anyway.

For a more complete and current copy of the history of the prime rate, you can call the Federal Reserve Bank in your district.

History of Prime Rate Changes

1987		1990	
April 1	7.75	Jan. 8	10.00
May 1	8.00		
May 15	8.25		
Sept. 4	8.75		
Oct. 7	9.25		
Oct. 22	9.00		
Nov. 5	8.75		

1988		1991	
Feb. 2	8.50	Jan. 2	9.50
May 11	9.00	Feb. 4	9.00
July 14	9.50	May 1	8.50
Aug. 11	10.00	Sept. 13	8.00
Nov. 28	10.50	Nov. 6	7.50
		Dec. 23	6.50

1989		1992	
Feb. 10	11.00	July 2	6.00
Feb. 24	11.50		
June 5	11.00		
July 31	10.50		

REFERENCE
Federal Reserve Bank

How to open an account

○ Once you have chosen two or three mutual fund families that meet all your requirements (and don't worry about finding *the best ever* mutual fund — you'll go crazy), call their toll-free numbers and request a prospectus on each fund in the family. Call again if you don't receive your package soon.

○ You don't have to read the prospectus word for word. Some of the numbers will look like gibberish. Do read carefully the information pertaining to investing, moving and withdrawing your money.

⊃ To open an account, complete the application they send you, and mail it along with your check to the address listed in the prospectus. Specifically state the name of the fund you want your money invested in at first.

Some mutual fund families' names and numbers to get you started

(This list is by no means complete, and it is not meant to be a recommendation of these particular fund families.)

AARP	800-253-AARP
Boston Co.	800-225-5267
Bull and Bear	800-847-4200
Dreyfus	800-645-6561
Fidelity	800-544-6666
Founders	800-525-2440
T. Rowe Price	800-638-5660
Scudder	800-225-2470
Twentieth Century	800-345-2021
Vanguard	800-622-7447

How to track your mutual fund investments

To track your investments, watch the newspaper. There you will find the fund's Net Asset Value (NAV), or the current value in dollars of one share of a mutual fund. The NAV is listed under "Mutual Funds" near the stock market quotes.

The mutual funds are listed by family, so all Fidelity funds are under "F." The load funds have two prices — the sell price (the lower figure) and the buy price. The difference is the commission.

If you purchased your shares at $10 each and they go up to $12 per share, you have made a 20-percent profit. If the fund earned dividends or interest and gave you the profits as additional shares, you may be getting a better return than you would think from just looking at the paper. Multiply the number of shares shown on your last statement by the current NAV and compare that number to your original investment to get your actual return.

REFERENCE

More Wealth Without Risk by Charles J. Givens, Simon & Schuster, New York, 1991.

Hot picks for cool bucks in mutual funds

The many, many mutual funds available make investing your money a major headache ... but you can pocket big bucks if you know how to pick 'em.

With mutual funds, smaller often means better. Small funds can move more quickly and take advantage of fast-growing, small companies. These stocks can more than double in a year and look great on a portfolio. Some excellent small funds are:

Delaware Value
Fam Value
Meridian
MIM Stock Appreciation
Skyline Special Equities
Wasatch Aggressive Equity

It's easy to make big money when you have big money, but options do exist for the small saver. **MIM Stock Appreciation** and **Berger One Hundred** have yielded great returns, and they both will open a new account for $250. You can invest as little as $50 at a time after you've opened the account. These funds are also "no-load," which means that you don't pay a salesperson's commission.

Don't be afraid to buy this year's winners. Just because they are hot now doesn't necessarily mean they will cool down later — except sector funds that focus on one industry or section of the economy, like gold or biotech companies. Those do go in cycles.

REFERENCE

Kiplinger's Personal Finance Magazine, September 1992.

How to read a mutual fund annual report

Reading the annual report of a mutual fund may seem like trying to read *Beowulf* in the original Old English: Most of the letters look familiar but put together they don't make any sense. Here are some definitions that might make the deciphering process a little easier.

Statement of Operations — How much money the mutual fund made and how much it cost to make it.

Net Realized Gain (or Loss) — "Net" means all the gains and losses are added together. "Realized" means the securities were sold.

Net Unrealized Gain (or Loss) — "Unrealized" means the investments are still held in the portfolio and "paper" gains and losses are netted together.

Statement of Changes in Net Assets — How much the total assets of the fund changed during the fiscal year. (The fiscal year is a twelve-month period, but its beginning and end don't necessarily correspond with the beginning and end of the calendar year.)

The total assets should correspond with the portfolio manager's objectives. For instance, if a fund specializes in small stocks, $500 million in assets may be large and $1 billion is absolutely unwieldy. A fund that invests in big "blue chip" companies can handle $3 billion in assets.

Bracketed figures ( ) — Indicates a negative value.

Ratio of Expenses to Average Net Assets — A percentage. Obviously, the higher the ratio of expenses, the lower your return will be. The average expense ratio for a stock fund is about 1.5 percent. For a bond fund it is closer to 1.0 percent.

Ratio of Net Investment Income to Average Net Assets — Indicates the amount of income the fund generates. Aggressive growth funds should have net income ratios in the 0 percent to 1 percent range, growth funds in the 1 percent to 3 percent range, and growth and income funds in the 3 percent to 5 percent range. Bond funds should have higher ratios and longer portfolio maturity funds should have the very highest.

Portfolio Turnover Rate — Purchases or sales (whichever is lower) compared to average assets. This averages around 100 percent for stock funds.

Schedule of Investments — All the stock and short-term fixed-income investments that the fund held at the end of its fiscal year.

REFERENCE

Consumers' Research, August 1992.

Mutual fund confusing facts

○ Bad funds sometimes rank as No. 1 performers. In fact, in the proper category and proper time period, almost any mutual fund can claim to be No. 1. On the other hand, even the best funds have terrible years.

○ Mutual fund names can mislead you: Dean Witter American Value Fund buys growth companies, not value stocks. Bond funds can have "government" in their names and still have 35 percent of their assets in securities other than government bonds. Growth funds don't necessarily buy growth stocks. A celebrated manager who runs one fund doesn't necessarily run another fund in the same family even though the names are almost identical (for instance, Vanguard Windsor and Vanguard Windsor II).

○ When a bond fund cuts its dividends, that's not always a bad sign. The fund manager may choose to buy lower-yielding securities in a time of falling interest rates to avoid risks.

○ If you can't meet a minimum-initial-investment requirement, that doesn't always mean the fund is not for you. Some funds will waive the requirement if you agree to pay a certain amount every month.

○ You don't always get what you pay for: No-load funds perform just as well or even better than funds that charge sales commissions.

○ "The more the merrier" isn't true in mutual funds. If you own more than a dozen, you probably own too many. Consolidate funds with the same investment style.

○ If the stock market crashes, don't rush to sell your mutual funds. Your shares won't be sold until the end of the day no matter how quickly you put in a sell order, and you will get absolute bottom prices.

REFERENCE ——————————————————————————
The Wall Street Journal, March 5, 1993.

How to spot the safest
money market funds for peaceful investing

The money market fund exists for people who don't like risks and want their money in one of the safest places that earns interest. The money market fund is a mutual fund that purchases short-term money market instruments. It pools investors' money to purchase jumbo CDs, treasury bills and commercial paper (a short-term corporate bond).

To find the money market fund that takes the least chances with your money, ignore the quoted yields and pay attention to the fund company's expense ratio. Some money market funds rake off over one percent a year in management fees and overhead costs. To finance these expenses and still produce high yields, the funds take more risks with your money.

Some funds with low expense ratios are:

Benham Government Agency/Benham

CoreFund-Cash Reserve/Fairfield

Dreyfus 100% U.S. Treasury MM/Dreyfus

Dreyfus Worldwide Dollar MM/Dreyfus

Fidelity U.S. Treasury Inc/Fidelity

Spartan Money Market/Fidelity

Spartan U.S. Treasury MM/Fidelity

Vanguard MM Reserves-Federal/Vanguard

Vanguard MM Reserves-Prime/Vanguard

Vanguard MM Reserves-U.S. Treasury/Vanguard

REFERENCE ——————————————————————————
Forbes, Aug. 31, 1992.

Billing yourself

The most important bill you pay every month should be the one to yourself. Every month, set aside a certain amount of money for savings. If you invest in money market mutual funds, you actually can bill yourself for your savings.

The statement you receive when you open a money market account has a stub you tear off and send in when you make your next deposit. Every month you make a deposit, you will receive a confirmation statement with a stub to send in. Most funds even send a return envelope. When you get the confirmation, tear off the stub and put it on top of the regular bills you pay every month.

Your savings will add up surprisingly fast.

REFERENCE
Terry Savage talks money: the common-sense guide to money matters by Terry Savage, Dearborn Financial Publishing Inc., Chicago, 1990.

Four hassle-free savings plans

You may be the type who can diet and lose 10 pounds at the drop of a hat. You may even jog in the morning. Willpower is your strong suit, until it comes to saving your money.

If you don't want to be bothered with writing a check to a savings account or money manager every month, try one of these savings plans that automatically deducts money from your paycheck or your bank account. With any of these plans, you can invest as little as $25 a month.

- ○ Mutual fund savings or reinvestment plans. Nearly all of the mutual fund companies will automatically transfer a set amount from your checking account to one of their funds.
  If you sign up for an automatic investment plan, you often don't have to make the fund's minimum initial investment. (Most funds require you to put in $1,000 to $3,000 when you open your account.) You can also save automatically by asking that any dividends or capital gains paid to you by the fund be reinvested.

- ○ U.S. Savings Bond payroll-deduction plans. At almost every company with over 100 employees, you can ask your employer to withhold money from your paycheck and invest it in Series EE savings bonds. You just fill out an enrollment form at your payroll department stating how much to withhold. The interest you get won't be astronomical, but it will be better than you'd get from a five-year CD at your bank.

○ Employee-benefit savings plans. These plans, called 401(k)s at private companies, 403(b)s at nonprofits, and 457 plans at government agencies, are some of the best automatic savings plans. You fill out a form at your payroll department stating how much to withhold from each paycheck, and your employer invests your pretax money for you. Most employers match some or all of your contribution.

○ Stock-dividend-reinvestment plans. Around 900 publicly traded companies offer dividend-reinvestment plans (DRIPs). These plans automatically use any dividends you receive to buy more stock.
Some companies even discount their DRIP share prices by 3 percent to 5 percent. Reinvesting dividends is smart: You end up buying more shares when stock prices are low and fewer when prices are high. To start a DRIP program, get a form from your broker or from the company itself.

REFERENCE ————————————————————————————————
Money, February 1993.

How to invest like a rich man

The really filthy rich people in the United States didn't get that way by playing the stock market. Wal-Mart's Sam Walton and The Limited's Leslie Wexler made a lot of their money *because* of the stock market, but they are owners of companies rather than savvy investors.

You can make a lot of money in the stock market if you follow the example of the wealthy and think like an owner.

Be an investor rather than a trader or speculator. Buy a big chunk of a good stock, sit back, be patient, and let it grow. The really rich didn't get that way in a hurry. Ross Perot held on through good periods and bad and came out way ahead in the end.

Invest in a company you believe in. If you have always used a Gillette Sensor shaving system and all your friends have, too, you might want to invest in Gillette stock. (Gillette stock has more than doubled since 1990.)

Contrary to conventional financial wisdom, the very rich don't seem to believe in diversification. Most of the fortunes come from a single shareholding in a simple, straightforward company. The rich haven't greatly diversified their holdings, and they seem to stay away from companies with tons of divisions and 18 unrelated lines of business.

You don't have to be a founder of a wildly successful company to think like one, or to get as rich as one, either.

REFERENCE
Laszlo Birinyi Jr., president of a financial consulting firm, in *Forbes*, Oct. 19, 1992.

Tips on investing in stock

- Recognize bad news when you hear it. If you own stock in a company that plans major job cutbacks in order to boost its bottom line, don't plan to buy more stock. Company restructurings and asset sales usually aren't good news. In the past, companies that have gone through a shake-up end up trailing the market.

- Don't think you've missed the boat if you hear the good news late. If a company reports strong quarterly earnings or other good news, the stock price will rise immediately. If you hear the news three day later, you can still buy the stock and reap the benefits of their good fortune. The strong earnings may be a sign of a long-term trend that will keep on rewarding shareholders for years.

- Remember, earnings alone do not a strong stock make. Company earnings are very important, but consider other factors, too — such as growth in revenues or the amount of cash a firm generates from its operations.

- Contrary to popular belief, it's not necessarily safer to keep investments at home. Actually, portfolios that include foreign stocks have performed better in the past. You may want to invest 20 percent to 30 percent of your equity holdings in foreign stocks.

REFERENCE ───────────────────────────────
Money, November 1992.

The insider to watch

Outsiders watching insiders' every move — it's the name of the game on the stock exchange. The insiders you might want to keep an eye on are company employees.

If employees own a big stake in the company where they work, you should consider buying the stock. When employees believe in the company and have their money in it, the company is bound to be more successful.

Several market studies show that the performance of companies with a sizable employee ownership beat the Standard and Poor's 500-stock index by around 10 percent.

By the same token, if employees start to sell their stock, follow suit. Trouble's sure to be ahead for the company.

REFERENCE ───────────────────────────────
The Wall Street Journal, Feb. 13, 1992.

What's the best time of year to invest in the stock market?

The best time of year to invest in the stock market is mid-December, especially if you are planning to buy small-firm stocks.

And the best time to sell?

Early February.

Stock market pros have long noticed the "January Effect" — the tendency of all stocks, and particularly the stocks issued by small companies, to perform well during the last trading days of the year and the first weeks of January.

In fact, during the last 50 Januarys, the "smallest-cap" stocks — those issued by companies with the smallest market capitalizations — have risen an average of 7.5 percent. That is amazing, especially considering that they usually return less than 1 percent per month during the rest of the year.

The "January Effect" has been around long enough for you to depend on it. Some investors will try to make a short-term quick buck by hopping into a mutual fund with no load and no redemption fees at the end of the year.

However, the average investor should plan to stay in the market for a while once he gets in it. (You can even be barred from investing if you try trading in and out of no-load, small cap mutual funds.)

Increase your odds of investment success: Just pay attention to the time of the year when you buy and sell stocks.

REFERENCE
Forbes, Dec. 7, 1992 and Dec. 21, 1992.

Making big bucks by playing with the big boys

If you have over $10,000 to invest in the stock market, here's one of the simplest and best ways to do it: Put $1,000 or more into the 10 highest yielding stocks among the 30 issues that make up the Dow Jones industrial average. After a year, sell any stocks that have fallen out of the top 10 and buy the new high yielding stocks.

This system is safe since you are investing in large, stable companies, and you have excellent odds of beating the market averages.

REFERENCE
Money, February 1993.

What professional investors do that you should do, too.

Mutual fund managers, pension plan managers and other Wall Street pros may have millions more to invest than you ever dreamed of, but all investors, big and small, have the same objective — to make money. You can use the strategies of professional investors to make your own investments less risky and more profitable.

Most important lessons from the big money managers:

○ **Only pick investments after creating an overall plan.** Your average investor puts his money in high-yielding mutual funds, in hot stocks, and so on, without having an investment plan. First decide what broad categories you want to invest in — such as stocks, real estate and bonds — then choose what types of stocks you want — such as small company stocks or blue chip stocks. Once you have a plan, don't make investments that don't fit into it.

○ **Keep your objectives in mind when you invest.** If you are saving for retirement, you can take more risk than if you're saving for a down payment on a home in three years. For a home down payment, you'd want to go with short-term bonds or certificates of deposit. For retirement savings, put your money in stocks. You have time to weather the ups and downs.

○ **Put at least 50 percent of your money in a long-term investment and leave it there.** To cut costs and reduce risks, many professionals put half their money in a stock or a bond fund. They gain enough security to play around with riskier investments with the rest of the money.

○ **Look towards a stock's future instead of focusing on its past results.** "Where you think a company can go" should be your main consideration. Common mistakes made by the average investor:

- Thinking a stock is a bargain because it dropped way down from its high.

- Assuming that a stock that has been rising steadily will continue to do so.

- Hanging on to a losing stock just because you don't want to sell at a loss. The professional money manager sells losing stocks much more quickly than the individual.

○ **When a stock falls 20 percent, either cut your losses and sell**

the stock, or double your investment. Make the choice based on the company's prospects.

○ **Put about 10 percent into foreign investments.** At the least, this strategy will keep your portfolio more steady since foreign markets swing up and down at different times from U.S. markets.

○ **Review your investments every quarter.** If you own a mutual fund that invests in small companies, make sure its performance equals that of other similar funds. Don't compare funds with totally different investment strategies (such as a growth fund and a value fund). It may just have been a bad quarter for certain types of funds.

REFERENCE
The Wall Street Journal, Jan. 8, 1993.

Stock market opening up to small investors

Most $50-a-month investors steer clear of the stock market and opt for mutual funds, CDs or simple savings accounts. Broker fees and commissions almost outweigh any money you'd make in the stock market anyway.

But if you've always wished you could own stock in one of the booming blue-chip companies, it's getting easier for you every day.

Many big companies are revamping their dividend reinvestment (DRIP) plans. These plans let you buy additional shares without going through a broker. Instead of giving you the stock dividends in hard cash, the company reinvests the money and gives you more shares.

More and more companies with these plans are allowing investors to buy shares by writing a check every month, too. You send it straight to the company instead of to a brokerage house.

These plans aren't for stock market players who like to buy and sell quickly at specific prices. They'll still need to go through a broker. The company itself will probably take about five days to issue the stock to the investor.

If you're interested in purchasing stock in your favorite company, call the company's shareholder relations department and ask about their DRIP plan.

REFERENCE ———————————————————————————————
The Wall Street Journal, March 3, 1993.

Seven ways to find
an economic prophet for you

Ready to play the stock market but don't know where to start? Never fear, hundreds of financial newsletters are out there, waiting to guide you through the demons of Wall Street. You can pay from $17 to $475 a year for the five to 10 pages worth of peeks into the economic crystal ball you will get regularly in the mail. Here are seven ways to find a newsletter that's right for you:

○ Chose a "fundamental" newsletter over a "technical" newsletter. A fundamental recommends stocks based on a company's bottom-line financial health. It takes an in-depth look at a fast-growing company and explains why now is the time to invest in it.
  A technical newsletter focuses mainly on stock prices. It draws conclusions about a stock's future based on its past. A new company will do well if similar companies did well. The fundamental newsletter has had better success.

○ Look for editors who run their own investment portfolios. They have a hands-on advantage.

○ Cut through the hype. Almost every letter has a gimmick to try to get your attention. There are letters for the environmentally aware, others that only follow companies in the health science field, even one called Harmonic Research that argues that solar eclipses have a slight bearing on investments. A newsletter should not have an agenda besides earning you money.

○ Make sure the newsletter is easy to understand. It should have clear buy and sell recommendations.

○ Find a newsletter that's in sync with you. If you are the edgy type who has trouble falling asleep, a newsletter that focuses on mutual funds may be right for you. Mutual funds allow more diversity and are less risky than volatile individual stocks.

○ Take advantage of the short-term trial subscriptions most newsletters offer. They usually cost about $50.

○ To learn all about the various newsletters, consult the *Hulbert Guide to Financial Newsletters.*

Three financial newsletters that have provided good returns for readers:

- Medical Technology Stock Letter, Editor Jim McCamant, +195 percent return
- BI Research, Editor Tom Bishop, +157 percent return
- Oberweis Report, Editor Jim Oberweis, +142 percent return

REFERENCE ————————————————————————
Fortune, 1993 Investor's Guide.

If they nailed Black Friday, shun 'em like the Black Plague

Certain investment advisors who publish their own financial newsletters correctly predicted the stock market crash of October 1987 — the worst crash in stock market history.

Wouldn't it make sense to turn to these seers when you need investment advice?

Not necessarily. In fact, advisors who correctly predicted the 1987 crash and even did well during the crash achieved a total return of just 6.8 percent from August 1987 through August 1992.

The financial newsletters that lost lots of money during the crash still managed to produce an average return of 25.3 percent during this five-year period.

The moral of the story is: Don't pick an advisor just because he happened to do well at predicting a particular event. A financial advisor may be great at seeing what is going to happen in the near future, but he may not be able to pull out the profits in the long run.

Don't worry so much about protecting yourself against crashes. Instead, choose a newsletter that has had long-term success, even if it has had ups and downs along the way.

REFERENCE
Forbes, Oct. 26, 1992.

For a middle-of-the-road investment, try a convertible bond

Eennee, Meennee, Miennee, Mo
My investments are at an all-time low
Stocks are scary and bonds are slow ...

In uncertain financial times, you sometimes feel you have to resort to child's games to plan your investment strategies. One hard decision is choosing between the steady income of a bond and the potential price appreciation of a stock.

So, instead of picking either a stock or a bond, consider the combination investment: a convertible bond fund. The convertible bonds sold by a company can be converted into a specified number of shares of the company's common stock. Since they can be converted into stock, their value is linked to the price of the stock. They have the potential to appreciate just as stocks do.

The convertible bond also offers the steady income of a bond. When stocks do poorly, that bond market yield is good to have.

In the 12 months ended September 1992, convertible bond funds returned an average of 16.3 percent, more than six percentage points better than the average stock fund and nearly three percentage points better than the average bond fund. That performance was probably unusual, but it is a good indication that convertible bonds are a safe, healthy investment in recessionary times.

REFERENCE
Fortune, Sept. 21, 1992.

What you need to know about investing in bonds

Bungee jumpers, gamblers, firemen and stock market players have one thing in common — they like risk, fear and uncertainty. On the other side of the world lives the knitters, the book lovers, the actuaries and those who invest in bonds. Bonds, issued by the federal government, cities, states and big corporations, are safe investments. Right?

It's surprising news for most people that you can lose money even in the safest of bonds.

When you buy a bond from a big corporation or a utility, you run the risk of losing your money if the company issuing the bonds defaults. The company, which has issued bonds to pay for new equipment, new buildings, etc., just doesn't pay the bondholders back.

You can generally avoid this rare catastrophe by checking the reputation of the company with a rating service such as Moody's or Standard and Poor's. Their top rating is AAA — for a company with almost no risk of default, then the ratings move down in investment safety — AA-1, AA, A-1, BAA-1, BAA, BA, B, ending with C.

"Junk bonds" are corporate bonds with ratings of double B or lower. They are tempting because they carry high interest rates, but conservative investors should stay away. Beware of insurance companies with huge junk bond portfolios funding their high-paying annuity contracts.

Never invest in bonds when interest rates are rising.

The other, more common way to lose money on a bond is through a rise in the interest rates. When the interest rates rise, bond prices drop.

Bonds are usually sold in $1,000 face value amounts. A $1,000 bond that sells for $1,000 is selling at par, or 100. A bond selling for less than face value is selling at a discount. Bonds sell at a discount because some new, higher-interest bond has come out. A $1,000 bond selling at a below-par price of 80 has a market value of $800.

If you buy a bond paying 8-percent interest, and a few years later interest rates are around 15 percent, your bond won't be worth very much. If you needed money quickly, you would have to sell at a large discount, probably only getting around $650 for your $1,000 bond.

To preserve or increase the market value of your bond, only buy bonds when you think interest rates are at their peak. If you think inflation is going to cause interest rates to rise, don't buy bonds. If it looks like the pressures of the federal deficit will force the Federal Reserve to create more money and cause inflation, don't buy bonds. If interest rates are sky-high and inflation is rampant, now is the time to buy bonds.

If you are stuck holding low-interest bonds in times of high interest rates, if at all possible, hold on to your bond until interest rates fall.

Make sure you don't pay too much for your bonds.

If you buy bonds through a stock broker or a specialty bond broker, you will pay a commission. If you don't see the commission marked clearly on the sales confirmation, you can be assured that one has been built in. Compare the price and yield of the bond with other brokers.

To avoid paying commission entirely when buying outstanding government bonds, don't go through your stock brokerage firm. Buy the bonds directly from the government at an auction given by the Federal Reserve Bank in your district. You can contact your local Federal Reserve Bank for auction dates.

Treasury bills (IOUs with maturities of one year or less) are auctioned weekly.

Treasury notes (IOUs with maturities of one year to ten years) are auctioned monthly, usually the third week of every month. Treasury bonds (IOUs with long-term maturities of up to 30 years) are sold at regular quarterly auctions.

Look out for "call provisions" when you buy bonds sold by corporations. Some companies pay off a small amount of bonds every year, but other companies have "call provisions," allowing them to pay off all the bonds in case interest rates take a plunge. After paying off the old bonds, they issue new ones at the lower interest rates.

If your bond is "called in" when interest rates are low, you are slapped with the problem of reinvesting your money at lower interest rates. Read the prospectus carefully before you buy.

Another tip on corporate bonds: Buy in lots of at least $5,000 face value or you may have trouble finding buyers. For easy selling, buy from major corporations.

Bonds to avoid

For the safest municipal bonds, check with Moody's or Standard and Poor's and stay away from revenue bonds. Revenue bonds are paid back out of the revenues of some specific city or state project, like a toll road. General obligation bonds are paid out of the general revenues of the city or state. That gives them higher priority and makes them safer.

Municipal bond packages: diversifying the easy way

If you would like to buy a package of municipal bonds to diversify your bond holdings, you can purchase a unit investment trust. You pay about five percent in commission for someone to manage your money for you. However, only buy unit investment trusts when they are being publicly offered for the first time.

If you buy a "resale" from a bond dealer, it is hard to know what you are buying. Some of the original bonds may have been paid off by the issuer, so you have no idea what the true value of the unit is.

REFERENCE ———————————————————————————————————
Terry Savage talks money, the common-sense guide to money matters by Terry Savage, Dearborn Financial Publishing Inc., Chicago, 1990.

The safe *and secret* municipal bond

One municipal bond you don't hear much about is the prerefunded municipal bond. Buy "pre-res" to get both the tax-free status of a conventional municipal bond and the security of a government-backed Treasury. These low-profile bonds are guaranteed by Treasury securities instead of by a city or state.

Governments issue pre-res when interest rates are high, and the bonds can't be retired right away when rates fall. The issuers sell new bonds at lower interest rates and use the money to buy Treasuries. They put the Treasuries in escrow to cover the old bonds. Since the money is there to pay off your high-interest bond as soon as possible, you can't get a much safer investment.

Most investors stay away from pre-res because the bonds sell at a premium. You are likely to pay $110 for the bond and get back $102 when the bond is called in. But pre-res offer higher yields than conventional bonds to compensate for the premium.

Warning: On rare occasions, a pre-re will be backed by certificates of deposit or Fannie Maes. These aren't as safe as those backed by Treasuries. Ask before you buy.

REFERENCE ───
Business Week, Jan. 11, 1993.

Making money as a landlord

Buying and managing an old, cheap, run-down apartment building on the wrong side of town may not be glamorous, but it's a good way to get rich.

If you want to get in on the real estate investment scene, find an old apartment building to buy, put down as little of your own money as possible and borrow as much as you can.

Why is this the way to go?

○ Since everyone needs a place to live, apartment buildings will always be in demand.

○ You can quickly upgrade and rejuvenate old properties and boost their value almost overnight.

○ By collecting rent, you can more than cover your mortgage and upkeep expenses. Since you get to make your monthly mortgage payments with rent money, you can sell the property for less than you paid for it and still make a big cash profit.

○ Commercial properties like strip malls or office buildings are not as safe for new investors as residential buildings. When a tenant of a shopping center moves his store out, that vacancy really hurts and can be hard to fill.
Utility bills are higher in office buildings because professional tenants, such as doctors and dentists, use a lot of electricity. Plus, you have to provide much more parking space for commercial properties than for apartment buildings.

○ If you buy an old, ugly property, you probably won't mind selling it quickly. It's not smart to hold on to an attractive property because you are proud of it.

With accelerated depreciation, you get fewer benefits each year from the depreciation allowance. You should sell quickly, and reinvest the money you made in another property.

REFERENCE

How You Can Become Financially Independent by Investing in Real Estate by Albert J. Lowry, Simon & Schuster, New York, 1982.

How to invest in real estate (or buy your house) with no money down

Invest in houses, factories, apartment buildings and fields, and you can hardly go wrong — the population is booming and nobody's making any more land. ...

What?

"No money in the bank," you say? "You got to have money to make money," you grumble?

Well, think again. You can buy real estate with no money down — at least, none of your money down — and then you can be on the road to riches.

Making sure the down payment doesn't come out of your pocket just takes a little creativity. Here are some ideas to get you started:

○ Ask the real estate agent to lend you part of his commission in return for a personal note guaranteeing to pay the money back. Real estate agents are sometimes willing to lend you money at a low interest rate if they think the deal won't go through otherwise. Use this money towards the down payment.

○ Satisfy the seller's needs. The seller may need to buy some items for his new home or new venture, such as a refrigerator. Offer to purchase these items for him if he will reduce your down payment. You can use credit cards or, better, store credit to buy the items.

○ Use rents and deposits. If you are buying a building with tenants, such as an apartment building, negotiate the closing date to fall on the date rents are due. Rent money and renter's security deposits become the property of the buyer on the closing day. You can use this money towards your down payment. (Make sure it is legal in your state to use renter's security deposits.)

○ Assume the seller's debts. People often sell property because they want to relieve some of their financial obligations. You could contact the seller's creditors, tell them you are going to pay the notes off instead of the seller, and even ask them to extend the due dates of the notes. You then could deduct the amount of the obligations you assumed from the down payment.

○ Use the seller's prepaid rent. The seller may need to stay in the apartment building or house while looking for another place to live. If the builder wants to continue using the building for a while after selling, total up the rent he will pay you and deduct it from the down payment.

○ Offer to pay the down payment in increasing installments. You could pay $1,000 at the time of the sale, $2,000 six months later and $2,500 after a year. This gives you time to find the rest of the money, or you could fix the property up and put it back on the market for a quick profit.

○ Use your talent instead of cash. If you are a builder, an accountant, a lawyer or even a salesman who can get merchandise at dealer's cost, offer your services to the seller in place of a down payment. An accountant can offer to do someone's taxes for the next ten years.

○ Offer to make monthly down payments. You could pay the seller $500 a month instead of paying up front. The property should appreciate, so your money will earn more than if you put it in a savings account. Plus, you earn equity.

○ Raise the price and lower the down payment. The seller may be more interested in the price the property sells for than in how much cash you give him up front. Offer him an extra $10,000 on the price if he'll let you pay no or little money down.

○ Consider splitting the property. If the property contains furniture or sits on a huge lot, you could sell the furniture or some of the land, and apply the money to your down payment.

An apartment building may be sold together with a small house or three duplexes may be sold as a group. You have to negotiate to give yourself time to make the sale of a piece of the property before the down payment is due.

Some of these suggestions work best if you plan on selling the property for a quick profit within a short time after you buy it. For instance, some sellers want to sell so badly that they'll take their equity in the form of mortgages on the property and notes secured against the property. Paying all these mortgages and notes means you could be paying out more for the property each month than you take in.

But if you plan on selling quickly after you fix up the house or the building or when the market gets better, you can still make a lot of money on the deal. But, be careful with negative cash flow situations.

REFERENCE ——————————————————————————————

Nothing Down for the '90s by Robert G. Allen, Simon & Schuster, New York, 1990.

Tax strategies

Sky-high taxes getting you down? Eight sure ways to cut your tax bill

Taxes are going up for everybody — not just the rich. The worst tax increases may be the ones that are slipped into law without your knowing about them — like when Congress phases out exemptions or trims deductions such as mortgage interest and business meals and entertainment.

You need to take some legal steps to shield your money from Uncle Sam. Here are some strategies for employees, retirees and the self-employed:

○ Contribute the maximum to 401(k)s and other employee-sponsored retirement plans. Contributions and interest earned aren't subject to federal income taxes and most state and local income taxes. You don't owe Social Security tax on the funds your employer puts in, either.

○ Set up a Flexible Spending Account (FSA). Many employers will deduct money from your paycheck before federal income taxes and Social Security taxes and put it into an FSA account for you. You can use this pre-tax money to pay your child-care expenses and your medical expenses that aren't covered by insurance.
If your adjusted gross income is more than $24,000, you should set up an FSA to pay for child care even though you will lose part or all of your dependent-care credit. The higher your income, the less the dependent-care credit helps you. On the other hand, the higher your income, the more the FSA helps you cut your taxes.

○ Take advantage of the tax break for commuters. Companies can give employees up to $720 a year tax free to pay for mass transit commuting costs. If you're in the 28-percent tax bracket, $720 in transportation tokens equals a $1,120 raise.

○ If you're self-employed, make sure you take all your write-offs —

business travel and entertainment, dues to professional organizations, subscriptions to business magazines and equipment depreciation.

○ Contribute to a Keogh retirement account if you're self-employed. Young business owners should start with a profit-sharing Keogh, which allows you to vary how much you contribute every year. Later, you can add a Keogh known as a money-purchase plan. These plans require you to contribute a fixed sum every year. If you are over 50 and you've never set up a Keogh, you might want to try a defined-benefit Keogh. These plans let you contribute annually whatever it takes to provide a high retirement payout at age 65.

○ Incorporate yourself. The self-employed may benefit from organizing themselves as a "C" corporation. (Small-business owners have to fill out a schedule "C" tax form.) This way, your business can pay and deduct your family's health and life insurance costs. Beware: If your business makes more than you pay yourself in salary, you could find yourself in a tax trap.

○ Consider investing in tax-free municipal bonds or Series EE savings bonds.

○ Have you set up investment accounts for your child? Don't automatically include that investment income on your federal tax return. In most states, your state tax liability is based on the income you report on your federal tax return. You increase your state tax when you add your child's income to your own. Consider filing separately for your child.

REFERENCE
Money, January 1993.

Cutting your chances of an IRS audit

The IRS doesn't audit taxpayers randomly — so you can quake in your boots unashamedly when you get the word that an audit of your return is pending.

You can, however, reduce your chances of being audited.

Certain items on a tax return are called audit triggers. Here are some of the most popular high-risk audit triggers:

- **Office in the Home deduction.** If the amount of the home-office deduction is small compared to your total income, consider not taking this deduction to reduce your chances of an audit.

- **Unreported Income.** High bank deposits without supporting reported income, failure to report interest or dividends, and the taxpayer's living style can suggest unreported income. Attach a statement explaining any situation that seems to indicate unreported income.

  Failing to report the sale of a residence is likely to cause an audit. If you are a senior taxpayer, don't attempt to use the one-time exclusion for the sale of a personal residence more than once. The IRS computers will catch you.

- **Travel and Entertainment Expenses.** When claiming travel or entertainment expenses, always attach a Form 2106 or Schedule C. Don't leave any questions unanswered. You can attach a statement justifying the expenses, but now is not the time to attach receipts.

- **Automobile expenses.** Always attach a statement and make sure these very high-risk expenses are correctly claimed.

- **Casualty and theft losses.** This deduction has been abused, so it is high risk. Include a statement explaining the loss, why it was not covered by insurance, and the methods used to arrive at the monetary value of the destroyed or stolen items. Also include a police report.

- **Hobby losses.** If you deduct hobby expenses as business expenses, make sure you substantiate that you engage in your hobby for profit, not just for pleasure.

- **Alternative minimum tax.** Use a Form 6251 if you have a large amount of deductions and exemptions and the alternative minimum tax applies. The alternative minimum tax assures that everyone pays a minimum amount of taxes.

Several other factors that seem to affect whether you are selected for an audit:

○ **Occupation.** The IRS looks at your occupation to make sure it relates to claimed business expenses and deductions. If the deduction or expense seems unusual considering your occupation, attach a statement justifying the item. Doctors and lawyers are often selected by the IRS for audits.

○ **Problem Tax Preparer.** Some tax preparers are listed with the IRS as problem tax preparers, and if you use one of them, you increase your chances of being picked for an audit. Unfortunately, this list isn't published. Try to use a local preparer with a good reputation whose clients are not normally audited.
Even better, prepare the return yourself and simply get tax advice or assistance. That way you can sign your return yourself. You'll reduce your chances of being audited by 20 percent.

○ **Exemptions.** If you list multiple exemptions or are a single taxpayer listing dependent children, explain the situation on an attached statement.

○ **Tax shelters.** Answer all the questions on Schedules C and F, even if the answers raise the issue of a tax shelter, and explain any item that appears to be an abusive tax shelter. In the past, the IRS has considered certain industries as tax shelters: hobby farming, movies, oil and gas, leasing investments and commodities.

○ **Alimony.** Be warned: The IRS frequently checks to make sure you report all your alimony.

REFERENCES ─────────────────────────────────
Fight the IRS and Win: A Self-defense Guide for Taxpayers by Cliff Roberson, Tab Books Inc., Blue Ridge Summit, Pa., 1988.
The Wall Street Journal, Feb. 24, 1993.

Divorce and filing taxes

Does the trauma of divorce never end? Just when you thought it was over,

April 15 loomed on the horizon. If you're recently divorced and it's tax time, you've got three more choices to make:

Should you file jointly or separately?

If you were divorced before January 1, you must file separately for the preceding year. If you were not divorced until January 1 or after, you may choose to file jointly or separately for the preceding year.

If you're not sure which way is better, roughly calculate the amounts you would pay if you filed jointly or separately. Even without the exact amount of your final tax, you can get some idea.

When in doubt, it is better to file separately. Filing separately may cost you more in dollars, but lessens your risk of connecting yourself to someone you don't completely trust.

If your spouse falsely states his income or expenses, you're liable for any back taxes, interest or penalties he may incur.

Plus, separate returns can be amended up to three years later if you see that joint returns would have worked out better. But jointly filed returns cannot later be amended to separate ones.

How are alimony and child support reported?

Generally, if you pay alimony, you may deduct it. If you receive alimony, it is considered taxable income.

If you have to pay an attorney to help you collect alimony, you may be able to deduct all the necessary fees. Be sure to ask your attorney for an itemized bill.

Child support payments don't affect either party when it comes to income taxes. It is neither a deduction for the parent who pays it, nor taxable income for the one it is paid to.

Who will claim the children as exemptions?

It is up to the parents to decide who claims the children as tax exemptions. Only one of you may claim the exemption, and usually the parent who has custody of the children makes the claim.

But if the two of you agree, the noncustodial parent may claim the exemption in exchange for paying more in child support. In this case, the custodial parent must sign an IRS Form 8332, Release of Claim to Exemption for Child of Divorced or Separated Parents, and give it to the noncustodial parent to file with his tax return.

If you have joint custody of your children, you may each claim one, or you may alternate claiming the exemption from year to year. But each of you must list the children's Social Security numbers on your tax returns each year, no matter which of you claims the exemption. That way the IRS can be sure that only one parent is claiming the exemption.

REFERENCE
Nolo Press, Spring 1993.

When a married couple should file separately

Occasionally, it does pay for a married couple to file separate returns. For instance, if one spouse has a lot of deductions, such as medical expenses, that spouse may be able to use all those deductions if he files separately but not if the couple files a joint return.

Medical expenses are deductible only if they exceed 7.5 percent of your adjusted gross income, and miscellaneous deductions have to exceed 2 percent of your adjusted gross income before you can claim them.

So, if you make $30,000 yourself and both of you together make $50,000, and one of you has $3,000 in medical expenses, you can probably claim those if you file separately but not if you file together.

REFERENCE
The Wall Street Journal, Feb. 23, 1993.

Whose tax debts are you liable for?

Think twice before you file a joint return with a live-in companion. You will be liable forevermore for that person's tax debts.

You can't just deny that you were married to him because the IRS accepted the returns as joint. You can't claim to be an "innocent spouse" either, because some states don't recognize common-law marriages.

REFERENCE
The Wall Street Journal, Feb. 24, 1993.

Last-minute tax savers

○ If you set up a Keogh (a self-employed retirement plan) before the end of the year, you can contribute up until April 15 of the next year (or until your extended due date) and still take the deduction. Self-employed workers or workers who free-lance, do consulting or serve as directors on the side can open Keogh accounts.

○ Take your records to your tax preparer neatly organized, and you can save 40 to 50 percent on your tax preparation fees compared with badly organized taxpayers.

REFERENCE
The Wall Street Journal, Feb. 23, 1993.

When not to trust your tax preparer

Need help preparing your taxes? Make sure you go to an honest professional.

Watch out for these tricks of a crooked tax preparer:

○ Asking you to sign a blank form or a return filled out in pencil.

○ Telling you to have the refund sent directly to the preparer.

○ Promising you a refund before they've even looked at your finances.

○ Promising you that, with their help, you will pay little or no taxes.

○ Charging you a percentage of what they "saved you" by preparing your return.

REFERENCE
The Business of Living by Stephen M. Pollan and Mark Levine, Simon & Schuster, New York, 1991.

When your job search is deductible

Your job search is not deductible if:

○ You are looking for work for the first time — a recent college graduate, for instance.

○ There is a long break between your last job and the beginning of your job search.

○ You are looking for work in a different field.

If your job search doesn't fall into any of these categories, you can deduct all your job-hunting expenses, including:

> • Resume preparation
> • Personnel agency fees
> • Carfare to and from interviews

You don't have to land a job to be able to deduct your expenses.

REFERENCE
The Wall Street Journal, Feb. 23, 1993.

New home-office laws

If you've been cutting your taxes with the home-office deduction, a new Supreme Court ruling may not be to your liking. To be deductible, the high court said, your home office must be your most important place of business or a place where you regularly meet with clients, patients or customers.

If you call customers at home, pay bills and keep records there, but provide your services elsewhere, you can no longer take the home-office deduction. If you are an anesthesiologist or a building contractor, for example, you're out of luck — you can't help but provide your services elsewhere. Claiming you have no other place of business doesn't hold water with the IRS, either.

How do you get around the ruling?

○ Regularly see clients or patients at your home.

○ Prove that you do most of your work at your home office.

To prove you spend most of your time there, document your working hours and keep good records. The court also ruled that each case must be judged on its own merit, so if you do your homework, you have a good chance of winning your case.

REFERENCE

The Wall Street Journal, Jan. 13, 1993.

How to deduct your health club membership

If you join a health club to improve your general health, even if your doctor suggests it, you can't deduct your dues.

But, if your doctor recommends exercise to help improve or relieve a particular condition, you may qualify for a deduction. (Remember, medical expenses must exceed 7.5 percent of your adjusted gross income before you can claim them as deductions.)

REFERENCE

Consumer Reports, March 1993.

Beating the IRS bully when you think you're right

The IRS can be a bully, but adults know that bullies can be beaten.

You stand about a one in five chance every year of receiving a penalty notice from the IRS in your mailbox, usually saying you paid too little or too late. Chances are good that either the IRS is wrong or that you have a valid excuse.

How do you fight the big guy when you think you're right?

First, don't automatically send off a check. You know the IRS makes lots of mistakes.

Don't ignore the notice. They know where you live.

Don't call the IRS. You will spend hours getting through, and it won't do any good.

The CP-2000 notice is the one you receive when the IRS computer decides that what you reported doesn't jibe with what your bank, your employer and your broker reported about you. The form provides a space for you to indicate that you think the IRS is wrong.

Check your records, and return the form along with a written explanation. Reply as soon as possible, because the IRS wants your response within 30 days of the date of its notice.

The IRS can also send a notice slapping you with a fine if you filed too late, if your check bounced or if you paid too little. Any offense will do.

Half of the people who fight these penalties don't have to pay them.

Write the IRS a short, calm letter explaining their error or your excuse (if it's a decent one). Ask for the penalty to be removed. If you are turned down, the rejection letter you get from the IRS will explain how to appeal their decision.

If you still haven't won, call the Problem Resolution Program (PRP) office nearest you. This program was set up to help you when the IRS makes a mistake. For the number of the nearest PRP office, call 1-800-829-1040.

Finally, you can contact your senators and representatives. Their staff is used to talking about your tax woes with problem resolution officers. Call a local congressional office or call the Capitol switchboard at 202-224-3121.

REFERENCE
Kiplinger's Personal Finance Magazine, September 1992.

What the IRS can't take if you don't pay your taxes

Never ignore any notice you receive from the IRS. If you owe taxes and you ignore the IRS letters, you will receive an "assessment notice," which states that liens are being filed against your property.

If you still don't respond within 30 days, an IRS agent can start taking your property. Not only can they take it, they can sell it for just enough to pay for the taxes you owe. They aren't exactly looking out for your best interests.

However, some of your property is exempt:

- Clothes and schoolbooks

- $1,650 worth of fuel, food, furniture and personal effects

- $1,100 worth of the books and tools you need for your trade, business or profession

- ○ Unemployment benefits

- ○ Mail that hasn't yet been delivered to you

- ○ Workmen's compensation benefits

- ○ Money you need to pay child support

- ○ A very small amount of your wages, salary and other income — around $100 a week if you could claim only one dependent. You get about $25 more for each additional dependent.

- ○ Some service-connected disability payments

- ○ Any assistance under the Job Training Partnership Act

- ○ It used to be true that the IRS would never take your house, but that's not so anymore. If the assistant district IRS director approves the seizure of your house or the Secretary of the IRS decides there's no other way to collect the taxes you owe, your house can be seized.

If you absolutely cannot pay your taxes, you need to apply for a Taxpayer Assistance Order to Relieve Hardship (TAO). If you've lost your job or you're overwhelmed by medical expenses, the IRS won't take your property. IRS employees will stop whatever action they're taking against you until your crisis is resolved.

To apply for a TAO, file the IRS Form 911. You can get the form by asking a Problem Resolution Officer to review your case. Call 1-800-829-1040.

REFERENCE ————————————————————————————————————
Debtors' Rights, A Legal Self Help Guide by Gudrun M. Nickel, Sphinx Publishing, Clearwater, Fla., 1992.

Are you letting the government earn interest on your money?

Don't rejoice over that fat refund check you get from the IRS every year. Do something about it.

A refund of $500 or more means you could have been earning interest on the money you handed over to the government with every paycheck. The government thanks you because it earned the interest for itself.

Ask your employer for a W-4 form and the accompanying sheet that helps you more accurately match your withholding with your tax bill. You may be entitled to more withholding allowances than you realized.

Consult the Internal Revenue Service Publication 505, *Tax Withholding and Estimated Tax*, for guidance in figuring out your withholding allowances. Order this publication by calling 1-800-829-3676.

REFERENCE ————————————————————————————
Kiplinger's Personal Finance Magazine, November 1992.

Cutting the taxes on your home

You may be paying more property taxes than you owe. In some areas of the United States, half the property tax assessments are wrong.

If you think you're paying too much in property taxes, appeal. Half the people who challenge their property tax bill end up cutting their bill by at least 10 percent.

Terms you need to know:

○ Fair market value — what your house would sell for

○ Assessment ratio — the percentage of fair market value subject to tax

○ Correct assessed value — the fair market value multiplied by the assessment ratio

○ Mill rate — the local tax rate

To get your tax bill, officials multiply the correct assessed value of your house by the local mill rate. You can't challenge the tax rate, but you can challenge the assessment of your house's value.

Make sure you know your community's assessment ratio. You may think you're getting a break if your house is worth $200,000 and is assessed at $180,000.

But if your city has an assessment ratio of 75 percent of market value, you're being overassessed by 20 percent and overtaxed.

You can find out your town's assessment ratio at the assessor's office.

While you're there, you should look at your property record card. This card lists features of your home, such as lot size, the age of your house and the number of rooms. Make sure the card is correct.

If your home's estimated value seems too high, you'll need to show the assessor that at least three similar properties sold for less fairly recently. Ask a real estate agent for some figures. You can also hire a real estate appraiser to evaluate your property.

If you know an area-wide revaluation is coming, invite the assessor to your home to see the cracks in your ceiling or other damage.

To receive a 12-page "How to Fight Property Taxes" brochure from the National Taxpayers Union, a Washington, D.C., lobbying group, send $2 to 713 Maryland Ave. N.E., Washington, D.C. 20002.

REFERENCE
Money, January 1993.

How to get your
mortgage money now if you need it

You've heard about the tax break you will get when you buy your new home. In fact, that's how you plan to afford the monthly mortgage payments, which are much higher than your present rent payments. But you need the cash each month when you pay the mortgage, not the following year when you file your tax return.

All you have to do is reduce the amount that is withheld from your paycheck. You will need to file a revised W-4 form with your employer. Your personnel office should have a copy of a W-4 form for you to use and a set of instructions.

A good rule of thumb: Each $2,000 of added itemized deductions should let you claim one extra withholding allowance. Each extra allowance you claim lets you take more money home every month to help pay your mortgage.

REFERENCE
Buying & Selling a Home by the staff of *Changing Times* magazine, The Kiplinger Washington Editors Inc., Washington, D.C., 1990.

How to top the 2% deduction limit

Shift your position when it comes to taxes.

If it doesn't seem to pay for you to itemize, try to shift your miscellaneous expenses so that you have a lot one year and a little the next. You can pay for two years of property taxes or state income taxes at once.

Since you can only deduct the portion of job, investment or tax expenses that add up to more than 2 percent of your adjusted gross income, you have a better chance of topping this limit if you bunch your miscellaneous deductions in one year.

One catch to shifting expenses: You can't write off mortgage interest payments in advance, but you can deduct more than 12 months' interest in one year.

Say your mortgage payments are due on the first of the month. You can make your payment for December on December 31 instead of January 1. Next year, you can deduct only 11 months' interest or you can keep accelerating your January payment.

REFERENCES ————————————————————————————
The Price Waterhouse Personal Tax Adviser, 1989-1990 Edition, Pocket Books, New York, 1989.
The Wall Street Journal, Feb. 24, 1993.

Beating the 20% withholding trap

When you retire, quit or lose your job, don't take the payout from your retirement plan. Roll it directly into an IRA or into your new employer's plan, never letting it grease your palms.

If you want to spend some of it right away, you should still put it into an IRA and then tap the IRA for the money. If you don't, you will be falling into an IRS trap.

If you accept the payout, the IRS will automatically withhold 20 percent of your money. You will get that 20 percent back at the end of the year if you put your money into an IRA within 60 days of receiving your retirement plan money.

But, of course, you will be unable to put that 20 percent the IRS withheld into your IRA within 60 days. So, that money they withheld will be taxed *and*, if you are under 55, will be subject to a 10-percent penalty.

Note: If you lose your job, you can also keep the money in your old employer's plan. The company is required by law to let you keep your account if you are under the company's retirement age and if your account is over $3,500.

REFERENCE ———————————————————

Kiplinger's Personal Finance Magazine, November 1992.

Tax-free investments

Are you in a very high tax bracket? The municipal bond may be the investment of choice for you.

Municipal bonds are issued by cities, states, water or sewer revenue systems, and other local taxing bodies, and the interest on them is free from federal income taxes.

Municipal bonds issued by your own state or local governments are often free from state income taxes, too.

Municipal bonds do pay lower interest rates because they are tax-free. You can compare a municipal bond to a taxable bond by figuring out what the yield would be on a municipal bond if it were taxable.

To do this, divide the municipal bond yield by 1 minus your marginal tax rate. If you are in the 33-percent tax bracket, you would divide the municipal bond yield by 1 minus 0.33, or 0.67.

If you are in a low tax bracket, municipal bonds will not be the best investment for you.

Other tax-free investments: Most people know that interest earned on U.S. Treasury securities is free from all state and local income taxes. But many people forget that interest and dividends from mutual funds that own only Treasury securities are also tax-free in most states.

REFERENCES ———————————————————

Terry Savage talks money, the common-sense guide to money matters by Terry Savage, Dearborn Financial Publishing Inc., Chicago, 1990.
The Wall Street Journal, Feb. 23, 1993.

Most common investment tax mistakes

When it comes to figuring your investment taxes, don't rely on your common sense, experts warn. It will most certainly lead you in the wrong direction.

Here are some tax tips and some warnings for owners of stocks, bonds or mutual funds:

○ For starters, separate your various sources of investment income. If you received more than $400 in interest or dividends, you will report that on Schedule B of Form 1040. Schedule D is for capital gains and losses. If you sell stocks, bonds, commodities or any other property, you'll need a Form 1099-B. (You should get this from your broker.) Details on real estate sales go on Form 1099-S. Mutual fund shareholders should receive Form 1099-DIV from their fund showing any dividends they made.

○ Also separate investments into long-term and short-term investments. Short-term investments are any held for a year or less. They are taxed at a higher maximum rate than the longer term investments.

○ If your capital losses exceeded your gains, you can deduct about $3,000 of the loss (or about $1,500 for a married person filing separately). You can carry the extra losses over into future years. See IRS Publication 17 for help on doing these calculations.

Stocks

○ When a company distributes shares of a subsidiary to its shareholders in a "stock spin-off," and you then sell some of those new shares, what do you use as your "cost basis" for those shares? You didn't pay hard cash for them, so figuring out your gain or loss seems impossible.

The solution: Call the company's shareholder relations department and ask for help. The company will most likely have a prepared answer for you.

Bonds

○ Bonds bought at a "premium," for more than their face value, pose problems for taxpayers. Say you bought a $1,000 bond for $1,200 and held it until it came due. Although logically you would think you could claim a loss of $200, you don't get to claim any loss at all.

Mutual funds

○ Mutual funds pay you in two ways: dividends and capital-gains distributions. The dividends come from your share of the dividends and interest paid by the stocks and bonds held by the mutual fund. Capital-gains distributions are your share of the money the fund makes when it sells stocks and bonds.
The trap: You're not completely safe from capital-gains tax if you are in a tax-free municipal bond fund. If the fund sells bonds from their portfolio at a profit, you have to pay taxes.

○ You are subject to the capital-gains tax every time you move money from one fund to another. You can even incur a capital gain or loss when you do a telephone transfer within a family of funds.

○ You owe taxes on dividends made payable in the fourth quarter even if you didn't receive the money until the next year.

○ If you have a fund that's free from federal income taxes but invests in out-of-state bonds, you may have to pay state income taxes. To avoid this, buy tax-free funds which invest only in bonds issued in your home state.

○ Don't forget about reinvested dividends. Most mutual fund investors instruct the fund to reinvest any dividends it pays out. You have to pay tax on those dividends just like you'd received the cash.

○ If your fund invests in foreign securities, you may get to claim a deduction for taxes paid to another country. You can claim a tax credit on Form 1116 or take an itemized deduction on Schedule A of Form 1040. Usually it's better to take the tax credit. See IRS Publication 514 for help in deciphering the complex Form 1116.

○ Fees or commissions you pay to buy a mutual fund can't be deducted, but you can add them to the fund share's purchase price when calculating your capital gains and losses.

○ To calculate capital gains and losses when you sell your shares, you have to figure out what you paid for your shares. This can be tough when you bought shares at several different times and prices. The easiest way to figure out what you paid for your shares is the "average basis" method. You just take the average of the prices you paid at various times, and use that as your cost.

To make sure you show the least capital gains possible, you may want to try these other methods:

— "First-in, first out." This method assumes that whatever shares you bought first will be sold first. This could be the best way of figuring for you if your fund's value has taken a nosedive since you bought your first shares. (With many funds, the shares you purchased first were the cheapest, so selling them gives you large capital gains and a big tax bill.)

— "Specific share identification." With this method you can specify which of your shares were sold, so you can cut your taxes by selecting the shares you bought at the highest price as the ones you sold. To use this method, you must tell your broker at the time of the sale to sell those particular shares you bought at a high price. And you need written confirmation from the fund that the shares that were sold were indeed those you bought at a high price.

For more information on your mutual fund investment taxes, see IRS Publication 564 — "Mutual Fund Distributions."

REFERENCE
The Wall Street Journal, Feb. 25, 1993.

Sales tax and your car

○ Trading your car in instead of selling it seems more attractive when you factor in sales tax. If you sell your old car instead of trading it in, you have to pay the full sales tax on your new car. If you trade your car in, sales tax is figured on the price of the new car minus the trade-in.

○ Don't think you can escape sales tax by leasing a new car instead of buying. When you lease a car, you have to pay sales tax on both your down payment and your regular lease payments.

REFERENCE
Consumer Reports, March 1993.

Estate planning

Why you need a will

If you die intestate — or without a will — the state will control the distribution of your assets. Most people like to have some say in the disposal of their property. The state probably wouldn't give your property away like you would.

Laws are different in every state, but in most states, the surviving spouse gets a third to half of your assets. Your children get the rest. In some instances, your parents and siblings will get part of your estate.

A will can provide for the unexpected — like who will inherit your property if you and your spouse die in the same accident. A will can also help decrease the taxes on your estate.

A simple will costs less than $200, and the cost of updating your will when circumstances change is low. If all your assets add up to more than $600,000, you may want to have an attorney who specializes in estates draw up your will. If your assets are less than $600,000, a good general practitioner will do just fine. The federal government doesn't tax estates under $600,000. You and your spouse should have your will drawn up at the same time to minimize costs and confusion.

REFERENCE
How to be your own financial planner by Elliot Raphaelson and Debra Raphaelson West, Scott, Foresman and Co., Glenview, Ill., 1990.

Leaving all your money to your children

Some states require you to leave a certain amount of money to your spouse when you die. Remember this when you remarry.

Many people, especially if they are widowed and older, want to leave all of their money to their children from their first marriage. You can do this with a little arranging. All you have to do is to get your husband or wife to agree to waive their legal inheritance. The two of you need to sign a contract specifically stating that your spouse is forfeiting his share in your estate and that your children will receive all your assets after your death.

The contract needs to fully reveal your financial situation so there can be no accusations of fraud later. Also, outline what is to be done with any jointly held property, like a house, a bank account or a boat. It's often best to sign this kind of contract before you marry in a "prenuptial agreement."

REFERENCE ———————————————————————————————————

The Family Legal Companion by Thomas Hauser, McGraw-Hill Book Co., New York, 1985.

When your children inherit money

It's not that you want to spend your children's allowance or milk money. You just need to get your hands on that $5,000 they have in the bank. And you don't want it to buy a car or anything; you just want to send them to a good college.

It's more and more common these days for children to inherit a good chunk of money from their grandparents. Can you use that money to send them to college or to put them in braces at the orthodontist? Probably so, especially if you take some steps to make sure it's all on the up and up.

Until a child reaches the age of majority (18 in some states, 21 in others), any money they inherit is invested and kept in safekeeping by a "custodian," usually a parent.

A custodian can be sued for mismanagement of the child's money, but few people would consider sending someone to college "mismanagement."

Just to ensure that you'd never be accused of it, you may want to apply for a court order which authorizes you to use the funds for college expenses.

What if you don't have much money yourself and you'd like to use your child's inheritance to give him some advantages like piano lessons or braces for his teeth? You need to get your court order extended to include these other nonessentials.

There should be no problem with using the money in this way if you can't afford to give your child these benefits otherwise.

REFERENCE ———————————————————————————————————

The Family Legal Companion by Thomas Hauser, McGraw-Hill Book Co., New York, 1985.

Drawing up a will for a second marriage

Your second marriage may be ideal, but you never know what will happen after you die. If you and your spouse have children from a first marriage, and you have children together, you better get a lawyer and do some estate planning.

It's only natural for a remaining spouse to favor her own children, and you don't want your offspring to be cheated. Even if you trust your spouse completely, you probably want to have some say in how your money is divided.

Most importantly, you need to plan your estate to avoid taxes. Estate taxes take from 37 percent to 60 percent of anything over $600,000.

The easiest way to avoid estate taxes is to simply leave everything to the surviving spouse. (If your spouse is not a U.S. citizen, she will have to pay estate taxes when you die even if you leave everything to her. You need to make special provisions to avoid this.)

But if you leave everything to your spouse, you can't control what happens to the money after your spouse dies.

To defer taxes and ensure that your assets go to your children, consider setting up a "qualified terminable interest property (QTIP) trust." Your property is left in trust for the use of your spouse, but all the assets go to whomever you specify after your spouse's death.

Afraid that a QTIP trust will cause a nasty situation with your children waiting for your spouse to die? An alternative: Will up to $600,000 to your first set of children (that much won't be taxed) and leave the rest to your spouse, possibly in a QTIP trust.

If you plan to divide your assets between your spouse and your kids, don't leave your individual retirement account to your children. They will have to pay a lot more taxes on an IRA than your spouse will.

You can also use life insurance to fund a trust for your first set of children. You pay the premiums of the life insurance by contributing funds to the trust. Since the policy is owned by the trust, it is exempt from estate taxes.

When you marry for the second time, always sign a premarital agreement. If you want to leave everything to your children, you can't unless you've gotten a written OK from your spouse. Most states require that the surviving spouse gets as much as 50 percent of the estate, depending on the length of the marriage.

If you want most of your assets to go to your children, be wary of acquiring new assets jointly with your spouse or giving your spouse your durable power of attorney or health-care proxy powers.

Let your kids know what your plans are for your estate. That way your survivors won't bicker or accuse your spouse of influencing you against them.

REFERENCE

The Wall Street Journal, July 22, 1992.

How to overrule a will

Your father was married to his third wife for just over a year, and he left all his money to her! What about the children who have been devoted to him for over 30 years? Can they protest if they've been cut out of the will?

Invalidating a will is very difficult. They are written to uphold a dying person's wishes, no matter how unreasonable. But we've found at least four situations in which a will can be overturned. Here are your best bets:

- ○ Prove that your father was mentally unable to make a will. In other words, he lacked "testamentary capacity." He couldn't understand the value of his estate and the will he was making, or he was under some strange delusion that changed the way he wrote the will. If you can prove that your father thought you were trying to poison him every time you came over for dinner, you might be able to get the will declared invalid.

- ○ Prove that your father was a victim of fraud when he wrote the will. If your stepmother told your father that his children had requested that he leave them nothing, the will would be overturned.

- ○ Prove that your father was under "undue influences" when he wrote the will. Your stepmother might have constantly threatened to put him in a nursing home unless he left her everything.

- ○ Find some technicality that would invalidate the will. The state you live in may have strict laws about wills and how they must be witnessed.

If you do get your father's last will invalidated, his last previous will goes into effect. So make sure that will is worth your trouble before you begin.

REFERENCE

The Family Legal Companion by Thomas Hauser, McGraw-Hill Book Co., New York, 1985.

Should you try to avoid probate court?

Probate is the process where the courts determine whether your will is legal and then transfer your property to your heirs.

Some of your property will pass through contract or law instead of through probate. Property that passes to a named beneficiary, like life insurance policies, IRA and Keogh accounts and United States savings bonds, passes by contract, not probate.

Laws in many states are being updated as to whether property owned jointly (such as when spouses jointly own a house) passes directly to the survivor or goes through probate and is divided among the children and the surviving spouse. Your deed may have to say that you are joint tenants with rights of survivorship to avoid probate. Check with your lawyer.

All your other property, unless you make other provisions, goes through probate. People who try to avoid the probate process do so because they don't want to pay the probate fees, their property can be transferred more quickly, and they can keep their affairs private.

One way to avoid probate court is to set up a living trust. You turn everything you own over to the trust, which provides for you while you live and then distributes your property to your heirs when you die.

If you have a lot of assets and you want the settlements after your death to be private, a living trust might be for you.

Find out how much the probate fees would be, and compare that with how much it would cost to have the trust documents drawn up and your assets transferred to the trust.

REFERENCE

How to be your own financial planner by Elliot Raphaelson and Debra Raphaelson West, Scott, Foresman and Co., Glenview, Ill., 1990.

Who's responsible for your debts when you die

What happens if your father dies owing a lot of people money? Are his creditors going to come knocking on your door asking you to pay up?

They may, but you don't have to pay. You're not legally responsible for a parent's debts. The creditors can take anything your father leaves behind — cash, stocks, Treasury bills, personal property or real estate — but they can't hold you responsible.

The exceptions to the rule:

ↄ If you've gone into business with your father. You might be held responsible for any debts from a business you two held jointly.

ↄ If you and your father co-signed a loan. You might be held responsible for any unpaid balance on the loan.

REFERENCE
The Family Legal Companion by Thomas Hauser, McGraw-Hill Book Co., New York, 1985.

Financial steps for the dying

Money doesn't matter much when someone you love is dying, but think: How would you feel if you were terminally ill and couldn't handle your own financial affairs? If you knew half your money was going down the tubes in estate taxes?

The family of a sick person needs to plan in advance, but you can also do much at the last minute to make sure a dying person's wishes are carried out, to reduce estate taxes and to make life easier on the survivors.

ↄ Get the sick person to sign a durable power of attorney. This allows a person you trust to sign tax returns and insurance policies, make gifts and take care of financial affairs when you can't.

ↄ Make a living will. You can make clear whether you want to be kept alive on a life-support system. The person with power of attorney can also make health care decisions.

ↄ Update your will, especially if it hasn't been changed since Sept. 13, 1981

— when an important federal estate-law change took place. Also, check insurance policies, profit-sharing and 401(k) savings plans to see that the beneficiary is whom the dying person wishes it to be.

○ Consider transferring real estate, bank accounts and stocks into a living trust. These take about a month to set up, but they can eliminate some of the cost, delay and lack of privacy in a probate court.

○ Save estate taxes by making a gift of up to $10,000 to heirs — children, grandchildren or others. You can make gifts up to $10,000 per person per year without incurring a gift tax. One woman wrote a $10,000 check to each of her 13 grandchildren before she passed away and saved her heirs $40,000 in estate taxes.

○ If the sick person needs cash for medical care, sell stocks with small gains or losses instead of stocks with large gains. Why? When heirs sell the stock, the IRS will "step up" the cost of the stock to the price at the time of death. That higher price will be used to figure the capital gain or loss. "Stepping up" greatly reduces the income tax on the sale of a stock which has made huge gains.

REFERENCE ————————————————————
The Wall Street Journal, July 2, 1992.

Saving money on a funeral

Did your eyes widen in disbelief at this title? Yes, funerals are a morbid subject. And to speak of saving money on one is crass beyond belief.

But it's this same unwillingness to talk about funerals, especially your own, that leads to the outrageous amounts of money that gets spent on them.

One of the nicest things you can do for your family is to prearrange your own funeral and put your plans in writing. That way your survivors won't feel pressured to hold an elaborate funeral to show their love for you.

To ensure a reasonably priced funeral for yourself, you can join a local memorial society for a small fee. These nonprofit societies help you plan an inexpensive cremation or burial service.

By making arrangements ahead of time, you'll also spare your family the rushed and harried decisions that always go along with funerals. Families rarely shop around for the best funeral prices, and shady funeral directors are more than willing to take advantage of the grieving.

When arranging a funeral for yourself or a family member, stay away from the funeral home packages. These often contain many unnecessary services. You'll do better buying á la carte.

If you don't like the idea of shopping around, take a look at the price ranges on some of these funeral services:

Casket	$200 - 25,000
Clergy	$25 - 350
Director's fee	$350 - 2,000
Embalming	$100 - 400
Entombment in mausoleum	$1,500 - 25,000
Niche for urn	$150 - 8,000
Refrigeration of body per day	$50 - 125
Visitation room	$50 - 300
Transporting remains to funeral home	$50 - 300

Funeral directors are required by the Federal Trade Commission to give you prices over the phone. That makes finding the best prices easier.

The simplest way to save money is not to have the body displayed. Embalming, elaborate caskets and clothing are expensive. A simple, direct burial or immediate cremation along with a memorial service without the body can be the most loving, comforting funeral.

REFERENCE ───

The Business of Living by Stephen M. Pollan and Mark Levine, Simon & Schuster, New York, 1991.

 # Retirement planning

Most common retirement plan mistakes

Many companies are getting away from traditional pension plans and providing "self-directed" retirement plans for their employees. You get to control your own money, but nobody is to blame but you if your investments go wrong.

Here are four common mistakes employees make and you should avoid when handling your own retirement plan:

- ○ ***Investing conservatively and staying out of stocks.*** Employees usually get to choose whether to put their money in money market funds, a guaranteed investment contract that pays a fixed rate for a set period, bond and stock mutual funds, or maybe their own company's stock. You should keep a big chunk of your money in stock funds, especially when you are young. It is tempting to play it safe, but your returns will be much higher over time if you invest in stocks than in fixed-income or money market options. You just have to ride out the stock roller coaster.

- ○ ***Not contributing to your retirement plan.*** You should contribute when you're young so that you can retire comfortably.

- ○ ***Taking money out early.*** Most of the new plans let you borrow funds or withdraw them when you change jobs. Don't use your retirement to pay bills, and don't withdraw without knowing the taxes and penalties you'll have to pay. You may discover it's wiser to get a loan against your 401(k) to pay for a child's education or an emergency.

- ○ ***Blindly putting your faith in a broker or brokerage firm.*** You often get all your money in a lump when you change jobs, are laid off or retire. Don't give it all to a broker without keeping your eye on what he's doing with it. Getting advice from a financial planner is a good idea.

REFERENCE ───────────────────────────────

The Wall Street Journal, July 7, 1992.

Uncovering hidden costs of retirement retreats

The harried and frazzled workers of the world dream a golden dream — it's called retirement.

Are you looking for an idyllic (and cheap) retirement spot where you can carry your financial savings and golf bags?

States that have no income tax and low property taxes aren't always as desirable as they seem.

There may be a high state and county sales tax, a big increase in property taxes may be coming up, you may have to pay a hefty intangibles tax, and other hidden financial traps may be waiting for you.

To uncover hidden taxes and costs before moving to a retirement area, follow these steps:

1) Ask the local Chamber of Commerce for an economic profile and details on area property taxes.

2) Call the state's tax department to find out state income, sales and inheritance taxes and special exemptions for retirees.

3) Subscribe to the Sunday edition of a local newspaper.

4) Call a local CPA to find out which taxes are rising.

5) Check with local utilities to estimate your energy costs.

6) Visit the area in different seasons. Talk with other retirees about costs of food, clothing, health care and auto insurance.

7) Consider renting for a short time instead of buying right away.

Five most expensive places to retire:*

Santa Barbara, California

Los Alamos, New Mexico

Santa Rosa-Petaluma, California

Carson City, Nevada

Honolulu, Hawaii

Five least expensive places to retire:*

McAllen, Texas

Brownsville, Texas

Grand Lake, Oklahoma

Deming, New Mexico

St. George, Utah

---

* Based on cost of living, state and local taxes and typical household incomes. Compiled by consultant David Savageau.

REFERENCE ─────────────────────
The Wall Street Journal, Nov. 6, 1992.

Protecting your pension from the source tax

You've decided to retire to an income-tax-free state, so you think your pension is safe from the IRS. But, don't relax yet.

Unfortunately, about twelve states have "source taxes," which means that even if you retire elsewhere, you have to pay taxes on your pension to your old state.

California will find you through a collection agency and may impose up to a 55-percent penalty and interest if you retired, moved away and failed to pay taxes.

Find out what your state's source-tax rules are before you move. New York, for instance, would tax you heavily on lump-sum withdrawals from your retirement account. But if you set up an annuity and receive regular payments every year, the state won't tax you at all.

If you are moving to a state with low income taxes, make sure your new state will give you credit for income taxes paid to the old state.

For information on source taxes, you can contact RESIST, or Retirees to Eliminate State Income Source Tax of America in Carson City, Nevada (701-887-1296).

REFERENCE ─────────────────────
Business Week, Nov. 30, 1992.

Turnabout is fair play:
Let your mortgage company pay *you* for a while

Most American retirees own their own homes, and many have even paid off their mortgages. But some of these retirees don't have enough income to live comfortably from day to day. They don't want to sell their homes, and they can't afford a home equity loan. The solution — arrange a "reverse mortgage."

With a reverse mortgage, the lender loans you money monthly for a certain number of years or for as long as you live in your home. The loan amount is usually from 60 to 80 percent of your home's value.

A fixed-term reverse mortgage means that you will pay the money back at an agreed-upon date — supposedly from the sale of your house. An open-ended reverse mortgage, or the tenure plan, has no set date for repayment — the loan is repaid when the house is sold or the owner dies.

If at any point you need some extra money — an emergency occurs or you need to build a bath on the ground floor so you don't have to climb the stairs — you can ask your lender for a lump-sum payment. This is called the line-of-credit reverse mortgage.

The monthly income from the reverse mortgage is tax-free and won't keep you from qualifying for Medicaid benefits. Your personal residence is not included when the government decides if you qualify for Medicaid.

REFERENCE
Finances after 50: financial planning for the rest of your life by Dorlene V. Shane, Harper & Row, Publishers, New York, 1989.

What the new
retiree-health-benefit law means to you

Bad news for retirees: Congress has passed a new rule that requires companies to show the liability for retirees' health benefits on their regular financial statements. That's going to make companies' bottom lines look worse, and that's going to scare shareholders away.

Employers will be trying harder than ever to trim medical costs for retirees, and that means you are going to be required to pay more of your health insurance premiums — if you are one of the lucky ones. Many companies are cutting out health benefits for retirees altogether.

What should you do about it?

○ First, read your health plan carefully and become familiar with its COBRA provisions (the rules that govern how long your company is required to offer you continued health insurance coverage).

○ Depending on your health plan and the state of your health, you may want to keep working past 65. Medicare would supplement your regular health benefits.

○ Decide whether you need to buy additional coverage. Medicare will not cover all your needs. A free booklet that will help you choose extra coverage is *Consumer's Guide to Medicare Supplement Insurance*, published by the Health Insurance Association of America, Box 41455, Washington, D.C. 20018.

○ Join a group that will help you get insurance at lower rates than you could on your own. Churches, fraternal organizations and professional organizations often can obtain low group rates.

○ Lobby your company about setting up a VEBA — a voluntary employee benefits association. VEBAs work sort of like 401(k)s. You put away pretax dollars in an investment account, but the money can only be used for health costs or health insurance premiums.

REFERENCE
Business Week, Nov. 30, 1992.

Time-saving tips
when you apply for Social Security

○ When you apply for benefits, take along proof of age (preferably a birth certificate, but school records or other evidence will do) and your most recent W-2 or tax return.

○ You can get Social Security checks deposited directly into your account if you give them a voided check or deposit slip. Payment should arrive on the third day after the end of the month.

○ Apply for benefits at least three months before you want checks to start coming in.

○ Call 1-800-772-1213 to order a form to send in for an estimate of your benefits. By calling the same number, you can also order a government booklet called *Retirement* that answers questions about Social Security.

○ In the federal government pages of many telephone directories, Social Security addresses and numbers can be found under "H" for Health & Human Services, not under "S."

REFERENCE ─────────────────────
Business Week, Jan. 11, 1993.

Early retirement —
a sweet deal for you or a sour one?

If your company is downsizing and cutting staff, should you accept their offer of an early-retirement deal or reject it? Should you try to negotiate or hold out for a better offer?

It's a time of uncertainty and decision making, but here are answers to a few of your questions:

○ *Am I being offered a fair deal?*

A good package will give you two to three weeks' salary for every year you've been at the company. The best packages will add five years to both your length of service and your age when computing your pension benefits. Health benefits are most important, and the best plans will extend your benefits until retirement age if you are over 50. If you are younger than 50, your company should agree to pay for or split the cost of your coverage under the COBRA law. The COBRA law requires the company to let you buy your company health insurance plan at group rates for up to 18 months.

○ *Should I negotiate?*

There are two basic types of buy-out offers — early-retirement programs and voluntary-separation packages. Early-retirement offers are more common if you are near retirement age, and, by law, they are not negotiable. If you are younger and are offered a voluntary-separation package, you may be able to negotiate for better benefits, more severance pay and, possibly, a future consulting contract.

○ *Should I accept the offer?*

If your company seems on shaky financial ground, if you are dissatisfied in any way with your job, or if you think you may be laid off if you don't accept the deal, then take the buy-out offer. Consider rejecting the offer if you think the company's problems are only temporary and the smaller staff will enable you to advance your career further.

○ *Should I hold out for a better offer?*

No. If you decide to accept a buy-out offer, don't wait, thinking the company will sweeten the offer in a year or two. More likely, the severance pay and benefits will be much slimmer the second time around.

REFERENCE ————————————————————————————————
Money, February 1993.

When times are tough, is your IRA the answer?

During hard times, the money you've stashed away in your individual retirement account shines out like a lighthouse in stormy weather. But, if at all possible, shield your eyes from that beckoning light and borrow the money instead.

If you withdraw, you'll only get about half the money you invested! For instance, if you withdraw $1,000, you'll actually get $550 after paying taxes at a combined 35-percent rate and paying the 10-percent early-withdrawal penalty.

Is there any way to get more of your money? You can avoid the 10-percent penalty if:

○ You are completely disabled.

○ You use the money to pay for medical expenses exceeding 7.5 percent of your adjusted gross income.

○ You make equal annual withdrawals based on your life expectancy. Older IRA holders with a lot of money put away could get a significant amount of money this way. On the other hand, a 35-year-old with $15,000 in an IRA account could only withdraw about $453 a year without paying the 10-percent penalty.

○ You are over age 55 and you take early retirement.

REFERENCE ─────────────────────────────────────
The Wall Street Journal, Jan. 17, 1992.

Travel smart

How to cut your travel costs in half

To grab bargain rates at hotels, restaurants, on cruises or even island tours, become a member of a travel club. Even if you're only an occasional traveler, travel clubs can save as much as 50 percent of your travel costs. Some clubs only offer hotel discounts, but others even include bargain deals on airfare.

Travel club membership prices range from $20 to $100, and every club offers something different. To find the best club for you, find out if the club provides deals on your favorite vacation spots. If you are a business traveler, choose a city you travel to often and ask the club for the names of the participating hotels there.

> **The Top 10 Travel Clubs**
>
> America at 50% Discount (800-248-2783)
>
> Concierge Card (800-346-1022)
>
> Entertainment Publications (800-285-5525)
>
> Great American Traveler (800-548-2812)
>
> International Travel Card (800-342-0558)
>
> Privilege Card (800-359-0066)
>
> Quest International (800-325-2400)
>
> See America (410-653-2616)
>
> Solid Gold (604-874-0821)
>
> Travel World Leisure Club (800-444-8952)

Once you join, the clubs will send you either a coupon book or a directory of hotels and restaurants that participate in the club. Before you visit a city, simply call the hotels listed in your directory. Tell them you are a club member and ask if any discounted rooms are available.

If a hotel you prefer is not listed in your directory, call anyway since it could have been added to the club's list recently. Don't use the toll-free reservation line because those operators may be unfamiliar with the discount programs. To get the best deal, call the hotel at least 30 days in advance.

Note: Most travel agents don't handle club reservations because club bookings don't yield commissions. Some clubs do provide their own travel agencies.

REFERENCE —————————————————————————————
Money, February 1993.

Affordable airfare

You can save almost 50 percent on airline tickets if you take advantage of what travel agents call "back-to-back tickets." This works when you travel more than once to the same city or to cities near each other, like New Orleans and Baton Rouge.

You buy two round-trip tickets and split them up, using one ticket one way and the other ticket for the return trip. It appears that you are making two extended visits to the city instead of two short trips, and this cuts your costs in half. This tactic is legal, but airlines don't like it.

Some airlines, such as Delta Air Lines, are fighting back against the back-to-back ploy by requiring travelers who stay over Saturday night to return home within 30 days.

This requirement makes it more difficult to use the second half of your back-to-back tickets. Most airlines have given up checking their computers for back-to-back tickets and charging travel agents who booked them.

Another cheap-fare ploy is to use a "hidden city." Airlines often offer discount tickets on flights that have to stop to make a connection. You may need to travel to that connecting city rather than to the flight's final destination. Simply buy a one-way ticket, carry your luggage with you, and get off when the plane stops to make the connection.

The "split city" method can be a dramatic fare-cutter, too. With this method, you split the trip into two legs.

If you need to travel from Los Angeles to Dallas-Fort Worth, you might be able to buy a cheap fare from Los Angeles to Albuquerque and from Albuquerque to Dallas.

The best deals on airfare go to senior citizens who buy coupon books from the airlines.

For cheaper airfares, try to:

○ Extend your trip over Saturday night.

○ Book over seven days in advance. (Airlines have discontinued the three-day advance price cut.)

○ Take advantage of fare wars.

REFERENCES ─────────────────────────

Parade Magazine, June 14, 1992.
The Wall Street Journal, April 9, 1993.

Getting others to pay your way

A round-trip ticket to Madrid for $150? That's all one man paid recently for a week's vacation in Spain. And all he had to do was carry a list of some electronic parts that were shipped in the plane's luggage compartment.

You can fly cheap as a "free-lance courier," too. When a U.S. corporation needs to make an urgent delivery to an international firm, they usually contact an air courier company.

These companies use ordinary people who are willing to travel on short notice to get an extraordinarily low airfare. Most often the delivery is a small item or some documents.

Getting a list of courier companies to let them know you're interested is easy. Look in your phone book or subscribe to a bimonthly newsletter published by the International Association of Air Travel Couriers in Lake Worth, Florida.

Some drawbacks to traveling as a courier:

○ You must be able to travel within a few days after being contacted.

○ Often only carry-on luggage is allowed.

○ You may not be able to stay as long as you'd like.

○ You may have to put down a deposit to guarantee you'll deliver the goods.

REFERENCE ─────────────────────────

The Wall Street Journal, Dec. 17, 1992.

Fighting the airlines: know your passenger rights

Missed connections, overbooked flights, lost luggage — airlines can quickly ruin the first days of a vacation and can wreak havoc on a tightly scheduled business trip. And travelers feel helpless in the face of it all.

Have you ever thought you would fight for your flight rights if only you knew them? Here's what airlines have to do legally when they screw up:

○ Airlines must compensate you for lost or damaged luggage. On domestic flights, airlines must pay up to $1,250 per person. On international flights, airlines must pay approximately $9 per pound. The maximum weight for a piece of luggage is about 70 pounds. Most international airlines will pay for the maximum weight instead of weighing every bag at check-in, so a lost bag is worth about $630.

Airlines owe you nothing when your luggage is delayed. Some airlines may provide a few personal items or money to buy necessities. To protect yourself against luggage thieves, carry expensive objects on board with you. If your bags are soft, a thief can feel for hard items like jewelry boxes, cameras or laptop computers.

Many lost bags can be prevented if you watch attendants carefully when you check your bag. Make sure they attach the right routing slips. If you don't recognize the code for the airport at your destination, ask.

If your luggage is damaged or stolen, don't leave the airport until you report the problem. Someone should file your complaint right away, and you should receive a copy. Take the name of the person handling your complaint.

○ Overbooked flights are common because airlines expect a certain number of no-shows. When an unexpected number of passengers do show up, airlines offer free tickets and sometimes cash bonuses to passengers who volunteer to take a later flight.

If you are bumped from a flight, you are entitled to one-half the cost of your round-trip ticket (up to $200) if you arrive at your destination between one and two hours later than your original flight, or the entire cost of your round-trip ticket (up to $400) if you arrive more than two hours late (four hours for international flights).

○ Airlines are not required by law to put you up in a hotel if they cause you to miss your connection or if your flight is diverted to another airport. Airlines want to maintain good customer relations so they usually will provide a hotel and put you on the next available flight. If the delay is due to a mechanical breakdown, the airline will probably be willing to sign your ticket over to another carrier.

○ If your flight is canceled or delayed, the airline has to comply with an industry rule called Rule 240. The rule says that the airline has to put you on another flight — whether on one of its own planes or on another carrier.

The airline won't provide alternate transportation automatically — the passenger has to ask. If the airline refuses, ask to see their "Terms and Conditions of Carriage." The airline must prove to you that it has no obligation to put you on another flight.

REFERENCES

Nolo News, Winter 1992.
Parade Magazine, June 14, 1992.

Flying safe

Despite all the reports that commercial airlines are one of the safest ways to travel, almost everyone has a niggling fear of flying in the corner of their mind. "It's just not natural," say those with flying phobias.

Although the risk of a fatal crash is about one in a million flights, airplanes could be safer. Here are the most common and very real safety concerns:

○ Seats are supposed to be flame-retardant, but many of them aren't. Flame-retardant seats and cabin materials became the law on Aug. 20, 1990, but airlines have a long way to go in redoing the planes built before then.

○ The "90-second factor" is more scary than reassuring. The Federal Aviation Administration requires that a full plane can be evacuated in 90 seconds with half its doors blocked. Why is that a rule? Because if you don't get out of a crashed plane in 90 seconds, you'll probably die from the fire and the toxic fumes. That's not much time.

○ There's no such thing as "the safest part of an airplane." Nobody can know what part of the airplane is going to be damaged in a crash, so a "safe seat" just doesn't exist.

○ Planes don't have automatic sprinkler systems. The FAA is testing a sprinkler system, but right now it's too heavy for a plane to carry.

○ Some planes look and sound as if they're falling apart. Airplanes have an average age of around 10 1/2 years. The Government Accounting Office reported that airframe repairs had been completed on only 28 of over 1,300 aging aircraft in the United States as of April 1991.

Best ways to protect yourself when flying:

○ Wear natural-fiber clothes that cover your whole body.

○ Don't wear high heels. Flat-heeled, sturdy shoes are best.

○ Count the rows from your seat to each of the exits so you can feel your way through heavy smoke.

○ Keep your seatbelt fastened tight.

REFERENCE
Parade Magazine, June 14, 1992.

The most dangerous places to fly

You can decrease your chances of crashing in an airplane: Just don't fly in Asia, Eastern Europe, Latin America and the Middle East. And never fly in Africa.

The rate of fatal accidents in Africa is 15 times greater than in North America. Fatal accidents are four times as likely in Asia, Eastern Europe, Latin America and the Middle East as they are in the United States and Canada.

What brings planes down in Africa? Terrorism. In the Middle East, terrorism is second to weather and terrain. In Eastern Europe, engine failure is the problem. Generally, more planes crash in Third-World countries because of poor aircraft, maintenance and pilot training. The poorer countries also are lacking sophisticated landing and weather-radar systems.

Even worse: If you do crash in a Third-World country, you're twice as likely to die than if you crash in the United States.

Optimistic view: Looking at airplane-crash statistics with these numbers in mind, you should feel pretty safe when you fly in North America.

REFERENCE ————————————————————————————
Why Airplanes Crash: Aviation Safety in a Changing World, cited in *The Wall Street Journal*, Jan. 8, 1993.

Don't like what airlines serve? Here's how to get what you want

Simply ask for a special-order meal.

You don't have to have a note from your doctor to order a special meal from an airline. All you have to do is ask. Low-sodium meals, seafood, kosher meals with cold cuts and vegetables, plates for the vegetarian and fruit platters with a slice of cheese can all be yours at no extra cost.

Airlines claim that there is no difference in quality between their regular meals and their special meals. But the special meals are often healthier and more freshly prepared. Airlines try to keep a low profile on their special-meal service because they create extra work for the flight crew.

Most airlines require a day's notice to prepare a special meal, so call early and enjoy your trip.

REFERENCE ————————————————————————————
The Wall Street Journal, Nov. 19, 1992.

Cruising for a good bargain

For a relaxing, pre-paid, all-decisions-made, exotic vacation, there's nothing like a cruise.

But before you get trapped on a little boat, in a tiny room, with bad food and no one to talk to, take some pre-cruise precautions.

- ○ Don't rely on flashy cruise-line advertisements. Get specific information on the size of the ship and the size of the room you plan to book. "The Love Boat" is 50,000 tons and carries 1,200 people, but the average cruise ship is 18,000 tons and holds 700 people. You are less likely to get seasick on the bigger ships, and you'll have more entertainment options on the big ships.

- ○ Find out what kind of passengers the cruise line caters to. You don't want to be the oldest (or youngest) person on board, or the only single person in a sea of honeymooners.

- ○ Choose to dine at a table that seats ten rather than a table that seats four. A foursome can be miserable if you have nothing in common with the other couple.

- ○ Whatever your travel agent or booking clerk advises, don't buy a "room guarantee" in order to save money. You won't be assigned a cabin until the day of departure, and you'll probably get the worst room on board. Go ahead and book a cabin with a porthole.

- ○ Check what is included in your "all-inclusive" cruise price. Day trips at ports of call are usually not included, and if you buy them ahead of time, you may get a discount. Tipping and drinks probably aren't included, either. Ask how much drinks are and what the cruise line's tipping policy is so that you can include these charges when you comparison shop.

- ○ Ask about special deals that may not be advertised: cash rebates, free airfare or cut rates for large groups.

- ○ Avoid cruise lines that require you to pay for the trip months in advance. These cruise lines may be in financial trouble.

- ○ Pay for your cruise with a major credit card. That way you're covered if the cruise line goes out of business.

○ Get prices for a cruise from several different travel agents and from the cruise company itself. You may find that someone is offering a special deal.

REFERENCE ————————————————————————————

The Business of Living by Stephen M. Pollan and Mark Levine, Simon & Schuster, New York, 1991.

Self-protection abroad

In many countries, the crime rate is far less than in the United States, and it is true that you can safely extend a handful of unfamiliar currency and trust a merchant to take only the correct amount.

Unfortunately, several experiences like that can lull you into trusting too easily.

Some rules for the road:

○ Sometimes foreign money doesn't seem real to us. Be careful not to flash wads of it or treat it nonchalantly, any more than you would U.S. greenbacks.

○ Don't divulge personal information to strangers anywhere. That includes Americans you encounter abroad.

○ Remember, the more you look like a tourist, the more the locals will think you are "loaded."

○ Pickpockets in most foreign countries make American pickpockets look like amateurs. Be extra careful in jostling crowds.

○ Be discreet about cameras and electronic gear; carry them inside jackets or pockets, not flung over a shoulder.

○ Spread your money, credit cards and I.D. over several pockets, purses or money belts.

○ Never leave jewelry and expensive gear in view in your room, even when you are present, and take them with you when you leave. You can store anything you don't want to lose in the hotel's vault.

REFERENCE ————————————————————————————
How to Avoid Burglary, Housebreaking and Other Crimes by Ulrich Kaufmann, Crown Publishers Inc., New York, 1967.

Sleeping securely in a hotel

When spending the night in a hotel or motel room in the States or overseas, a little Yankee ingenuity goes a long way to help you sleep more securely.

- If the mechanism permits, leave your room key in the lock after locking yourself in at night. The hook end of a coat hanger, threaded through the key and hung over the knob, will help hold it in place.

- The hanger-over-the-knob trick works as an alarm, too, if you hang a ring of keys or another clattery device over it so that the door cannot be opened without disturbing the hanger.

- The back of a chair jammed under the knob will make forced entry more difficult. If there is no carpet to help hold the legs, place them in the heels of a pair of men's shoes, toes pointed toward the door.

- After locking up, hang a small, empty desk drawer or nightstand drawer over the upper corner of the door frame so that the door will dislodge it when opened. If the door opens out, hang the drawer over the doorknob, and the frame will make it fall when the door is opened.

- Add more racket by setting a couple of empty glasses in the drawer.

REFERENCE ————————————————————————————
How to Avoid Burglary, Housebreaking and Other Crimes by Ulrich Kaufmann, Crown Publishers Inc., New York, 1967.

Hotel fires: almost anything beats jumping

Fire in a high-rise building — everyone's nightmare. Plan how to take care of yourself before the unthinkable happens and there is no time.

Whether in a tall hotel or an office building, take note of the location of at least two emergency exits. Count the number of doors between your room and each exit. In case of fire, the only safe escape may be to crawl below the smoke, close to the wall, counting doors because you will not be able to see.

Look for smoke detectors and automatic sprinklers in the rooms. If possible, choose hotels with these safety devices — they mean your safety is important to the management. Pack a portable smoke detector just in case.

At night, leave your room key on the bedside table where you can find it easily in an emergency. If there is a fire and you discover the hall exits are blocked, you need to be able to get back into your room. You'll be glad you packed a flashlight if the lights fail in an emergency.

The same rules apply as at home. Feel the door before opening it, and don't open if it feels hot. If the hall seems safe, cover your face with a wet towel and crawl out, counting doors to the exit. Once in the exit stairway, it should be safe to stand and start down, unless going down seems to lead into smoke and fire. In that case, go to the roof and wait for rescue.

If that option does not appear safe, return to your room, and stuff dampened towels around doors to block poisonous gases. Call the fire department and the front desk, so your location is known.

If the room becomes smoky, crawl to the window, open it and hang a sheet or light-colored item out the window to signal rescuers. Break open a sealed window if you must, but use care not to drop a heavy object to the street — you could injure someone else.

Sometimes smoke blows back in through an open window. Block it by hanging a wet sheet over the opening, or wet and close the curtains.

Never use elevators in case of fire, even if they are operating. They can become death traps.

Wait to be rescued. Do not jump if you are above the second floor — few people survive jumps above that level.

REFERENCES ————————————————————————————

Smoke Signals, 2nd edition. A service of the International Society of Fire Service Instructors, Ashland, Mass., 1986.

Safe and Alive by Terry Dobson and Judith Shepherd-Chow, published by J.P. Tarcher, Inc., Los Angeles, 1981.

Worry-free vacations

A sure way to have a stressful vacation: Work at the office frantically before you leave in order to get the next week's work done, pack at the last minute, and fill every minute of your trip with sight-seeing excursions and other plans.

Make an effort to have a relaxing, rejuvenating vacation by trying these tips:

- Pack everything you can a few days early.

- Delegate your responsibilities at the office or just leave things undone.

- Get to the airport, bus station or dock an hour early, but don't be the first one to rush on or off the plane or boat.

- Don't completely change your routine. If a daily activity is important to you, like jogging or walking, keep it up on vacation.

- Your likes and dislikes aren't going to change completely on a trip. If operas or art galleries bore you at home, they probably will while you're on vacation.

- Business papers, of course, aren't allowed on vacation. You're permitted one call to the office a day.

- If you get fidgety on two-week vacations, take two or three shorter ones instead. Just make sure you give yourself time to relax.

REFERENCE ——————————————————————————————————————

The Business of Living by Stephen M. Pollan and Mark Levine, Simon & Schuster, New York, 1991.

Should you stop
your newspaper when you leave home?

Contrary to conventional wisdom, having the newspaper stop delivery while you are on vacation can tip off a potential burglar that the place is all his. Instead, tip your newspaper carrier to swap out yesterday's edition for today's.

Leave the hose out, if it's usually out, and some trash in the can. Have the grass cut regularly. Invite a neighbor to park his car in your driveway.

A few inexpensive timers, set at irregular intervals to turn lights off downstairs and on upstairs, will make the house look occupied.

Notify the police department of your planned absence. Some cities provide routine house checks for absent homeowners. Leave shades up and curtains open so the police can see into your house easily. A light on where it shouldn't be is also a sign to neighbors that an intruder is in the house.

And let your neighbors know you'll be gone. Burglars agree that your best protection against them is a watchful neighbor.

REFERENCES
Home Sense by Mike McClintock, Charles Scribner's Sons, New York, 1986.
The Family Handyman Magazine's Home Emergencies and Repairs, Harper & Row, New York, 1971.

What to look for in luggage

When you travel frequently, especially on business, the right kind of luggage can help make your trip more enjoyable. Unbalanced luggage that falls into every rain puddle at the airport, a carry-on "under-the-seat" bag that won't quite fit under the seat, or a bag that's too small or poorly designed won't help you look your best when you arrive at your destination.

The luggage of choice for business travelers and frequent flyers is the garment bag.

These bags are flexible, they can be stuffed into an overhead compartment easily, they weigh a lot less than other luggage and hold just as much, and they let you pack clothes still on the hanger, making the clothes a little less wrinkled and unpacking easier.

There are around 100 different garment bags, and the more expensive ones aren't necessarily more durable or more useful. They just look fancier. Here are some guidelines for finding a bag that will make traveling a little less painful:

○ **Frame:** A bag with a frame holds its shape better than the soft variety.

○ **Length:** The main compartment should be long enough to hold a suit jacket or a short dress without folding. Some bags have a pouch or a panel called an extender which is made to hold the bottom of an average-size dress. The length extender helps somewhat to prevent wrinkles.

○ **Straps**: Straps that crisscross to hold clothes in place work better than a single strap or multiple straps.

○ **Zipper**: Plastic zippers work more smoothly than metal ones. The "coil" zippers are easier to fix if they separate than the "toothed" zippers. Large pulls on zippers are handy, too.

○ **Opening**: Bags that open like a book to allow you to get to the clothes are easier than bags with a zipper than runs straight down the center or diagonally. Main compartments with an "I" opening require too much zipping. Bags with a fold-down front flap are also easy to open.

○ **Pockets**: Look for plenty of small compartments designed to hold a travel iron, shoes, sweaters, hair dryer, shaver, etc. There should be a long, thin pocket for ties and a large, flat pocket for folded shirts. Pockets made of see-through mesh are handy, and outside pockets are useful for items you may need during the flight.

○ **Expansion**: Some bags have extra fabric stored behind a zipper. You just unzip the zipper and the bag's main compartment can hold almost twice as much.

○ **Hanger**: Look for a jawlike metal bracket to hold the clothes hangers in place. You open these brackets, insert the hangers, then close them to lock the hangers in so they won't slide off. Two brackets help distribute the clothes more evenly than one bracket.

○ **Bag hook**: Passengers who've had the hook snatched off their garment bag know that you need to be able to put the hook away. Detaching it is too much trouble, so look for a bag with a pouch for the hook or a strap that snaps to hold the hook down against the bag.

○ **Shoulder straps and handles**: Shoulder straps should be wide with a nonskid underside. If you think you may want to carry the bag unfolded, look for a handle on the top of the bag as well as one at the center. Some bags even have wheels and a leash for pulling.

REFERENCE ——————————————————————————————
Consumer Reports, March 1993.

How to avoid lost luggage

There's nothing more frustrating than getting to an airport only to discover that your bags have been sent to another city — or even worse, luggage never-never land. Airlines handle thousands of pieces of luggage each day, and for the most part, it goes where it's supposed to go.

With a little effort on your part, you can increase the odds of your bags making it not only to the right city, but to your hotel room as well.

- ○ Remove all old flight tags. This will prevent confusion about the destination. Check to make sure the flight tag on the bag is the right one.

- ○ Avoid overly expensive luggage. It attracts thieves.

- ○ To further avoid theft, pick up your bags as soon as possible. The longer it sits in the claim area, the better the chances of it being stolen.

- ○ Never, ever leave bags unattended. Thieves move fast.

REFERENCE ——————————————————————————————
Heloise From A to Z, Perigee Books, New York, 1992.

Quenching your thirst in Europe

- ○ As with all northern European countries, tap water is perfectly safe in Germany. Germans find it incomprehensible that anyone would drink it, however, and will bring Perrier if you should ask for water. Since "ice" — *eis* — means "ice cream" in German, confusion escalates if you ask for *eis wasser*.

- ○ Americans accustomed to water fountains in public places are dismayed to discover these simply don't exist in most of Europe. One possible solution: Carry a small cup and quench your thirst in rest rooms, or carry water in a plastic bottle.

REFERENCE ————————————————————————————

The Federal Express World Business Advisory and Calendar, Educational Extension Systems, Clarks Summit, Pa., 1992.

'I'm lost!' How to get directions from the locals

The problem with asking directions of local folks is that they know the territory and you don't. Sounds obvious, but that's exactly why getting directions sometimes confuses us more than ever.

Local people tend to refer to "Old National Highway" instead of Route 279 which is how your map shows it, and they seldom know Interstate exit numbers.

The most useful tool for getting or giving directions is a map. Be sure to have one with you when you ask for help. It is much clearer to mark out a route than to describe it.

Be sure you are stating your destination clearly. Better still, write it down. Ask the person to point out the place on your map.

No map? Ask her to sketch the route. And ask her to estimate distances in blocks or miles.

Write down instructions, with notes on landmarks, and read them back. Don't be embarrassed to ask for clarification.

REFERENCE ————————————————————————————

Reader's Digest Practical Problem Solver, The Reader's Digest Association Inc., Pleasantville, N.Y., 1991.

Shopping in Mexico: how to bargain like a native

As Americans, we consider Mexico to be our personal exotic next-door neighbor bargain town. For vacationers, the lure of quality goods at dirt-cheap prices is often greater than the lure of the sparkling white beaches in the fancy (and inexpensive) resort towns of Cancun and Cozumel.

The only problem is, we never know if our last purchase was a great deal or a great scam. Scamming is, after all, a way of life in Mexico.

But you can beat the system if you are armed with a lot of nerve and an interest in bargaining, haggling and fighting for your rights.

- Your best defense against being taken by the Mexican market vendors is the ability to speak the language. Even if you have only had high-school Spanish, you can still improve your position if you are a pretty good actor. You need to gesture wildly and say contemptuously "No soy turista" (I'm not a tourist).

   The right price for an item is probably 10 percent to 25 percent of the asking price. You certainly don't want to pay more than $40 for an item priced at $100 — so offer $20. If they laugh, just walk away.

   On the other hand, if you are in an authentic marketplace where tourists are rare, you may get barely 10 percent off the asking price. In fact, prices may be so low that you are happy to bargain very little and pay the asking price.

- Never express how much you love something. Play good buyer, bad buyer, if possible. The bad buyer should make all the appropriate gestures to show that he is not impressed.

- Don't be rude to a vendor. If you are truly not interested, say "I will not insult you with an offer," or make a gesture like a traffic cop signaling a car to stop in order to cut short bargaining.

- If you shop in a place that accepts credit cards, use one. If you buy an item that turns out to be cheap (it breaks the third day you use it), you can get your money back from the credit card company. They also cover lost or stolen merchandise.

Popular scams

- A popular scam in Mexico is to switch sizes. You may make an offer on a liter bottle of vanilla and the salesman may quickly begin to wrap a 750 ml bottle. Keep your eye on the merchandise and know what size you should be getting.

○ To avoid another scam, make sure you don't misread a peso price (also written with a $ sign) as a dollar price. To confuse tourists, a retailer might abbreviate the peso price, putting $30 on the tag instead of $30,000. This item really has an asking price of around $10 American dollars.

○ Beware of the "Sale" sign scam. Some shops put American prices on their tags and calculate those prices at the beginning of the season. If the value of the peso falls during the season, instead of changing all the price tags, the store has a "sale." The retailer offers you 20 percent off any marked price. If you believe you are getting a good deal, you've been had.

○ Don't change money with guides or taxi drivers. They act as though you can trust them, but you won't get a good exchange rate. If you are in desperate need of pesos and you have to change money with them, don't give a tip at the end of the day.

○ Kid vendors will scam you as fast as adults will. There are a lot of kid vendors in Mexico so if you are a softie for youngsters, avoid them.

○ You should know that if a taxi driver or tour driver takes you by a shop, he is getting a kickback from that shop. The person handing out brochures at your hotel for a particular tour is getting a kickback or bribe from the tour coordinator. Don't expect impartial advice on shopping and entertainment.

Shop with care when buying these items

Perfumes and cosmetics — French perfume seems like a great buy in Mexico. But the perfume you buy in Mexico is rarely what you would get in France. Fragrances are often watered down, mixed from concentrate, or made in America or the Caribbean. Some perfumes are made in Mexico through a licensing agreement, and some are complete fakes.

Mexican-made pharmaceuticals — Avoid these if at all possible. Particularly resist the temptation of cheap Mexican-made birth control pills.

Ready-to-wear clothes — Look carefully before you buy because some items, even some designer clothes, are poorly made.

Silver — Sterling silver can be a great buy, but if you want real silver, buy from a reputable shop instead of the street vendors. Look for the stamp ".925," which means that of 1,000 grams of metal, 925 grams are pure silver. With street vendors, even if it is stamped .925, be wary.

Vanilla — Vanilla is a Mexican original, but don't buy the cheapest vanilla you can find. Fake vanilla is big business in Mexico. They use tonka beans, which taste and smell like vanilla. The extract from tonka is coumarin, a blood thinner sometimes used as rat poison and banned in the United States. Look for a picture of a vanilla bean and the logo of the Vanilla Association.

Where to get the best buys

Arts and crafts are the best buys in Mexico, and you will find them cheapest in or near the city where they are made. The great exception to this rule is silver, which is not cheaper in the Silver Cities.

These cities — Taxco, San Miguel de Allends, Queretaro and Guanajuato — are tourist traps.

Here is a list of cities that specialize in certain craft items:

> **Oaxaca**: Black pottery and carved wooden animals
>
> **Tlaquepaque**: Pottery and glass
>
> **Puebla**: Tiles
>
> **Olinalá**: Pin-dot lacquer work
>
> **Mérida**: Hammocks and henequen rugs
>
> **Pátzcuaro**: Pottery
>
> **Tijuana**: Liquor
>
> **Toluca**: Wool, pottery, baskets
>
> **Michoacán**: Black lacquer
>
> **Guatemala**: Weaving

If the poor people in Mexico make you too miserable to shop, keep your pockets filled with 100-peso coins. That will buy a loaf of bread or a roll. Give out one to all who ask.

REFERENCE
Born to Shop: Mexico by Suzy Gershman and Judith Thomas, Bantam Books, New York, 1989.

Recreation and sports

Improving your putt

Whether you're a serious golfer or not, improving your putting can be lots of fun.

But, like any other sporting activity, improving your game takes practice. Keep the following hints in mind:

- Keep the distance to the hole in mind. Practice uphill putting and downhill putting to learn to gauge your strength.

- Practice your stroke by putting between a pair of two-by-fours. This will help you develop a good path.

- Don't move your head when putting.

- Keep still from the waist down.

- Be creative! Come up with a pre-putt routine and do it every time. (It may be a little frustrating for others to watch, but it will help you relax.)

- Set up your shot. Line the putter up with the hole and consider the distance.

- As you approach the ball, study the green. From a distance you can usually detect slopes and other potential hurdles.

- Check your grip. If you're not sinking the ball, you might want to consider making a change.

- Sorry, but you can't blame your putter. With a good stroke, you can make a hole with just about anything in your hands.

- Practice by putting at small objects, such as a tee stuck into the ground.

- You can also set numerous balls at equal distances from the hole and work on making the shots. This way you learn to shoot with and against the grain of the grass. Start relatively close and move out.

REFERENCE
Golf Made Easier ... Not Easy by Bruce Fossum, Golfish Inc., Okemos, Mich., 1989.

Making tricky golf shots

Just about anyone can hit a golf ball on a flat fairway. And with a little practice, you can make it go where you want it to. But, those same moderately talented golfers fall to pieces when an incline comes into play.

Hills don't have to turn birdies into bogies. With the proper stance, you can actually use them to your advantage.

When shooting uphill, keep your weight on your left side, balancing yourself with your right. Aim a little right of your target since you're likely to pull the ball. Balls tend to fly higher when shot from this angle, so use more club.

Downhill shots require an open stance, with your body weight resting on your right leg. Here, aim left of your target and use less club.

REFERENCE
Golf Made Easier ... Not Easy by Bruce Fossum, Golfish Inc., Okemos, Mich., 1989.

Tennis: different strokes for different courts

The clay court. Want to go to the courts for a quick match? Better not go to the clay courts. On clay, the first set may take as long as the entire match would take on a hard court. So take your lunch and plan to be there for a while.

Since the ball moves slower on the clay court, it may be easier to place your shots and maneuver your opponent. You can make sure he has a long way to run to get to the next shot. The counterpunching that can result is what makes tennis on clay very exciting.

One trick to playing well on clay is getting just the right speed on your serve. You don't have to serve hard, but if you serve too softly, your opponent will pass you on the return.

You must have good balance to play on clay, because the footing can be so uncertain. If you rush the net and stop abruptly, you may end up flat on your face.

The grass court. Since balls don't bounce well on grass, don't give them a chance to try. Your emphasis on this unpredictable surface should be on getting to the net, volleying and taking the ball in the air.

Sadly, the grass is dying on tennis courts. If you have a chance to play on a grass court, you should try it before they're all gone.

The indoor court. Indoor courts shield you from the elements, giving you truly ideal conditions to enhance your concentration. The ball is easier to see against a consistent indoor background, but there are some drawbacks if you are not used to playing indoors. The low and sometimes V-shaped ceiling can be a problem unless you practice.

Because indoor court time can be very expensive, many people don't take the time to warm up properly. This may result in injuries that certainly cost more than the extra five minutes a good warm-up takes.

One problem with indoor courts is that they spoil you. Returning to the outdoor court and facing the elements again can be a shock to your game.

Hard courts. There are no hard and fast rules for your average hard court. Hard court surfaces can also vary. A little practice will get you used to a new court and help determine whether the ball will move fast or slow.

If the court is very fast, much of the play is simply blocking the ball back. You don't have time for complex strategies. A point usually lasts only two or three shots.

A hard court is the place to play a quick match.

REFERENCE
Total Tennis: A Complete Guide for Today's Player by Peter Burwash and John Tullius, Macmillan Publishing Co., New York, 1989.

Successfully selecting racquetball equipment

Sure, practice makes perfect, but wouldn't you like a little extra help in your racquetball game? Equipment is sometimes just as important as strategy and fitness when playing this businessperson's sport.

To improve your game, keep a few things in mind when you're at the sporting goods store:

○ A smaller grip gives the player better control and power.

○ If possible, try hitting a ball with a number of different racquets before settling with one racquet. The variety will help you decide what's best for your game.

○ Buy a racquet with a flat top and sides. This makes it easier to play balls that hug the walls and floor.

○ Always buy brand-name products. They cost more, but the quality construction is worth the price.

○ Power players should lean towards heavyweight racquets, while control players are better off with lightweights. Determine whether you're looking for power (heavy) or maneuverability (light).

○ Beware of "new" products. If you've been able to play the game this long without them, why do you need them now?

○ Tighten the strings on your racquet for control, loosen them for more power.

○ Buy quality eye guards. Eye injury is a strong risk in the game.

○ Wear a glove to prevent blisters and to keep perspiration off your equipment.

○ Choose shoes made for racquetball to enhance your movement and prevent injuries. Running shoes and the like may not give you the protection you require.

REFERENCE

Skills and Strategies for Winning Racquetball by Ed Turner and Marty Hogan, Leisure Press, Champaign, Ill., 1988.

Avoiding common racquetball injuries

It's funny that a distant sports cousin of tennis is almost a contact sport, but racquetball players suffer more than their share of injuries.

The most common injuries, by far, are eye injuries. That's why eye guards are such a necessary part of the game. With the ball flying at speeds of up to 40 miles per hour, glasses don't do the trick. To fully protect yourself, choose eye guards without hinges that completely cover your eyes on all sides.

You should also be careful that your racquet doesn't fly out of your hands and hit other players. Secure it with the thong attached at the end. Some players like to make a slip knot while others twist the thong tight then grasp the racquet.

To avoid ankle injuries, make sure the court's floor is dry. Take the extra time to wipe up sweat spots if a player dives or falls on the court. High-top shoes can also cut down on ankle injuries.

Stretching is important to avoid back pain or pulled muscles. Warm up thoroughly before you step on the court.

REFERENCE
Skills and Strategies for Winning Racquetball by Ed Turner and Marty Hogan, Leisure Press, Champaign, Ill., 1988.

What the hockey rule book doesn't tell you

You might learn all about cross-checking, icing and power plays if you study the official rules of hockey, but if you're unfamiliar with the sport, you'll probably still walk away with a few questions running through your head.

For example, did you know that some slap-shooters hit the puck at speeds of more than 100 miles per hour? Some shots have even been clocked at 120 mph.

The ice on a hockey rink that looks so thick is actually only three-fourths of an inch in depth. Because thicker ice is softer, players move slower.

The red and blue lines on the ice — as well as the "crease" (the half circle in front of the goal) and the face-off circles — are painted on after one-half of an inch of ice is frozen, then covered with another one-fourth of an inch.

Despite the catcalls of some fans, referees aren't all that stupid, either. That's why when two players begin to slug it out, they often stand clear for as long as possible. Between the flying sticks and punches, the ref (who wears only a helmet as protection) might get hit and seriously injured.

At the same time, the referee does watch the fight closely, determining who has earned what penalties.

REFERENCE ——————————————————————————

Knighttime (the official program of the Atlanta Knights).

Debunking swimming myths

Bad news, swimmers! All that good press your favorite sport has received may not have been quite accurate. Sure, swimming is a fantastic way to exercise, but it might not be the best way.

For years, water lovers have boasted that, because you use all of your muscles, swimming is the quickest way to get in shape. Alas, the only way to use all your muscles is to swim wrong.

You don't really sculpt a body in the water, either, though you do tone your muscles some. And you've got to learn to swim before you do any toning at all.

Swimming is also not the best way to lose weight. While most other forms of exercise, such as running, cause you to lose your appetite, swimming actually makes you more hungry.

Speaking of food, at some point in your life, you've probably been told not to eat or drink anything for at least an hour before you swim, lest you run the risk of getting a stomach cramp and dying. Bunk!

Just as marathon runners bulk up on carbohydrates the night before a race, so do professional swimmers. As long as you have eaten a normal meal, you're safe to get in the water.

As a matter of fact, it's often necessary to drink some fresh water when you're working out in the pool. Swimmers sweat as much as any other athlete, though it's not as noticeable. If you find yourself tiring quickly, you could be dehydrated. Drink a glass of water and watch yourself revive.

To get in shape, you don't have to swim fast. In fact, when you're just beginning, you should take it slow. Otherwise, you're putting a tremendous strain on your body's systems.

Good swimming shape doesn't equal good all-around athletic shape.

Don't assume that a good competitive time in the 100-meter butterfly will make you a whiz on the basketball court.

Swimming is an upper body sport. (Legs are used more for balance than anything else.) So while your heart and lungs are in good shape, your legs might not be as strong as you think they are.

REFERENCE
Swim Swim: A Complete Handbook for Fitness Swimmers by Katherine Vaz and Chip Zempel, Contemporary Books, Inc., Chicago, 1986.

Build your confidence by building your muscles

Just for once you'd like to stand up to your boss instead of cringing when he loses his temper in a meeting. Or you'd like to discipline that employee who walks all over you. And you'd like to look in the mirror and admire what you see instead of wrinkling your nose in distaste.

New research shows that one of the best ways to pump yourself up for everyday life is to pump iron. In fact, in a study of 89 college students, the students who exercised through strength training improved their self-esteem while students who participated in a program of swimming, an aerobic exercise, didn't.

Why does lifting weights lift your confidence so well?

- You can see almost immediate results. Muscle strength and toning becomes obvious quickly.

- Strength training doesn't require talent, so you don't have the frustration factor that you get with sports like basketball or tennis.

- The strength and physical power you acquire gives you a feeling of power in all areas of life. You feel mentally tough.

- Exercise stimulates the release of neurotransmitters and chemicals such as endorphins that give you a natural high and stave off depression.

To build your confidence and your muscles, start small, lifting an amount that is easy for you and adding slowly. Perform your exercises slowly.

Keep a schedule of your workouts that includes how much weight you are lifting for each exercise. Give yourself an incentive, such as new clothes, when you reach your goals.

Work with a partner, if possible. You'll have support to keep you going, and you'll have more fun.

REFERENCE ───────────────────────────

Prevention, December 1992.

How to train for a road race

Twisted ankles and dehydration are just the tip of the iceberg when it comes to running injuries. Every time you start to jog, you put pressure on your heart and lungs, among other organs.

Done right, running will get you in terrific shape. Run recklessly and you could regret it for a long time.

The same training errors cause most running injuries. Watch out for these training mistakes:

- ⊃ Don't overtrain. Let your body adapt to its current level of conditioning before you head to a new plateau. Running too far, too soon is the chief cause of injury to runners. Even if you decide to race for speed, build up slowly.

- ⊃ Don't undertrain. Before you're ready for a race, especially a marathon, you have to be comfortable with the distance you'll be required to run. Don't rush your training — there will always be another road race.

- ⊃ Don't get greedy. Let your body fully rest after each race. Even when you're not running, you have to pace yourself.

- ⊃ Give yourself regular, easy workout days, or even days off. This allows your body to recover from the stress of training.

- ⊃ Let your body heal. If you've been injured, get a doctor's approval before you hit the track again.

- ⊃ Watch that form. Poor technique might put extra pressure on your legs and lower back.

○ Stretch! Stretch! Stretch! If you're not flexible, you can't run. Be careful not to overstretch, and never jerk or bounce as you loosen up.

○ Gradually cool down after a race. Stretch lightly and walk around. As tempting as that chair might be, you'll regret it later.

REFERENCE
The Injured Runner's Training Handbook by Bob Glover and Murray Weisenfeld, Penguin Books, New York, 1985.

Runners, listen to your body

Most running injuries don't occur spontaneously. Chances are that if you suffer a jogging-related ailment, your body tried to give you advance warning.

Do any of these symptoms sound familiar? If so, it might be time for a little rest before you hit the road again.

○ Mild tenderness or stiffness that doesn't go away after a day or two of rest.

○ Unexplained poor performance in workouts and races.

○ You're tired after a full night's sleep or feel sluggish for several days.

○ Your morning pulse rate increases. (Keep a diary. If your body isn't recovering from the stress of a workout, the pulse will increase.)

○ Continual thirst, despite a replenishment of fluids.

○ Significant weight loss.

○ Sore throat, fever or runny nose. As your body fights off a cold, it's best to reduce activities that stress your body, such as running.

○ Muscle cramping.

○ Upset stomach, constipation and/or diarrhea.

○ Loss of appetite.

○ Increased irritability.

REFERENCE ─────────────────────────────

The Injured Runners Training Handbook by Bob Glover and Murray Weisenfeld, Penguin Books, New York, 1985.

How to avoid shin splints

Running might not be considered a contact sport — but just tell that to your legs!

The stress of regular running and jumping can inflame the muscles and tendons on the front of your leg above the ankle so badly that you're actually unable to run.

Runners call this condition shin splints because it hurts along the shinbone, but the real name for this injury is medial tibial stress syndrome, and it is the most common of all running injuries.

Even if you are only running two miles daily, you're taking more than 3,000 strides.

Furthermore, for each step you run, your leg absorbs two to three times your body weight. It's easy to understand how almost 20 percent of all runners get this painful injury at one time or another.

Fortunately, there are steps you can take to prevent shin splints, and you can exercise while you're getting over a bad case.

Try these tips to avoid getting shin splints in the first place:

○ Stretch carefully before running.

○ Warm up and cool down slowly.

○ Wear the right shoes (some runners believe the shock-absorbing power of running shoes wears out by about 300 miles).

○ Alternate two different brands of running shoes to give your feet and legs a break.

Shin splints often start as pain that accompanies the beginning of your workout and then disappears during your run.

If your shin splints get worse, you might feel the pain throughout your workout and into the cool-down. At their worst, the pain of shin splints persists into your everyday routine, and the front of your leg above the ankle will feel tender to the touch.

These changes in your routine might help you recover from shin splints:

○ If pain doesn't prevent you from running, continue your workouts, taking special care to warm up and cool down slowly.

○ If pain persists throughout your run, give your legs a rest from running. Change to no-impact activities like riding a stationary bicycle, using a stair-climbing machine or swimming.

○ Massage your shins with ice for eight to 10 minutes three times daily, especially after your workout.

○ Take an anti-inflammatory, such as ibuprofen.

○ As your shin splints improve, move up to treadmill running or running on a flat, even surface.

○ Stretch your leg muscles carefully (if it doesn't cause any pain).

○ Ease back into your running routine by running every other day or alternating running with a no-impact activity.

You'll probably be able to start running again about four to eight weeks after your injury.

Follow the rule of the "toos" to prevent shin splints or to avoid reinjury: don't run too much, too soon, too fast.

See your doctor if pain persists or occurs on the shinbone itself.

REFERENCE
The Physician and Sportsmedicine, December 1992.

The biking commuter

Concern for good health and the environment has sent more and more Americans back to an old form of travel: bicycling.

Bicycling has most of the advantages of recreational walking. Properly done, cycling is a low-impact aerobic exercise, perfect for over-all toning of muscles and the cardiovascular system.

Biking makes you feel better and relieves tension, and you don't even need a team, greens fees or lessons.

Best of all, biking gets you there, wherever your particular "there" happens to be, sometimes faster than a car and with absolutely none of the pollution — unless good honest sweat counts as pollution.

Count the "whys" of commuting to work by bicycle:

- Bikes zoom right past gas stations, except for an occasional sip from the air pump.

- Although traffic rules apply to cyclists as well as motorists, there are short cuts available that drivers can't use — like cutting through a park or narrow alley.

- Couriers use bikes to carry packages or documents across busy cities faster than they can in cars.

- Just being outdoors is important for a lot of people.

- Regular fitness workouts — on the way to and from work.

- Parking is a snap, sometimes right inside your building.

- You may even be able to say good-bye to the high cost of auto-ownership, insurance, parking fees and car repairs.

- The energizing effects of biking will improve your performance at work and get you home without the usual day's end exhaustion.

REFERENCES

The Cyclist's Companion by John Howard, The Stephen Greene Press, Brattleboro, Vt., 1984.

Bicycling by George S. Fichter, Golden Press, New York, 1974.

How to buy a bike

Bike size. Men should be able to straddle their bikes with both feet flat on the ground and have one to three inches between crotch and the top tube. The length of the top tube (for men's bikes) is measured by holding your elbow at the front edge of the saddle and extending your arm to the handlebar stem. Your hand should overlap by about the fingers' length.

Saddle. The front edge of the saddle should be about two inches behind an imaginary line drawn vertically from the center of the pedal crank. If your legs are especially long, it may even be located an inch or two further back.

The saddle should parallel the ground, tipped slightly forward or backward according to your preference. When riding in a seated position, your leg should be almost but not fully extended. Saddles are usually adjustable, so have someone critique your form as you ride, or watch yourself passing a plate glass window:

- If your hips rock with every stroke, the saddle is probably too high.

- If you appear to bounce with every stroke, it is probably too low.

- If your leg is fully extended, lower the saddle just until your knee has a very slight bend in it at the bottom of the stroke.

Handlebars. The type of handlebar is also largely a matter of personal preference. Dropped bars allow a lower profile and decreased wind resistance, and they are often preferred by men and boys. Women usually like the standard handlebar that allows a more upright position. Experienced cyclists feel that the "racing" position of dropped handlebars is more comfortable and less tiring than riding upright. The body's weight is more evenly distributed when shared by the arms.

Standard handlebars should also be slightly lower than the top of the saddle. When the arms are correctly used in bicycling, they contribute to the rider's efficiency, especially in climbing hills.

Toe clips. Experienced riders strongly recommend toe clips — metal stirrups that fit on rat-trap pedals (metal with toothed edges to grip the shoe sole). Here's why:

- They position your foot correctly, ball of foot over pedal, and prevent it from sliding forward, even with hard pushing.

- They aid in "ankling," turning the foot down so that on the lowest part of the stroke, you are pushing backward and getting as much power from your stroke as possible.

- You can pull your foot up in the backstroke, thus continuing to drive through the entire circle your pedals make.

Gears. Bikes come with gears, without gears and in every combination of gears that you can imagine. The choice is yours, based on how you will be using your bike: on hills? to race? for casual rides in a flat neighborhood?

The more gears on a bike, the more choices you can make to get exactly the ratio you want for your circumstances. Most riders, however, find they use only a fraction of the many available to them. A 10-speed or even a 5-speed bike gives you plenty of options.

REFERENCES

The Cyclist's Companion by John Howard, The Stephen Greene Press, Brattleboro, Vt., 1984.
Bicycling by George S. Fichter, Golden Press, New York, 1974.

Walking your way to health

When you consider the advantages walking has over other forms of recreational exercise, you'll start to wonder why it took you so long to get started.

High on the list of reasons walkers give for feeling strongly about their particular form of exercise is that it simply makes them feel good. They're not imagining that.

Exercise releases endorphins in the brain, mood-enhancers that doctors call natural opiates. They reduce stress and produce a certain euphoria.

When people say they have become almost addicted to exercise, they are describing the "high" that results from endorphin production.

Other walking pluses:

- Can be done virtually anywhere, anytime and by anyone — no reservations or lessons needed.

○ It's cheap. The only equipment you need is a decent pair of walking shoes.

○ Less chance of injury, less risk of twisting your legs than with more strenuous exercise.

○ Uses almost as many calories as more strenuous workouts — a 12-minute walking mile uses only 26 fewer calories than jogging a mile in 8 1/2 minutes.

○ Improves circulation and the efficiency of lungs.

○ Helps you lose weight and sleep better. Walking actually helps curb the appetite.

○ Helps prevent or reverse certain types of osteoporosis, arthritis and cardiovascular disease.

REFERENCES

Walking for the Health of it by Jeannie Ralston, an AARP Book, Scott, Foresman and Co., Glenview, Ill., 1986.
Take Care of Yourself by Donald Vickery, M.D. and James Fries, M.D., Addison-Wesley Publishing Company, Reading, Mass., 1981.

Calories burned when walking at various speeds

Speed (miles per hour)	Calories burned (per hour)
2 (30 min./mile)	120-150
3 (20 min./mile)	240-300
3 1/2 (17 min./mile)	300-360
4 (15 min./mile)	360-420
5 (12 min./mile)	500-600

REFERENCES

Walking for the Health of it by Jeannie Ralston, an AARP Book, Scott, Foresman and Co., Glenview, Ill., 1986.
Walking — The Pleasure Exercise by Mort Malkin, Rodale Press, Emmaus, Pa., 1986.

An answer for every objection to walking

○ *I don't have time for exercise.*

Walking fits into your schedule easier than any other exercise. Just change shoes.

○ *Bo-o-o-oring!*

Use walking time to plan or reflect on your day, clear your mind of tensions, listen to music or talk with a friend.

○ *It's hard to get up a team.*

You don't need a partner or a team to walk, as you do in other sports, but it is nicer when you have company.

○ *We get so much bad weather here.*

You can walk in the heat or the cold, the sun, rain or snow.

○ *By the time I get home, I'm too tired. I have no energy.*

Walking gives you energy; improved circulation and deep breathing are invigorating.

○ *But I hate to sweat!*

Walking seldom makes you perspire enough to need a shower.

○ *And the gym and pool are so crowded!*

There's plenty of room to walk, even on city streets.

○ *My schedule is so irregular; I might not stay with it.*

Walk all or part of the way to work, when you do errands or after work. Walking has the lowest dropout rate of any kind of exercise.

○ *Well, what if I hurt myself?*

Walkers get the benefit of strenuous exercise without serious injuries.

○ *I'm not athletic — how will I learn?*

You already know how to walk; you've been doing it for years!

○ *I'm under too much pressure at work.*

Walking actually reduces tension, and it has a relaxing effect on the body.

○ *Why start now? I've done fine for years without exercise of any kind.*

You may be in perfect health now, but walking helps prevent illness and the aches and pains of old age.

REFERENCES

Walking for the Health of it by Jeannie Ralston, an AARP Book, Scott, Foresman and Co., Glenview, Ill., 1986.

Walking — The Pleasure Exercise by Mort Malkin, Rodale Press, Emmaus, Pa., 1986.

Best way to keep walking

Convinced walking's the right exercise for you, but you can't seem to stick with it? Probably the single most helpful motivation is having a walking partner.

○ When you know someone is out there at the corner waiting for you, you can resist the temptation to sleep in.

○ Time seems to fly by when you have someone to talk to.

○ You don't have to be bosom buddies (although you may get to be), but it does help if you and your partner move at the same speed and can commit to a similar amount of time.

○ A spouse makes a good walking companion. For some couples, going for a walk together is a great way to decompress after work. It may be the only time you have for each other all day.

REFERENCES

Walking for the Health of it by Jeannie Ralston, an AARP Book, Scott, Foresman and Co., Glenview, Ill., 1986.

Walking — The Pleasure Exercise by Mort Malkin, Rodale Press, Emmaus, Pa., 1986.

Improving your aim with darts

If you've spent any time in a sports bar — or even a neighbor's basement

— chances are you've thrown a dart or two. Without an abundance of practice, it's a safe bet that you didn't score too many bull's-eyes.

Repetition is the only way to make yourself an expert thrower, but you can avoid embarrassing yourself if you know what you're doing when you approach the line.

Your stance determines the accuracy and consistency of your throw. Keep both of your feet flat and firmly on the ground. And when you throw, keep 'em planted! Balance is important, too, so don't lean into your throw or bend your knees.

Keep both your eyes open when tossing a dart. Closing one won't improve your aim, though it will distort your perspective.

Relax. When your throw is complete, you should be (with the exception of your arm, of course) in the exact same position as when you started.

As for the throw, start with your arm at a right angle to your body, with your hand tucked back, and with the dart alongside your eye.

Relax your wrist and toss it firmly. (The dart should hit the board at close to 40 miles per hour.) If the dart lobs — sorry, but you've got a lot of work to do.

REFERENCE ——————————————————————

All About Darts by I.L. Brackin and W. Fitzgerald, Contemporary Books, Inc., Chicago, 1986.

Making Monopoly fun again

There's no denying that Monopoly is one of the great American board games. But, play it a few hundred times, and it does tend to get a bit bland. After all, it doesn't take that long to figure out which properties are the big breadwinners.

There is an alternative: Change some of the rules. Purists might balk, but changing the terms of play can bring new life to an old favorite.

○ Double the price of property. If you decide not to buy, put the property up for auction, with the money going to the bank.

○ Do away with mortgages, but allow players to resell property to the bank (for half of its list price).

○ Treat Water Works and Electric Company like railroads. Instead of paying a percentage of the dice roll, add them to the railroad fee schedule. (For example: Four railroads earns the player $200, five "railroads" earns $300 and six earns $400.)

○ Allow voluntary bankruptcy. A player who is not in debt is allowed to declare Chapter 7 and receive $800 and the dark-purple monopoly (Mediterranean and Baltic Avenues).

○ Create "Go" cards. Whenever a player lands on "go," she draws a card similar to a "Chance" or "Community Chest" card. Be creative!

○ Ban the use of $1 bills. Round all rents up to the closest $5 figure.

○ Don't make jail a haven. Players who have been arrested cannot bid on property, cannot build houses and can only collect half of the normal rent when someone lands on their property.

○ Build unevenly. Own Boardwalk and Park Place? Put a hotel on Boardwalk, but leave Park Place vacant.

○ Make Free Parking a cash bonanza. Most families already follow this rule, putting taxes and house improvements in the center of the board.

○ Only allow building immediately before a player's turn.

○ If a player lands on Income Tax, he is allowed to count his money before deciding whether to pay $200 or 10 percent.

REFERENCE ───

Beyond Boardwalk and Park Place by Noel Gunther and Richard Hutton, Bantam Books, Toronto, 1986.

Improving your luck at pool

Another of those favorite basement and bar games, pool takes practice — and lots of it — before you can claim boasting rights. Improving your shot is, for the most part, trial and error, but there are a few things you should keep in mind.

- ○ Know what you plan to do before you bend over. Once you aim, don't stall.

- ○ Keep your left hand closer to the cue ball and grip the butt of the cue farther forward for softer shots.

- ○ Put the cue tip virtually against the cue ball at the exact spot you want to strike it.

- ○ Keep your bridge (made of your spread fingers) firm.

- ○ Your cue should be as level as possible at all times.

- ○ Take a few warm-up strokes (usually between three and six) before actually shooting at the ball. This will help you get a feel of how much force is required.

- ○ Remember, smooth, easy strokes are the best.

- ○ Avoid locking your right wrist.

- ○ Use wrist action when you're hitting the cue ball.

- ○ Make sure your follow-through is at least as far as you draw back.

- ○ Don't move anything except your right arm when shooting. Moving the head and shoulders, even slightly, can throw off your shot's strength and accuracy.

REFERENCE

Byrne's Standard Book of Pool and Billiards by Robert Byrne, Harcourt Brace Jovanovich, San Diego, 1987.

Know the odds in Las Vegas

Roulette! Craps! Blackjack! Viva Las Vegas!

Even the occasional gambler can get caught up in the excitement of the casinos, but your chances of walking away a winner are slim at best. Knowing that going in will make it a lot easier to walk away a happy person.

Realize that the majority of the games in a casino are based solely on luck.

Skill doesn't help much when you're at a slot machine, or even a craps table.

The name of the game is gambling. If you're willing to take a risk, you could walk away with loads of money. (Remember, never bring in more than you're willing to lose.)

The house always has the mathematical advantage over the gambler, regardless of the bid. Because of this, the casino stands to win between one-half of a cent and 20 cents on every dollar you bet.

Whatever your game, keep your bets low until you determine if Lady Luck is with you that evening. If so, increase your bets. If not, walk away. Never press your luck when you're losing. The "law of averages" gets broken all the time.

Once you start winning — and are playing with house money — that's the time to start upping your bids. After all, it's always easier to spend someone else's cash, and big bets are the only way to earn big bucks in a casino.

REFERENCE
Las Vegas Experts Guide to Craps, Blackjack and Card Games by Robert Scharff, Coles Publishing Co., 1978.

How to make the most of a Frisbee

Frisbees, on first glance, seem pretty easy to use — simply throw the disk in the air and watch it soar. Unfortunately, there are thousands of folks whose lack of coordination becomes immediately obvious the minute they loosen their grip.

Accurate Frisbee throwing isn't a real trick, but you do have to keep a few things in mind. Always keep your eye on the target, even when you're about to let go of the Frisbee.

Make sure your body is positioned properly (legs apart and limbs loose) and, just as you release, point your finger at your target. Follow-throughs, while fancy, don't do anything to increase accuracy.

If it's distance you're looking for, however, a follow-through will be required. A running start doesn't hurt either.

Curl your wrist as you bring your arm back and tilt the Frisbee toward your body and uncurl completely as you bring your arm forward. The disk will zoom outward.

REFERENCE
Frisbee Fun by Margaret Poynter, Julian Messner, New York, 1977.

Turning heads with your Frisbee know-how

OK, so you've got the basics down. Your throws get the Frisbee to your partner most of the time and catching it is a breeze. Now, how to impress people.

Why not with a few tricks? How about a spectacular catch? How about simply showing off?

○ Behind-the-Back Catches: The trick here is to get your partner to throw the Frisbee at about waist level. To catch the disk with your right hand, twist to the right, which will leave your left hand facing the thrower. Reach your right hand behind your back and catch the Frisbee as it passes.

○ Between-the-Legs Catches: Low throws are the perfect opportunity to use this trick. As the Frisbee gets closer, move so it will pass between your legs, then simply reach down and grab it through your legs.

○ Tipping: This is the fun trick of Frisbee, keeping the disk in the air and making it hover. It will also give you a little extra time to make a trick catch.
As the Frisbee approaches you at head level or above, hold all of your fingers together and straight up. Hit the bottom of the Frisbee (near the center) to keep it aloft, but watch out for calluses.

REFERENCE
Frisbee Fun by Margaret Poynter, Julian Messner, New York, 1977.

Making your pictures spectacular

Trick photography isn't only for the pros. If backyard snapshots of your pets and children and countless slides of summer vacations are starting to get a bit boring, you can add special effects to your photographs with only a little effort on your part.

Your flash is one of the easiest ways to create optical illusions. Set your shutter speed so that it stays open a full second or so (as opposed to the normal 1/15th of a second) and take a picture in dim light. The flash will fire normally, giving things in the foreground a ghostlike image, while the rest of the shot appears normal.

In darkness, try using multiple flashes with an open shutter. If things go well, you can get two or three images of the same person in different poses. (Because there is no light to expose the film, you can pose once, hit the flash, move, pose again and once again hit the flash. The only image that will appear is the person that the flash is aimed at.)

With a little work, you can also "defy gravity" through photography. This special effect usually requires some sort of preparation, such as setting the shot up with fishing line or fine wire. (Both are fine enough to turn invisible when set against a matching background.)

Screens and filters also give amateur photographers the chance to create special effects easily. You can buy screens, filters and special lenses at photographic stores.

Not all trick shots of this sort require special equipment. Try shooting your pictures through textured glass. Perhaps smear some petroleum jelly on your lens. The effects are both startling and beautiful.

REFERENCE ——————————————————————
Creating Special Effects edited by Jack Tresidder, The Kodak Library of Creative Photography, Time-Life Books and Kodak, Salvat Editores, South America, 1984.

The world's abuzz over beekeeping

Got a little of the Pooh Bear in you? Do you crave honey with the ferocity of a grizzly? Beekeeping might be the hobby for you.

A relatively inexpensive amusement, beekeeping is an old tradition that, if done right, carries minimal risk. (Still, if you're allergic to bee stings, you might want to think twice.)

Starting out as a beekeeper is as easy as mail order. Membership houses and bee-keeping companies sell packages containing equipment and collections of bees for fairly affordable prices.

Advanced beekeepers can try capturing a swarm, removing a colony from a bee tree or buying a secondhand colony, but beginners should go through companies. If nothing else, you lessen your chances of getting diseased bees.

Buy your bees in early spring. (Major honey flow is usually in late June or early July.) Packages come with anywhere from one to five pounds of bees, with 4,000 bees to the pound. Three pounds is usually best for the beginner.

When they arrive, put the bees (in their package, of course) in a dark room kept at about 70 degrees Fahrenheit. Feed them almost immediately with a half water, half sugar mixture. Once they have gorged themselves, transfer the bees to their new home. Don't worry too much about being stung, full bees are docile bees.

After the bees are stored in their house, put out two pails of the sugar-water mixture for the worker bees to eat and bring in to the queen, then leave them alone. Check the food supply occasionally (bees will generally consume 20 pounds in a week to 10 days), but do not open the house for at least 10 days.

When you do finally peek, make it quick and only to ensure that the queen is still alive and laying. If this isn't the case, your package is lost. A colony cannot survive without its queen.

REFERENCE

The Complete Guide to Beekeeping by Roger A. Morse, E. P. Dutton, New York, 1986.

Bird-watching secrets

Birds are everywhere, which is one reason birding has such universal appeal. (Birding, by the way, is the term preferred by folks who used to be called "bird watchers.")

Besides your own backyard and the neighborhood park or greenbelt, there are countless sanctuaries, shorelines, wildlife refuges, national and state parks and forests.

When you take a trip for business or pleasure, pack some small, fold-up binoculars and a field guide to use in your free time. In every city, you get a chance to study a variety of birds in new habitats.

Some helpful hints for observing our feathered friends:

○ Leave bright colored clothes behind.

○ Walk quietly and slowly.

○ Concentrate on margins, where woods meet fields, sea meets marshes or low shrubs meet mowed lawns — birds concentrate in such areas. Birds of prey may often be found near interstate highways, where litter attracts rodents and utility poles provide great perches.

○ Birds are most active early in the morning, just before and after sunup. Around sundown there is another burst of activity.

○ Birds are busiest in the spring. Fall migration is also good birding season, but midsummer is the pits.

○ Your car is a good blind. Birds will come closer when you are in your parked car than if you are on foot.

○ Birders have a secret for bringing birds in close. It's called "pishing," and consists simply of whistling air through the teeth, somewhat explosively, like "pshhwshhwshh" or a soft "tchtt-tchtt-tchtt." The sound apparently resembles a scolding or alarm sound and most birds can't resist coming to see what's going on.

○ You can also call birds by loudly kissing the back of your hand, or playing back bird songs on a portable tape recorder. Do take care not to disturb them during the nesting season.

○ You'll need one or two good bird guidebooks so you'll know what you're looking at. Choose a book with colored drawings instead of photographs. People who believe the camera never lies will change their minds when they've had some in-the-field experience. Light and shadows, angles, positions, age of the bird, season, background — all these may be distorted in a photo but not in a well-drawn picture. The handiest books have illustrations opposite descriptions and maps of where you can find the bird.

REFERENCES

Birds of North America by Chandler Robbins, Bertel Bruun and Herbert Zim, Golden Press, New York, 1983.
How to Attract, House, and Feed Birds by Walter E. Schutz, Macmillan Publishing Co., New York, 1974.
The Birder's Catalogue by Sheila Buff, Simon & Schuster Inc., New York, 1989.

How to make your yard a bird haven

Busy people who find it difficult to get away to indulge their bird-watching hobby find ways to bring the birds to them. Your own yard can be an avian haven with very little effort on your part.

Everyone knows bird feeders and birdbaths attract birds, but there's more you can do:

- Provide cover for birds by planting shrubs and bushes. They feel more secure if they can approach feeders through branches.

- In the spring, crush eggshells on the ground where the birds can find them. They need the calcium for their own egg production.

- Clean out your own hairbrush or the one you use to groom your dog or cat, and hang bunches of hair in low shrubs. Most birds love soft hair to line their nests. They'll even use clothes dryer lint.

- Birds love sweet pastries with lots of shortening in them, like stale doughnuts. Put them out along with more healthful seed mixes.

- Spread cracked corn on bare ground or on your sun-deck. Ground feeders love it, and it won't sprout like other seeds.

- Too much trouble to cook down suet? Birds aren't really that particular. Put chunks of raw fat in the suet feeder.

- Better still, buy cheap peanut butter and lay the open jar on its side on a platform feeder. Most birds love it, and the fat helps keep them warm in winter. (Stir in corn meal if you like, but don't pay attention to fables about birds choking on plain peanut butter.)

- Hang a shallow pan of water from a window bracket or provide a raised birdbath. In cities, birds sometimes find it harder to locate a dependable source of fresh water than food.

- Concrete or ceramic birdbaths may crack in winter if water freezes in them. A block of wood in the water will help a little.

- If you can devise a drip or gentle bubbler for your birdbath, you'll find that your feathered guests are fascinated by moving water.

○ Birds love old, dead trees. After Christmas, remove all tinsel and ornaments from your tree and toss it into an out-of-the-way corner of your yard. You may want to leave trees felled by storms. Rotting bark provides great habitat for insects and worms, hence birds. One conservation group calls dead trees Animal Inns.

○ If you're fond of hummingbirds, buy a red hummingbird feeder and fill it with sugar water. (Boil tap water and stir in ordinary white sugar — 4 parts water to 1 part sugar — until it dissolves.) Since a hummingbird feeder should be cleaned out once a week, choose one that doesn't require an engineer to open, clean, refill and hang without spilling. To clean, try a weak solution of chlorine bleach to help kill mildew and bacteria, rinse well and follow with a vinegar rinse.

REFERENCES

Attracting Birds: from the Prairies to the Atlantic by Verne E. Davison, Thomas Y. Crowell Co., New York, 1967.
The Birder's Catalogue by Sheila Buff, Simon & Schuster Inc., New York, 1989.
Mary Ellen's Best of Helpful Hints by Mary Ellen Pinkham and Pearl Higginbotham, Warner Books Inc., New York, 1980.
How to Attract, House, and Feed Birds by Walter E. Schutz, Macmillan Publishing Company, New York, 1974.

Waving off seasickness

It can ruin a boating or fishing trip faster than anything. But that queasy feeling or outright seasickness shouldn't ruin your reputation as a sailor. It happens to virtually everyone at some time or another, even professional seamen. And woe unto him who mocks your discomfort — his time will come.

If you know the early symptoms, you may be able to head off a bout. They are:

○ Yawning, mouth-watering, a need for fresh air.

○ Dizziness, cold sweats, a slight headache.

○ A queasy stomach, proceeding on to outright nausea, vomiting and dry heaves.

Some pointers:

○ Eat frequent, light meals before and after boarding.

○ Another tried and true remedy: ginger candy. Studies prove that ginger fights nausea.

○ A berth low in the middle of a large ship is more stable than one in the bow or stern of a smaller vessel.

○ Fresh air and activity often help relieve symptoms; lying down below decks often aggravates them. (However, for some sufferers, the opposite is true.)

○ Fixing your eyes on something stable like the horizon usually helps.

○ Over-the-counter motion-sickness remedies, such as Dramamine, are effective, but they might cause drowsiness. (Check with your doctor to make sure any pills you take are compatible with any other medication you may be taking.)

○ Scopolamine patches, available by prescription, are perhaps the most effective of all.

REFERENCE ─────────────────────────────────
Practical Boating by W.S. Kals, Wilshire Book Company, N. Hollywood, Calif., 1973.

Drownproof yourself

Want to enjoy a day boating, fishing or just playing at the beach without worrying about drowning? When you can't swim, spending time near the water isn't always fun.

The U.S. Coast Guard estimates that half of all Americans can't swim 50 feet. Half of all drownings occur within 20 feet of safety.

Knowing how to swim is less important than knowing how to float. By learning "drownproofing," a technique developed in the early 1940s to keep even an injured person afloat in fresh or salt water, in rough seas or a quiet pool, you can also conquer your greatest enemy — panic.

With drownproofing, you can survive for hours in the water, long enough for help to come or to work your way to shallow water. No book is a good substitute for in-the-water training, available through YMCA and Red Cross courses. But here are the basic principles:

○ Ease into water about as deep as you are tall and go limp, in a standing position. Feel how your body remains more or less upright, head sagging toward chest, back curved, arms and legs dangling. Kids call this the "jellyfish float."

○ Bring your hands slowly to your forehead (keep all movements very slow and lazy to conserve energy) and extend your arms. Make a lazy sweep downward, just enough to straighten your neck and raise your mouth above water to grab a shallow breath. You're wasting energy if your neck and shoulders emerge.

○ Go limp again, resting, and let about half the air out through your nose, under water. What remains helps your lungs act as buoys.

○ Once you get the hang of it, you'll find your desire to breathe reduces to just a few times per minute, and less effort is required to raise your head that minimal amount.

○ Now try holding your hands behind your back and giving just a gentle kick, scissors or frog-style, to convince yourself you could survive this way if your arms or shoulders were injured.

○ When you have mastered survival floating, try flattening out slightly into a tiny glide between breaths. Nonswimmers have covered a mile in less than an hour using this technique.

○ Note that much less effort is required in salt water and when you are wearing a bathing suit; somewhat more is needed in fresh water or when fully clothed. Weigh carefully the decision to remove clothing: If the water is cold and there is a risk of your body temperature dropping too low (hypothermia), the clothes will help reduce heat loss.

Practice in a pool, then teach your family and crew this life-saving skill.

REFERENCE ———————————————————————————————————
Practical Boating by W.S. Kals, Wilshire Book Company, N. Hollywood, Calif., 1973.

Collector's confidential

Doing 'bid-ness' at an auction

While the odds of getting a pretty good deal at an auction are fairly high, people often don't get the best deals they can. Carried away in the heat of a frenzied bid, some folks will often spend a lot more than they can afford for something they don't really need — or even want all that bad.

Discipline is the key to being successful at an auction. Follow these rules and you should be able to escape without being burned.

- Inspect an item you are considering bidding on very carefully. If you're not an expert on the item, bring along someone who is.

- Do your homework. Read about items of interest. Know the going market rate. And know how to spot potential problems.

- Get to know the rules of the auction. (These are often explained by the auctioneer before bidding begins and are occasionally printed in the auction guide.) You don't want to scratch an itch at the wrong time and end up with a piece of junk.

- Set a bidding limit for yourself and stick to it. Many novices will break this rule, which only benefits the seller.

REFERENCE ────────────────────────
How to Save Money on Just About Everything by William Roberts, Strebor Publications, Laguna Beach, Calif., 1991.

How to collect autographs

With America's fascination with paparazzi, it shouldn't come as any surprise that autographs are such a popular collector's item. Letters, manuscripts and documents signed by notable folks from history are fast becoming investments rather than mementos.

Historical autographs are the most prized by collectors, and often the most expensive. Prices vary greatly depending on the document signed and its historical significance. Abraham Lincoln's "house divided" speech, for example, recently sold at auction for $1.54 million. A letter signed by Theodore Roosevelt, however, sells for a mere $250.

Presidents and historical figures aren't the only signatures hunted by collectors. Movie stars and sports greats can fetch big prices as well.

If you're planning to start gathering autographs, be aware: Forgery runs rampant in the industry. Before investing a substantial sum of money, be sure to get some good advice, either through a dealer or through one of the collectors' groups. You can find names, addresses and phone numbers of both in Autograph Collector, a monthly magazine.

REFERENCE
Forbes, March 1, 1993.

Beer cans for fun and profit

An unlikely art form, beer cans are becoming increasingly popular among today's collectors. Believe it or not, that container of hops and barley in your refrigerator could be a collector's item someday.

Introduced in the mid-1930s, beer cans command prices of up to $2,000 these days. Collectors are not looking for names like Miller and Budweiser, but they are looking for names like Chief Oshkosh and Krueger's.

Over 80 percent of the breweries that were open when cans were introduced are now closed. The scarcity and condition of the cans determines their value. If you're lucky enough to get a cone-topped or defective antique can, a collector is often willing to pay handsomely for it.

Your search for antique beer cans might take you to some unusual places. Dumps and abandoned buildings are good locations to find collection additions.

The beer can collector's market is bottoming out these days, however. If you're looking to make a profit off your collection, it might be wise to hang on to it for a few years.

REFERENCE
Hidden Treasures by Alan Crittenen, Union Square Books, 1985.

How to collect firearms

If you're looking to put together a collection fast, set your sights somewhere other than on gun collecting. Patience isn't so much a virtue in this hobby as a necessity.

Generally, you should spend your first few months as a collector in the library. Without a firm knowledge of firearms, you're making yourself a target for scam artists and unethical dealers.

Pick a specialty and start studying. (Most collectors focus on either a particular type of gun, such as the Colt or Winchester, or a certain time period, like the Civil War.)

Join the local collectors' clubs, too. You will find them to be an excellent source of information, not to mention extra guns.

Counterfeiting runs wild in this hobby, and the scammers are quite bold. So be careful when ordering from the back of a magazine or newspaper.

Be sure to maintain your collection carefully if you want it to keep its value. Rust and scratches detract greatly from the value of a weapon.

These little details make it hard to tell whether a gun is worth its asking price. If you're not sure, take an expert with you when you want to buy.

If you have good business skills, you can make a profit from gun collecting. Specialty collections sell more readily and make a better profit than haphazard collections. You can also make an extra few dollars if you have a documented history of the gun's ownership.

REFERENCE ─────────────────────────

The Gun Collector's Handbook of Values by Charles Edward Chapel, Coward-McCann, New York, 1983.

A hobby that's just ducky

Are these collectors quackers? Spending up to $50,000 for a wooden duck? A high price, unquestionably, but that's what a William Bowman Golden Plover fetched at auction in 1985. Granted, not all decoys are that expensive, but if you're looking for something by celebrated carvers like Bowman or Nathan Cobb, be willing to pay handsomely.

Of course, most people are looking to start or add to their collection with a less substantial investment. Flea markets and antique shops are often the best place to look.

Be on the lookout for counterfeit or replica collectible decoys. A new head nailed to an old body is one of the more popular scams.

Decoy dealers exist, but they tend to charge a bit more. "The National Directory of Decoy Collectors" will give you a complete list of reputable outlets of all sorts of decoys.

REFERENCE

Hidden Treasures by Alan Crittenden, Union Square Books, 1985.

Marbles roll into collectors' hearts

Believe it or not, those marbles you shot with reckless abandon as a child are now considered a collector's item. Cateyes, aggies, bumblebees and more are now sought by collectors who are willing to pay top dollar for them.

Rarity, size and condition help determine the price of a marble, but pizzazz is where the real value lies. If it can capture the eye or imagination of a collector, it can capture their wallet as well.

Stone, clay, crockery and china marbles are a bit more rare than the glass variety, and thus command higher prices. The rarest marbles are made of clear glass with white or silvery figures inside. Individually made in the 1850s and 1860s, these "sulphides" are now worth up to $4,000 each.

If you've long since lost your own childhood marble collection, try flea markets and antique shows. New collectors will probably want to specialize in a particular type of marble. This will allow you to familiarize yourself with the field and learn the difference between rare and common.

REFERENCE

Collecting Antique Marbles by Paul Baumann, Wallace-Homestead, Radner, Pa., 1991.

How to collect posters

The trick to collecting posters is determining what interests you. Do you like movies? Historical events? Political statements? The direction you choose will determine what your collection will be worth.

Movies are the overwhelming choice of most poster collectors. Generally, people will focus on one star, such as Marilyn Monroe or John Wayne, and devote themselves to obtaining a poster from each of that star's films. Depending on the star, the posters usually range in price from $40 to $200.

The posters of World Wars I and II are also quite popular. James Flagg's "I Want You" poster has become a symbol for the World War II era and is highly sought after by collectors. Prices in this category run from $25 to $600.

Posters of the 1960s by such artists as Andy Warhol and Roy Lichenstein have also had a resurgence of late. The fusion of art, fun, advertising and protest has once more caught collector's eyes.

Other popular posters come from circuses (though these are hard to find) and travel companies (old ships and railways are particularly popular).

The type of poster you want to collect will determine the best place to search for it. It's usually best to start in used bookstores or antique shops. Remember to store them carefully since the paper is so fragile to the elements.

REFERENCE —————————————————————————————————
Hidden Treasures by Alan Crittenden, Union Square Books, Novato, Calif., 1985.

Making a profit off politics

Election time is bonanza time for political junkies. Besides getting to watch history turn another page, they get to add to their memorabilia collection.

Since George Washington's day, politicians have used trinkets to try to sway public opinion. And modern collectors are paying top dollar for the knickknacks of old.

Political buttons are by far the object most desired by collectors. Other items, like cameo brooches, ribbons, canes and coins, remain quite popular as well.

Scarcity, historical value and age determine how much a political item is worth. It also helps to have something by one of the more popular presidents. (Chester Arthur memorabilia has never appreciated very much.)

Garage sales and flea markets are the best places to find bargain buttons. You're also likely to run across something at a collector's show (especially one focusing on coins and stamps).

A warning for collectors: Don't clean your political items. Because so many are paper-based, it may damage them. And with demand on the rise, you want things in the best condition possible.

REFERENCE
Hidden Treasures by Alan Crittenden, Union Square Books, Novato, Calif., 1985.

Have a Coke collection and a smile

Coca-Cola isn't just one of America's favorite soft drinks, it's also one of the country's favorite memorabilia suppliers. From the Haddon Sundblom Santa Claus that has become a holiday tradition to recordings of the successful advertising jingle "It's the Real Thing," the company has put out a steady stream of noteworthy items throughout its history.

Simply put, if an item has the word "Coke" on it somewhere, it's probably worth something to somebody. Prices on the cola collectibles range from mere pennies to $3,500 and up. Swap meets and auctions are the best place to buy and sell the memorabilia, but come armed with a handy price guide to avoid paying too much.

Like most collectibles, the older an item is, the more it's generally worth. The fastest, surest test of age is the advertising slogan on the Coke product. Since Coke started in the late 1800s, the company has switched slogans more than 100 times.

REFERENCE
Price Guide to Coca-Cola Collectibles by Deborah Goldstein Hill, Wallace-Homestead Book Co., West Des Moines, Iowa, 1984.

How to collect comic books

Comic books aren't just for kids anymore. As a matter of fact, they're more an adult plaything now than ever. Not only have the story lines and art become more issue-oriented and graphic, but the prices for new issues have climbed steadily over the past few years.

Prices on older comics, however, have skyrocketed. Popular titles featuring Spider-Man, Batman, X-Men and Superman are among the safest investments around. However, knowing what's popular won't make you an expert collector. Arm yourself with a reliable price guide (*Overstreet's Comic Book Price Guide* is the favorite) and get to know your local dealer to learn the ins and outs of the industry.

Eventually, all comic collectors become specialists of sorts. The variety of books and characters is too wide for anyone to gather them all. Perhaps the most popular specialty is trying to collect a complete set of any given title, but there are other specialties that can be just as exciting:

- ◯ Choose your favorite characters and gather all books in which they appear. "Crossovers" (a well-known hero appearing with a newer one) are a popular way for comic companies to build interest in a new book.

- ◯ Pick a subject. Super heroes aren't the only theme in the comic world. There are also horror, romance, humorous and science-fiction books.

- ◯ Collect your favorite writer or artist. Comics have developed into an intricate art form, telling complex stories and displaying masterful art. Some writers and artists have developed followings: Frank Miller (Daredevil, Wolverine, The Spectacular Spider-Man), John Byrne (The X-Men, Avengers) and Berni Wrightson (Swamp Thing).

Comic shops have sprung up all over the country, so finding a place to add to your collection isn't hard. Do your homework, and know the value of what you want to buy.

Carefully inspect before you buy. Condition is everything to a true collector. Also, be sure you don't accidentally buy a reprint of a popular issue.

Buying duplicate issues can also increase the value of your collection in a hurry, especially if you buy premier issues or books with special covers.

Other good sources to find comics are fan magazines, newsstands, conventions, friends and (of all places) trash cans. Those stories about people accidentally throwing out extremely rare comics are true. Always be on the lookout.

REFERENCE
Collecting Comic Books by Marcia Leiter, Little Brown & Co., Boston, 1983.

Collecting coins just takes a little common cents

Virtually everybody is a coin collector to some extent. Whether it's that quirky quarter you received as change last week or the silver dollar your uncle gave you for your seventh birthday, chances are you've got a coin tucked away somewhere. As a result, it's easy to see why numismatics (coin collecting) is such a popular hobby.

Most collections are started by accident. Once enthusiasts decide to collect, it's usually for one of three reasons. Some love the challenge of getting a complete set of coins, such as all the Lincoln pennies ever issued. Others simply have a love of history. And then there are the people who seek out the freakish, odd or controversial coins (such as the 1907 "Godless Eagle," a $10 gold piece which didn't have the words "In God We Trust" imprinted on it.)

Because there are so many varieties, simply collecting any type of coin can get boring real fast. Decide what type of coins interest you, and begin your search.

Aside from the local convenience store and gas station, the best places to find coins are at shows and coin clubs. There are also several "coin stores" scattered throughout the country.

REFERENCE
The Official Investor's Guide to Coin Collecting by Marc Hudgeons, The House of Collectibles, Orlando, Fla., 1985.

Doll collecting isn't for the financially weak

Not too long ago, doll collecting was an easy and affordable hobby for just about anybody. Times change.

These days collecting antique dolls requires a serious capital investment. Spurred by an upsurge in interest, porcelain and china dolls are commanding all-time high prices, and even cloth dolls are fetching handsome sums.

If you do decide to start collecting, do it carefully. Buy from an established dealer, not an antique shop. Unless your seller is a specialist, she can't guarantee authenticity and may (intentionally or not) overcharge you.

Beware of old dolls that are in perfect condition. They probably aren't authentic. Standard wear and tear over the years makes mint specimens virtually nonexistent.

If the doll you buy is a bit scuffed, it may not be worth your while to get it restored. While condition is important, restored dolls do not fetch much more than damaged ones.

Careful storage of your dolls is also of utmost importance. Never expose them to direct sunlight. (It's best to store them in frosted-glass cases.) Also, handling the dolls isn't recommended.

REFERENCE ─────────────────────────────

Dolls and Dolls' Houses by Constance Eileen King, Arco Publishing, New York, 1984.

Caring for a record collection

While compact discs are all the rage today, there's not much of a collector's market for them yet. Records, those old grooved plastic dinosaurs, however, are hotter than ever.

While they have proven to be the most desirable and long-lasting music archives for collectors, records are by no means indestructible. And broken or badly warped records are essentially worthless.

While the records themselves are what music lovers are after, the condition of your album cover helps determine value. There are ways to ensure that your collection stays in pristine shape and doesn't deteriorate over the years:

- Keep the surrounding temperature and relative humidity low.

- Records should be kept in a dark room.

- Use metal containers, enclosed cabinets or acid-free boards to store your records.

- Use a high-quality, polyester film sleeve for permanent storage. If you only plan to keep the records for a short time, the common polyethylene bags are OK.

- Be especially careful when playing your albums. Even a minor scratch can reduce the value significantly.

REFERENCE

Osborne and Hamilton's Original Record Collector's Price Guide by Jerry Osborne O'Sullivan, Woodside & Co., Phoenix, Ariz., 1982.

How to collect stamps

Can't afford a world cruise? Try collecting stamps. You'll get to see all the exotic ports of call, natural wonders and even a celebrity or two. And you won't have to leave your living room.

Whether world or U.S. stamps, gathering a collection is a fairly easy process. If you are planning to collect for profitability, there are a few things to keep in mind.

Stamp collectors need to do research. (Catalogs and dealers are the best sources.) And to keep your collection in pristine condition, you'll need to get specific tools to help handle and display your stamps: stamp tongs (ranging in price from $2 to $10), a magnifying glass and stamp hinges or sleeves.

Condition is everything to a stamp collector. The most desirable postage is centered and colorful (not faded by the sun). More importantly, the glue on the back of the stamp (referred to as the gum) should be in perfect condition.

American stamps are often easier to obtain than international. If you're looking to boost the value of your foreign stamp collection, you probably don't want to buy any Communist, Third World or "sand dune" stamps. With very few exceptions, they are not a good investment.

REFERENCE

Collecting Stamps For Pleasure and Profit by Barry Krause, Betterway Publications, Crozet, Va., 1988.

Stay sharp when collecting swords

With some, it's a fascination with history. For others, it's an obsession with military affairs. But once someone starts collecting swords, it's hard to get them to stop.

Sword collecting is gaining popularity. It's a field that requires study, however. Ignorance can be especially costly.

There are several books on swords that can give a collector an edge. Visiting museums, stately homes and castles is another good way to stay sharp.

Regularly check auction catalogues to keep abreast of the latest pricing trends. Even if you don't bid, you will know how much to pay should you see the same item on display in a shop.

REFERENCE ———————————

Edged Weapons: A Collectors Guide by Frederick J. Stephens, Spurbooks Ltd., 1976, Bourne End, England.

How to care for your swords

Sword collecting can be expensive, so most collections grow very slowly. For that reason, maintenance is more important than ever.

Neglecting your edged weapons or letting time ravage them makes any investment on your part foolish. There are, however, easy ways to ensure that your collection is always an eye-catcher.

○ Always wipe blades with a clean, dry cloth after handling.

○ Clean intricate parts of the sword with a soft bristle brush instead of a metal brush.

○ If you can't remove ingrained dirt by brushing, use hot water with a small amount of mild detergent. (Be sure to wipe the areas afterwards to avoid rust.)

○ Lightly polish swords with nonabrasive cleaners to remove tarnish.

○ Remove rust by repeatedly polishing with a paper towel. It takes more elbow grease, but you won't scratch the blade.

○ Treat leather scabbards with leather polish to avoid cracking.

REFERENCE ———————————

Edged Weapons: A Collector's Guide by Frederick J. Stephens, Spurbooks Ltd., 1976, Bourne End, England.

Pet pointers

Basic pet safety tips

Dogs and cats are a lot like children. You're constantly both annoyed and scared silly about what they will do. A little common sense can help you keep your pets out of danger.

- Don't leave a choke collar on an unattended pet.

- Avoid feeding your pet prior to a car ride. (It increases the chance of vomiting.)

- Don't leave your pet in a hot or partially closed car or chain your pet without shade or water. (If your pet seems to be suffering from heatstroke, place him in cool water, then take him straight to the veterinarian.)

- Never chain your pet where it can hang itself.

- Have your dog checked out by a veterinarian before starting it on heartworm prevention medication. Otherwise, your pet could have a fatal reaction.

- Unless your veterinarian recommends it, don't feed your dog real bones.

- Don't give dog food to a cat.

- Never, ever give aspirin to a cat or chocolate to a dog. (Both are poisonous.)

- Avoid using lindane (pesticide) or phenol (antiseptic) products on a cat.

- Don't leave the dryer or oven door open if you have a cat. They like small spaces.

- Don't keep sewing needles and thread where pets can get at them.

○ Never use lead paints or lead objects in or around a bird cage.

○ Don't chain your bird to a perch.

○ Don't keep your bird in the kitchen. Some fumes, such as from oven-heated Teflon pans, can be hazardous.

REFERENCE ───────────────────────────────────

The Pet-First Aid Book by Dan Hill, Ann Morrison, Bernard Myers, Glenn Finnell, Genye Hawkins and Robert Hess, McGraw-Hill Book Co., New York, 1986.

Introducing a new pet to your home

A playmate for your pet can be a great idea, but it's not one you should rush into. Getting animals acquainted can be awkward, and if you're not careful, it could result in fights.

Much like children, animals have to be taught to share. Social rules must be established, and you must firmly adhere to them.

Dogs and cats are social animals and bringing in more than one will often prevent pet boredom. But, don't assume the addition of another pet will cure your problems as an owner. It might double them.

If your pet constantly misbehaves, it's probably not a good time to bring home another one. Teach your dog or cat obedience first, then see if you truly want another pet.

If your pet is older, a major change may be traumatic. On the other hand, older animals can sometimes help new additions learn manners and act as a baby-sitter.

Avoid introducing males to males and females to females. It can breed competitiveness and hostility. While it is best to introduce a younger animal to your household, don't make that dog or cat too young. Your pet might see it as prey to be hunted.

Bring the new pet home when you have the chance to spend a few days with both animals. Your presence will reassure your pets and give you a chance to "referee." Play it cool when you and the new animal do arrive. If you're nervous and looking for a fight, your pet will be on edge.

Give each pet equal time. If one starts to get jealous, reassure it by touching it and looking at it while you speak, then do the same to the other animal.

Growling, hissing and even an occasional scuffle are normal. You pets are simply determining who's in charge. If things start looking ugly, throw a blanket over one of the animals and drag it out of the room. Never pick up an angry or frightened animal.

Schedule playtime with each animal separately and together. Teach the animals that they are part of the same family. Feed them together (though on different sides of the room).

REFERENCE
Atlanta Humane Society.

Helping your pet adjust to a new baby

Bringing home your newborn from the hospital can result in two infants in your house if you haven't prepared your pet for the change. Since most of your attention will now be focused elsewhere, the transition might be a difficult one for your dog or cat.

As you start making changes in your life to welcome your child, do the same for your pet.

○ Sounds and smells are an important part of a pet's world. When the baby arrives, these will change dramatically. If vacuum cleaners and telephones disturb your dog or cat, give yourself extra time to introduce "baby sounds."
Borrow a friend's crib (or something with a baby scent) and make a tape of the usual baby sounds — gurgling, crying, laughing, etc. Start playing the tape daily at different times. Keep the volume low at first, gradually increasing it as your pet gets used to it.

○ If you plan to remodel or rebuild parts of your house, do it early. Give the pet time to explore the area and then forbid it from entering "off-limit areas." A screen-door is usually best. It lets the dog see what's going on without jumping in.

○ Recognize your pet's need for privacy. Give it a private area, complete with a water bowl, its bed and some old worn clothes with your scent on them.

○ Enforcing your position as leader of the house is more important than ever. Re-train your dog to sit and lie down, and forbid jumping. If your pet likes to sit in your lap, teach it to "ask permission" first.

○ Don't eliminate your private time with your pet. You'll need some time away from the baby occasionally, and your dog or cat will still require your love. Set some time aside each day to play exclusively with your pet.

REFERENCE ————————————————————————
Atlanta Humane Society.

Approaching and transporting injured animals

Whether it's your own pet or a stray, true animal lovers can't simply pass by an injured animal on the road without trying to help. Recklessness on your part, however, can result in further injuries to the dog or cat and possibly put you at risk.

Approach any injured dog or cat in a slow manner, talking in a soft, calm, soothing voice.

If you see any signs of resistance, such as hissing from a cat or growling from a dog, protect yourself before going any further. Before you can do any good, you must earn the animal's trust.

For cats, leisurely lower yourself to their level, gently petting the animal's head. Slowly pick it up by reaching over the shoulders and under the chest, bringing it slowly under your arm. Use one hand to hold the front legs and the other to support the head and neck, resting the bulk of the cat's weight against your body with your elbow.

Dogs, especially unfamiliar ones, should always be muzzled when injured. (When in pain, they tend to snap.) A soft bandage or tape will do.

If the animal must be moved, place one hand in front on the shoulders below the neck and the other under his hindquarters, behind both back legs. Go slowly when picking the dog up.

With both dogs and cats, if the animal can't move, secure it to a stretcher (a board or stiff cardboard) before taking it to a veterinarian. At least wrap the animal in a blanket so the body is evenly supported.

Never attempt to move a wild animal. Call your local humane society or animal control office instead.

REFERENCE

The Pet First-Aid Book by Dan Hill, Ann Morrison, Bernard Myers, Glenn Finnell, Genye Hawkins and Robert Hess, McGraw-Hill Book Co., New York, 1986.

Man's best friend

Man's best friend might offer more than the morning newspaper and your evening slippers.

Sometimes a dog can be nature's best remedy for stress or illness.

The presence of a dog can act as a "natural drug" for its human owner by helping to lower blood pressure and other bodily responses to stress.

Dogs seem to help reduce the effects of stress because they provide unconditional love and support without criticizing the owner's actions.

Dogs often help buffer their owners from illness, too, a study reports.

Researchers studied 96 people with heart disease released after care in a heart unit at a hospital.

They found that the people who owned pets had a higher survival rate one year after release from the hospital than the people who did not have pets, even after accounting for individual differences in the extent of heart damage and other medical problems.

In fact, owning a pet seemed to be a better indicator of a positive recovery than the presence of a spouse or extensive family support.

In another study, 345 elderly pet owners reported fewer doctor visits over one year than did 593 elderly people without pets.

Some studies indicate that touching, stroking and cuddling pets reduces a person's heart rate and blood pressure.

Scientists state, however, that these benefits probably do not extend to those people who are afraid of animals or are uncomfortable around animals.

But for those who enjoy the company of a pet, the benefits of those faithful companions might help you enjoy a longer, more stress-free life.

REFERENCE

Science News, Nov. 2, 1991.

How old is your dog?

We've all heard the old wives' tale (or is that tail?) that one year of a dog's life is equal to seven of ours, but how realistic is that?

Dogs live upwards of 21 years, which would make senior citizen canines 147 years old! That makes them eligible for doggy social security at nine years, three months.

To get a better, more realistic age gauge of your dog, use this chart instead:

Dog's Age	Equivalent Human Age (in years)
6 months	10
8 months	13
10 months	14
12 months	15
18 months	20
2 years	24
4 years	32
6 years	40
8 years	48
10 years	56
12 years	64
14 years	72
16 years	80
18 years	88
20 years	96
21 years	100

REFERENCE

The Pet First-Aid Book by Dan Hill, Ann Morrison, Bernard Myers, Glenn Finnell, Genye Hawkins, Robert Hess, McGraw-Hill Book Company, New York, 1986.

How sensitive are dog's ears?

While they don't have ESP, dogs often seem to ... thanks to their spectacular hearing. Noises that are well beyond our hearing range are clearly audible to a dog. If your pet is sitting by the door wagging its tail furiously when you get home from work, chances are he heard you walking up the driveway a long time ago.

Humans and dogs are about equal on low sounds. When it comes to higher pitches, though, we can't compete.

REFERENCE
Dogwatching by Desmond Morris, Crown Publishers, New York, 1986.

Are those dogs playing?

It's sometimes hard to tell the difference between two dogs who are best friends and two who are ferocious enemies. Rough-housing is the status quo when puppies get together. Knowing the signals of playing can help alert you when a dog fight is around the corner.

The most popular canine invitation to play is the play-bow, where the dog lowers its front end while keeping its rear in the air. The animal will usually stare at its companion and make small jerking motions.

Remember that dogs participate in essentially two games: Play chase and play fight. In the former, they run around at breakneck speeds in wide circles, often stopping and reversing roles. In the latter, the dogs will roll on the ground nipping each other, but doing no real damage.

If your dog looks to be "smiling," then it's probably in a playful mood. Snarls, however, where the teeth are bared are not an invitation to play.

To entice play, some dogs will nudge potential playmates with their nose or give them a little slap with their paw.

Humans aren't exempt from dog games, either. Your pet may "offer" to play by bringing a ball or stick to your feet and dropping it. When you reach for it, the dog will snatch it and run off. If you give chase, the game's afoot. If not, the dog will usually try again.

REFERENCE
Dogwatching by Desmond Morris, Crown Publishers, New York, 1986.

How to avoid getting bitten by a dog

Remember, a dog's bite is much worse than its bark.

Let sleeping dogs lie. And injured ones, too. Otherwise, you're risking a serious injury.

The average dog bites down with the force of 150 to 200 pounds per square inch. Trained attack dogs can increase that to 400 to 450 pounds per square inch. Regardless of the pressure exerted, a bite can cause severe damage. There are ways, however, to reduce your chances of being chomped.

If you're around an unfamiliar dog, go slowly. Let the animal get to know you. Dogs that feel threatened will often bite. By all means, avoid a stare-off with a dog. By maintaining eye contact, you are threatening the animal and inviting a bite.

Also, never try to take food or a toy away from a dog, even if it's yours. Distract it first. (Maybe throw a stick a short distance away.) Then, after the dog has left to retrieve the stick, pick up the object.

If an animal approaches you on the street barking and growling, do not run. This will trigger a dog's chase instinct. Don't yell, either. You'll only further excite the dog.

Instead, stand still, with your arms to the side, and look away. There's a good chance that the dog will get bored with you and walk away.

REFERENCE

101 Questions and Answers About Pets and People by Ann Squire, Macmillan Publishing Co., New York, 1988.

CPR: Canine Pulmonary Resuscitation

Cardiopulmonary Resuscitation (CPR) and artificial respiration aren't the easiest techniques to learn on humans, and they're even harder on dogs and cats. But, there may come a time when knowing these techniques could save your pet's life, especially if they tend to play near the road.

Of the two stimuli, artificial respiration is the easier, though it's not for the squeamish. First, clear your pet's mouth of any foreign material. Cup your hands around the muzzle to prevent air from escaping. If the snout is short or awkwardly shaped, you may have to put your mouth completely over your pet's nose.

Blow gently into the animal's nostrils between eight and 10 times per minute. This should inflate the chest. Let it deflate naturally. Continue until the dog or cat begins breathing naturally or starts to cough.

CPR for pets is tricky even for the experts. If the animal is severely injured and no veterinarian is nearby, you may have to attempt it.

Lay the animal on its right side, checking for a heartbeat by pressing your fingers firmly on the lower side of its chest, below the elbow. If you can't detect a heartbeat, start CPR.

Place the heel of your hand on the chest, behind the elbow (if your animal weighs more than 45 pounds, use both hands), and rapidly compress the chest six times. Allow one to 10 seconds between compressions.

Next give three breaths via artificial respiration. Continue alternating the six compressions and three breaths for five minutes or until the heart starts beating.

If there's still no beat after five minutes, get someone to drive you and your pet to the nearest veterinarian. Continue your efforts to revive the dog in the car.

REFERENCE —————————————————————————————————————
The Pet First-Aid Book by Dan Hill, Ann Morrison, Bernard Myers, Glenn Finnell, Genye Hawkins and Robert Hess, McGraw-Hill Book Co., New York, 1986.

Why do dogs chase their tails?

Chances are you've seen it at least once. A dog will get a look of sudden inspiration on its face, then begin in a … well … dogged pursuit of its own tail, spinning and circling until it collapses in dizziness and confusion.

In most cases, it's a puppy behaving this way, but the habit sometimes extends into a dog's adult life. Nine out of 10 times, this is due to boredom.

Dogs are extremely social animals, and if they're not given the chance to properly exercise and play, they tend to amuse themselves, thus the tail chasing. Increase the animal's social interaction and adventure and your pet will usually discontinue the "game."

Occasionally, tail chasing indicates an irritation in the tail region. This is usually accompanied by other symptoms as well, such as rump-dragging and tail-nibbling.

REFERENCE ————————————————————
Dogwatching by Desmond Morris, Crown Publishers, New York, 1986.

Why puppies chew slippers

One of the questionable joys of owning a puppy is watching some of your favorite belongings become chew toys. Slippers, newspapers, toys, books and just about anything else a young dog can get its mouth on is fair game.

Part of the reason for this oral fixation is simple playfulness. As the dog gets more comfortable with its surroundings, it begins to explore. And as with small children, exploration often means destruction.

Puppies that chew are also usually teething. Anything tough helps new teeth break through the skin. Don't expect crunchy dog food to do the trick.

Remember, dogs were bred from wolves. Your puppy is probably going through a "pre-hunting phase" where it is large enough to be interested in the hunt, but not coordinated enough to catch anything.

Adult wolves will leave chunks of meat for their pups, which allows the young to survive. When a human leaves something lying on the ground, the puppy looks upon it as a "present."

Booda bones (rope tied in knots at each end) and rawhide chews help the teething process along and save your personal belongings. If you haven't invested in either of these yet, now's the time to do so.

REFERENCE ————————————————————
Dogwatching by Desmond Morris, Crown Publishers, New York, 1986.

Crating your dog: Is it cruel?

Controversy rages between dog experts who believe in confining a dog to a small crate occasionally and those who oppose this measure as cruel.

They seem to agree on a few points:

○ Crating should not be used for punishment.

○ A crate is a good short-term container for the safety of the dog, such as during travel or when the dog is being badgered by small children.

○ A crate should be designed so the dog cannot be caught by the head or collar, and cannot tear loose splinters.

○ Provision should always be made for a water dish that cannot be spilled and for a quilt or pad to make sleeping comfortable.

○ The dog should be accustomed to crating gradually:

— As with any training, begin when the pup is still young.

— At first, keep crate sessions very brief, and leave the door open. As the puppy seems to feel completely at ease with each experience, close the door briefly and leave him alone for very short periods of time.

— Make going into the crate a happy experience: Give treats, toys and praise. Rub the dog's toys with your hands or let her have an item of your clothing so she senses your presence.

○ As the dog matures and outgrows youthful indiscretions like chewing or wetting, consider phasing out the use of the crate.

○ Some dogs never adapt to crating. If despite your best efforts to accustom the dog to the crate he howls and claws frantically to get out, do not crate. Such trauma will not allow your dog to develop into a happy, secure family pet.

Consider aiming a video camera at the crate and recording what happens when you are gone. You'll feel better about leaving your dog if you see that she seems happy with the arrangement.

REFERENCES ─────────────────────────────────

The Guilt-Free Dog Owner's Guide by Diana Delmar, Story Communications Inc., 1990.
Pet Clean-up Made Easy by Don Aslett, Writer's Digest Books, Cincinnati, Ohio, 1988.

House-training your dog

There's nothing worse than finding those "presents" your puppy likes to leave all over your rug. And while you could train the dog to go on newspaper, that doesn't make your house smell any better.

If you have a backyard, or even a nearby patch of grass, outdoors is the best place for dogs to "go." Training your puppy that the Persian rug in your living room isn't a toilet can be fairly simple, too.

Take your dog outside at specific times. It might mean coming home for lunch, but you'll have less to clean up after work. As your pet gets older, you can take it out less.

Remember that you're working with a baby. Punishing your dog for eliminating never works. Rubbing a dog's nose in its mess doesn't teach it house-training, it only humiliates the animal.

Every time you and your dog go outside, take it to the same spot. Keep your pet on a leash, and do not let it play or exercise. (This trip is for one purpose only.) Even if you have a fenced yard, use a leash. This will teach the dog to only use a certain area.

As the animal relieves itself, praise it generously. (Don't overdo it, though. This might be interpreted as an invitation to play.) Give the dog a little time to sniff around.

Once your animal completes its task, reward it with a little play time and take it back inside. Do not reward animals that don't "make" during these trips. But, don't punish them.

REFERENCE ———————————————————————————————————
Atlanta Humane Society.

Best way to clean up pet urine

The most effective and least expensive cleanup for urine is good old white vinegar, promptly applied. It neutralizes, deodorizes and is safe for most floors and carpets. Club soda is a good alternative if you're out of vinegar.

Do not use ammonia or ammonia-based cleaning products. Ammonia smells enough like urine to leave a signal to the animal that this is a good place to "go."

First absorb as much of the liquid as possible by laying layers of newspapers on the spot and stepping on them until each stack of papers is soaked. (Blot gently; never scrub.) Repeat until the papers come up virtually dry. Then spray or sprinkle on generous amounts of vinegar, either straight or diluted, and pick it back up in the same way.

If further cleaning is needed, use a solution of liquid dishwashing detergent and water or a commercial carpet cleaner.

This treatment should remove the urine's odor so well that the animal will not return to the spot to use it again based on the familiar smell.

If the pet's diet contains food coloring, as many pet foods do, you may have a stain that a professional carpet cleaner will have to deal with.

REFERENCE

The Guilt-Free Dog Owner's Guide by Diana Delmar, Story Communications Inc., 1990.

What to do when your cat won't use its litter box

One of the nicer features of owning a cat is the cleanliness. Generally, picking up after "accidents" is a rare occurrence. Every once in a while, however, cats ignore their litter boxes, urinating and defecating wherever they please.

This is usually an attempt on the part of your cat to communicate some problem to you. Your first step should always be the veterinarian. Because the behavior is so rare, it often means a serious physical problem, such as a bladder or kidney infection, a blockage or even diabetes.

If the vet gives your cat a clean bill of health, the problem is probably in the litter box itself. Ask yourself the following questions:

○ Is the box kept clean? If you can smell an odor, your cat certainly can. And no one likes to use a filthy toilet.

○ Does your cat feel safe in the box? Put it in a secluded corner away from your cat's food and bed. Avoid any high-traffic areas. Make litter box moves slowly, allowing the animal time to adjust.

○ How many litter boxes do you have? If you live in a large home, one might not be enough.

○ Do you use plastic liners in the box? Cats dislike the movement of a liner when they scratch their feet to bury their waste. If you must use some sort of a liner beneath the litter, consider switching to newspaper.

○ Is the litter box hooded? Your cat might feel insecure because it can't see what's coming. After all, it is in a vulnerable position.

○ Are you using too much litter? Cats often get alarmed when their feet sink.

○ Is your litter perfumed? If so, you might be offending the cat's sensitive sense of smell. Find a plain, low-dust litter and try that.

○ Have there been any recent major stresses in the cat's life? Moving and other major commotion can have traumatic effects on cats. A side effect of that trauma might be reckless elimination.

REFERENCE ——————————————————————
Atlanta Humane Society.

How to get a cat out of a tree

Despite what Hollywood tells you, you do not have to call the fire department when Fluffy gets caught up in the neighborhood oak tree. A calm head and a little common sense will keep the fire fighters available for real emergencies and get your cat down at the same time.

Most cats can climb down trees whenever they feel like it. They just need a little help and encouragement on your part.

First and foremost, stay calm. Keep other pets and people away. After all, it's humiliating enough for the cat to be stuck, but a crowd will only add to its tensions.

Make sure the animal isn't injured. Chances are it's not. If so, call the local humane society or animal control division for help.

Open a can of its favorite food (or even better, tuna fish) and put it at the bottom of the tree. Then beat it. It may take a little time, but eventually the cat will get hungry and shimmy down.

REFERENCE ——————————————————————
101 Questions and Answers about Pets and People by Ann Squire, Macmillan Publishing Co., New York, 1988.

How to tell if your cat is right- or left-handed

Humans aren't the only species that favor a particular hand. Animals, too, prefer a certain paw to conduct their business. Generally, cats are left-handed. But, there are exceptions.

Here's an easy way to find out which paw your pet prefers:

Tape an empty tube from a roll of paper towels to the floor and allow your kitty to become familiar with it.

Once that's done, put a piece of its favorite food directly in front of the tube. After it eats the food, the fun begins.

Put another piece inside the tube, where the cat will have to use its paw to get it. Make a mental note of the paw it uses. Repeat the test ten times, keeping track of the paw used each time.

If your cat prefers its right paw, it's right-handed (and vice versa). If the numbers are pretty much even, chances are you own an ambidextrous cat.

REFERENCE ─────────
101 Questions and Answers about Pets and People by Ann Squire, Macmillan Publishing Co., New York, 1988.

How to bathe your cat without getting killed

Bathing a cat may be a matter of life or death — yours, that is. A cat does a good job of keeping himself clean, and usually makes it very clear he doesn't need any help that involves water.

Actually, he's right. A cat seldom needs to be bathed, but if it does become necessary, here are some good commonsense rules:

- Don't bathe a young kitten (under three months) or a sick animal.

- Provide a warm, quiet place afterwards until your cat is thoroughly dry.

- If possible, have another person help you by holding the cat's feet — firmly, perhaps with thick cotton garden gloves.

- If you are comfortable with trimming your cat's claws, do so a day or two before a bath is planned.

○ A thick towel or an ordinary window screen in the bottom of the sink or tub will give your cat something to grip and help him feel secure.

○ Start with an empty sink and pour pitchers of lukewarm water gently over the cat. Lather well, and rinse thoroughly in the same way. Use a cloth on the cat's face. Wrap him in a thick towel and soak up as much water as possible before letting him finish drying.

REFERENCE ─────────────────────────────

Pet Clean-up Made Easy by Don Aslett, Writer's Digest Books, Cincinnati, Ohio, 1988.

Fighting fleas

Did you know that fleas don't live on animals? They spend 90 percent of their lives in rugs, bedding, upholstery, floor cracks, leaves and grass. They jump on warm-blooded animals only long enough to eat.

Killing fleas on your pet without attacking your entire house is useless. And the whole job must be done at once, or the fleas will simply evacuate one area for the safety of another.

Keeping your house and pet clean will go a long way toward preventing an infestation of fleas in the first place. Vacuum often, then burn the vacuum cleaner bag or seal it in plastic and throw it away.

Steam-cleaning the carpet works, too. Water temperature as high as 170 degrees applied under pressure will kill fleas.

To keep the pet's bed free of fleas, clean it with hot water and strong detergent once a week. Sprinkle flea powder in the bed every few weeks.

For a homemade, environmentally safe flea trap, rig a lamp with a low-watt bulb (60 watts or less) so it shines all night on a light-colored pan of water on the floor.

Add a tablespoon of dish detergent; fleas will jump or fall in, sink and drown. Keep in place until you no longer find dead fleas in the dish in the morning, then move to another room. Repeat until no more fleas are collected.

Here's a list of products to free your pets of fleas:

○ **Systemics** — injected or in pill-form; puts a low level of pesticide in pet's bloodstream at all times. Possible serious side-effects; should be used only under a vet's supervision, and never on cats.

○ **Sprays** — used directly on pet, kill fleas quickly. The hiss and chill of aerosols are not popular with pets; try a pump spray, or spray on a brush and apply. Avoid animal's face and genitals, and don't let him lick until the spray dries. Wear plastic gloves and wash hands well afterwards.

○ **Powders** — messy, short lived, but generally safer and less frightening to animals. Rub powder through hair to the skin, taking care to get areas around ears, hindquarters and base of tail. Leave on at least ten minutes, then brush or comb out.

○ **Flea bag** — a cloth bag into which a cat is tucked (except for head); contains flea powder.

○ **Flea comb** — fairly effective. Dip into hot water or alcohol to kill fleas caught in it.

○ **Dips** — strong chemicals actually sponged on pets; very effective, with good residual protection when allowed to dry on coat. Apply in a well-ventilated area, avoiding eyes, mouth and nose. For cats, use only dips specifically designed for them.

○ **Flea shampoos** — must be used weekly; allow lather to remain on body as long as directions indicate; rinse thoroughly.

○ **Flea collars** — plastic strips filled with pesticides; work slowly and tend to concentrate power away from tail and hindquarters where problem is usually the worst. Risks: allergic reaction, choking, too strong a dose if allowed to become wet.

○ **Orange oil or shampoo containing citrus extracts** — moderately effective, environmentally responsible.

REFERENCES

Pet Clean-up Made Easy by Don Aslett, Writer's Digest Books, Cincinnati, Ohio, 1988.
Reader's Digest Practical Problem Solver, The Reader's Digest Association Inc., Pleasantville, N.Y., 1991.

Two ways to keep your pet off your furniture

If your pet gets up on furniture while you're gone, try these harmless booby traps.

○ Set several mousetraps, place them upside down on the couch, and cover with a sheet of newspaper lightly taped on top (to keep paws from actually being caught).

   When the dog or cat jumps onto the surface, the traps will snap noisily and startle him off. After a few such experiences, he'll probably give up on that piece of furniture as a good place to nap.

○ Drop 10 or 12 pennies into an empty aluminum soda can, then close the hole with strong tape. When your pet starts to do something he shouldn't, say "No" firmly and shake the can vigorously. The sudden loud noise will startle the animal into compliance. Make several shake cans so they can be kept around the house.

   Build a booby trap by stacking cans so that your pet's misbehavior knocks them down with a crash — for example, on the garbage-can lid. Eventually, just the sight of the shake can — guarding the couch, for example — should do the trick.

REFERENCE
Pet Clean-up Made Easy by Don Aslett, Writer's Digest Books, Cincinnati, Ohio, 1988.

Training your fish to do tricks

While chances are you will never teach your guppy or goldfish to fetch your slippers or even shake hands (or fins as the case may be), that doesn't mean your aquatic pal can't do some tricks.

Know the fish's limitations and have a lot of patience when training this particular type of pet. One of the best tricks to teach your fish is to come to the top of its tank on "command" (usually a tap on the side of the bowl).

Notice that when you feed your fish, it comes to the top of the tank. So every time you feed it, tap first, then lightly spread the food onto the water.

It may take several weeks, but eventually your fish will learn that the tap means dinner time. But, don't overfeed your pet as you teach it the trick.

REFERENCE ———

101 Questions and Answers About Pets and People by Ann Squire, Macmillan Publishing Co., New York, 1988.

Cleaning your fish tank

You can do a quick cleaning of your tropical fish aquarium each week, at the same time replacing about a third of the water with fresh, and your fish will love you for it.

The easiest way is to use an old hose or a piece of plastic tubing as a siphon. Pinching the bottom end tightly, fill the tube with tap water. Place the top end in the aquarium, the bottom in a bucket below the level of the tank, and let the bottom end open.

While the water is draining you can take advantage of the vacuum effect by "sweeping" the tube over debris small enough to pass through it. When the level is down, wipe the accumulated algae and film off the inside of the glass using strong paper towels or a clean washcloth.

Gently refill tank with water that has been sitting at room temperature for several hours or overnight.

You can speed up this de-chlorinating process somewhat by heating the water to near-boiling, then allowing it to cool down to the same temperature as the water in the aquarium.

REFERENCE ———

Reader's Digest Practical Problem Solver, The Reader's Digest Association, Inc., Pleasantville, N.Y., 1991.

Is your bird sick?

Birds should receive routine health examinations two to three times a year. Illness, however, can strike with life-threatening swiftness — never delay taking a pet to the vet if he shows any of the following signs of illness:

○ A discharge from the eyes, or a change in their clarity or color

○ A discharge or plugging of a nostril

○ An inability to eat or manipulate seeds

○ Fluffed feathers, closing of the eyes, inactivity

○ A loss of appetite, loss of weight

○ Change or stopping of vocalization

○ Sneezing (more than the normal two to three times a day) or open-mouth breathing

○ Inability to perch, loss of balance

○ Change in quantity or quality of droppings

○ Crusty deposits on nonfeathered parts of body

○ Bleeding

○ Bobbing, pumping of tail

REFERENCE ————————————————————————————

The Pet First-Aid Book by Dan Hill, Ann Morrison, Bernard Myers, Glenn Finnell, Genye Hawkins and Robert Hess, McGraw-Hill Book Co., New York, 1986.

Wild birds as pets?

It's actually against the law to keep a songbird as a pet — even if you found an abandoned baby bird, or you're trying to heal a bird that's badly injured.

The story that touching a bird will make its parents abandon it is useful in discouraging children from picking up nestlings, but it is, in fact, not true. Birds have a poor sense of smell and will never know the difference.

When an "abandoned" baby bird is found, it is best to place it on a branch or in dense brush where the parents can care for it.

Badly injured birds should be taken to a wildlife rehabilitator.

Birds sometimes fly into windows, even if you close curtains or put up an owl silhouette.

In the spring, when territorial battles send birds chasing each other almost blindly, such collisions inevitably happen.

Birds may look fragile, but they're amazingly tough. Unless killed out-right by a broken neck or caught by a cat while stunned, they can survive such an impact — with proper treatment.

That means no treatment at all, beyond protection. It's possible that more birds are "cared for" to death than die by crashing into windows.

Here's what you do:

- ○ Be ready to act quickly. Keep an empty shoe box, lined with a bit of tissue, where you can find it readily. When a bird hits the glass, pick it up gently, place it in the box on its belly in as natural a position as possible, and close the lid. (It is especially important to get a bird off a wet surface so it doesn't lose body temperature.)

- ○ This is the hard part: Leave the bird alone. If the weather is cold, bring it indoors and place it in a quiet place, with the box lid weighted. Resist the temptation to show it to the kids, give it water, stroke it or talk to it.

- ○ After 30 to 45 minutes, take the box outside again, and gently remove the lid. Odds are good the bird will have recovered. He may blink for a moment, but then will fly to a nearby branch where he will rest for a while until his senses clear.

REFERENCE ——
The Birder's Catalogue by Sheila Buff, Simon & Schuster Inc., New York, 1989.

Marriage and family life

Love and money

Paychecks, shopping, entertaining, investing — money. It causes tension and resentment between you and your spouse, arguments in most marriages, even divorces in some. When one spouse believes you make money to enjoy it and the other equates money with security, it can sabotage the best of relationships.

Many money problems are unique to our generation of the two-paycheck family: How will we share our wages? Who will pay for what? Who supports kids from previous marriages? How do we manage investments or paying the bills when our habits are so different?

It's not easy, but you and your spouse can work to solve money conflicts before they destroy your marriage.

First, look at your past to figure out what money means to you. If you find yourself raging about a trivial matter and you think, "I sound just like my parents," you've recognized your deeply ingrained money beliefs.

Money beliefs come from parents, friends, religion, the social environment around you, past experiences (like when you bounced three checks) — and they are hard to shake.

Note: If you are feeling smug right now because you never worry or talk about money, you have a "money attitude" left over from your past, too. Maybe, for some reason or another, money was a taboo subject in your family.

Or maybe you're rebelling against your parents' focus on money. Now, your refusal to be concerned over money can cause problems with a spouse who doesn't feel the same way.

Sit down with your spouse and discuss:

○ How did your parents treat each other concerning money?

○ How did they treat you concerning money? What was their advice to you? Are you still trying to please your parents?

○ Were your parents' actions consistent with their advice? Did they flaunt their money or were they secretive about it?

○ What have your adult "money experiences" been? Do you watch your second wife's spending habits with an eagle eye because you were burned in a messy divorce? Sure, you should learn from mistakes, but are you going overboard?

○ Do you have a selective memory when it comes to how your spouse spends money? If you've decided your spouse is a spendthrift, do you forget about times when she saves money? Or maybe you've decided she's a cheapskate, and you remember only the fast-food-dinner-and-rented-video dates while forgetting the good, quality purchases she makes.

You may not want to discard all the money beliefs you got from your parents, friends and past experiences, but you should be able to recognize them so you'll know where you and your spouse are coming from.

Remember you're dealing with the opposite sex. As much as we'd like to think we're not all that different, we are. When discussing money with a spouse, the old communication problems between genders are going to arise.

Men communicate through interpretations ("What he probably meant was"), advice ("Here's what you should do"), and jokes. Women communicate through confidences ("I have to let you know how much this is bothering me"), emotional expressions ("Oh no! They're going to cancel our account!"), and confrontation ("You need to take care of this right now!").

When men joke, women think they don't care. When men interpret, women think they don't trust her point of view. When men advise, women think they're patronizing.

When women confide, men think they're being burdened with unnecessary information. When women express emotions, men think they're making a mountain out of a molehill. When women confront, men think they are henpecking or nagging.

If you remember the differences in how men and women communicate, you can try to control your instinctive reactions to your spouse's words. Try to be supportive and try not to get your feelings hurt.

Escape traditional gender roles when it comes to money. For instance, men shouldn't be ashamed when their wives make more than they do. They don't have to be the main provider.

Examine your beliefs about money and the opposite sex. Do you secretly believe all men are money-scheming or all women are miserly? Do you think the opposite sex is disorganized or incompetent concerning money matters?

Don't get into "power plays" with your spouse. You may not know what a "power play" is, but have you ever noticed these remarks?:

○ *"Don't worry your pretty little head about it."* If your husband controls all the family finances because he doesn't think you would understand, he's on a power trip. After a divorce or his death, you're going to be in trouble. Many wives get their revenge by "skimming." They overestimate the cost of groceries, kid's clothes, etc., and keep the extra money for themselves.

○ *"I work so hard for you, and this is the thanks I get"* or *"I can't possibly buy that dress I need. The kids need Reebok sneakers so they'll fit in at school."* These suffering "money martyrs" get power by making their spouses feel guilty and undeserving.

○ *"I'll do what I please with my own money, thank you."* This person feels their power through spending money, and they are likely to buy clothes, jewelry, a new stereo, even a new car, without consulting their spouse. The spouse may get revenge by splurging on purchases, too.

○ *"I'll do it when I want to ... if I want to."* The "money rebel" hates financial responsibility and resists paying taxes, sending the rent payment and recording checks. Spouses are seen as parent substitutes to rebel against.

○ *"You're making a mountain out of a molehill. Have I ever let you down, honey?"* These "benevolent manipulators" soothe and disarm spouses, making them feel like they overreacted. They make promises (*"When we can afford it, you'll get everything you want"*) that never materialize.

○ *"I just can't understand all this financial stuff. You'll handle the money for me won't you?"* Is this "helpless manipulator," usually female, unable to take financial responsibility, or is she just not willing to?

○ *"Thank God I came along in your life."* These "money saviors" feel powerful because they think they've saved their loved one from certain financial ruin. But they're hurting their spouse because the spouse will always be uncertain of himself and will never learn from his mistakes.

Recognize these power plays for what they are, and don't be a victim of a power-hungry spouse. You may need a marriage counselor to work through major problems.

Map your personal financial turf. Keeping in mind each other's self-esteem needs, decide who will be in charge of what. The wife may want to be an equal partner in all money decisions, and she may want to keep some of the money she brought into the relationship for her private use. The husband may want to keep some of his money for his own use, too.

If one of you hates dealing with paperwork and financial details, you may decide to let the other spouse handle those matters. That doesn't mean one spouse has power over the money decisions, but it does mean he has power over some of the details and shouldn't be constantly questioned about them.

Bring financial matters to the open without blowing your top.

○ Tell the truth about your money. Don't "forget" to mention a shopping spree.

○ When your partner flares up at you, take a deep breath and count to ten before you answer. Or take a time-out and come back to the problem later when your emotions are under control.

○ Ask your partner about his feelings when you see an argument coming on. Try to shift the focus away from blaming you and onto how the problem makes him feel.

○ Find a safe place and time to discuss money. You may want to hold hands or walk in the park. Bad times to discuss money: when someone is rushing out the door or in bed.

○ Confine the discussion to the problem at hand. If you're talking about bills, don't talk about earnings. Don't bring alimony payments into the discussion when your partner bounced a check.

○ Repeat what you hear your spouse say. This technique will show you're listening and may reveal communication gaps.

○ Stick with "I" messages instead of "you" messages: "I feel frustrated that our books are in a mess" instead of "You are so disorganized."

○ Don't let small disagreements go unresolved. If you have a problem with balancing checkbooks and bouncing checks, agree to record every check as soon as you write it and then balance the checkbook weekly. Small problems will only get bigger.

Switch roles for a week. If one spouse is a spender and the other is a saver, switch roles for at least a week so you can learn to value your spouse's habits. If you're a spender, budget your money so that you'll have some left over at the end of the week. Question every purchase you make.

If you're a saver, buy one thing you don't really need every day. Allow your partner to handle all the savings — you have to learn to trust your spouse. Switching roles may help you see the other person's differences as sources of strength.

Most of all, when you're inclined to argue over money, remember: While money is important, it is always secondary to love.

REFERENCE ———————————————————————————————

Couples and Money by Victoria Felton-Collins with Suzanne Blair Brown, Bantam Books, New York, 1990.

Building reserves
in the 'emotional bank account'

You can make mistakes, hurt others, lose your temper, break promises and get away with it.

You just have to have plenty of cushion in your "emotional bank account."

The emotional bank account is the amount of trust in your relationship with another person — your boss, your child or your spouse. If you build up a reserve of trust with another person, you can make mistakes and they will love and understand you anyway.

Here are six ways to build up the reserve in your emotional bank account:

- Seek to understand the other person. What is important to you may not be important to them.

- Pay attention to the little kindnesses and courtesies. The little things in a relationship are really the big things.

- Keep commitments. If something comes up and you think it would be unwise to keep a promise, explain the situation thoroughly and ask for a release from the promise.

- Clarify expectations. Unclear expectations in a job, a marriage or a family will lead to misunderstandings and withdrawals of trust. When you start a job, a project or a marriage, get all your expectations out on the table.

- Show personal integrity. Be honest and, especially, be loyal to people behind their backs. Don't betray others' secrets. No one will trust you if they see you bad-mouthing and betraying others.

- Apologize sincerely when you make a withdrawal from the emotional bank account. Admit your mistakes; admit you were wrong. You have to be a strong person to be able to apologize.

REFERENCE

The 7 Habits of Highly Effective People by Stephen R. Covey, Simon & Schuster, New York, 1989.

Secrets of a great marriage

You can't create a formula for a wonderful relationship, but it doesn't hurt to keep looking for what makes the best marriages thrive. Here are three major components to make a marriage last:

○ Security. Both people must feel secure in a marriage. You have to let the other person know that you are committed to them even if they aren't perfect. You do this by spending time with the family, making sacrifices and showing interest in their life.

○ Meaningful conversation. Provide sufficient, consistent time to talk about important issues. You can be a good listener if you try to restate what the other person said in your own words, if you lovingly hold your tongue when you're tempted to judge, and if you try to recognize what they mean behind what they say. Look for the issue behind the issue.

○ Courtship. Romance in marriage most often dies because it is linked to sex. Plan romantic times. Contrary to popular belief, they don't just happen.

How much money you spend doesn't determine how romantic the time is. You can write love notes, watch a sunset together, or rent each other's all-time favorite movies and play a double feature. Ask your spouse what their romantic "10" is, and celebrate birthdays, anniversaries and holidays.

Make sure you don't have a hidden motive behind your romance. Don't send flowers so that your wife won't get angry when you tell her about the fishing trip you're planning with your friends.

REFERENCE ————————————————————————————
Love is a Decision by Gary Smalley with John Trent, Word Publishing, Dallas, 1989.

R-E-S-P-E-C-T

"Honor" is a more important word when it comes to relationships than love. Honoring someone means showing respect and believing that person to be special and important. Here are the top ten ways to dishonor a family member and to ruin a good marriage.

○ Ignore or degrade another person's opinions, advice or beliefs.

○ Bury yourself in the television or newspaper when another person is trying to communicate with you.

○ Create jokes about another person's weak areas or shortcomings. (Sarcasm or cutting jokes do lasting harm in a relationship.)

○ Make regular verbal attacks on loved ones. Criticize harshly, be judgmental, deliver uncaring lectures, especially in front of others.

○ Treat in-laws or other relatives as unimportant while making plans or communicating.

○ Ignore or simply don't express appreciation for kind deeds done for you. Take your spouse for granted.

○ Practice distasteful habits in front of the family — even after you are asked to stop.

○ Overcommit yourself to other projects or people so that everything outside the home seems more important than those inside the home.

○ Participate in power struggles that leave one person feeling childish or harshly dominated.

○ Be unwilling to admit that you are wrong or to ask for forgiveness.

REFERENCE ————————————————————————————
Love is a Decision by Gary Smalley with John Trent, Word Publishing, Dallas, 1989.

Making joint custody work

Joint custody has gotten a bad rap, say researchers at Stanford University. In the past, studies have shown that children who alternate living with divorced parents are torn between the two. They are caught in conflicting loyalties.

But, if the divorced parents can communicate and cooperate in a friendly way with each other, the children function as well or better than children living with a single parent.

If you are in conflict with your former spouse, don't ask your child to spy or carry messages. Children will feel trapped and will be more likely to be anxious or depressed and exhibit behavior problems, like smoking, drinking and cutting class.

REFERENCE ————————————————————————————
The Wall Street Journal, Nov. 15, 1991.

Beating the monsters under your child's bed

Be it things that go bump in the night or simply loud household appliances, children's fears are real. And while it might be easy to laugh them off now that we know better, it's important to listen to your child when he comes to you afraid.

Teasing can cause children to express their fears through aggression or, in some instances, make them withdrawn. Instead, help them face up to their phobias.

- Always take a child's fear seriously. Check for "monsters" under the bed or remove a "scary" lamp from his room.

- If a child is afraid of the vacuum, get her to help you when operating it. Let her push it and turn it on or off. If the child is particularly young, hold her while you clean.

- Confront irrational fears irrationally. Got a child who's convinced there are monsters just waiting to gobble him up once the lights go out? Bring out your "magic anti-monster spray" (a spray can or atomizer filled with cologne or something scented to calm the child after you leave).

- Go over possibilities with children. Give them something to do in the event of an accident.

- Admit that you, as an adult, still have fears. And tell your child how you have overcome some of the ones you used to have.

- Don't discourage "security blankets" or other soothing objects.

- Hang a picture of a police officer in the child's room to "patrol" things when you're not there.

- Have the child draw a picture of what's bothering him. Then correct the negative points with positive ones. (Draw a smile on the monster, for example.)

○ Bad dreams a problem? Turn over your child's pillow and tell them that there are only good dreams on that side.

REFERENCE ——————————————————
Practical Parenting Tips by Vicki Lansky, Meadowbrook Press, New York, 1992.

Keeping children quiet

Short attention spans and restlessness can make even the most well-behaved child a little too noisy at times. Try these tips to make life easier for everybody:

○ Sit in the front row at religious ceremonies or other events where children tend to get fidgety or loud. Knowing they're being watched helps some kids behave. The better view doesn't hurt either.

○ Alternatively, sit in the back. If you are unable to quiet your child, you can make a quick (and relatively anonymous) exit.

○ Sit the child between two adults at a gathering.

○ Teach your child to whisper. Teach her the difference between "indoor" and "outdoor" talking.

○ Find things for children to do. Get them to count the number of redheads in the audience or the number of children in a certain row.

○ Bring along some quiet toys or objects for the child to play with.

○ A last ditch alternative is quiet food, such as raisins.

REFERENCE ——————————————————
Practical Parenting Tips by Vicki Lansky, Meadowbrook Press, New York, 1992.

How not to listen to your child

You can bridge the gap between you and your child. If you think your child doesn't understand you, then the problem probably is that you don't understand your child.

When you talk to your child, don't rush in and try to "fix" things with good advice before you really get a handle on the problem. You have to learn to listen without thinking about your reply.

Here are four ways not to listen:

- ○ Evaluate. Agree or disagree with his words.

- ○ Probe. Play 20 questions. Invade her privacy and ask questions from your point of view.

- ○ Advise. Give advice based on your own experience. Your son or daughter will be ready for your advice after you've listened and understood.

- ○ Interpret. Try to figure out and explain your child's motives and behavior based on your own motives and behavior.

When you want other people to understand you, you have to show that you understand where they are coming from. Don't get on a soapbox or get wrapped up in your own thing.

REFERENCE ————————————————————
The 7 Habits of Highly Effective People by Stephen R. Covey, Simon & Schuster, New York, 1989.

Dealing with a child's temper tantrums

Sure, they're angels most of the time, but when children work up a really good temper tantrum, they can make your hair stand on end. But children, like adults, need to blow their stacks every now and then.

The reason behind the explosion is often beside the point. Right or wrong, you just want them to stop. Here are a few ways to keep a grip on your sanity without forcing your young one to repress her feelings.

- ○ Occasionally let the child scream to his heart's content.

- ○ If disciplinary action is the cause of the screaming session, tell the child that the rule stands, then ignore the tantrum.

○ Distract your child by doing something silly. Stage your own mock tantrum or flick the lights on and off. Both are wonderful distractions.

○ Pick your child up without anger or hostility and gently shake the "mads" out in a fun fashion.

○ Vanish into another room. Without someone to complain to, the child will stop wailing. If they follow you, move again.

○ Tell the child to go to his room until his mood improves.

○ If the child decides to hold his breath, try stopping it by gently blowing on their face or dashing them with a small amount of water. If the child does turn blue or pass out, don't panic. Breathing will automatically resume.

○ When away from home, escort the child to a more private location. When the tantrum is over, return to whatever you were doing.

REFERENCE
Practical Parenting Tips by Vicki Lansky, Meadowbrook Press, New York, 1992.

Choosing your child's summer camp

While summer camp should be more than sitting around the campfire singing "Great Green Gobs of Greasy Grimy Gopher Guts ..." it should always be fun. But, your child's enjoyment doesn't have to come at the expense of education. Search around and you can probably find the perfect blend of pleasure and knowledge.

Keep in mind that camp isn't really the place for Junior to polish his subject-verb agreement. Because most camps only run for a few weeks, there's not much knowledge they can impart that will stick with your child.

Life lessons are what children are more likely to walk away with. Camp-goers learn to make friends, address their strengths and weaknesses and get along with others.

As a parent, you should know exactly what you want a summer camp to offer your child. Consider factors like:

○ Location. Is it too far away for your tastes? What are the physical surroundings of the camp like?

○ Size. Are there big groups or small groups? Which is best for your child?

○ Age of campers. Will your son or daughter have friends their own age to play with?

○ Geographic representation. Is there a good mix of campers from different areas? What good is camp if it doesn't offer exposure to diversity?

○ Duration of stay.

○ Cost. How much are you willing to pay?

○ Camp structure. Are there enough activities to occupy your child's time? Is there enough free time?

○ Staff. What are their qualifications? How old are counselors? What's their background?

○ Health and safety. What if something happens to your child? What is the camp's procedure.

○ Feeding. Camp food may not be the best in the world, but is it a healthy mix?

○ Intuition. If a camp doesn't "feel" right to you, pass on it. Gut feelings tend to be right.

REFERENCE ————————————————————————————————
Choosing the Right Camp by Richard C. Kennedy and Michael Kimball, Times Books, New York, 1992.

Tired of hassling over homework?

Problem: Most kids hate homework.

Bigger problem: Most parents don't know how to deal with kids who hate homework.

If you've tried everything from nagging to screaming to speaking with the teacher, you may be ready to give up on the Homework Wars. You may have decided just to ignore the whole subject.

Don't do it. Research has shown that children do better in school when parents help with homework. The time it takes to help children with homework is an investment in their future.

○ **Don't lecture, plead or argue** about homework with your child. Listen to him and respond firmly and positively. Don't give your child a choice unless you mean it. Don't say "Would you like to do your math now?" when you mean "It's time to work on your math."

○ **Do try to find a homework time** that works for your child. Right after dinner usually works well since kids have time to relax after school, and they aren't too hungry to concentrate.

○ **Take breaks** and try switching from one subject to another for variety. Young children can't concentrate for long periods of time.

○ **Praise children** and build their self-esteem. A compliment for completing an assignment is usually more appropriate than a gift or a promise. Don't go overboard with praise — children can tell when you aren't being sincere. Be specific: "You spelled eight out of ten words right. Much better." For children who are hard to motivate, give small and frequent rewards for completing projects and small punishments for not doing them. Avoid criticism of a child's performance.

○ **Be enthusiastic and humorous.** Enjoy tickles and giggles. Don't downgrade teachers in front of children, either.

○ **When checking work,** help your child discover his errors by prompting him: "There are two spelling errors and one capitalization error. Can you find them?" Do check with the teacher before you correct homework. Teachers may want to see the errors so they'll know what they need to work on in class.

○ **If your child hates to read,** suggest alternating the task: "You read a page, then I'll read a page." Encourage your child to read aloud to you. When your elementary-school child doesn't understand a word, never have him stop reading to look it up in the dictionary. This interrupts the flow. Explain the word, act it out or draw a picture.

○ **The best way to learn spelling** is to see words spelled correctly and to recognize patterns (bright, light; made, trade). You can write the words on flash cards, hold the cards up, then take them away and ask your child to spell these words. Writing words over and over again and looking words up in the dictionary does not seem to help.

○ **Math** is a subject that gets a lot of bad press. Don't participate in math-bashing. Use real-life examples of math: Calculate the interest on $100 in a savings account or look for the geometric shapes in your house. When working on word problems, children should draw pictures to visualize the problems. Build associations between new concepts and things the child already knows: "Multiplying fractions is like regular multiplying except … " With young children especially, use blocks and pictures to help with math. Encourage your small children to move around when they learn math, such as counting the number of times they jump or clap.

○ **To teach handwriting** to a child, have her trace letters. Tape examples of good handwriting to her desk. Do not try to correct children when their hand hooks around the pencil. That handwriting position is perfectly normal, and it may be harmful to correct it. Some children who write poorly should just be taught to type.

REFERENCES ————————————————————————————

How to Help Your Child With Homework by Marguerite C. Radencich and Jeanne Shay Schumm, Free Spirit Publishing Inc., Minneapolis, 1988.
Hassle-Free Homework by Faith Clark and Cecil Clark with Marta Vogel, Doubleday, New York, 1989.

Don't let your children fool you about homework time

Parents are often puzzled when kids say, "I finished my homework at school" or "I don't have any homework tonight." You are right to expect your child to do a certain amount of homework every night. By fifth grade, a child should not have time to complete his homework in class and get enough practice to properly learn.

Some guidelines on how much time your child should spend on homework:

Second and third grades:	1/2 to 1 hour
Fourth to sixth grades:	1 to 2 hours
Seventh and eighth grades:	1 1/2 to 2 1/2 hours
Ninth to twelfth grades:	2 to 4 hours

REFERENCE ————————————————————————

Hassle-Free Homework by Faith Clark and Cecil Clark with Marta Vogel, Doubleday, New York, 1989.

Getting your child organized

Does your child bring home assignments sticking out of schoolbooks, crumpled in pants pockets, or stuffed in the bottom of his book bag? No homework hints will help this child until he gets organized. Help him create the Big Perfect Notebook.

◯ In the front, put a zippered plastic envelope for pens, pencils, erasers, highlighters and colored markers.

◯ Include a 5 x 7 assignment notebook. Your child can use one sheet a day to write the subject name, date and homework assignment for each subject. This will be a big adjustment for a child used to writing assignments on little slips of paper. Replace this notebook as many times as your child loses it.

◯ A three-hole-punched school calendar is important. Your child can write in when long-term assignments are due.

◯ The notebook should have plenty of darkly lined loose-leaf paper separated by colored dividers for each subject. As your child gets older, she may prefer to keep separate small notebooks for each subject. She can keep these notebooks in the bigger one.

○ Put a set of pocket folders in the back — one for each subject, one labeled "For Parents," and one for "General Junk." On the outside of the folders for each subject, your child should write the subject and how the final grade will be determined (50 percent from tests, 30 percent from class participation, etc.). Your child should also list his grades here as he earns them.

REFERENCE ──────────────
Hassle-Free Homework by Faith Clark and Cecil Clark with Marta Vogel, Doubleday, New York, 1989.

Money matters for children

"Money doesn't grow on trees!"

How many times did you hear this wonderful philosophical insight from your parents, and how many times have you said it to your kids?

Most kids have no concept of the value of money, and most kids have never been taught anything about finances — beyond the fact that dollar bills and apples come from different places.

Maybe you're worried that you're spoiling your children because you give them so much of what they want. Or maybe you just want to teach them good spending habits and guard them from a life of financial woe.

Here are eight steps to teaching your children financial responsibility:

○ At age 3, when children usually begin to learn to count, they can learn about dollars and cents. Use play money and picture books that show how coins add up to dollars.

○ At the grocery store, show that money can be exchanged to buy the food they eat.

○ Begin an allowance at an early age. Pay children for extra work they do around the house (not their expected chores), and let them make some purchases.

○ Explain the benefits of saving money. If you save your allowance for three weeks instead of spending it right away, you can buy that big toy you want.

○ Start a bank account for your child and encourage her to put a little money in every week, even if it's just a dollar. Some institutions, like credit unions and small regional banks, have very low minimum balance requirements.

○ Once your children start school, use board games to help them learn supply and demand basics and more subtle money issues. Make sure you play with your kids so you can help steer them in the right direction. The Game of Life is one of the best classic board games. You win when you collect the most wealth — not the most cash. You make major life decisions like whether to go to college or start working right after high school. You even get monetary credit for doing good deeds — like adopting a child or recycling.

○ Encourage entrepreneurship in children who would rather strike out on their own than mow lawns or deliver papers, but don't let money-making take over their lives. *Biz Kids Guide to Success* by Terri Thompson and *A Teen's Guide to Business* by Linda Menzies are two books that help children start their own little businesses and make money.

○ You may want to buy your teen-age children a few shares of stock in a company they like. They can learn to watch the stock price in the newspaper and to reinvest dividends. Kids may enjoy companies that give presents, discounts and coupons along with dividends: Wrigley sends boxes of gum to stockholders in December, and Tandy sends Radio Shack coupons.

If you teach your kids how to handle money and how to be financially responsible, they will make better life decisions for themselves. And, jumping out of the family nest and flying on their own won't be such a shock.

REFERENCE
Business Week, Feb. 1, 1993.

How to talk to your child about postponing sex

Your parents didn't talk to you about it, so why should you talk to your child?

Telling your children about sex is like the old "Don't put beans up your nose" story — they would never have done it if you hadn't mentioned it. ...

If you've decided that the best conversation you can have with your child about sex is no conversation, think again. Children are having sex earlier and earlier these days. They are bombarded with the concept on television, in movies and even on greeting cards.

Because of better nutrition and health care, girls and boys are reaching puberty and becoming fertile at a younger and younger age. Premarital sex is becoming more accepted as people are postponing marriage until after college and job success. Plus, this age of easy and effective birth control is turning society's attitude more towards sex as a means of recreation instead of procreation.

The point is: Sex is a much bigger issue for adolescents today than it was when you were a child.

Even if a parent has no religious or moral scruples about premarital sex, moms and dads are concerned about pregnancy and their child's emotional immaturity. Children aren't equipped to handle the issues of trust and confidentiality sexual relationships need. Early sex might damage a child's self-esteem, especially if she feels used and guilty. Also, sex at a young age may hamper a child's ability to develop positive, loving relationships later in life.

But how do you communicate about sexual relationships?

The first step is "the birds and the bees" conversation. Be accurate and factual; use details and correct terms. If you give factual information, children won't be encouraged to find out on their own.

The saddest cases of teenage pregnancy are girls who were misinformed by parents too embarrassed to give anything more than vague warnings or cute stories about "planting seeds." Think about how much you didn't know about your body or the other sex until long after you were married.

Next, talk to children about what will happen to them if they become involved with someone physically or if they get pregnant. Parents don't understand why "You could get pregnant" or "You could get AIDS" isn't enough of a warning.

Adolescents have not yet fully developed adult thinking skills. They think in a much more concrete way than adults do, and they have trouble seeing beyond the present. Even if they worry about getting pregnant, they aren't really thinking about how their life will change.

Ask your child what his plans for the future are, and explain how having a child or supporting a child will affect those plans. Talk about child-care payments, not being able to fit into a desk at school, and having no more free time without the baby.

Abortion seems to be an easy option for the concrete-thinking teen. Talk with them about how difficult it is to go through with an abortion and how they may have bad feelings or regrets about their decision for the rest of their lives.

Explain that their relationship with their "friend" will change after a pregnancy — whether they decide to keep the baby, put it up for adoption or have an abortion.

Explain that having sex could change their self-image, and it could hurt a future relationship that could be much more important to them than the person they are choosing to have sex with now. Talk about healthy relationships and how they develop. Explain that physical attraction is just one part of a good relationship.

Understand how important it is to teens to be accepted by their peers. Tell them that, no matter what their friends say, it's not true that "everybody's doing it." There are more young people who aren't having sex than who are. And many adolescents who have had sex were pressured into it.

Help teens understand that, while friends are important, it's more important to develop your own beliefs and stick to them. Teens need self-confidence to stand up to friends. Help them think positively about themselves.

Tell teens that they have the right to say no, without an explanation, and that no one has the right to pressure them into doing anything they don't want to do. They don't have the right to pressure others, either.

Children need someone to talk to about sex and about how to handle their feelings and their sexual growth. They need someone who will listen and not be judgmental.

Look for natural opportunities to talk about sex — they are everywhere — on TV, in newspapers, perhaps a relative's pregnancy. And always remember to show your love for your child so he won't need to look for affection elsewhere.

REFERENCE ——

How to Help Your Teenager Postpone Sexual Involvement by Marion Howard, The Continuum Publishing Co., New York, 1988.

How to find a good nursing home

Finding a good nursing home for an aging parent or spouse can be an emotional trauma for a family. Everyone feels anxious and guilty about putting their loved one in a home, even when they want to go. The fact that so many nursing homes have terrible reputations of neglect and poor care just makes the situation worse.

But that doesn't mean there aren't any good nursing homes out there. You just have to find them.

The U.S. Department of Health and Human Services has made the search a lot easier. They have put together three-page reports on every Medicare- and Medicaid-certified nursing home in the United States.

You can find these reports in your state Medicare and Medicaid offices, in your state health and welfare office and, probably, in your local library. These reports are a much better place to start the nursing-home search than the Yellow Pages.

Use the *Medicare/Medicaid Nursing Home Information* report to pick several nursing homes to visit. If possible, three or four family members, including the prospective resident, should make the trip. The more people making the decision, the better everyone will feel about it.

Set up interviews with the administrator, the director of nursing, the director of social services and the activities director. Tell the home you'd also like to meet with several residents, preferably ones about the same age and sex as your prospective resident.

In your interviews, you want to find out the background and experience of the people running the nursing home, what they see as the strengths and weaknesses of the home, and how many residents transferred out last year and why. Ask how many nurses and other staff members there are, how much the staff gets paid, and whether the home has special care units.

Ask how the home is funded and governed. You are likely to get the best care for your money in a government-owned nursing home or a not-for-profit home owned by a religious or charitable organization. The Veterans Administration, the Masons and the Odd Fellows, for instance, all own excellent homes. Nursing homes should have active governing boards or advisory boards constantly looking over the management's shoulders.

Find out what activities and counseling services are offered to the residents. What programs are available for evening and weekend recreation? Excellent nursing homes provide services to meet both the emotional and physical needs of the residents: social-service counseling for residents and their families, art therapy, gardening therapy, pet therapy, music therapy and dance therapy.

Do residents get to take regular trips to parks, local restaurants or shopping centers? Are there plenty of activities besides bingo? Homes should provide places to exercise, to play, well-stocked libraries with audio books and large-print books, perhaps even beauty parlors and barbershops.

Find out how much time the medical director spends at the home. A home with more than a hundred beds needs a medical director who is around at least ten to twenty hours a week. He should be in charge of staff training, drug therapy, bowel and bladder problems, patient care, etc.

The nursing home should be clean and should not smell of urine. If the home smells bad, that means the staff does not deal with continence problems properly — a sign of neglect beyond just the problem of smell.

Don't be fooled by plush lobbies with grand pianos and antique furniture. These trappings of wealth are there to impress you. They may mask inadequate staffing and poor medical care.

See if you can buy a meal at the nursing home. You can test the food and the atmosphere of the dining room for yourself.

Look closely at the residents. They should be dressed in neat, clean clothes that are appropriate for the weather. Fingernails should be clean and cut, and eyes should be free of crust.

Look for evidence of restraints, like cloth straps on the beds and wheelchairs. If there seem to be a lot of these, ask about the home's policy on restraints.

The nursing staff and the patients should look as though they like each other. Nurses should be helping the residents rather than busy at their stations writing charts. Are there plenty of nurses around? The best nursing homes will have about 3.5 nursing hours per resident per day.

After you've visited the nursing home twice and your visiting team has compared notes and shared impressions, you're ready to make a decision.

REFERENCE

Choosing a Nursing Home by Seth B. Goldsmith, Prentice Hall Press, New York, 1990.

Wedding bells

Dressing for the occasion

What to wear to a wedding depends on whether you're a guest or a member of the wedding party and whether it is a daytime or evening ceremony.

The wedding party takes its cue from the bride. After the bride and groom have decided on the time and place of the wedding and the degree of formality, they tell their attendants exactly what type of dress they expect.

In general, the rules are:

Formal daytime (before 6 p.m.) wedding:

Bride: Floor-length white or off-white gown with train and coordinating veil, matching shoes, gloves and blusher veil optional.

Bride's attendants: Floor-length or tea-length dresses with matching shoes, head covering, gloves.

Groom: Cutaway coat, striped trousers, pearl gray waistcoat, white stiff shirt, turndown collar with four-in-hand tie, or wing collar with ascot, gray gloves, optional top hat and spats.

Groomsmen and father of the bride: Same as the groom.

Mothers of the couple: Long or short dresses, head coverings, gloves.

Women guests: Street-length cocktail dresses, preferably not black, white or red. Head coverings and gloves optional.

Men guests: Dark suits.

Formal evening (after 6 p.m.) wedding:

Bride: Same as formal daytime wedding.

Bride's attendants: Same as formal daytime wedding.

Groom: Black full dress, white pique waistcoat, formal shirt, wing collar, white bow tie, white gloves, black dress shoes.

Groomsmen and father of the bride: Same as the groom.

Mothers of the couple: Long evening dresses, tea-length or short, dressy cocktail dresses, head coverings appropriate to the dress, gloves.

Women guests: Long or short dresses, depending on local custom, head covering and gloves optional.

Men guests: If women wear long dresses, tuxedos; if they wear short dresses, then dark suits.

Semiformal daytime:

Bride: Floor-length or tea-length dress with short veil or pouf, gloves optional.

Bride's attendants: Same as formal daytime wedding.

Groom: Gray stroller (not tails) with striped trousers, gray vest, four-in-hand tie with white pleated formal shirt, homburg and gloves optional.

Groomsmen and father of the bride: Same as groom.

Mothers of the couple: Floor-length, tea-length or street-length dresses, head coverings appropriate to dress, gloves optional.

Women guests: Short afternoon or cocktail dresses.

Men guests: Dark suits.

Semiformal evening:

Bride: Same as semiformal daytime.

Bride's attendants: Same length and degree of formality as bride's attire.

Groom: Winter — black tuxedo, summer — white jacket and formal trousers, pleated or pique soft shirt, black cummerbund, black bow tie, no gloves.

Groomsmen and father of the bride: Same as the groom.

Mothers of the couple: Same as semiformal daytime.

Women guests: Cocktail dresses, gloves, small hat or veil.

Men guests: Dark suits.

Informal daytime:

Bride: Short afternoon dress, cocktail dress or suit.

Bride's attendants: Same style as the bride.

Groom: Winter — dark suit, summer — either dark trousers with white linen jacket or white trousers with navy or charcoal jacket, soft shirt, conservative four-in-hand tie. Hot climate — white suit.

Groomsmen and father of the bride: Same as the groom.

Mothers of the couple: Same as semiformal daytime.

Women guests: Afternoon dresses, gloves, head coverings optional.

Men guests: Dark suits, light trousers and dark blazers in summer.

Informal evening:

Bride: Long dinner dress, short cocktail dress or suit.

Bride's attendants: Same style as bride.

Groom: Tuxedo if bride wears dinner dress; otherwise, dark suit in winter, lighter suit in summer.

Groomsmen and father of the bride: Same as the groom.

Mothers of the couple: Same length dresses as bride.

Women guests: Afternoon or cocktail dresses, gloves, head coverings optional.

Men guests: Dark suits.

The groom's father may dress like the groom and his attendants if he has a part to play in the wedding. For instance, the father of the groom sometimes serves as his son's best man or the father of the groom is often asked to stand in the receiving line. If he has no part to play in the wedding and has no desire to dress formally, the father of the groom may wear the same type of clothing as the men guests.

REFERENCE ——————————————————————————————————

Emily Post's Etiquette, A Guide to Modern Manners by Elizabeth L. Post, Harper & Row, New York, 1984.

What to wear the second time around

The second time around presents a whole new set of fashion dictates for the bride and groom. There once was a time in the not-so-distant past when a long, white dress for the second-time bride would have been considered in poor taste because the white dress was supposedly symbolic of the bride's virginity and purity.

"But since virginity is no longer an assumption for first-time brides, the question of wearing white loses some of its impact," writes Judith Slawson.

Perhaps the best rule is to combine two-thirds common sense with one-third desire. For example, if the bride's first marriage was short and she's still of an age where a traditional bridal gown looks appropriate, then it's reasonable that she should wear one.

On the other hand, if the second-time bride is on the far side of 40, a traditional white gown could make her look ridiculous. In either case, the blusher veil — the veil that covers the bride's face — is inappropriate because it is a symbol of virginity.

Usually, the second-time bride makes up for her lost dewy youth in sophistication and chic, and there are numerous wedding dress options available to showcase that hard-won maturity.

For example, an under-30, second-time bride might opt for a traditional style of bridal gown, but in a pastel color. If the second-time bride has her heart set on wearing white, she might consider a vintage gown — say a flapper outfit reminiscent of the 1920s — with bright flowers or jewelry.

Or, the second-time bride might use the occasion to splurge on a high-fashion, designer suit, custom-made for her.

The bride should let the groom decide how he and his groomsmen will dress for the occasion. The only guide should be that the men and the women in the wedding party blend appropriately.

REFERENCE ———————————————————————————————————
The Second Wedding Book by Judith Slawson, Doubleday, New York, 1989.

Who does what when there's more than one of a kind

Who does what and sits where when there's more or less than one of a kind? Those are the questions bridal couples ask as divorce and remarriage are more and more a fact of American family life.

When you face the altar, the pews to the left are for the bride's family and friends. The pews to the right are for the groom's family and friends.

The sides are reversed for Conservative and Orthodox Jewish weddings. They are also reversed in a church that has two main aisles. In those churches, the middle section of pews serves for both families, with the bride's family and friends on the right side of the section, and the groom's family and friends on the left.

Wedding guests tell the usher whether they are friends of the bride or the groom or of both. In the latter case, the usher will seat them wherever there is a vacant place.

If one of the parents of the couple is a widow or widower, he or she may ask a long-standing family friend to serve as escort. The friend would not participate in the ceremony in any way.

Naturally, if the relations between the bride and groom and the "family friend" are hostile, the widowed parent may choose to sit by him or herself. The widow or widower may also ask a relative who is not involved in the wedding to serve as escort.

In families in which there has been a divorce, the two guiding principles should be: Who's paying? and How well do the divorced parents get along?

If the divorced parents are friendly, the bride's mother and stepfather sit in the front pew on the left side. The bride's stepbrothers and stepsisters or half-brothers and half-sisters sit in the second pew behind the mother of the bride.

The next pew is for the bride's grandparents, aunts and uncles, both maternal and paternal.

Finally, the fourth pew is for the bride's father, his wife and their family. The groom's side observes the same order.

If divorced parents are included in the Jewish processional, only the parent and the stepparent with whom the bride or groom lives takes part.

In families where the divorced parents are hostile to one another, the father still may walk the bride down the aisle, after which he would sit behind the bride's mother's family. His wife or companion would be seated discreetly along with other guests of the couple.

There are, of course, lots of variations on this theme. For example, the father of the bride may choose to absent himself immediately after the ceremony, if he thinks that his or his wife's presence would be disruptive at the reception. But, if he receives an invitation to the reception and plans to attend, he should — for the day, at least — put aside all bitterness and ill feeling.

All of that, of course, assumes the mother of the bride is hosting the wedding and the reception.

If the father of the bride is hosting the occasion, and he and the bride's mother are friendly, he joins his former wife in the front pew. If they are decidedly unfriendly, he sits further back with his present wife and family.

Again, there are many variations. For instance, if the bride or groom is closer to a stepparent than a biological one, that relationship should be honored.

Brides and grooms should always remember that the ceremony should fit them and not the other way around. If the rules don't seem to apply to a particular family situation, the couple might want to meet with a wedding consultant or with the clergy who will be involved in the ceremony. Usually these professionals have dealt with a variety of family tangles and can offer sound, practical solutions for most situations.

REFERENCES ————————————————————————————

Emily Post's Etiquette, A Guide to Modern Manners by Elizabeth L. Post, Harper & Row, New York, 1984.

Bride's Book of Etiquette by the editors of *Bride's*, Grosset & Dunlap, New York, 1973.

Who pays for what?

The question of who pays for what in a wedding has become blurry in recent years because of the number of couples who pay for their own weddings.

Traditionally, the bride's family paid for the following:

- The paper trail — invitations, announcements and bride's personalized stationary
- Bride's gown, accessories
- Bride's trousseau
- Flowers for maid of honor, bridesmaids, flower girl, place of ceremony and reception
- Engagement and wedding photographs
- Rental fee for church or room
- Fees for sexton, musicians
- Rental fees for aisle carpet, canopy, candelabra or other equipment
- Transportation of the bridal party to the ceremony and reception
- All costs of the reception, including food, beverages, hall rental, music, decor, photographs, video
- Groom's wedding ring
- Groom's wedding gift
- Lodging for out-of-town bride's attendants
- Physical examination and blood test
- Wedding consultant fees

The groom's family paid for:

- Bride's engagement and wedding rings
- Marriage license

- Clergy fees

- Bride's bouquet and going-away flowers

- Boutonnieres for the men in the wedding party

- Flowers for the mothers and grandmothers

- Gloves and ties (or ascots) for the men in the wedding party

- Bride's wedding gift

- Gifts for best man and ushers

- Lodging for ushers from out of town

- Wedding trip expenses

- The rehearsal dinner

Female attendants could expect the following expenses:

- The dresses, shoes and head coverings they wear during the ceremony

- Transportation to and from the place of the wedding

- A wedding gift to the couple

- A share of the gift given by all the bridesmaids

- Participation in one or more showers, including appropriate gifts

Male attendants could expect the following expenses:

- Rental of wedding clothes

- Transportation to and from the place of the wedding

- A gift to the couple

- A share of the ushers' joint gift

- Part of the expense of the bachelor dinner

Some of the items on these traditional lists differ from place to place, in which case local custom should prevail.

Specific costs may be borne by others, depending upon the situation. As always, the prospective bride and groom should look to the traditional list as a guide and not something set in concrete.

REFERENCE

Emily Post's Etiquette, A Guide to Modern Manners by Elizabeth L. Post, Harper & Row, New York, 1984.

What to do with the boss and co-workers

Inviting the boss to the wedding depends on how well you know him. If you work for Mega Company, the company CEO may not know who you are, in which case it could be embarrassing to send her an invitation.

But, if you work for Small Company in Tiny Town and the CEO is a personal friend, naturally you would want to send him and spouse an invitation.

Problems usually arise when your relationship with the boss falls between these extremes. The first thing to do is to ask around the office discreetly to see what others have done in similar circumstances. Second, ask friends in other offices how they've handled the situation to find out what the local custom is.

If you have determined that you really don't want to invite any of your business friends to your wedding and reception, you might host a party several weeks before the wedding for all your office acquaintances to allow them the opportunity to meet your fiancee. Be sure during the course of the evening to mention (several times) how limited the wedding and reception guest list must be.

You may send a blanket invitation to your office to be posted on the bulletin board only if everyone who reads that bulletin board is invited. You may also post a note and a sheet of blank paper with the invitation asking people to sign their names if they plan to attend the wedding and reception. Be sure your note accounts for inviting office friends' spouses or fiancees. Including "dates" is neither necessary nor expected.

You may invite office friends to the reception or the wedding, not necessarily both. For example, if the church or hall is huge, a few more people won't matter much, but if the reception is a sit-down dinner at $25 a person, you begin to think very carefully about each guest.

Or, perhaps, the chapel where the ceremony is being held is so small that every seat makes a difference, but the reception is an inexpensive punch and cake affair in a large reception hall. In that case, you might want to send out more reception cards than wedding invitations.

REFERENCE ——

Emily Post's Etiquette, A Guide to Modern Manners by Elizabeth L. Post, Harper & Row, New York, 1984.

Who to invite where

If your friend asks you (subtly or bluntly) to invite his fiancee/date/ significant other to the wedding and reception and you have extra invitations, as well as space at the wedding and reception, you may do so either by asking your friend for the correct address and sending a separate invitation or by indicating both names on the inside envelope.

Even though you are not obligated to include someone else's friend in your wedding, it is nice if you can, simply because your friend will — presumably — have a better time at the festivities.

There is no direct way of telling people not to bring their children, though not including the children's names on the invitation would seem to be a strong clue.

Some brides are adamant about excluding children from the ceremony, and certainly, young children can be disruptive. If the bride feels this strongly about children, she should make arrangements for a nursery attendant. It would be the duty of the ushers to suggest to parents of small children that there is a nursery and attendant available and offer to escort the parent and child to the nursery.

The bride should also make her wishes known by word-of-mouth in the weeks before the wedding. If, in spite of everything, parents bring children to the ceremony and won't relinquish them to the nursery, make the best of it.

Some people prefer children of manageable age at the wedding, but don't want them at the reception, saying the reception is, in essence, a large party and the presence of small children is inappropriate.

People with small children would be advised to think twice and look thrice at their invitations before taking their children with them to a wedding and reception.

REFERENCE ———————————————————————

Emily Post's Etiquette, A Guide to Modern Manners by Elizabeth L. Post, Harper & Row, New York, 1984.

Please and thank you

Saying please and thank you both verbally and on paper will go a long way toward smoothing the rough edges of a wedding.

Verbal assurances that you plan to attend the wedding or the reception are not adequate. You must send a written response, if you plan to attend or not, so the hosts — usually the bride's family — will know how many to plan for at the ceremony and reception.

REFERENCE ———————————————————————

Emily Post's Etiquette, A Guide to Modern Manners by Elizabeth L. Post, Harper & Row, New York, 1984.

Cutting wedding costs

There are lots of ways to cut the cost of a traditional wedding. Try these 10 suggestions for cutting costs:

- ○ Rent a bridal gown, buy a second-hand gown, have one made or re-do your mother's.

- ○ Use the church social hall or your own home for the reception.

- ○ Serve light refreshments and nonalcoholic beverages at the reception.

- ○ Decorate with more ribbons than flowers or use friends' garden flowers.

- ○ If possible, plan your wedding for several hours after another wedding in the same church so you and the other family can split the cost of the flowers or any rental equipment.

- ○ Ask a friend of the family who has a big car, maybe even a vintage vehicle, to drive the wedding party to and from the church.

○ Plan your wedding in a public garden with a picnic reception.

○ Ask hometown friends to house out-of-town guests and relatives.

○ Ask a musical friend to sing and play at the wedding.

○ Ask several musical friends to play for the reception or to put together a selection of tapes and rig a sound system.

REFERENCE
Emily Post's Etiquette, A Guide to Modern Manners by Elizabeth L. Post, Harper & Row, New York, 1984.

Things not to skimp on

The following are wedding expenses you should not skimp on:

○ Photographs: More than one bride and groom have been sorely disappointed when their good-friend-the-amateur-photographer took 10 rolls of film with the camera lens cap on. Hire a professional and tell him exactly what you want.

○ Fair pay for those professionals who assist you with your wedding. Some, of course, have set rates, but others, such as the clergy, depend on contributions. Don't insult them by offering less than you would tip the fellow who parks your car.

○ No matter how light the refreshments, make sure they are pleasing to the palate and the eye.

○ Don't use the newspaper engagement announcement as a wedding invitation. If you can't afford engraved or printed invitations, buy attractive note paper and write your own.

○ Be sure to write thank-you notes not only to those who give gifts, but also to those who assisted with the wedding.

REFERENCE
Emily Post's Etiquette, A Guide to Modern Manners by Elizabeth L. Post, Harper & Row, New York, 1984.

Social strategies

How to be a welcome guest

For many, the rules of etiquette have come to be associated with an excessively formal lifestyle that has, in large part, been abandoned. However, good manners are still important, especially when it's party time.

Party hosts usually go to a lot of trouble to make an event special and to show their guests a good time. If you act inappropriately or don't do your part in making the party enjoyable, you run the risk of being struck from the guest lists. To make sure you don't become the social outcast, follow this advice:

- Always, without exception, respond to an invitation. If the invitation includes a telephone number, call it. Otherwise, send a written response.

- Arrive on time, neither early nor late.

- The time to leave a party is when you're still having fun. Don't wait until the host is yawning and picking up plates.

- Nobody's interested in what you don't like. Try to eat whatever the host is serving without comment about your own dietary likes and dislikes. Find something you do like and rave about it.

- Don't ask who else will be present or what the host is serving before accepting or declining your invitation.

- If the host does not offer alcoholic beverages, don't ask for one. But, if alcoholic beverages are all that the host offers, you may request something else.

- It's always a nice gesture to take a small gift for your host and hostess. But don't make them uncomfortable by implying that they should open the gift right then.

- Ask if you may help in the kitchen. If your host says no, don't push it. Some people just don't like having others in the kitchen with them.

○ Do not bring your dog, cat or child unless they have been specifically invited.

○ Always, without exception, call or write the day after to thank your host for the lovely party, even if it was the most miserable night of your life.

REFERENCE ──────────────────────────────
Emily Post's Etiquette, A Guide to Modern Manners by Elizabeth L. Post, Harper & Row, New York, 1984.

What a good host never asks

The words to be avoided are: "Well, what would you like to do?"

When you are the host of out-of-towners, especially those from other countries, you should prepare a choice of activities for your time together. Don't ask what they'd like to do in a vague, open-ended sort of way. Sharing your favorite restaurant or special get-away spot is a gesture of real friendship.

Some other helpful gestures:

○ Offer maps and brochures for your city — most towns of any size regularly publish a "What's happening" kind of guidebook that a visitor will find helpful.

○ Line up transportation. Imagine how nice it would be for you to have a car and driver at your beck and call in London!

○ An especially nice touch: Arrange for delivery of your guest's home-town newspaper while he is here.

REFERENCE ──────────────────────────────
The Concise Guide to Executive Etiquette by Linda and Wayne Phillips, Doubleday, New York, 1990.

The designated nondrinker

Most people know that one member of any group of party-goers should remain stone-cold sober to drive everyone home.

But have you ever thought of a designated nondrinker for at-home parties?

A house after a party is at high risk for a fire. Fire studies reveal that nearly half of those who die in fires had blood-alcohol levels high enough to be legally drunk.

People who have been drinking tend to be more careless. They drop cigarettes and matches into upholstered furniture or even onto their own clothing without realizing what has happened. Embers may smolder for hours before bursting into flame.

People who drink heavily fall asleep easily and are hard to wake up. When they do wake up, they may be too confused to save themselves.

The designated nondrinker at every party can make sure no guest drives after having too much to drink. He will wake up if a smoke alarm sounds, and he'll be able to help people get to safety.

REFERENCE
   Smoke Signals, 2nd edition, The International Society of Fire Service Instructors, Ashland, Mass., 1986.

Good restaurants: How to pick 'em

Crispy, crunchy fried chicken; plump ravioli simmering in sauce; succulent, tender, thick cuts of steak. ...

Think about it. Nothing can make or break your long-awaited vacation week faster than food. Sure, beautiful beaches and sunsets over mountain ranges are nice, but food — that's where it's at.

The pressure is on when you have to pick out the restaurant to top off your vacation day, so here is some advice from the pros on how to spot a good eatery:

○ Is the restaurant parking lot crowded? Check the license plates for local folks, not just out-of-towners like yourself.

○ Instead of asking your hotel concierge or taxi driver for a recommendation, ask a policeman, an antique dealer or a bookshop owner. If a good restaurant is recommended to you and it is all booked up, ask there what other restaurant you should try.

○ Restaurants named after a person are sometimes good — if the person is still living and connected to the restaurant. You can usually trust restaurants named for two people, especially when one is a woman. Restaurants named after a location are the best bet, whether the location is its own or some other place — the Florida Avenue Grill or the Santa Fe Bar & Grill, for instance.

○ If you have a hankering for a good steakhouse, find one that makes its own french fries. The best places for steak are often outside of town in a near suburb.

○ Want a simple meal in a good cafe? Ask if their mashed potatoes and pie crusts are homemade. Waitresses or customers wearing house-dresses are a sign of good home cooking. And children sitting around the cafe doing homework can almost ensure a good meal.

○ To choose between two unfamiliar restaurants, pick the one with the smaller menu, especially one-dish menus. A newly written sign in a bar, cafe or roadhouse advertising "today's special" indicates that somebody is probably cooking in the kitchen.

○ When Chinese food would suit your fancy, pick the restaurant with the lowest number of chow meins.

○ Stay away from restaurants with reviews on the wall when the newest review is more than three years old.

○ Never opt for a restaurant in a small city where the waiters wear ruffled shirts.

○ Don't turn up your nose at restaurants connected to bowling alleys or housed in former gas stations. They are a safer choice than similar, more conventionally housed restaurants.

○ For authentic local food, try church suppers, outdoor food festivals and firehouse breakfasts. Check the classifieds in small local newspapers and posters tacked to trees and telephone poles.

REFERENCE

Phyllis C. Richman, restaurant critic, *The Washington Post*, in *Great American Food Almanac*, Harper & Row, Publishers, New York, 1986.

What never to order when you're eating out

After finding a good restaurant, you have to decide what to order. Local specialties that are in season can't be missed. Ordering several appetizers instead of a regular meal can be smart since appetizers are often the best part of the meal. If the restaurant displays something as available for carryout, it's probably good.

Some dishes should never be ordered in a restaurant:

○ Complex dishes on an otherwise simple menu — the Chicken Kiev, Veal Cordon Bleu and Beef Wellington are likely to be frozen.

○ Lobster dishes, if you don't see whole lobsters anywhere. The lobsters are likely to be frozen or made from frozen lobster tails or, in the case of lobster bisque, from a powdered mix.

○ Potato skins, if no other potato dishes are on the menu. The potatoes are probably frozen. Also, stay away from fried clams when you don't see clams on the half shell, oyster dishes when there are no oysters on the half shell, and fish fillets stuffed with crab, if there are no other crab dishes.

○ Steaks, in restaurants that don't specialize in steak.

○ Beef, when you are in sight of an ocean, or seafood, when you are more than three states away from the water (except in major cities.)

REFERENCE

Phyllis C. Richman, restaurant critic, *The Washington Post*, in *Great American Food Almanac*, Harper & Row, Publishers, New York, 1986.

Dealing with dining dilemmas

Whether you are the guest or the host at a business luncheon, you are usually acutely aware that the purpose of the occasion is more than just food. You are there to check out your business associates, to convince them to work with you or to wrap up a deal.

To keep the focus where it belongs — and not on your struggles with fly-away pasta or unruly chops — order manageable food.

When the food has already been selected and you have to deal with it, here are some tips for coping with unwieldy edibles:

○ Artichokes: Tear off leaves one by one, dip the broad end into the accompanying sauce (usually melted butter), then draw between the teeth to remove the "meat." Place leaves on your plate or on a dish provided. Remove the fuzzy choke with knife and fork, cut up the heart and eat it with a fork.

○ Asparagus: If cooked crisp-tender, asparagus may be picked up at the base, using the fingers, dipped into a sauce and eaten down to the "woody" part of the stalk. Since many people do not realize that asparagus is a finger food, your guest or host may use a fork. In that case, you should follow suit. (Asparagus that has been overcooked and limp should be eaten with a fork.)

○ Bacon: Eat with a fork. If very crisp and dry, you may use your fingers.

○ Baked potato: Cut an X across the top, then squeeze gently and add butter, sour cream or both. The butter should be put on the potato with a fork, not a knife.

○ Chicken: Not a finger food, except at picnics and barbecues. Always use your knife and fork.

○ Clams or oysters in the shell: With one hand, remove meat with oyster fork and eat whole. It is okay to pick up the shell and drink the juice from it.

○ Corn on the cob: If the ear is large, break it and butter only small portions at a time. Hold with both hands.

○ Long pasta: A few strands at a time, twirl around a fork, prongs against the edge of the plate, not in the bowl of a spoon.

○ Whole fruits like apples and pears: Quarter and peel (if you wish), then cut into bite-sized pieces and eat with a fork.

Which fork do I use first?

When dining in a formal setting, don't be intimidated by ranks of forks, knives and spoons. As a general rule, you begin at the outside and work your way in as courses appear. Place used utensils diagonally across the upper right edge of the plate to be removed by the server.

A handy way to remember that plates will be removed from your right in a formal meal: "remove" and "right" both begin with R. Food will be served from your left. Beverages will be poured on your right side.

Salad on your left

Have you ever been dismayed to discover that the diner to your left at a banquet has forked into your salad? He forgot the rule that beverages are set on the right of the place setting, food on plates to the left. Depending on the formality of the occasion, there is probably no graceful way for you to suggest he pass you his uneaten lettuce — it would only embarrass him.

Fork up or fork down? Continental vs. American style

Europeans hold the fork in the left hand, tines down, while cutting food with the knife held in the right. Instead of shifting the fork to the right hand to eat, as Americans do, they simply eat "left-handed." Either is perfectly acceptable, in the States or on the Continent.

It's interesting to note that early in the seventeenth century, when the use of knives and forks became popular, diners on both sides of the Atlantic ate as most Americans do today. European aristocracy wanted to distinguish themselves from the common folks, and adopted the habit of keeping the fork in the left hand. Eventually, all Europeans switched forks to the left.

(For left-handed people, the reverse of the above is also quite acceptable.)

Handling inedibles

When can you use your fingers to remove something inedible from your mouth? The rule is, if it was finger food when it went in, it's all right to remove it the same way.

Same thing goes for other utensils: gristle or fat should be removed with a fork, seeds from fruit with a spoon. Fish bones are the only exception. You may use your fingers to take a fish bone from your mouth, placing it at the edge of your plate.

REFERENCE —————————————————————————————
The Concise Guide to Executive Etiquette by Linda and Wayne Phillips, Doubleday, New York, 1990.

Mealtime manners in strange locales

To try to appreciate how offended your Saudi Arabian host might be by your refusing to eat sheep's eyes, a delicacy in his country, imagine how you would feel if he declined to taste your prize-winning pumpkin pie recipe.

When gracious acceptance is a must, there are ways to overcome your disinclination to sample the unfamiliar:

○ Slice strange food very thin and swallow quickly.

○ Don't even look at the English translation on the menu. Let your host order.

○ In Chinese cultures, leave tea in your cup and rice in your bowl to signal that you are full and cannot possibly eat more.

○ In Africa, your host may take offense if you don't at least sip the proffered whiskey or gin, and promise to finish the rest later.

REFERENCE
Do's and Taboos Around the World edited by Roger E. Axtell, compiled by the Parker Pen Company, produced by The Benjamin Company Inc., Elmsford, N.Y., 1985.

Chopsticks: There's more to 'em than getting the food to your mouth

Chopsticks have their own rules of etiquette. When serving yourself from communal bowls, use either serving chopsticks or the wider end of your own (the end that has not been in your mouth).

Don't plant your chopsticks vertically in a bowl of rice or wave them about to illustrate a point. Don't spear food with them as you would with a fork, and don't cross them in an empty bowl. Replace your chopsticks on the rest provided when you are finished with your meal.

More Japanese restaurant rules:

○ In a traditional Japanese room, the place of honor is in front of the alcove, and the least favored location is by the door.

○ Never pour your own sake before offering it to your neighbors, and always raise your cup to receive it. Please note that while drinking is considered a good way to foster informal communication, drunk driving is not tolerated.

○ Rice and soup bowls may be picked up while eating. If they have lids, replace them when you are done.

REFERENCE
Simply Japan, News from the Consulate General of Japan in Atlanta, January 1992.

Be a class act: audience etiquette at theater, concert or ballet

Whether you are host or guest, if you are an infrequent theater- or concert-goer, you'll make a better impression by keeping your lack of experience to yourself. Here are several tips that will help:

○ Familiarize yourself with the music or plot ahead of time. This will almost certainly enhance your own enjoyment of the evening, and if you're having fun, so will your companions.

○ Read reviews and whatever else you can find about the author, composer and performers to improve your anecdotal skills for the evening.

○ Eat lightly before a performance, and avoid alcohol. A heavy meal, a few drinks and a comfortable seat in a dark theater could result in the embarrassment of falling asleep.

Tickets and seating

○ Buy tickets in advance, if possible. Keep in mind that orchestra seats, usually the most expensive, are not necessarily preferable for every event. Seats in the lower balconies usually provide the best overall view of the stage.

○ If there is a chance someone in your party may be called to the telephone during a performance, ask for aisle seats. The same is also advisable if someone in your group is handicapped.

○ Arrive early. Tickets that have not been picked up by 20 minutes before curtain may be sold to someone awaiting a cancellation. An early arrival also ensures time to check coats and be seated comfortably. Late arrivals are usually not seated until the first break in the program.

○ When there is an usher, the proper order for seating is for the guest and her spouse to follow the usher; the host-couple enters last. If there is no usher, the host leads the way to the seats.

○ When there are two couples, one of the men enters the row first, followed by the two women and then by the other man. Traditionally, each woman sits by the man who is not her spouse.

○ When the party is large, a woman should lead the way into the row, the others alternating: man, woman, man, etc. Except as noted above, a man should take the aisle seat.

The don'ts

While it may appear obvious, it cannot be overemphasized: Absolute silence should be maintained during the performance of a play, ballet, concert or recital.

Whispering, talking, humming along, unwrapping candy or lozenges, jangling jewelry, rustling programs, cracking gum or tapping feet or fingers are simply inexcusable and will make the worst possible impression on others.

The same may be said for leaving your seat during a performance. Nothing short of an extreme emergency excuses this kind of disruption.

Applause

At a concert, it is permissible to applaud when the conductor enters and, of course, when the work is completed. Do not applaud after a solo, which is part of the ongoing work, or between movements. If in doubt, watch the conductor.

He usually remains facing the orchestra with hands raised in preparation for the next movement.

Interestingly, applause is welcome after a solo or pas de deux (a duet of dancers) within a ballet, as well as following an aria in an opera. As each scene or act concludes, applause is also appropriate.

At the theater, do not applaud entrances, even to show that you recognize a star. However, it is OK to applaud when he exits following a big scene.

Likewise, you may applaud at the end of a song or dance, but not when it is introduced. Applause is appropriate at the end of a scene or an act, and also when some especially complicated bit of mechanical stage work is carried off well.

REFERENCE ————————————————————
The Concise Guide to Executive Etiquette by Linda and Wayne Phillips, Doubleday, New York, 1990.

Dating data

If you are lonely, you're not alone. One in five Americans is single and searching for a mate. The number of singles has grown 85 percent since 1970, and the number of married people has grown only 19 percent.

The singles boom isn't all due to the aging population. More than one in three singles are baby boomers ages 25 to 44. Two-thirds of this group have never been married, and about a third are divorced. Most of the baby boomers are single parents and people whose busy careers make social lives difficult.

Business is booming for dating services. Most of their customers are business owners, physicians, attorneys and people with careers in computers, high-tech sales, health care and schools. Dating services are usually expensive, so they attract affluent singles.

Men are more likely to take out ads in the classifieds. Women should be aware that men aren't nearly as likely as women to mention children in their ads, and 40 percent of them ask for women's photographs.

Men are also concerned with their own appearance, and nearly 75 percent of men include their weight in their ads, while only 43 percent of women mention their weight.

Least desirable characteristics: Short and undereducated men are hard to match, and overweight women have a difficult time on the dating scene. Women's education doesn't seem to matter so much. Smoking is a definite turn-off for both sexes. Southerners are very concerned about religious preference.

Most difficult to match up with a mate: men in their early 20s and women ages 45 to 74. Women in their 20s tend to like older men, and men often prefer younger women.

REFERENCE ————————————————————————————————
American Demographics, April 1992.

Been single for too long? How to meet your mate.

There are plenty of fish in the sea, but you won't find them in your bathtub.

Everyone knows that you have to get out of your house in order to meet others. But, the problem is, many people who are lonely are also shy. When shy people go out on the town, they are much more likely to go to a movie theater than to the local dance hall, and it's hard to meet someone when you are all sitting in the dark staring at a movie screen.

Try taking a continuing education class at your local college or community center. Talking with fellow students is very easy. You can ask about homework assignments, join a study group, discuss the lecture after class, and you'll probably be forced into several group projects.

Continuing education students are good people to meet because they are interested in life and are trying to improve themselves.

Sports clubs and sporting events are also good meeting grounds for the shy and lonely. You have to at least make eye contact and smile when you are sweating beside someone on a treadmill. If you play tennis, basketball, golf, etc., you can sign up for a coed tournament.

Once you get out in the world, view everyone as a potential mate or friend and be determined to enjoy yourself. Your zest for life will attract others.

Never say, "I felt no chemistry." These words sound a death knell to potential relationships.

"No chemistry" usually means "no sexual chemistry," and while sex is important, it isn't a solid basis for a long-term relationship. Sexual attraction sometimes develops after you have come to appreciate another person.

"No chemistry" can also be an excuse if you think the other person is going to reject you. If you or your date is nervous, a "no chemistry" situation can develop.

If you are tempted to write off a nice, compatible person as a potential mate because there wasn't some mysterious attraction between you, give your date another chance.

Fear of Rejection: That's what's holding most of us shy people back. How do you get over it?

When you walk into a room, instead of looking down at your toes or at a spot on the back wall, say a big hello — loud enough so that there is no doubt everyone heard you. If someone ignores you or snubs you, you'll have no doubt that it was intentional. More likely, you will get several friendly responses.

To show a certain person that you like them, try:

> * A friendly smile whenever you meet
> * Compliments on clothing or appearance
> * Helping without being asked
> * Holding the door for her
> * Waiting for him to walk down the hall with you
> * Laughing at his jokes
> * Paying close attention and being a good listener

Blind Date Dos and Don'ts

○ Never double date on your first date with someone. Often a young married couple will match up some friends and plan an entire evening for the four of them. Everyone feels awkward and can't act naturally. You don't only worry about what your date thinks of you, but about what your friends think about how you're acting. Even though the first few moments may be awkward, you'll get to know someone much more quickly and easily one-on-one.

○ Avoid large cocktail parties or other public functions for your first date. A big party can doom a potential relationship. You can't get to know each other, and it is too easy for you to hide, get lost or let your eyes wander if you feel uncomfortable.

○ Don't reveal every one of your personal secrets on a first date. You should tell about yourself, but your date may be overwhelmed if you get too intimate.

○ Don't give up on blind dates because they seem boring. Blind dates can be boring because you anticipate them so much or because you enjoy the comfort and ease of a long-term relationship rather than the flirtatiousness of a first date. However, keep on going — your next blind date may be your last!

Want to know if you are compatible? Listen for these three words.

The three words that should shout "Watch Out!" are "What's so funny?"

If you are laughing hilariously with your friends or crying with laughter over a movie, and your date says, "I don't see what's so funny," you should know that your relationship probably won't work.

A happy marriage has a compatible sense of humor at its core. Successful couples usually laugh at the same things, so if your date's laughter bewilders you or if you have to stop to explain what's so funny, beware!

When should you stay single?

Some single people haven't been single long enough, especially if they've recently gone through a divorce or are grieving for a spouse who has died.

Some signs that you're not ready to find a permanent mate are:

○ You only want to date your "fantasy mate." If you are looking for perfection — intelligence, good looks, a certain height, athletic, dignified, etc., you could be suffering from the effects of a bad marriage. Your previous husband was a slob, so you expect your next mate to be just right. No one will ever live up to your fantasy.

○ You are looking desperately for your next mate. This problem is the opposite of the first. You want to be happily married so badly that you believe anyone will do.

○ If you haven't had much dating experince, you shouldn't rush into a marriage. You need to date for a while so that you can get the experience and knowledge necessary to choose a life partner.

REFERENCE
Haven't You Been Single Long Enough?: A Practical Guide For Men Or Women Who Want To Get Married by Milton Fisher, Wildcat Publishing Co., Green Farms, Conn., 1992.

Courting your sweetheart

Courtship in the 1990s? Some people think that old-fashioned wooing isn't a bad idea, better than the dating pattern we've established in the last century.

Some people who believe that dating can be a disappointing and painful experience are using the term "courtship" to describe an alternative way of meeting a mate. Instead of dating, teen-agers and older singles interact with others at work, school and church and build open friendships.

When two people are attracted to each other, they tell their parents and friends and get to know one another through group activities and family gatherings. In this way, they find out if they would be compatible marriage partners.

REFERENCE
Dating and Courtship from a Biblical Perspective by Paul Jehle, Heritage Institute Ministries, 1990.

Looking your best

How to dress like a millionaire without being one

Clothes don't make the man. ... They just control whether or not he gets anywhere in the business world of images and first impressions.

If you want to dress like the president of IBM but you think paying for your kid's education seems more important, try this advice for buying your clothes cheap:

○ Plan ahead to buy your clothes on sale. Fall-winter clothes are usually on sale from about Jan. 10 to Feb. 5, and spring-summer merchandise goes on sale after the July 4 weekend until the end of August. Buy extra clothes during sales times so you won't have to pay full price when you need them.

○ Compute a garment's true cost. If clothes have to be dry-cleaned, figure in that expense. Don't buy cotton shirts if you want to save money. Cotton costs more than cotton/polyester in the first place, the shirt will probably have to be dry-cleaned since cotton is so difficult to iron, and the cotton shirt will last about half as long.

○ Learn to "cross-shop." Go to a range of stores with various prices — the expensive shops, the department stores, the chain stores and discount stores. Take a notebook with you to write down what you find. For instance, if you are looking for a suit, follow these steps:

- Write down your needs and your preferences — you'd like a gray suit but you'll take a dark blue, etc.

- Notice the look of the materials in the different stores. Is the suit soft-looking or hard and shiny?

- Look at specifics — the buttons, the lining, the fit, interior pockets and whether the pattern matches where the suit is sewn together.

- Go to a store you can afford and try to find a suit most like the expensive ones you saw. You may not always find exactly what you want right away, but you will learn to determine what is a good deal. In the expensive stores, write down brand names and prices so you'll know what to look for in the discount stores.

- Don't buy designer labels. You are paying extra for the name. You will get the most for your money if you look for the store's own label. (Sometimes a store label won't have the same name as the store. It is a made-up name which is usually put on the cheapest merchandise.)

- Consider the discount stores. They buy manufacturers' overruns and merchandise from stores that aren't doing well. If you are a selective shopper, you can get quality clothes at great prices. Be careful at a discount store to stay away from the store's own labels. When discount stores bring in their own merchandise, it is often poor quality. Avoid labels that only appear at that store and nowhere else. Also, know what's in style because some clothes will be out of date.

- Try factory outlets. They sell seconds, so check clothes carefully and unwrap shirts to make sure they have no obvious flaws. In factory outlets that sell several brands, look for labels you recognize. If you wear unusual sizes, you will do well to shop in factory outlets.

- Look for imported bargains. Some countries consistently offer the best buys on certain items, such as Brazil's shoes; the Orient's suits; America's polyester/cotton shirts, socks and underwear; Italy's silk ties; and Mexico's sweaters.

REFERENCE
Dress for Success by John T. Molloy, Warner Books Inc., New York, 1988.

Building a wardrobe on a budget

How many times have women heard that you must coordinate your wardrobe — buy basic colors that mix and match, then a few accessories to dress up plain outfits?

Well, get ready to hear it again. The only way to dress well for work every day without spending a fortune is to color-coordinate your clothes. If your closet looks like a rainbow, you probably have too many mornings when you're at a loss for something to wear.

The first step in building a workplace wardrobe is to take an inventory of your closet. Make a chart of your clothes, including color, description and what the item can be worn with. You will find the gaps this way — you may have a perfect winter collection but nothing to wear in the summer.

Next, if you want to be trendy, visit the expensive designer shops or specialty sections in department stores. You can see what's in style, then go to the budget departments or discount stores to find imitations. You may decide to forget about trendiness and go for a classic look.

Choose a basic color — black is one of the easiest and classiest for all seasons — and build your wardrobe on it.

Here are the clothes you need that, when color-coordinated, will combine for over a hundred outfits:

- One suit in a basic color.

- One blazer that matches your skirts, blouses and dress.

- Three skirts (a gray skirt and two black skirts, one short and one long).

- Three sweaters.

- Three to five quality blouses (good summer colors are white, red and blue; for winter you might try gray, red or burgundy).

- One dress. If you don't need to be dressy too often, buy a basic black dress that can be dressed up or down with scarves, jewelry and, possibly, a beautiful jacket.

- Two pairs of slacks.

- Two pairs of shoes (black leather pumps are versatile).

- One quality handbag.

- One pair of boots.

- One expensive coat. Many people will only see the coat and not what's underneath. A raincoat with a zip-in lining that will fit over suit jackets will do for all seasons.

○ Other clothes that aren't essential to your wardrobe but are nice to have are an unconstructed jacket and a sweater jacket that will go with most of your skirts, slacks and dresses.

○ For play clothes, you may want to look in the men's department. The fleecy knit shorts, sweat pants and shirts you can find there in plain gray, navy, black and white will be better quality and less expensive than what you can find in the women's department.

REFERENCE
Heloise's Beauty Book, Avon Books, New York, 1985.

How to be fashionable *and* comfortable: Putting the squeeze on tight shirt collars

What with necks thickening and shirts shrinking, too many men are choking themselves at work these days — literally.

If you unbutton your shirt collar and loosen your tie the minute you step out of the office, you are probably wearing your shirt too tight. Don't feel silly — 70 percent of working men do.

But being uncomfortable should be the least of your worries. A tight collar squeezes the carotid artery, causing blurred vision and a feeling of dizziness. In the long run, your eyes could be permanently damaged.

You can easily solve this problem by making sure your shirts fit. Don't figure out your neck size by putting a tape measure around your neck as so many salesmen do. Instead, get out your most comfortable shirt, spread the collar out flat, and measure from the center of the collar button to the far end of the buttonhole. Then add a half neck size to allow for shrinkage.

To ensure that your shirt collar is stylish as well as comfortable, take note that the "in" collar today is more pointed, longer and narrower than the wider collar of the 1980s. The shirt collar should form an upside-down V, with about one-half inch of shirt material showing above the collar of the jacket.

Choose a shirt collar that looks best with your face. Big men should wear large collars, while men with short necks should wear a collar that lies flat. If you have a thin, long face, look for a medium to wide collar.

REFERENCE
Forbes, Nov. 9, 1992.

Ties you should never wear

With ties these days, almost anything goes. But there are still some ties that should never be worn:

- ○ "Storybook" or "big picture" ties.

- ○ Ties that show signs of poor dyeing — harsh colors, washed-out patterns or patterns that run into each other.

- ○ Ties that are too short. They should reach your belt buckle.

- ○ Black ties, except for funerals.

- ○ Bright purple ties, or any pattern that is hard to look at.

REFERENCE
Dress for Success by John T. Molloy, Warner Books Inc., New York, 1988.

Looks that say 'I don't mean business'

Want to be taken seriously as a woman? Then you've got to look like a professional, and that means not looking like you're dressed for Easter Sunday or a night on the town when you come to work.

Women's work clothes don't have to be boring, but you should stick with dark, uncluttered, quality clothes with simple lines and classic accessories. Have your own style, but don't stray too far from what the women above you in the company hierarchy wear.

Some clothes and accessories should never be worn to work:

- ○ Jangling bracelets or other jewelry.

- ○ A scarf tied in such a complex knot that it needs constant adjusting.

○ A blouse with such a high or low neckline that you're constantly pulling at it.

○ A shirt that slips to show bra or slip straps.

○ Skirts or slacks that reveal panty outlines.

○ Any clothes not in good condition: loose or missing buttons, ripped hemlines, spots, scuffed shoes, run-down heels.

○ Strapless pumps that go clackety-clack.

○ Spiky heels that get hung in grates and rugs.

○ Pantyhose with runs or reinforced toes that show through open-toed shoes.

○ Bare legs or bare feet in sandals.

○ Ridiculously long fingernails.

○ Slit or wraparound skirts that show too much leg when you walk or sit.

REFERENCE ——————————————————————————————
Heloise's Beauty Book, Avon Books, New York, 1985.

Slimming clothes for the overweight man

Is there anything a man can do with his limited workplace wardrobe to make himself look thinner? Well, we've come up with a few clothing tips for the overweight man:

○ Avoid large patterns and light colors. Instead, choose dark solids.

○ Long jackets are much more slimming than short jackets.

○ Wear single-breasted jackets rather than double-breasted. Single-breasted jackets slim the figure much more than their more formal counterparts.

○ Pants that fit properly and are tailored to fit are slimming. Have the waistline of your pants let out rather than squeezing into a size too small.

REFERENCE ——————————————————————————————
Letitia Baldridge's Complete Guide to a Great Social Life by Letitia Baldridge, Rawson Associates, New York, 1987.

Dressing thin in women's wear

Women are lucky because they can do more to hide a few extra pounds than men can. Women, even company presidents, just have more flexibility. Some tips for the overweight woman:

○ Wear longer jackets with dresses. Avoid the waist-length suit jacket.

○ Choose dark or neutral colors rather than pastels.

○ Choose prints with vertical lines. Vertical lines make the eyes go up and down rather than around. Stay away from polka dots, geometric or checkerboard plaids.

○ Create vertical lines with your accessories. Wear long strands of beads or pearls and long, colorful scarves against dark or neutral dresses.

○ Wear narrow belts that blend in with the rest of your outfit rather than tight, colorful belts or wrap-and-tie belts. You don't want to cut yourself in half or draw attention to bulky parts. If your weight is in your tummy, try straight-line dresses without a belt.

○ Wear matching tops and bottoms for longer, slimmer lines.

○ Wear medium-length hemlines — not too long or too short.

○ If your problem is a too-large bust, don't wear clinging fabrics or fitted garments to work. The more a dress hugs your waist, the bigger your bust will look. Stick with jackets that hang straight down without pinching in at the waist.

○ Stay away from bulky fabrics like thick wool or mohair and from flimsy, see-through fabrics. Don't choose clothes with big puffy sleeves or huge ruffles and bows.

○ Buy quality garments that fit. Clothes shouldn't show stress at the seams. You'll stand a better chance at buying clothes in the right proportions if you'll shop in stores for large women.

REFERENCE

Heloise's Beauty Book, Avon Books, New York, 1985.

Being cool in a short-sleeved shirt

Good news for men who want to stay cool and be "cool": Short-sleeved dress shirts aren't the fashion faux pas they once were. In other words, you're not necessarily a nerd if you wear one. But make sure your shirt is loose with longer sleeves that brush the elbow rather than sticking out like a wing. And still avoid them for formal occasions.

REFERENCE

The Wall Street Journal, June 11, 1992.

Going native

What should you wear when you're doing business in a foreign country? The best advice is: Dress like the American businessperson you are, but have a sense of the prevailing local tastes. While imitation is flattering in most circumstances, it's silly for you to go native.

By the same token, however, a woman in a tailored business suit is going to look severe in India. A colorful dress is just as professional and better suited to the land of saris.

As a general rule, men should wear a conservative suit and tie and women a dress or suit with skirt for business, for dining out and for visiting people in their home. Denim and jogging shoes are great for sightseeing, but for sightseeing only.

If in other lands you make at least an effort to follow your hosts' lead or observe what other guests are doing, your instincts should guide you through the maze of unfamiliar customs.

Here are a few specifics:

○ Shoes are forbidden in Muslim mosques, Buddhist temples and Japanese homes and restaurants.

○ If your host in India or in Indonesia removes his shoes, you should do the same.

○ Wherever you take your shoes off, place them together facing the door by which you entered.

○ In most Arab countries, even in your hotel, women should dress modestly — no shorts, mini-skirts, sleeveless blouses or low neck-lines. Suffice it to say, a bikini, even at the pool, will shock your hosts.

REFERENCE ────────────────────────────────

Do's and Taboos Around the World edited by Roger E. Axtell, compiled by the Parker Pen Company, produced by The Benjamin Company Inc., Elmsford, N.Y., 1985.

Looking younger when you're feeling old

A hard day's work or a poor night's sleep can make looking in the mirror downright scary. Some days you look ten years older than you normally do.

Here are eight age-busters that will keep you looking, and feeling, your best:

○ Try some egg on your face. An egg-yolk or yogurt mask can moisturize your skin and help you shed a dry, flaky surface. Whip the yolk of one large egg. Apply it to your face and throat and leave on for five or ten minutes. Rinse off with warm water and cotton pads. Now apply a moisturizer to keep your skin smooth and soft.

○ Imitate young looks with makeup. When faces are exposed to sun, skin color will eventually become blotchy and uneven. To even out your skin color, use a tinted moisturizer followed by a lightweight foundation. The foundation should be only slightly darker than your skin color. Use a moisturizer with sunscreen to prevent further dark spots. Use a blusher on cheeks and temples to get the color of youth. Make sure your blush looks natural — brush a nonfrosted shade from the apple of your cheeks to your hairline. If you can see the edges, blend them in with a cotton pad.

○ Give your face a lift by the eyebrows. Well-groomed eyebrows that sweep up and out at the corners can make your face look younger. Use an eyebrow brush or a toothbrush to brush the hairs up. Then, if Mother Nature made your eyebrows sparse, fill in with a makeup pencil in your natural color — neutral, soft brown or blonde. If your hairs would rather point down than up, brush them with a clear mascara to hold them in place.

○ Get rid of dark circles and puffy eyes — sure signs of hard work and sleepless nights. If morning puffiness is your problem, try sleeping on your back or putting several pillows under your head so fluid won't pool in your face. Cut back on the liquids you drink at bedtime and watch out for salt in your diet. Splashing your face with cold water will reduce puffiness, and so will placing wet, lukewarm tea bags on your eyes. The best solution for dark circles is concealer patted gently around your eyes. Make sure you pat upwards toward your eye and in toward your nose so you won't help your wrinkles along.

○ Moisturize and outline those weather-aged lips. Apply a light lotion around your lips and a sunscreen to your lips to prevent weathering. Use a neutral-colored lip pencil to outline your lip line. It should be harder than lipstick so it won't bleed.

○ Get rid of stress with a quick relaxer:

— Blot your face and eyes with a cool, wet paper towel.

— Relax your shoulders, tilt your head back and lower your jaw as far as you can, then allow your jaw to raise naturally.

— Stand up and reach for your toes. Dangle your arms and totally relax your body for a few minutes.

— Add a quart or two of milk to a lukewarm bath and soak your skin for 20 minutes.

○ Keep sunscreen on your hands. Hands can be one of the first signs of age. Keep a moisturizer with an SPF (sun protection factor) of at least 15 at your desk and apply it several times a day.

○ Stand up straight and smile. A good posture and a smile that draws your face upwards are the best natural anti-aging ploys there are.

REFERENCE ⸻
Prevention, January 1993.

Economic personal hygiene

You have to bathe. You have to brush your teeth. You even have to blow your nose. You do not, however, have to pay a lot to do so.

Personal tastes and preferences play a large role in picking your personal hygiene items. For instance, you may like scented soaps even though they cost more than other brands. You may buy the more expensive, specially packaged items because they're cute and handy.

Hand and bath soaps are essentially equal when it comes to getting you clean. What you prefer and what you can afford will most likely be your guidelines.

Liquid soaps are usually more expensive than bar soaps. (Of course, if you buy the more expensive, scented brands of bar soap, the difference in cost tends to vanish.)

Shampoos are a lot like soap. There really is no "best" brand. Go with what makes your hair feel good. But there's no reason to spend a lot of money for clean, healthy hair.

Don't believe the ads. If you want to buy an expensive "hair care system," realize that you're doing more for your ego than your hair.

If bad breath is a concern, you don't have to buy brand-name mouthwashes to avoid offending someone. Store brands usually do the same job for less money.

When it comes to toothpaste, go with quality (usually signified with the American Dental Association seal of approval). It will save you money on dental bills down the road.

Taste is an important factor as well. Obviously, don't buy a toothpaste that you can't stand. For your gums' sake, try to find one that isn't abrasive. (However, people with heavily stained teeth might need something with a little scrubbing power.)

Buy toothpaste in tubes, rather than in pumps or squeeze bottles. The fancy packaging might look fun, but it sends the price up.

Facial tissues don't vary a great deal from brand name to brand name. Experiment with various tissues and determine what works best for your needs.

When it comes to toilet paper, you do have to pay more to get your money's worth. Stick with a two-ply tissue. However, you don't need name brands. Often, a good two-ply supermarket brand will be just as good and save you a few cents.

REFERENCE

How to Clean Practically Anything by the editors of *Consumer Reports* with Monte Florman, Consumers Union, Mount Vernon, N.Y., 1986.

Making sense of cosmetic claims

Every industry has its "buzzwords"—those phrases that confuse you, but you're afraid to ask what they mean.

Should you buy one of those "pH Balanced" products? Are you helping the environment by buying something "organic"?

Don't worry! Here's a glossary for the industry jargon.

- ○ "Hypoallergenic." While it sure sounds safe, this is a made-up word. It basically means that the product won't make your face break out in a rash or some other allergic reaction. Think twice before paying more for a "hypoallergenic" product. No manufacturer wants its product associated with skin rash, hypoallergenic or not. Generally, a product isn't put on the market unless the chance of a reaction is less than 1 in 10,000.

- ○ "Organic." Again, there's no set definition for an "organic" product. "Organic" means the product came from the earth, so it's supposed to be cleaner and purer. But it's hard to pin down proof of this. Also, keep in mind that those "organic" ingredients have to be loaded with preservatives to keep them from spoiling.

○ "Dermatologist Tested." It's a nice boast, but the dermatologists probably can't dig any deeper than the 1 in 10,000 standard all products have.

○ "Nourishing." Most often used with hair and fingernail products, the ads using this word usually forget to remind you that hair and nails are simply dead cells. Nail polish strengthens nails with plastics and polymers. These will overwhelm any conditioner. Ditto for hair products. Conditioners boasting vitamins are overwhelmed by the soap in the shampoo.

○ "pH Balanced." Cosmetic manufacturers constantly underestimate the human body. Here, they try to fool the consumers into believing that adding to or reducing the acidity or alkalinity of their skin is a horrible thing. Nope. Soap is an alkaline and strips the skin of oils. No problem, though. Your body adjusts and replenishes the acid. Don't waste your money.

○ "Natural Cell Renewal." You probably know this term better as "scrubbing." These products remove the upper layer of skin, remove oils and improve circulation. A good washcloth will do the job just as well.

REFERENCE —————————————————————————————
Secrets From the Underground Shopper by Sue Goldstein, Taylor Publishing Co., Dallas, Texas, 1986.

Making sense of moisturizers

As the Baby Boomers get older, one product you're going to see more and more of is the cosmetic moisturizer. How do you know which moisturizer you should use?

The trick to keeping your skin smooth is to keep it, well, moist — with water. Oils then lock that water in.

Listen to the ads and you'll think that the last thing you ever want on your face is oil. Instead, they suggest trying "emollients" (oil), "collagen" or "lanolin" (wood wax or oil). In fact, most products promising to be "oil free" have some oil-based product in them.

Your best bet is to keep your environment humid. Avoid hot showers, which sap moisture. Pat water on your face. Then, lock in the moisture with, of all things, petroleum jelly, such as Vaseline. Sounds kind of crazy, perhaps, but it's all your skin needs.

If you can't bring yourself to do that, remember that the oil-water combination is equal in all moisturizers. So when you're at the store, don't pay three or four dollars more just for a recognizable name.

REFERENCE ───────────────────────────────────

Secrets From the Underground Shopper by Sue Goldstein, Taylor Publishing Co., Dallas, Texas, 1986.

Better looking skin the natural way

With a little forethought, you can save yourself a bundle of money in cosmetics down the road. Skin care doesn't have to be packaged. And it certainly doesn't have to cost a bundle. Care for your skin on a day-to-day basis and you'll be able to pass by moisturizers and wrinkle creams without a second glance.

○ Quit smoking. Besides doing your lungs a favor, you'll be replenishing oxygen to your skin that nicotine robs. You'll also lower hormone levels which make existing skin problems worse.

○ Drink less. Alcohol can break blood capillaries in your face, giving you a rugged appearance.

○ Eat better. Good nutrition and good skin go hand in hand. Avoid junk food, caffeine, sugar and salt whenever possible. Spicy foods also break blood capillaries.

○ Avoid tanning salons. Ultraviolet rays wrinkle skin at an amazing rate.

○ Chill out! Learn to deal with stress. Staying up all night worrying about some problem or another is no way to improve your complexion.

○ Got a pimple? Try an ice-pack, followed by a cream that lists the ingredient "sulfur resorcinol."

○ Remember, if it makes you feel any better, bad skin is something you can blame your folks for — it's in the genes.

REFERENCE —————————————————————————————

Secrets From the Underground Shopper by Sue Goldstein, Taylor Publishing Co., Dallas, Texas, 1986.

Dry skin relief

Does your skin remind you more of an alligator's hide than it does of smooth, supple baby's skin? About 80 percent of people over age 60 suffer from dry skin, and 50 percent of all women over age 40 suffer from dry facial skin.

Even children experience dry skin from time to time. Fortunately, there are some simple remedies that should help smooth out your skin:

○ Try to avoid rubbing or scratching your skin — this only makes it worse. Instead, try using an over-the-counter, anti-itch medication.

○ Avoid wearing clothes that aggravate your skin, such as wool and other rough fabrics. When you wear clothing made from rough or coarse fabrics, wear a cotton shirt, blouse or other garment under it.

○ Cover your skin with a scarf and gloves when outside in the winter to protect yourself from the chapping effects of the cold wind and chilly air.

○ Drink about six to eight glasses of water each day to keep enough moisture in your body. Try to avoid caffeine and alcoholic drinks — they pull moisture out of your system.

○ Keep the air in your home moist. You can do this by putting a bowl of water on your heater during the winter months or using a humidifier that you can buy at your local pharmacy or retail store.

○ Wear rubber gloves when washing your car, washing dishes or other chores that involve putting your hands in soapy water.

○ Avoid using strong detergent soaps when bathing. These soaps strip away natural oils and moisture in your skin. Try mild, unperfumed soaps instead.

○ Try to avoid bathing or showering too often (more than once a day). This also robs your body of natural moisturizing oils. Don't sit in whirlpools or hot tubs, and avoid saunas and steam baths.

○ Try some oatmeal. Put some colloidal (powdered) oatmeal in your bath water, much like you would put bath oils in the water and soak for a while. You can find colloidal oatmeal at most pharmacies or supermarkets. Just follow the instructions on the label and let the oatmeal do its thing.

○ If possible, avoid putting makeup or other perfumed products on your dry skin.

○ After bathing, do not rub your skin with a towel. Instead, gently blot your skin dry.

○ Try the "soak-grease" method of soothing your dry skin. This might be just the home remedy that your skin needs to get back to normal. Follow the steps below:

1) Soak your dry skin in water for about five to 10 minutes. You can do this in the bathtub or the sink, depending on how much of your body has dry skin. Soaking in water allows your skin to pull in water, much like a sponge.

2) Blot the skin dry gently with a soft towel — remember not to rub the skin with the towel.

3) Apply a thin layer of lotion, oil or petroleum jelly on your skin to keep the moisture from escaping. These things form a kind of shield against the environment and keep water from being pulled back out of your skin.

Some lotions and creams work better than others. The thicker and more oily, the better — but these kinds of creams can stain your clothes. So, if you do this in the morning before work, you might want to use a thin, nonoily lotion. However, before you go to bed, try the soak-grease steps again and use a thicker cream or some petroleum jelly.

If your dry skin does not get better after trying these remedies, call your doctor. Sometimes dry skin is a warning sign of a more serious illness, like diabetes or thyroid problems.

REFERENCE
U.S. Pharmacist Skin Care Supplement, June 1992.

Keeping makeup infection-free

Heed this warning when waving that mascara wand: Eye makeup can be dangerous if not used properly!

Follow these steps to prevent eye infections and even blindness:

○ Throw away eye cosmetics when they are three months old.

○ Wash your hands before applying eye makeup since your hands contain bacteria.

○ Keep the outside of your makeup clean to prevent the inside from contamination.

○ Don't share your mascara. Another person's bacteria may be harmful to you.

○ Don't keep makeup in the car or in any place that gets very hot. The preservatives will deteriorate.

○ Don't use eye makeup when you have an eye infection or when the skin around the eye is inflamed.

REFERENCE
Consumer Survival Kit adapted by John Dorfman from the television series by Maryland Center for Public Broadcasting, 1975.

Removing perspiration stains from work shirts

Don't sweat it!

You don't have to live with those embarrassing antiperspirant or deodorant stains on your work shirts, and you certainly don't have to throw the shirts away.

To help avoid the stains, let your deodorant dry completely before you get dressed.

Never wash your sweaty shirts with laundry detergent and cold water. The aluminum salts in the deodorant combine with the water and detergent and become difficult to wash out. Rinse the sweaty areas in plain water before washing the shirts in warm or hot, sudsy water.

Use diluted ammonia to remove fresh perspiration stains. Rinse out with water.

To remove old stains, apply white vinegar and rinse with water.

REFERENCE

All-New Hints from Heloise: A Household Guide for the '90s, The Putnam Publishing Group, New York, 1989.

Sure cures for stubborn stains

The first rule of thumb for stains is that the sooner you attack them, the more likely you will succeed in removing them.

And the second rule of thumb is this: Always test an inconspicuous corner of the garment or cloth to be sure the remedy doesn't harm it.

○ Ballpoint ink: Spray liberally with hair spray and rub with a clean, dry cloth.

○ Blood: Soak in cool water at once, then wash with detergent. If the fabric is colorfast, hydrogen peroxide (the 3-percent solution found in the medicine cabinet) will "boil" dried blood loose. Or cover stain with a paste of cool water and meat tenderizer; sponge with cool water after allowing to set for 15 to 30 minutes.

○ Fruit stains: Even those as dark as cranberry sauce or blackberry jam yield quickly to boiling water poured through the taut fabric from a foot or so above it.

○ Grass stains: Rub in liquid detergent or naphtha soap, then rinse. A pad soaked in diluted alcohol will also help. Use a weak solution of hydrogen peroxide or household bleach only if safe for the fabric.

○ Grease spots on fabric: Club soda works wonders on double knit. On a rough-surfaced fabric, a liberal sprinkling of corn meal absorbs grease. Leave for several hours, and repeat as needed. The same goes for cornstarch on smooth fabric, and talcum powder on polyester. Remember that shampoo cuts grease, too.

○ Perspiration: Soak garment in warm vinegar water.

○ Red wine: On washable fabric, dunk into cold water and rub before washing as usual in detergent. Remember that red wine may be treated like a fruit stain, if safe for the fabric. Club soda and salt works well on carpet.

○ Rust stains: Apply lemon juice and salt; then let sit in the sun. Several commercial rust removers are available, including Barkeeper's Friend and Zud.

REFERENCES ──────────────────────────

Mary Ellen's Best of Helpful Hints by Mary Ellen Pinkham and Pearl Higginbotham, Warner Books, Inc., New York, 1980.
Reader's Digest Practical Problem Solver, The Reader's Digest Association Inc., Pleasantville, New York, 1991.

Do-it-yourself dry-cleaning

Do you feel as though you're being taken to the cleaners by your dry-cleaner? Do you send sweaters and silks that aren't very dirty just because you've worn them so many times?

A home dry-cleaning solution is on the way. Inventors are busy coming up with products that you can use in your dryer to clean lightly soiled clothes.

One product that's already on the market is Sweater Fresh, made from a sunflower-oil base. The warmth of a dryer sets the plant oils to work on your clothes. Sweater Fresh does remove light soil and odors, but it isn't very effective on heavier soils.

There's more research to be done, but even now home dry-cleaning products can help you cut down the dry-cleaning bill. Be on the lookout for new cleaners sure to appear soon on your grocery-store shelves.

REFERENCE ───────────────────────────────────

The Wall Street Journal, March 8, 1993.

Health secrets

Always sick? Improve your immune system with vitamins

They are not "magic pills" that contain mysterious wonders that can prolong your life.

But they can help prolong your years of illness-free living by cutting your rate of sickness by up to 50 percent.

"They" are vitamins, and scientists have recently discovered that multivitamin-multimineral therapies can improve immune responses in elderly people.

Apparently, more than 40 percent of elderly men and women suffer from some type of vitamin and mineral deficiency. These deficiencies can weaken the immune system and increase the risk of minor and major illnesses.

Only 25 percent of elderly people have immune responses as vigorous and healthy as those of younger people.

A research team from Memorial University of Newfoundland enlisted 96 volunteers (all over the age of 65) to test the effects of vitamin and mineral supplements on immune response.

The group was randomly divided into two small groups. Group one received a daily placebo (fake pill). Group two received a daily supplement that contained several different vitamins and minerals. Each volunteer took the assigned pill once a day for 12 months.

The study had remarkable results.

The volunteers who were taking the placebo experienced no increased "immune components" in their blood. But, the volunteers who took the vitamin-mineral supplements enjoyed an increase in the amounts of these immune components.

Those suffering from vitamin deficiencies at the beginning of the study enjoyed an improvement in their nutritional status if they received the supplement pill.

And, most significantly, those volunteers in the supplement group enjoyed a 50-percent decrease in the number of infection-related illnesses compared to the placebo group.

The researchers stress that the supplements used in the study did not contain huge amounts of vitamins or minerals. Some supplements contain as much as 30 times the RDA. But the amounts of vitamins and minerals in the supplement were close to the recommended daily allowances for each of the nutrients.

Taking large doses of vitamins and minerals can actually impair immune responses. In other words, getting too much of the nutrients can be just as bad as getting too little.

REFERENCE —————————————————————
The Lancet, Nov. 7, 1992.

Why most diets don't work

You want to get rid of that spare tire around your waist, but you have been discouraged with dieting attempts in the past. And now you're hesitant about starting another one.

A large number of people either fail to lose weight or fail to keep it off for a few simple reasons:

○ You set unrealistic goals and get discouraged early on and give up.

○ You use unsafe, crash-diet methods of weight loss that do not involve any kind of long-term maintenance programs. These methods may work in the short term, but you are left with the same old bad habits after you lose weight.

○ You fail to get support from friends and family or from local diet support groups to help encourage you through slow periods of weight loss.

○ You start easing up on your diet habits after losing some weight, and end up putting the weight back on.

REFERENCE —————————————————————
Nutrition Today, July/August 1992.

How to find the
best weight-loss program for you

Weight-loss programs can prove to be enormously successful and life-changing, but you need to consider several things before you enlist.

You will need to decide what will work best for you: a program that meets three days a week or just once a month, a program that meets in the mornings or evenings, an inexpensive program or a costly one, and so on.

One rule-of-thumb to remember is this: Don't judge a weight-loss program based on the "success" stories that they publish or advertise. These success stories don't always reflect the true success of the program as a whole.

Try to get the following information:

○ How many people who enroll in the program actually complete it?

○ How many of the people who enrolled and finished the program lost the amount of weight they wanted to?

○ How many who lost their desired amounts of weight kept them off for one, two and five years after the program?

○ Have many people experienced any kind of emotional, mental or physical problems related to the program?

If the program you are looking at does not have this information available, you might be able to find it in some published studies. Ask your local librarian to help you locate this information. After getting the answers to those first questions, it's time to begin looking into the more specific details of the program. Take time to find out about the following:

○ Does this program require that you buy and use its food, or can you prepare your own meals using food you buy at the grocery store?

○ Does the exercise program require you to use specialized equipment from its program, or can you learn the proper exercises and then do them at home or at your own private health club?

○ How does this program blend together a mix of diet, exercise and behavior modifications? Is there a good mix of all three, or are one or two areas stressed more than the others?

○ Does this program combine counseling with the weight-loss program? If so, is it a group setting or individual counseling? If it is group counseling, will there be open or closed groups? (Open groups allow people to drop out or join randomly. Closed groups start with a small group of people and don't add newcomers, even if some drop out.)

○ If this program does provide counseling, how are the counselors trained? Are they professionals with the appropriate educational degrees, or were they "trained" at a weekend seminar?

○ Does this program offer any type of continuing education — for example, classes on nutrition, preparing healthy meals, exercise safety, etc.? If so, are the teachers properly trained?

○ Does this program stress long-term behavior changes that will help you keep the weight off and live a healthier life, or does it focus on quick weight-loss gimmicks?

○ Do you set your own weight-loss goals, or do program directors help you decide how much weight to lose?

Professional weight-loss programs are certainly not the only way to effectively lose weight and keep it off. However, if a professional weight-loss program is the route you choose to follow, doing your "homework" will help you make the right decision on the best program to suit your needs and improve your chances of creating a new, slimmer you.

REFERENCE ——————————————————————————————
Nutrition Today, July/August 1992.

Exercising without upsetting your stomach

Whether you're a weekend warrior or a serious endurance athlete, gastrointestinal (GI) disturbances can be a real pain in the stomach at just the wrong time.

But if you plan ahead, you can avoid exercise-induced stomach pain and cramping, nausea, gas, diarrhea, heartburn and rectal bleeding.

The reason these digestive problems happen during exercise is that when you exercise vigorously, your body automatically reduces activity in your digestive system.

This is due to our built-in "fight or flight" mechanism that says exercise (being able to run away or fight) is more critical to survival than digestion.

Suppose you've just had a meal, and then you go out for a jog.

Both digestion and exercise require a huge blood flow, but your body simply can't serve two masters at one time.

Your working muscles take priority and most of the blood flow is diverted away from your digestive system.

Dr. Stamford says that gastrointestinal problems can also occur for any or all of these reasons:

○ Working out can disrupt the normal function of hormones and nutrients that aid in the absorption of nutrients.

○ Moving and breathing vigorously can agitate and squeeze the digestive system, forcing food through the intestines too quickly.

○ Taking anti-inflammatories like aspirin and ibuprofen before or during your workout can cause bleeding in your stomach.

○ Sweating and diarrhea can cause dehydration that lowers the amount of blood in your body. You can actually sweat two to eight cups of water an hour if you're working out strenuously on a hot day.

Stomach upsets may persist even after you stop exercising, because it takes your body several hours to readjust after a hard workout.

Postponing your workout for two to three hours after a meal will help solve some of your GI problems. But you don't have to give up the idea of exercising after eating.

A brisk walk not only speeds the passage of food through the GI tract, it also relaxes the mind, and your body digests food better when your mind and body are relaxed.

Ways to avoid stomach problems while exercising:

○ Wait two to three hours after a meal to begin exercising.

○ Choose foods that are high in carbohydrates, not in fat or protein.

○ Liquid meals can help you avoid diarrhea.

○ Avoid gassy foods like broccoli and beans.

○ Drink water or low-sugar sports drinks to avoid dehydration.

○ Reduce the need for nonsteroidal anti-inflammatory drugs, or NSAIDs (aspirin, ibuprofen, etc.) — warm up before you exercise and reduce the intensity of your workout. If you must use NSAIDs, take them after you exercise.

○ If you'll be participating in a particular event, train at the hour of day the event will start to allow your body to get accustomed to exercising at that time.

REFERENCE
The Physician and Sportsmedicine, November 1992.

Exercising for senior citizens

What prevents joint and muscle injury and helps with stress, depression, anxiety, blood pressure, obesity, diabetes, coronary artery disease, cholesterol and constipation?

The answer is simple: regular exercise.

Although we hear lots of talk about staying healthy these days, the truth is that less than two out of 10 older adults are taking advantage of this marvelous natural health aid.

If you once believed that the risks of vigorous exercise outweighed the benefits for seniors, that's not the case anymore. Doctors are now saying that if you don't use it, you lose it.

In other words, acting like a couch potato can lead to glucose intolerance, lower resistance to infection, heart trouble and deterioration of your bones, among other problems.

On the plus side, doctors now believe that exercise helps older people stay active and independent longer and can even prevent cancer. And don't worry that you might not be able to get fit again.

No matter what your age is, older bodies seem to adapt to exercise in the same way that younger bodies do, according to the report.

But before you join a bench-aerobics class, ask your doctor's advice about a program that's right for you.

Heart trouble, breathing problems like emphysema or chronic bronchitis, uncontrolled diabetes, seizures or arthritis prevent some people from starting or maintaining an exercise program. Certain medicines can also affect your ability to exercise.

When you do get the OK from your doctor, design your exercise program with these three goals in mind:

○ Flexibility — Be sure you learn to stretch properly. Since men tend to be less flexible than women, stretching is especially important for them.

○ Increased strength — This helps you avoid joint and muscle injury and prevents bone thinning (osteoporosis), a serious problem for many women.

○ Cardiovascular endurance — This should be your most important goal. You can reach this goal by swimming, walking, rowing, biking, water aerobics and other activities.

Whatever exercises you choose, you'll find it's easier to stick with your program if you enjoy the activities and find an exercise group or a setting that you like.

A word of caution: Stop exercising and call your doctor if you experience any of these symptoms:

---

chest pain

shortness of breath

pain in neck or jaw

faintness or dizziness

excessive fatigue

nausea or vomiting

heart racing

extreme muscle or joint pain

REFERENCE

Geriatrics, Aug. 8, 1992.

Is your heart rate on target?

Exercise specialists love to come up with new ways to measure the effectiveness of your exercise program. Here's one way to see if your heart is working hard enough:

○ Subtract your age from 220 — that gives you your maximum heart rate.

○ Multiply by 70 to 80 percent — that should be your target heart rate if you are under 50. People over 50 should go for 60 or 70 percent.

○ So, a 45-year-old might aim for a rate of 123 to 140 beats per minute while exercising, while a 60-year-old should be striving toward a rate of 96 to 120 beats.

○ Once you reach your target and work at that rate for a while, you'll find your heart rate decreasing as it adapts to the exercise. When that happens, increase your output of effort — but don't be surprised if it becomes difficult to increase your rate. Your heart is doing more work at the same number of beats.

REFERENCES
Walking for the Health of it by Jeannie Ralston, an AARP Book, Scott, Foresman and Company, Glenview, Ill., 1986.
Fitness Walking by Robert Sweetgall, Putnam Publishing Group, New York, 1985.

Exercise and breast-feeding

If your newborn bundle of joy could speak in complete sentences that you could understand, she might come out with a heart-felt groan something like this: "Oh no — she's putting on her running shoes — well, there goes dinner."

Why such a groan? Because your breast milk tastes sour after you exercise.

Dr. Janet Wallace from Indiana University noticed that nursing mothers often complained that their infants refused to nurse or fussed while nursing after the mothers had exercised. So Dr. Wallace conducted a study to find out if the breast milk was different after exercise.

The study involved 26 volunteer mothers and their 2- to 6-month-old babies. The mothers each volunteered some pre-exercise breast milk to use in the study. Then, they all exercised vigorously on treadmills, and immediately afterwards they expressed some more breast milk.

The researchers put the pre-exercise and post-exercise milk samples in separate coded bottles so that the mothers would not know which was which. The babies were offered both bottles, and the researchers and mothers rated the babies' responses to the milk samples.

Results: The babies preferred the pre-exercise milk samples over the post-exercise milk samples.

Why? The after-exercise milk tasted sour, researchers believe. The sour taste comes from excess lactic acid produced during exercise.

Lactic acid is a natural by-product of vigorous or extended exercise. And while you exercise, your body uses sugars and carbohydrates as energy sources. Lactic acid is produced as your body breaks down the sugars and carbohydrates for energy while you are exercising.

The more you exercise, the more energy you need from sugars and carbohydrates. And the more energy you use, the higher the level of lactic acid in your blood.

Shortly after exercise, your body breaks down the lactic acid, and the level of lactic acid in the blood returns to the pre-exercise level. However, immediately after exercise, the levels of lactic acid in the blood are high, and it spills over into the breast milk.

Fortunately, the lactic acid is not harmful to your baby. But it does make the milk taste sour. And the level of lactic acid in the milk usually stays high for about 90 minutes — which means sour-tasting milk for at least an hour and a half after exercising.

So should I stop exercising? you ask. The answer is, no. For your health's sake, keep exercising regularly.

To avoid a baby that fusses or refuses to nurse after exercising, try nursing your baby before you exercise or try expressing your milk before exercising and saving it for a feeding after your workout.

REFERENCE ——————————————————————

Pediatrics, June 6, 1992.

Make the most of your hours in bed

Nothing's worse than waking up in the morning tired and cranky. Especially when you went to bed early the night before just so you'd feel better.

You can cut the amount of time you spend in bed by two hours and feel less sleepy during the day if you improve the quality of your sleep time.

- Follow your own sleep rhythms. If you don't get sleepy until 2 a.m., you may benefit more by getting four quality hours of sleep than by forcing yourself to go to bed at 11 p.m.

- Resist the Saturday and Sunday morning sleep-in. You throw off your body's clock when you wake up later than usual on the weekend.

- Eat balanced meals on a regular schedule and have a light snack before bedtime. The snack should be high in carbohydrates: a glass of milk, cereal or a light sandwich.

- Exercise regularly, but don't exercise vigorously late in the evening. Your body will be stimulated instead of relaxed. Mild stretching can be relaxing at bedtime.

- If you smoke or chew tobacco, stop well before bedtime. Nicotine is a stimulant.

- Don't rely on an alcoholic "nightcap" to help you get to sleep. You won't sleep deeply, and you'll wake up often.

- Caffeine from coffee, tea or cola affects you for at least six hours, so watch what you drink in the evening. Caffeine makes your sleep restless as well as keeping you from falling asleep.

- Your bedroom should be dark, quiet and comfortable with no drafts or fans blowing on you.

- Follow a regular routine each night. If you brush your teeth, wash your face, set the alarm and turn off the lights every night, the routine will be a signal to your body that it's time to go to sleep.

- Read a boring or difficult book to help you fall asleep. Think about pleasant things that are happening in your life, but don't get excited over them.

○ If you lie in bed unable to sleep for twenty minutes, get out of bed and go into another room. Do something that relaxes you.

How you sleep determines whether your body will be able to erase the strain and stress it suffers during your workday. Your sleeping posture can either help your body relax or it can make your body fatigue worse.

○ Sleep on your back or side. Sleeping on your stomach night after night can cause back strain. It also forces you to keep your neck twisted.

○ Make sure your pillow is neither too thick nor too thin. Your neck should be level with the bed. When sleeping on your back, use a thin pillow and curl it slightly under your neck. You can buy a specially designed pillow that helps keep your neck and shoulders level.

○ Don't sleep for long periods on your back with your arms above your head, or on your side with your arms under your head or neck. This will strain your shoulders and upper arms and can cause numbness and tingling in your arms and hands.

○ When you sleep on your side, your legs should be on top of each other with your knees bent. If you have bony knees, place a thin pillow between them. You may place the top knee slightly behind the other one. When you throw your top leg across the bed, you twist your spine, straining your lower back.

Sleep should be an enjoyable time. If you can't get comfortable in these "proper" positions, you may have a back or joint problem that you should discuss with your doctor.

REFERENCE ——————————————————————
Sitting on the Job by Scott W. Donkin, Houghton Mifflin Co., Boston, 1989.

Easing office pains and job strains

Back strain, eye strain, neck pain, fatigue and headaches — a typical day at the office involves at least one of these problems for most people. It's hard to believe that just sitting around causes more aches and pains than hard labor. The solution is sometimes a trip to the doctor, but you can do a lot yourself.

Eye strain: When you've been concentrating on small print or small objects for a long period of time, frequently look away to an object in the distance. Look at the other end of the room or out the window.

Roll your eyes around, too. Look to the extreme right and left, up and down, diagonally upward and downward. Exercising the eye muscles instead of constantly holding them in one position reduces eye fatigue.

Close your eyes occasionally for thirty to sixty seconds and lightly place your hands over your eyes.

Avoid computer screen glare: Make sure you can tilt your computer screen to reduce glare. Position the screen so that it is not in direct sunlight.

If possible, use indirect lighting — a desk lamp or lamp on a flexible arm. The brightness of the screen and the surrounding area should be about the same so your eyes won't have to keep adjusting. Remove any bright objects directly opposite the screen that are creating a distracting reflection. Consider installing an anti-glare filter.

Back and neck pain: Your chair should support the curves of your body. Your lower back curves forward, so your chair back should, too. If you have a straight-backed chair, a special pillow can help support your back. The seat of your chair shouldn't dig into your hamstrings, and your feet should be planted on the floor or on a footrest.

Don't slump or sit with your back twisted.

Take small breaks to shrug your shoulders and roll them in circular motions. Turn your head slowly from side to side and tilt your head slowly from one shoulder to another.

Push back into your chair's back support to stretch. Straighten your legs and move your ankles and feet.

Do the cat stretch — stand up at your work station and place your hands on your work surface at about shoulder width. Arch your back like a cat, looking at the floor, then push your back downward, looking at the ceiling.

Occasionally take a deep breath or two — breathe in slowly through your nose and slowly out through your mouth. This helps relax the rib cage and upper body.

The best way to avoid fatigue is to exercise vigorously three to four times per week. If your company provides exercise facilities, take advantage of them during lunch. Concentrate on the abdominal, buttock, and front and inner thigh muscles to counteract the effects of sitting all day.

REFERENCE ———————————————————————————————————————
   Sitting on the Job by Scott W. Donkin, Houghton Mifflin Co, Boston, 1989.

Back pain hot lines

The Texas Back Institute based in Austin offers two free services for people who suffer from back pain.

The Back Pain Hot Line, 1-800-247-BACK. Registered nurses answer questions for individuals from Monday through Friday, 9 a.m. to 6 p.m. Eastern Standard Time.

The MoneyBack program, 1-800-233-0589. Professionals provide verbal, printed and on-site counsel for businesses and employees to try to eliminate high-risk back-injury settings.

The professionals give information and advice such as:

> - Provide adjustable chairs, so hips and knees line up and feet stay flat on the floor.
> - Place a small rolled-up towel at the small of the back while sitting.
> - Adjust computer screens to eye level.
> - Provide headsets for frequent telephone users.
> - Avoid sitting too long.
> - Don't be a weekend warrior.

REFERENCE ———————————————————————————————————————
   Inc., October 1992.

How to cut out computer-screen cancer

Worried about the hazardous emissions from your computer screen? Or have you philosophically decided not to worry since there isn't a thing you can do about having to sit in front of your computer every day?

Scientists have given us no definite answer about whether computer radiation is really hazardous to our health. They do know, however, that video display terminals give off low-frequency electromagnetic fields, which have been linked to cancer, brain tumors, leukemia and miscarriages.

If you decide it's better to be safe than sorry, here are four ways to cut down your exposure to computer-screen radiation:

○ Sit at least an arm's length from the front of your screen and sit at least twice that distance from the back or sides of someone else's terminal.

○ Buy a simple, fairly inexpensive product to reduce emissions. Metal strips that fit inside the monitor at the back or metal bands that can be placed around the outside of the monitor are available. The cheapest emission-blockers are grounded mesh or glass screens that you can attach to the front of your monitor.

○ Buy a low-emission monitor. Most computer manufacturers now sell low-emission monitors that only cost about $100 more than the average monitor.

○ If you plan on buying a personal computer and you don't need sophisticated graphics, consider purchasing a laptop with a liquid-crystal display screen. These screens give off very little radiation.

REFERENCE ————————————————————————
Business Week, Nov. 30, 1992.

When your phone could give you a brain tumor

Remember when microwaves were new, and everyone was afraid of getting cancer from the radiation? The microwave-oven industry immediately started designing ovens that don't leak radiation.

Now there are other sources of radiation to worry about: power lines, electric blankets, video display terminals and — the latest — hand-held cellular phones.

The cellular phone controversy is a little different because cellular phones work at a much higher frequency than power lines and electric blankets. Very little research and no conclusive studies have been done on these higher frequency levels.

Also, at least one scientific study seems to show a link between tumor growth and cellular frequencies. Stephen F. Cleary of the Medical College of Virginia used tumor cells that had been removed from the brain and showed that cellular frequencies stimulated the growth of those cells.

More research needs to be done on the danger of cellular phones, but, for now, you might want to limit your use of the hand-held variety with the antenna that goes alongside your head. Make sure the antenna doesn't touch your head while you are using the phone.

If you have a cordless home phone, don't worry. Their signals are 100 times lower-powered than the cellular phone signals, so no one is questioning their safety.

REFERENCE ———————————————————————————
Business Week, Feb. 8, 1993.

How to swallow medicine painlessly

Do you dread the thought of taking medicine or vitamin supplements? Has swallowing pills become more and more difficult as you've gotten older?

You're not alone. Many people, both young and old, have trouble swallowing pills of any size.

Below are six simple ways of swallowing pills that might make taking medicine a little less threatening:

○ Take a sip of water (or other liquid) and drop the pill in your mouth. Then hold your head back as if you were going to gargle. The water and the pill will fall toward the back of your throat, and you can swallow the pill easily with the water.

○ Place the pill in a spoonful of soft food such as applesauce, ice cream, jello or yogurt. When you swallow the food, the pill goes with it.

○ To make the pill a little more "slippery," cover it with a thin layer of butter or margarine to help you swallow it.

○ If the tablet is large, break it in half. The smaller halves will be easier to swallow. Just remember to take both halves.

○ Ask your pharmacist if the pill comes in liquid form.

○ Ask your pharmacist if grinding the pill to a powder will affect the potency of the drug (some pills are "time-released" and grinding them up will interfere with the activity of the pill). If the pharmacist says that grinding the pill is okay, place the pill in a zip-lock bag and crush it. Then put the powder in a teaspoon. You can wash it down with some water, or you can mix it with a teaspoon of soft food (applesauce, etc.) to help swallow it.

REFERENCE
American Family Physician, January 1993.

Home remedies for hiccups

Your grandmother may have told you that if you drink a glass of water without stopping for air that it would stop your hiccups.

If that didn't work, she may have moved on to one of the other popular home remedies such as holding your breath; blowing into a paper bag; swallowing several times while holding your nose; or maybe swallowing a spoonful of dry, granulated sugar. Were these effective treatments for hiccups or merely old wives' tales?

Excluding hiccups caused by underlying medical problems, you probably get hiccups most often after eating too fast, experiencing sudden changes in temperature, emotional stress, drinking alcohol or some other irritation to the nerves that control the diaphragm.

When you hiccup, your diaphragm contracts involuntarily. As you inhale, the space between the vocal cords at the upper part of the larynx closes quickly, thus making the hiccup sound and also interfering with the flow of air.

Researchers report that raising carbon dioxide pressure helps reduce hiccup frequency. This may explain why holding your breath and other techniques designed to interrupt your respiratory rhythm are effective.

Other home remedies, such as swallowing a spoonful of dry, granulated sugar, begin to make sense also when considering the report of researchers who were able to inhibit hiccups by using a catheter to stimulate the pharynx.

The pharynx is the part of the digestive tract that extends from the nasal passages to the larynx and becomes part of the esophagus.

Home remedies such as sipping ice water, swallowing granulated sugar, and various other manipulations of the diaphragm could have the same inhibiting effect on hiccups as the frictional movement of the catheter within the pharynx.

If you tickle your baby's tummy or otherwise cause him to hold his breath for a few seconds, you may be employing the same treatment a doctor might use to cure an occasional case of the hiccups.

However, as with any persistent symptom, see your doctor if hiccups persist for more than a day or two.

Other at-home remedies to get rid of those pesky hiccups:

○ Hold your breath for as long as you can, and swallow each time you feel the urge to hiccup. Try this a few times, and the hiccups should go away.

○ Try the old paper-bag remedy. Breathe for about a minute into a paper bag gathered tightly to your lips. The buildup of carbon dioxide might shut down the hiccups. Don't try this for more than a minute at most.

○ Chug-a-lug a glass of water quickly.

○ Eat some dry bread.

○ Swallow some crushed ice.

○ Tickle the top of your mouth with a cotton swab.

REFERENCE ─────────────────────────────

British Medical Journal, Nov. 21, 1992.

What your dizziness may mean

"I'm so dizzy; my head is spinning." If you have the same sensations Tommy Roe sang about in 1969, you may be worried that something besides falling in love is making you dizzy.

Although some eight million of us visit doctors for dizziness each year, it might be comforting to know that most of the time it doesn't signal a serious disorder.

One study found that dizziness in middle-aged and elderly people is commonly caused by ear infections or psychological disorders.

The balance mechanism of the inner ear is a factor in about half of all dizziness complaints. A disruption in this balance mechanism causes feelings of spinning or moving.

Usually these spells of dizziness, also called vertigo, last less than a minute. The most common type of vertigo occurs after a change in head position. Simply rolling over in bed can sometimes cause dizziness.

Vertigo can be almost completely cured with specific exercises designed for this complaint. Rehabilitation therapists can show you how they are done. Walking can help improve loss of balance caused by vertigo.

Other conditions that can affect the balance mechanisms of the inner ear and cause dizziness include shingles of the ear and Meniere's disease.

Shingles of the ear is characterized by a rash inside the ear canal, severe vertigo and, occasionally, facial weakness. Rest is the best treatment. Prescribed medicines may be helpful in some severe cases.

Meniere's disease is characterized by dizziness, periods of hearing loss, ringing in the ears and a feeling of fullness in the ears. The dizziness can persist for several hours up to several days, and the hearing loss usually worsens. In addition to medical treatment, a low-salt diet may help.

Dizziness may accompany a migraine headache. It may also occur if you get up too fast.

If your doctor can find no physical cause of dizziness, it may be related to depression, anxiety or panic.

Psychological problems are the primary cause of dizziness in 16 percent of people who complain of dizziness and a contributory cause in 40 percent of people complaining of dizziness.

This type of dizziness may be accompanied by feelings of sadness or hopelessness, memory loss, sleep and appetite changes and suicidal thoughts. Counseling or short-term medication can help.

Often dizziness has more than one cause. It is usually brief, disappearing quite often in two weeks or less. It rarely signals a life-threatening disease. However, you should consult your doctor if you have prolonged or recurrent dizziness.

REFERENCES ————————————————————————

Annals of Internal Medicine, Dec. 1, 1992.

Medical Tribune, Dec. 24, 1992.

'Dyeing' risks — hair color turns lethal?

Color your hair? Then this shocking news might make your hair stand on end — women who use hair coloring products have a 50-percent greater risk of developing non-Hodgkin's lymphoma (cancer of the lymph tissues) than people who don't color their hair.

According to the National Cancer Institute, animal studies have shown that hair coloring products are known to contain various carcinogenic (cancer-causing) and mutagenic (causing permanent cell damage) chemicals.

Researchers have found that women who use permanent hair dyes have an increased risk of developing the disease compared with women who have never used hair coloring products. Women using semi-permanent or non-permanent products don't have as great a risk as those using permanent hair dyes. The risk for non-Hodgkin's lymphoma increased 70 percent in women who used permanent hair dyes, and 40 percent in women who used semi- or nonpermanent hair coloring products.

Among women who used permanent dyes, risks were slightly higher with darker colors such as black, brown, brunette and red hair dyes compared with those who used lighter color hair dyes. Blonde colors weren't linked with the risk of lymphoma at all.

Study results showed that women who had used the dyes for at least 11 years had double the risk of developing non-Hodgkin's lymphomas compared with women who had never used them.

Multiple myeloma (bone marrow cancer) and Hodgkin's disease (malignant tumor of the lymph glands) were also linked to the use of hair coloring products, but fewer people with those diseases have been studied.

Researchers at the National Cancer Institute also interviewed men about their use of hair coloring products and their exposure to pesticides, tobacco and other chemicals.

Results of the study showed that the risk of developing multiple myeloma was almost doubled in men who colored their hair compared with those who did not. The risk was greater for men who colored their hair at least once a month for a year or more.

Coal-tar-based hair dyes make up the majority of hair dyes on the market, according to the Federal Drug Administration (FDA). Past studies have shown that coal-tar-based hair dyes contain cancer-causing chemicals.

Both the Federal Drug Administration and the National Cancer Institute believe further studies need to be performed and do not recommend that you stop using hair dyes.

However, Dr. Bailey of the FDA advises you to be on the lookout for this caution statement (which usually indicates that the hair-coloring product is a coal-tar dye):

"This product contains ingredients which may cause skin irritation in certain individuals. A preliminary test according to accompanying directions should first be made. This product should not be used for dyeing the eyelashes or eyebrows. To do so might cause blindness."

REFERENCES
American Journal of Public Health, July 1992.
Journal of the National Cancer Institute, Aug. 5, 1992.
American Journal of Public Health, Jan. 18, 1993.
Medical Tribune, July 23, 1992.

Can you be allergic to cold weather?

Most people who brave frigid weather to exercise don't need to worry about being allergic to the cold.

But occasionally, an athlete will come home from a run or a cold-water swim with more than the pleasant glow that comes from an aerobic workout.

One running enthusiast returned from a cold and windy run of 35 minutes. During his cool down, the runner started to itch all over, and then developed hives. He also felt slightly dizzy and anxious.

Although he didn't know it, this runner was experiencing a form of physical allergy called cold urticaria. Fortunately, a warm shower took care of the problem, and the itching went away.

Exercise in combination with certain foods can also cause the same itchy reaction, and so can heat and emotions.

Usually, cold urticaria occurs just in areas that are exposed to the cold, such as the head and neck. It is generally not dangerous and does improve with time.

However, cold urticaria can cause more serious and even life-threatening reactions in some people.

The most extreme reactions are angioedema and anaphylaxis. Angioedema means swelling around the lips and eyes that can spread to the neck and obstruct breathing. Anaphylaxis is a reaction that can lead to shock because it dilates the blood vessels so that blood pressure drops dangerously low.

Doctors test for cold urticaria by using, guess what? An ice cube held against the skin for up to 10 minutes. If you get hives under the ice cube, you're prone to develop cold urticaria.

To avoid the itch of cold urticaria:

- Avoid being out in the cold for extended periods of time.

- If you desire to exercise in the cold, take an antihistamine before exercising.

- Those who have severe reactions to cold should exercise with a buddy who knows how and when to give them an epinephrine shot in case of anaphylaxis or angioedema.

REFERENCE
The Physician and Sportsmedicine, December 1992.

How to fight the urge to scratch

Have an itch that won't quit? The causes of itching are numerous: Kidney failure, thyroid problems, HIV, iron deficiency, infections, fungi and even parasites are possible reasons for constant itching. Although you might need to consult your physician to discover the origin of an itch, these remedies can help you fight the urge to scratch:

○   Cool, moist washcloth placed on the area that itches.

○   Pressure applied with the palm of your hand.

○   Moisturizer applied to your skin.

○   Bath oils applied directly to your skin.

○   Antihistamines.

If symptoms persist, talk to your doctor about causes of your itching and treatments for relief.

REFERENCE ────────────────────────────────
Postgraduate Medicine, Nov. 15, 1992.

Cold, hay fever or sinus infection? How to tell them apart

Suffering from sneezing, sniffling, coughing? You could have hay fever, a cold or a sinus infection. The symptoms often overlap, sometimes making diagnosis difficult even for the family doctor.

Researchers have found five consistently reliable indicators of infected sinuses. The last two will only be evident to a doctor.

○   Ache in the upper jaws.

○   Creamy yellow or greenish colored discharge from the nose.

○   Condition is not improved by taking antihistamines or decongestants.

○   Pus and mucus are found in nose or sinus cavities.

○   Abnormal transillumination. This means that the light from the flashlight the doctor uses to examine the nose will not pass through the cartilage that divides the nose into two passages.

Other possible symptoms are listed below. These are generally not as reliable as the ones previously mentioned.

- Nasal speech
- Difficulty sleeping
- Sinus tenderness
- Sore throat
- Loss of sense of smell
- Sneezing
- Aching muscles
- General ill feeling
- Cough
- Headache
- Recent upper respiratory infection
- Facial pain

If you suspect that you have a sinus infection, see your doctor immediately. A confirmed sinus infection should be quickly treated with antibiotics.

If left untreated, it can lead to serious disorders, such as bacterial meningitis, which can cause brain damage and death.

Your best bet is to avoid sinus infections completely. Here's how:

- If you have allergies or a cold, sleep with your head elevated. This will help keep the infected mucus from draining back into your sinuses and infecting them.

- Avoid tobacco smoke.

- You may also want to take decongestants. They will decrease the amount of mucus produced, making it less likely that mucus will drain into your sinuses and cause an infection. Caution: Do not take decongestants for long periods of time or if you have high blood pressure, heart disease, irregular heartbeat or glaucoma.

REFERENCES ———————————————————————

Annals of Internal Medicine, Nov. 1, 1992.
Drug Topics, Sept. 7, 1992.

Asthma sufferers should plan for a rainy day

If it's raining outside — you might want to stay inside to avoid having an asthma attack.

Asthma sufferers learn early on to stay away from things that can trigger an asthma attack such as smoke, dust, heavy perfumes or other irritants. And many people say that their asthma tends to get worse after a heavy rainstorm. What does the weather have to do with an asthma attack?

Pollen granules are known lung irritants. And when dry, these granules are sometimes too large to get down deep into the lungs. But when it rains, water causes these particles to swell and burst. The rupture of the pollen then releases starch granules into the air. These starch granules are small enough to be inhaled deep into the lungs and cause the airways to narrow which triggers bouts of wheezing.

If you suffer from allergies and asthma, you should try to stay indoors as much as possible the day after a rainstorm (when pollen usually ruptures) and use your air conditioners and air filters. You should also avoid venturing out into the woods, fields, parks and other areas where pollen is most likely to be a problem.

REFERENCE
The Lancet, March 7, 1992.

Treating insect stings

If you and your family spend any time in the great outdoors, you are bound to have a run-in with a bee, a yellow jacket or another pesky, little insect. But there are some simple ways to take care of bee stings so you can get on with your family fun.

Although the wasp and hornet can cause their fair share of pain, the stings from the honeybee and the yellow jacket usually cause the most problems. The sting is usually followed by intense pain or stinging for a few minutes. Then the area around the sting usually begins to turn red and may start to swell. If you are not allergic to bee stings, the sting will usually go away in a few days with only an occasional itch.

The honeybee is the only bee that leaves its stinger and sack of poison in your skin. When you get stung by a honeybee, you need to get the stinger out as soon as you can.

Do not try to pull the stinger out with your fingers or tweezers, and try not to squeeze the area around the stinger — this will force more poison (venom) out of the venom sac and cause more trouble.

To remove the stinger, gently scrape it with a knife blade or your clean fingernail until the stinger comes out. Then clean your hands and the sting with soap and water.

After removing the stinger, put some ice or a cold compress on the sting for about 20 to 30 minutes. This will help reduce pain and swelling.

Mix together some baking soda and meat tenderizer and a few drops of water to make a paste to put on the sting. The meat tenderizer contains an ingredient called papain that can make the bee venom ineffective and relieve some of the symptoms.

If you got stung on your leg or foot, keep it elevated and still for a little while.

People who are allergic to bee stings might start to experience wheezing, dizziness and cramps, or in serious cases, choking, unconsciousness and even death. These people should receive emergency medical treatment.

If you have ever experienced mild symptoms like dizziness, shortness of breath, difficulty breathing or cramps after a sting, but didn't go to the doctor because the symptoms went away, you need to tell your doctor about it.

In some cases, a person who experiences a mild allergic reaction to a bee sting on one occasion may experience a serious allergic reaction the next time he comes into contact with a bee. Next time, your symptoms might be much worse —even deadly.

To avoid symptoms of a bee sting, try to avoid getting stung in the first place. Here are some simple precautions:

○ Stay away from insect nests. If you need to remove one from an area close to your house, use a bug spray that has a six-foot or nine-foot sprayer. If you are allergic to bees, call an exterminator to get rid of any bee nests or hives.

○ Don't wear bright-colored, flowery clothes — the bee could mistake you for a flower and be attracted to you. Avoid wearing dark, rough clothes. Light-colored, smooth fabrics are the best things to wear to avoid being stung. Also, don't wear brightly colored jewelry, hair ribbons, shiny jewelry or other shiny metal objects that might attract the bees.

○ Wear insect repellent when you go outside. Put the repellent on your clothes and on any exposed skin.

○ Keep your garbage cans covered to avoid attracting bees. Also, keep screens on your windows and doors to keep the bees outside.

○ Always wear shoes outside. Many bees gather food from clover and other flowers that are close to the ground, and some bees even live in the ground. Going barefoot makes your feet a prime target.

○ Use caution when cutting or smelling fresh flowers. And carry some bug spray out to the garden in case you run into some angry bees that don't want to leave you alone.

REFERENCES ───────────────────────────────
Emergency Medicine, May 15, 1992.
The Physician and Sportsmedicine, May 1992.

Smoking could put your eyes 'on the blink'

You can now add cataracts to the list of reasons why you should give up smoking.

People who smoke cigarettes are twice as likely to develop cataracts as people who have never smoked. Cataracts, which cloud the normally clear lens of the eye, are the world's leading cause of blindness.

Studies have yet to pinpoint how smoking causes cataract formation. However, one possibility is that cigarette smoking may reduce blood levels of nutrients that are responsible for maintaining the transparency of the lens.

Researchers don't know exactly what causes changes in the chemical composition of the eye that results in the formation of cataracts. Known cataract-risk factors include:

- Aging
- Diabetes
- Nutrition
- Exposure to sunlight
- Smoking
- Heredity
- Eye injury

Cataracts develop slowly and without pain, redness or tearing in the eyes. You may first discover a problem when you have trouble passing a vision test to obtain your driver's license.

Symptoms include fuzzy, blurred or double vision; frequent changes in eyeglass prescriptions; a feeling of having film over your eyes; changes in color of pupil; and problems finding the right amount of light for reading. If you have any of these symptoms, talk to your doctor immediately.

People who quit smoking can reduce their risk of developing cataracts. So don't lose sight of what smoking does to your health. In this case, a quitter is a winner!

REFERENCE ───────────────────────
The Journal of the American Medical Association, Aug. 26, 1992.

Are you giving yourself an ulcer?

It started out as just mild discomfort after you ate your meals. But, lately you've noticed that the former dull aching has turned into a sharp, knife-like pain after meals. Sometimes it even strikes in the middle of the night.

You might be suffering from peptic ulcer disease. Peptic ulcer disease occurs when you develop ulcers (small, open sores) on the lining of your stomach or intestines. This can happen because something damages the lining of the digestive system or because the stomach acid has "eaten away" part of the lining. Some of the most common causes of ulcers in the digestive tract lining are things that you can avoid.

The use of nonsteroidal anti-inflammatory drugs (NSAIDs) is one of the most frequent risk factors. Aspirin, ibuprofen and naproxen are some of the more well-known NSAIDs. These substances disturb the sensitive lining in the stomach and intestines, and using them frequently increases your risk of ulcer by about 50 percent.

Another common cause of peptic ulcer is an infection by the bacteria *H. pylori*. Scientists report that *H. pylori* is present in up to 95 percent of people with intestinal ulcers and in 75 percent of the people with stomach ulcers. Getting rid of the bacteria usually gets rid of the ulcer.

Diet is the third major culprit behind peptic ulcer disease. Caffeine, alcohol, tobacco and spicy foods can irritate the stomach and intestinal lining which might cause bleeding and the development of ulcers. And, surprisingly, milk can also lead to ulcers.

Although milk is bland and would seem to soothe the digestive tract, the calcium in the milk actually increases the amount of acid in the stomach. The increased acid level could cause ulcers.

One final risk factor for peptic ulcer disease is stress. Stress could cause higher levels of acid to be produced in the digestive tract, and it can also lead to high-risk behaviors like drinking alcohol and smoking.

Stop smoking, stop drinking alcohol and cut down on NSAID use to help your ulcer heal and help protect you from getting another one.

Then, ask your pharmacist for a good antacid that you can buy over-the-counter. An antacid will lower the amount of acid in your digestive tract. This will create a better environment for the ulcer to heal. In many cases, the ulcer will heal within six to eight weeks. If, however, the ulcer does not seem to be getting any better, you should see your doctor. If the ulcer is caused by the bacteria *H. pylori*, you will need an antibiotic to get rid of it.

REFERENCE ————————————————————
American Family Physician, July 1992.

The best antacids

For every 100 people with heartburn, 84 of them take antacids. These chemical combinations work by neutralizing the acid parts of gastric juices (primarily hydrochloric acid) that are attacking the sensitive lining of the esophagus. Here are some tips concerning antacids:

  ○ Most effective nonprescription antacids: Liquid forms containing aluminum (Maalox), magnesium (milk of magnesia) or calcium (Tums). Antacids containing alginic acid seem to work best in preventing heartburn.

○ If you use tablets, chew them thoroughly before swallowing, and drink some water with them.

○ Avoid taking calcium antacids for more than a few days for two reasons: They might cause acid rebound, in which your stomach is stimulated to produce even more acids, or they can lead to formation of kidney stones.

○ Don't take sodium bicarbonate (baking soda). It releases carbon dioxide, which can cause bloating and can increase the amount of acid sloshing back into your esophagus. Carbon dioxide is what causes the bubbles in the fizzy antacids.

○ Take the antacid every four to six hours as directed to help stop acid buildup.

○ Start with the lowest dose suggested on the label and increase only as needed, according to the directions.

○ Watch out for interactions with other medicines: tetracyclines, quinolones, digitalis and iron-containing preparations. If you have to take both antacids and these other drugs, separate the doses by at least one hour, but preferably two.

○ Unless you have gas along with your heartburn, avoid antacids containing simethicone.

REFERENCE ————————————————————————————————
U.S. Pharmacist, October 1992.

How to keep breathing while you sleep

If your spouse falls asleep while you're talking to him, it's not necessarily because you're boring him or because he didn't get his eight hours of sleep last night. His daytime sleepiness might be part of a larger, potentially dangerous health problem.

The Greeks called it "apnea" or want of breath. Sleep apnea is a sleeping disorder that can place stress on your heart and possibly increase the risk of stroke and heart attack. People with sleep apnea actually stop breathing for 10 to 20 second intervals throughout the night. After each breathless pause, the sleeper gasps for air, then repeats the cycle.

Although snoring and snorting during sleep are common symptoms of sleep apnea, not all snorers suffer from apnea. While one in 10 adults snores, only one in 10 snorers has sleep apnea.

Additional symptoms of apnea include:

○ daytime sleepiness

○ headache, irritability, forgetfulness upon awakening

○ loss of interest in sex

○ depression

Sleep apnea is extremely dangerous for your health because it puts "stop and go" stress on your blood vessels and heart every night. And drivers with sleep apnea are up to five times more likely to fall asleep at the wheel. Most researchers agree that any or all of these factors can play a role in sleep apnea:

○ obesity (20 percent above ideal weight)

○ sleeping on your back

○ hypothyroidism (deficient activity of the thyroid gland)

○ jaw abnormalities

○ longer than normal tongue or soft palate

○ drinking alcohol or taking tranquilizers

○ antihistamines (Try not to take them at night if you think you are prone to sleep apnea.)

If you have sleep apnea, any of these influences can temporarily cut off air flow through your breathing passages while you sleep. And when you've stopped breathing, you won't inhale again until the amount of oxygen in your blood gets so low that your brain gets a signal to jump start your breathing again.

REFERENCES
British Medical Journal, June 16, 1990.
FDA Consumer, June 1992.
Emergency Medicine, April 30, 1992.

The best dental floss

The best kind of dental floss is dental floss that is used.

In a five-week study, investigators found no significant differences between waxed, nylon floss made by Johnson and Johnson and Glide expanded polytetrafluoroethylene floss (PTFE) made by W.L. Gore. Both were equally effective in removing plaque and reducing gum swelling and bleeding.

The only difference that the investigators found was that almost 75 percent of the 57 people participating in the study preferred the PTFE floss — mostly because it didn't fray during flossing.

REFERENCE
Clinical Preventive Dentistry, May 1992.

Getting the most out of your eyedrops

Close your eyes for a full two minutes after you put in the eyedrops to help increase the action of the eyedrop medication and resist the urge to blink.

If you blink, the medication is washed away with the film of tears that automatically develops when you administer eyedrops. The medication is not properly absorbed by the eye, so you really don't get the intended effect.

Keeping the eye closed gives the medication enough time to be absorbed before it's washed away. This also helps cut down on side effects from eye medications, the report claims. Since the fluid from the eye drains into the nose and throat, any medication that isn't absorbed into the eye tissue is flushed away into the nose or throat. This often results in the circulation of that medication throughout the body and possible side effects.

REFERENCE
American Family Physician, January 1991.

Tips to help prevent bone loss

○ Be sure you get the recommended daily allowance of calcium. The RDA for calcium in females ages 11 to 24 is 1,200 milligrams, 800 milligrams for women ages 25 and over, and 1,200 milligrams for pregnant women.

○ Milk, cheese, yogurt and other dairy products are great sources of calcium. However, they are also sources of fat. So try to use the low-fat versions.

○ Wheat bread is a good source of calcium. Although it does not contain a large amount of calcium, the calcium in wheat bread is easily absorbed and used in the body.

○ Yeast helps increase the availability of calcium in the body. Eating breads with yeast ensures that the calcium present in the bread will be easily digested and utilized in the body.

○ Several different types of beans (such as soybeans, navy beans, pinto beans and red beans) are good sources of calcium. However, the availability of the calcium in soybeans is almost as good as that in milk.

○ Green, leafy vegetables are good, natural sources of calcium. Broccoli, kale and collards are good examples.

○ If you take vitamin supplements, talk to your doctor or pharmacist about how much to take and what kind to take. Never take more than is recommended on the package.

○ Begin exercising regularly to increase your bone mass. Try to do smooth, nonjarring exercises such as walking, bicycling, swimming and low-impact aerobics instead of high-stress, high-impact sports such as basketball, long-distance running and high-impact aerobics.

○ If you are past the age of menopause, you cannot increase your bone mass, but you can slow or prevent the rate of bone loss. Take the recommended daily allowance of calcium and exercise regularly.

REFERENCES

The Journal of the American Medical Association, Nov. 4, 1992.
The Atlanta Journal/Constitution, Oct. 16, 1992.

How to read medical mumbo-jumbo

Have you ever looked at your medical records at your doctor's office or at the medical chart hanging on your bed at the hospital? If you haven't, you should. You should be an informed consumer when it comes to medical care.

If you have tried to read your medical records, you may have found the technical jargon impossible to decipher. The abbreviations alone make medical talk sound like a different language.

Here's a guide to a few of the more common abbreviations you might find on charts, records, forms or prescriptions:

a	—	before
aa	—	of each
a.c.	—	before meals
ad	—	to, up to
ad lib	—	as needed
agit	—	shake, stir
A.M.A.	—	against medical advice
b.i.d.	—	twice a day
BM	—	bowel movement
Bx	—	biopsy
CA	—	cancer
CBC	—	complete blood count
CC	—	chief complaint
Cl. time	—	clotting time
cont rem	—	continue the medicine
CSF	—	cerebrospinal fluid
d	—	give
dd in d	—	from day to day
dec	—	pour off
dur dolor	—	while pain lasts
Dx	—	diagnosis

emp	—	as directed
FH	—	family history
gravida	—	pregnancies
h.s.	—	at bedtime
I&D	—	incision and drainage
ind	—	daily
m et n	—	morning and night
MI	—	heart attack (myocardial infarction)
mor. dict.	—	in the manner directed
o	—	none
O.L.	—	left eye
p.c.	—	after meals
p.r.n.	—	as needed
q.	—	every
q.o.d.	—	every other day
ROM	—	range of motion
SOS	—	can repeat in emergency
ss	—	half
stat	—	right away, immediately
TPR	—	temperature, pulse and respiration
ung	—	ointment
WBC	—	while blood cell count

REFERENCE

Take This Book to the Hospital With You by Charles B. Inlander and Ed Weiner, The People's Medical Society, Pantheon Books, 1991.

The food you eat

America's top food myths

Can you separate the wheat from the chaff in the deluge of nutrition advice we get every day? A lot of nutrition "facts" have been around forever. So they must be true, right? Not necessarily.

Here are some of America's top food myths:

○ **Fresh vegetables are more nutritious than frozen.**

Actually, frozen vegetables are more likely than fresh to hang on to their vitamins by the time they reach your plate. Vegetables begin to lose their vitamins as soon as they are picked, but frozen and canned vegetables are usually processed close to the field with a quick heat treatment to halt decay. (The vitamins in canned vegetables tend to leach into the liquid, so don't drain that liquid off.)

Vegetables that are destined to be processed are often allowed to get more ripe than fresh vegetables, and this increases their vitamin content, too.

○ **Baked goods with 'no tropical oils' are healthier.**

Baked goods without fatty tropical oils contain substitutes that are just as bad for your blood cholesterol level. A product that says "made from 100 percent vegetable oil" is providing false reassurance.

○ **Chicken is a better choice than beef or pork.**

Farmers are breeding lean animals these days, and some cuts of beef and pork are just as low in fat as chicken. In fact, roasted pork tenderloin has a third of the calories of skinless, roasted chicken.

○ **Rinsing fruits and vegetables removes pesticides.**

No such luck. You might remove some dirt, but it would take a scrubbing with soapy water to remove pesticides farmers use and the fungicides in the wax many grocery stores apply. Best advice: Don't worry about it.

○ **Shellfish is bad for your heart.**

Shellfish is loaded with cholesterol, but it is extremely low in saturated fat. Saturated fat is worse for you than cholesterol.

○ **Salty foods raise blood pressure.**

Four out of every five people can eat as much salt as they want without increasing their blood pressure. Of course, it's hard to know if you are that one person in five who is salt sensitive.

○ **Margarine is less fattening than butter.**

The truth is, a tablespoon of both margarine and butter has 100 calories. (Butter does have a lot of highly saturated fat, which probably raises your cholesterol slightly more than the "trans fatty acids" found in margarine. Margarine does have some "good fat" — the "polyunsaturated fatty acids." These help to balance out the bad "trans fatty acids." Soft margarines have fewer "trans fatty acids" than the hard stick margarines.)

○ **Vitamin pills energize you.**

Only carbohydrates, fats, protein and alcohol give you energy.

○ **Sugar is bad for you.**

Starchy foods and dried fruits stick to your teeth and cause them to decay more than sugar does. Fatty foods make you gain more weight than sugary foods since fat has more calories than sugar. And in spite of parents' complaints, sugar doesn't make your kids hyper.

REFERENCE ——
Health, October 1992.

Hard-boiled facts you might rather not know

Ever wonder why every slice of hard-boiled egg you get on an airplane or in a cafeteria looks eggsactly the same? You probably aren't getting a slice from a single egg, but from a very long "egg roll." Food processors create a long roll of cooked yolks and encase it with a long ring of cooked whites. The egg slices look perfect with the yolk in the very center.

REFERENCE
Great American Food Almanac, Harper & Row, Publishers, New York, 1986.

Don't eat those green potatoes!

Peel your potatoes if they have been bruised, cut or exposed to sunlight, and particularly if they have a greenish tinge.

Potato skins contain natural toxins that repel predators, and bruised or green potatoes contain enough to cause headaches, nausea and diarrhea. The potato peels are also covered with a mildly toxic chemical used by growers to keep spuds from sprouting while in storage.

Most of the nutrients are inside anyway, in spite of what Mother always said.

REFERENCE
Health, October 1992.

Natural remedies to ease your aches and pains

They have been around for hundreds of years, but researchers have only recently begun to rediscover their value. Herbs — they can provide relief for many common ailments, and you can grow many of them in your own backyard.

Below is a list of some of the more well-known herbs that many researchers think might become popular remedies.

Horseradish is usually thought of as a sauce or spice, but herb specialists claim that it is useful in helping your digestion. This member of the mustard family can also be used as a pain-relieving remedy for neck and back pain. Or, you can use a mixture of grated horseradish, honey and water as a way to ease hoarseness.

Rosemary is a member of the mint family, and the oil from this herb can be rubbed on the skin to help ease the pain of arthritis, bruises, cuts, sores and skin problems like eczema.

Catnip is Mother Nature's version of Alka Seltzer. It helps soothe and relieve upset stomachs, headaches and baby colic. Catnip tea causes the body to sweat, so it can be used to help reduce fever. This herb with the heart-shaped leaves also helps bring relief from the coughing and congestion of the common cold, and it's also used as a sleeping aid.

Peppermint is known far and wide for its minty smell, but few people know of its ability to relieve indigestion, upset stomach, colic, flatulence and even menstrual cramping. Rubbing oil from peppermint herbs on the skin can help soothe aching muscles and joints, and a cup of warm peppermint tea will help clear your sinuses.

Garlic is also a well-known herb that many chefs refuse to cook without. Keep up the good work, chefs — garlic seems to be helpful in lowering high blood pressure, lowering blood cholesterol levels and helping to unclog arteries that are coated with atherosclerotic plaques. Garlic can also be applied directly onto the skin to get relief from insect stings.

Chamomile is one of the oldest known herbs with an age-old ability to relieve inflammation of the skin. Applying the ground-up leaves directly to the inflamed area helps reduce swelling and tenderness. Tea made from the oil of the chamomile plant is helpful in treating digestion problems, colic and menstrual cramps. You can even add the oil to your bath water if you want a natural relaxer, or you can use chamomile oil as a natural insect repellent.

Comfrey is another herb that can be used to reduce inflammation, especially around cuts and sores, insect bites, burns, bruises, sprains and skin problems. Grinding the leaves in a blender makes an ointment that you can rub directly on the skin to help reduce pain and swelling.

Sage is a member of the mint family that is unbeatable for relief of sore throats, mouth and gum problems, cuts and sores, bruises and skin problems. Sage tea is even used to bring relief for nervousness or irritability — its relaxant effects can help you settle down after a long day at work.

Many amateur gardeners have been enjoying the benefits of herbs for years. Fortunately, doctors and researchers are beginning to rediscover the medicinal value of herbs, and we soon may see a return to more natural ways of dealing with common, everyday ailments.

REFERENCE ————————————————————
Alive, January 1991.

Garlic may do more than spice up your life ... it could prolong it.

If you are like most Americans, you probably have some garlic on hand to spice up anything from chicken to potato salad.

This potent herb does more than spice up your favorite dishes. Eating garlic appears to slow down or inhibit the growth of cancerous tumors and slow down the first stages of skin cancer.

And good news for people with cancer already: Garlic seems to reduce the toxicity of certain cancer-therapy drugs without interfering with the drugs' effectiveness. It tends to lessen damage to organs and tissues from toxic chemotherapy drugs and radiation treatments.

Researchers conducting animal studies at the American Health Foundation in Valhalla, New York, found that garlic helps prevent almost 80 percent of tumors from colon cancer and reduces the risk of lung cancer.

Garlic (Allium sativum) is a member of the allium family. Onions, scallions, chives, leeks and shallots are also members of this group.

Onions have garlic's healing and preventative characteristics, too. Studies show both onions and garlic help prevent blood clots and may also lower cholesterol.

Another advantage: Eating lots of garlic has been known to ward off mosquitoes and other pesky bugs.

While it is probably not feasible to eat a pound of garlic and onions each week and still maintain a social life, include as many members of the allium family in your diet as possible.

You may want to talk with your doctor about taking garlic tablets as a supplement to your daily diet. Many tablets are odorless and have no aftertaste.

REFERENCES ———————————————————————————————————————
Nutrition and Cancer, 1992.
Medical Tribune, Sept. 24, 1992.

Snacking during labor

Probably the last thing you want to do while you're in labor is eat, right? But that's just what a new study suggests you do — if you want to shorten the time you're in labor, that is.

Although many doctors still advise women in labor to drink clear liquids and not to eat, a new study may change that advice.

Angela Flanagan, a midwife at Jubilee Hospital in Belfast, Ireland, conducted a study of 90 women in labor at the hospital. Half the women followed the traditional recommendation of fasting (going without food), and the other half were allowed to eat until they went into the advanced stages of labor.

The women who were allowed to choose from foods such as ice cream, scrambled eggs and toast with jelly not only reduced labor time by one-and-a-half hours, but they also required fewer labor-inducing drugs and painkillers than those who fasted.

Dr. Kieran Fitzpatrick, who participated in the study, said that the infants born to the "snacking" mothers also had stronger heartbeats and better muscle tone than those born to the fasting mothers.

One possible reason for the increased heartbeats of the babies could be that the babies were less sleepy because mothers used fewer painkillers during labor.

Of course, any woman who is a candidate for surgery requiring general anesthesia, such as a Caesarean section, should not eat while in labor. But, where there are no complications, a little snack may strengthen both mother and child.

REFERENCES ———————————————————————————————————————
Medical Tribune, Sept. 24, 1992.
Medical World News, September 1992.

Eating this when
you're pregnant is no fish story!

"There's something fishy about your eating habits," should be the claim of husbands of pregnant women.

But "something fishy" doesn't mean ice cream and pickles.

It means fish.

Eating fish throughout the pregnancy seems to improve the health of the baby.

Women who eat a lot of fish rich in omega-3 oils tend to have fewer premature births, and the babies tend to weigh more at birth. Full-term deliveries and higher birth weights usually indicate stronger, healthier babies.

However, researchers recommend eating fish to increase your omega-3-oil intake instead of taking fish-oil supplements. Apparently, the supplements have the same beneficial effects for the baby, but the mother might suffer negative effects.

One of the actions of fish-oil supplements is to reduce the amount of "sticky" clotting factors in the blood. In nonpregnant women, this can reduce the risk of strokes due to blood clots.

However, the reduction in clotting factors can be dangerous in pregnant women, because the women tend to bleed more during delivery than they should. Too much blood loss during delivery can be dangerous, and even life-threatening.

To avoid side effects, stay away from fish-oil supplements. Instead, eat more fresh fish, and enjoy a long and healthy pregnancy.

REFERENCE
The Lancet, July 11, 1992.

Fiber lowers risk of colon cancer

Fiber — it's what we used to call "roughage."

And, by now, we all know that adding roughage to our diets each day can help keep us healthy.

Numerous studies have shown that eating a high-fat diet can increase your risk of colorectal cancer, but eating a high-fiber diet actually helps lower your risk of cancer.

Researchers say that people get much less of the total amount of fiber than they should every day from vegetables, fruits and grains.

In addition to fiber, researchers found that vitamin C and beta-carotene (gives carrots their orange color) slightly reduced the risk of colon cancer.

Research strongly suggests that increasing your fiber intake to 39 grams a day can reduce your risk of developing colorectal cancer by one-third.

This could mean that as many as 50,000 fewer cases of colon cancer would be diagnosed in the United States every year.

Estimating that the average person takes in about 23 grams of fiber every day, studies showed that it would take a 70-percent increase to reach 39 grams a day.

Fiber is the part of plants that your body can't digest because enzymes in the intestinal tract won't break it down. But, that's what makes it beneficial to you.

Dietary fiber increases stool weight and helps move waste more quickly through the intestines. This helps reduce levels of cancer-causing agents in the intestines and the bacteria that produce cancer-causing agents.

How much fiber should you eat? The National Cancer Institute recommends that you eat five or more servings of a combination of fruits and vegetables, especially green and yellow vegetables and citrus fruits every day.

And increase your intake of starches and complex carbohydrates (beans, peas, lentils, breads, rice and cereals) by eating six or more servings each day.

Complex carbohydrates are an excellent source of energy without adding extra calories. (Carbohydrates have only four calories per gram, whereas fats have nine calories per gram).

An average serving is approximately a half cup for most cooked or fresh vegetables, fruits, dry or cooked cereals and legumes (beans, peas and lentils), or one medium-size piece of fruit, a slice of bread, a roll or muffin.

REFERENCES ———————————————————————————————

Journal of the National Cancer Institute, Dec. 16, 1992.

Medical Tribune, May 7, 1992.

Diet and Health, National Academy Press, Washington, D.C., 1989.

Ways to preserve nutrients in fruits and veggies

- Select produce that is not bruised or damaged.

- Choose dark green, orange and yellow vegetables and fruits — these are high in beta-carotene.

- Pick fresh vegetables and fruits rather than canned.

- Try to shop on the first day your grocery store receives its produce for the freshest selection.

- Place your fruits and vegetables near a window to sun-ripen them.

- Avoid storing produce that has already been cut or sliced — exposure to air can destroy vitamins.

- Rinse your fruits and veggies with water just before you serve them.

- Don't soak your produce — it can remove valuable nutrients.

- Try not to remove the peelings or skins (nutrients are concentrated in the skins).

- Steaming, stir-frying or microwaving foods seems to preserve the most nutrients.

- Be sure not to overcook foods — you can lose vitamins and nutrients.

- Avoid deep-frying foods to save fat and calories.

- Don't cook vegetables with baking soda — it can damage the vitamin contents.

REFERENCE
American Institute for Cancer Research.

Soup it up for your health

Chicken soup will cure what ails you — or so mom says, anyway.

Even though a bowl of mom's soup can warm and comfort you, soup doesn't make a whole meal.

But, when you combine your soup with salad and whole-grain bread, you have a wonderfully comforting meal that's also good for you.

Busy cooks find soups a time-saver, too, because a large pot can carry you through a whole week.

Suppose you don't have time to cook a pot of soup. You can just open a can of prepared soup for the same benefits, right? Not so fast.

You have to read the label first. Some soups are high in sodium — not good for people with high blood pressure and heart disease. Some canned soups even contain sugar or sweeteners, a no-no for diabetics.

You may be better off taking the time to put together your own soup, after all. That way, you control the ingredients. For a healthier homemade soup, try these nutritious tricks:

○ Substitute skim or low-fat milk to cut fat in a cream soup.

○ Substitute herbs for salt.

○ Let your meat stock cool, then skim off the fat.

○ Use a vegetable stock as a basis for your soup.

○ Combine green, orange and yellow vegetables for a soup that contains cancer-fighters like beta-carotene and vitamin A.

○ Add grains to your soup for iron, thiamin, niacin and riboflavin.

○ Get the protein and carbohydrates you need from beans or peas.

○ If you prefer a vegetarian soup, you'll need a side dish to complete your protein requirements.

Grains, nuts or seeds complete a pea or bean soup, and dairy products or eggs add protein to vegetable soups. All of these soups will add fiber to your diet.

Athletes, take note: Soup transports well in a vacuum bottle, and it can replenish needed liquid as well as nutrients.

Soups are also great for jocks because they can be low in fat and easy to digest. Bean and pea soups are so high in fiber that they are harder to digest, so you might want to avoid eating soups containing legumes before you work out.

REFERENCE ————————————————————————
The Physician and Sportsmedicine, December 1992.

Copper deficiency and heart disease

You might not realize you're eating copper when you're sitting at the breakfast table eating your whole-grain cereal, but you'd better hope you're getting an adequate supply of this essential mineral!

Doctors say that too little copper in your diet can contribute to heart disease. But the problem is how much copper is enough, and do women and men have different requirements?

The Estimated Safe and Adequate Daily Dietary Intakes of Selected Vitamins and Minerals says that you can safely take between 1.5 to 3 milligrams of copper each day.

There is no current recommended daily amount of copper.

However, women might need less copper in their daily diets than men. When nutrition experts served the same copper-rich breakfast to men and women of all ages, tests indicated that the women absorbed more copper than the men.

Although men might normally consume more food (and thus more copper), women's bodies actually seem to absorb the copper better.

Researchers found that hormones, such as birth control pills and hormone replacement therapy, made no difference in the way women absorbed copper.

Some natural sources of copper include whole-grain cereal, liver, seafood, legumes (beans, peas and lentils), nuts and seeds.

REFERENCES

Recommended Dietary Allowances, *10th Edition*, National Academy Press, Washington, D.C., 1989.

The American Journal of Clinical Nutrition, November 1992.

Is your food 'intoxicating' you?

You don't drink alcoholic beverages or allow your children to, but you serve chicken baked in a wine sauce without batting an eye.

"The alcohol is burned off," you explain.

Guess again.

People have heard, and believed, that the alcohol in cooking liquors is burned off during the cooking process, but that theory was never scientifically tested.

Until now.

A team of researchers recently prepared six recipes, each recipe calling for some type of cooking liquor, and measured the amount of alcohol that remained in the entrée after the preparation. The results were quite dizzying.

The following recipes were prepared for the test: pot roast Milano, orange chicken burgundy, scalloped oysters, brandy alexander pie, cherries jubilee, and Grand Marnier sauce. The different liquors that were used in the various recipes included burgundy, dry sherry, brandy, creme de cocoa and Grand Marnier.

After each of the recipes were prepared, the researchers measured the amount of alcohol that remained in each sample.

The pot roast Milano still contained 4 to 6 percent of the alcohol that had been used in the recipe. The orange chicken burgundy contained up to 60 percent of the original amount of alcohol used.

The scalloped oysters retained up to 49 percent of the original alcohol amount, and the brandy Alexander pie kept up to 77 percent of the recipe's amount.

The cherries jubilee and the Grand Marnier sauce retained up to 78 and 85 percent of the original amount of alcohol from the recipes.

Researchers were astonished at these results, especially because all but one of the recipes had been "cooked" in some manner.

The pot roast had been simmered at 185 degrees Fahrenheit for two and a half hours.

The oysters had been baked at 375 degrees for 25 minutes, and the cherries jubilee had been flamed for 48 seconds. Yet, in spite of the cooking, a great deal of alcohol had not been "cooked off."

The researchers found that the longer a recipe is cooked, the more alcohol is cooked off; and the larger the surface area of the cooking pan, the more alcohol evaporates during the cooking process.

However, all cooks should be aware that even after cooking a recipe for a long time in a large pan, some alcohol might still be present in the food.

REFERENCE ————————————————————————
Journal of the American Dietetic Association, April 1992.

Grape juice lowers heart disease risk

By now you might have heard results of studies that say alcohol is associated with a reduced risk of coronary heart disease.

But did you know that you can get the same protective benefits from drinking a natural, nonalcoholic beverage?

Studies show heart disease is linked to a diet high in saturated fats. But in France, where a typical meal has an abundance of fatty sauces and creams (saturated fats), they have a relatively low death rate from heart disease. Researchers believe this is due partly to the French's higher consumption of red wine.

But, all-natural, purple, concord grape juice contains the same chemical, resveratrol, which is believed to lower blood cholesterol levels and lower your risk of heart disease.

Wine contains a chemical which is naturally produced in grapes. Levels of resveratrol differ from wine to wine but are usually higher in red wines made from grapes fermented in their skins. (Resveratrol is concentrated in the skins of grapes.)

Purple grape juice actually contains more of the protective chemical than most wines.

White wine and white grape juice contain very little resveratrol. And just eating grapes themselves won't work because the actual fruits contain only slight amounts of the protective chemical.

Researchers plan to study jams, jellies and other grape products to find out how much resveratrol they contain and to see if we can substitute other natural foods for wine in the prevention of heart disease. But for now it's "bottoms up" with grape juice for your heart's sake.

REFERENCE ————————————————
Science News, July 18, 1992.

Pop your eyes at this news:
Spinach can save your eyesight

A big medical study indicates that eating a lot of spinach, broccoli, sweet potatoes and winter squash can shield your eyes from blinding cataracts.

The big boost in eye protection seems to come from the vitamin A and carotene compounds in the vegetables.

The women who participated in the study and took in the most vitamin A — by eating high-A foods, rather than by taking vitamin-A supplements — cut 40 percent off their risk of developing cataracts.

You also get added anti-cataract protection by taking vitamin-C supplements — 250 to 500 milligrams a day — researchers suggest. That's about four to eight times the RDA for vitamin C.

Surprisingly, carrots lose out as cataract preventers, and the better-known carotene — beta-carotene — is not the star of this study. Carrots are among the richest sources of beta-carotene, a nutrient that your body turns into vitamin A as needed. Other carotenes besides the beta variety provide the protection against lens-clouding cataracts. Spinach is naturally high in carotenes known as lutein and zeaxanthin, while carrots are low in these nutrients.

Taking regular multivitamin supplements doesn't seem to help fight cataracts. Foods are your best bet, along with tablets that contain large amounts of vitamin C. Most multivitamins include only enough vitamin C to meet the RDA.

Cataracts cloud the lens, the clear part of your eye. That blocks out light and causes the light that reaches the retina to be unfocused and blurred.

People with diabetes run a big risk for cataracts. Getting older, smoking, getting too much sun, and eye injuries also increase your risk.

Now, some cautions. Don't overdose on vitamin A. This is a so-called fat-soluble vitamin, meaning that it doesn't dissolve well in water. Your body stores excess vitamin A in the liver. Too much of this vitamin can cause liver and bone damage.

The RDA for vitamin A is one milligram for adult males and 800 micrograms for adult women. Many people start feeling the toxic effects of vitamin A at about five to 10 times the RDA.

Although vitamin C is considered to be among the least toxic of all vitamins, megadosing yourself with vitamin C can cause diarrhea and digestive upsets.

REFERENCES ——————————————————————————

British Medical Journal, Aug. 8, 1992.

Recommended Dietary Allowances, 10th Edition, National Academy Press, Washington, D.C., 1989.

Eat high-fiber food to stay regular

○ Fiber is a natural laxative — it can help keep you regular.

○ To up your fiber intake, substitute whole-wheat flour instead of white and whole-wheat or spinach pasta instead of regular, and try brown rice instead of white.

○ Eat vegetables with their skins (the skins contain high levels of fiber).

○ Fruits with seeds such as blackberries, raspberries, strawberries and figs are good sources of fiber. (Avoid fruits with seeds and nuts if you have diverticulosis.)

○ You can eat a wide variety of fruits and vegetables and not use up a bunch of calories for the day.

○ Drink plenty of liquids to help pass foods through your body.

REFERENCES

Diet and Health, National Academy Press, Washington, D.C., 1989.

Nutrition Prescription, Crown Publishers Inc., New York, 1987.

Lowering risk of breast cancer

You don't need to speak Spanish to understand this: A traditional Hispanic diet might help lower the risk of breast cancer.

According to the results of a test recently conducted by the American Health Foundation, Hispanic women have lower rates of breast cancer than Caucasian women. And the researchers believe that the high intake of beans and other low-fat foods in a Hispanic diet could be one of the keys.

The study revealed that Hispanic women typically eat twice as many beans as Caucasian women. The beans seem to contain anti-cancer properties due to their low-fat, high-nutrient makeup. Eating a diet high in beans turns into lower risk of breast cancer.

The study also revealed that the Hispanic women used large amounts of olive oil, which is high in monounsaturated fat (a "good" kind of fat). This also seems to reduce the risk of breast cancer.

Another study conducted by the American Health Foundation found that fruits and vegetables in the diet also reduce the risk of breast cancer in women.

After studying 626 women, the researchers found that the women in the study who did not suffer from breast cancer ate more fruits and vegetables than those women who did suffer from the disease.

Scientists are still conducting tests, but they suggest that a diet high in fruits and vegetables and low in fat "shows promise" for reducing the risk of breast cancer in women.

REFERENCE
Medical Tribune, July 9, 1992.

Diet to prevent impotence

Men! Watching your fat and cholesterol intake now might prevent impotence years down the road.

Researchers in New Zealand discovered that rabbits fed a high-fat, high-cholesterol diet developed impotence from plaque buildup in the arteries of the penis.

The same conditions have been found in men with similar diets. Problems from the buildup of plaque in these arteries can be even worse for those whose arteries are already damaged by smoking and high blood pressure.

Blockages from cholesterol are one of the chief causes of impotence, the report says.

And, changing your diet after you've found out about the problem may not reverse it, doctors say. But you can reduce your chances of ever developing this problem if you start a low-fat, low-cholesterol diet now — before it's too late.

REFERENCE
Medical Tribune, June 25, 1992.

Coffee does not cause heart disease

The final word on coffee and heart disease is that the two are not related.

Drinking coffee does not increase your risk of heart disease, indicates the combined study of 11 major coffee-and-cholesterol studies done in the past 25 years.

Dr. Martin B. Myers of the University of Toronto and his colleagues grouped all of the studies together to determine if drinking coffee every day is a risk factor for heart disease.

Out of a total of 11 studies, eight concluded that there was no relationship, whatsoever, between the consumption of coffee and the development of coronary heart disease.

The researchers concluded that the risk of heart disease was the same for people who drank one cup of coffee each day as it was for people who drank six cups a day — there is no increased risk of coronary heart disease among coffee drinkers.

The question has also been raised, "Does drinking coffee raise cholesterol levels and, therefore, increase your risk of heart disease?"

Coffee has been standing "trial" on the charge that filtered coffee is a health hazard. Some researchers believe that filtered coffee can raise cholesterol levels and increase your risk of heart disease.

A team of researchers at the Johns Hopkins Medical Institute did a study to settle the issue, and their results also turned out to be in favor of coffee.

The investigators recruited 100 volunteers for the study. Each of the volunteers had to be between the ages of 20 and 60 years with no history of diabetes, ulcers, obesity, high cholesterol levels or cardiovascular disease.

The volunteers also were recruited based on their coffee-drinking habits — they had to have a regular "coffee habit" of more than one and less than six cups of coffee a day.

The final results of an eight-week, carefully controlled study showed a slight increase in the amount of blood cholesterol in the volunteers who drank 24 ounces of regular caffeinated coffee each day. None of the volunteers who drank 12 ounces of regular coffee or 24 ounces of decaffeinated coffee experienced a rise in blood cholesterol levels.

The researchers concluded that even though the volunteers in the 24-ounce regular coffee group experienced a slight increase in blood cholesterol, the increase was so small that it shouldn't have any effect on the risk of heart disease.

In other words, now you don't have to hide your face at the coffee shop anymore. You can drink coffee to your heart's content.

REFERENCES
  Archives of Internal Medicine, September 1992.
  The Journal of the American Medical Association, Feb. 12, 1992.

For the coffee gourmet

For the ultimate flavor, grind fresh coffee beans just before brewing. Store unused coffee — whether whole beans or ground — tightly sealed in the freezer to preserve flavor and aroma. Use fresh, cold water when making coffee. If your water is heavily chlorinated, buy bottled water to make a better brew.

Clean your coffee maker regularly by running a vinegar solution through the brewing cycle. Accumulations of oil spoil fresh coffee's flavor.

Serve fresh-made coffee promptly. If necessary, keep warm in a thermal bottle or carafe, or reheat in the microwave. But coffee kept on a hot plate will turn harsh and bitter.

REFERENCE
  1,001 Helpful Tips, Facts & Hints from Consumer Reports by the editors of *Consumer Reports Books* with Monte Florman, Consumers Union, Mount Vernon, N.Y., 1989.

Food tips from the pros

○ Lettuce can be notoriously short-lived in the fridge. Here's how a chef keeps lettuce fresh: Cut out the core, enough to expose the base of the head. Soak the head for about 15 minutes in warm water, then "shock" it in ice water for 15 minutes more. Shake well, wrap in paper towels, and store with core end up in the refrigerator.

○ Plunge a ripe tomato into boiling water for 20 seconds or so, then into ice water to stop the cooking process. The skin should slip off easily. Works for peaches, too.

○ Squeeze almost twice as much juice from a lemon by heating it first in the microwave. Ten to 20 seconds on high should do it.

○ Spin an egg to determine if it has been cooked or is still raw. Spins easily? Hard-boiled. Spins not at all? It's raw.

○ To peel and mince a clove of garlic easily, smash it on the cutting board with the flat side of the knife. The skin will break and snap off. A wet towel placed under the cutting board will keep it from sliding while you mince. And if you soak the garlic overnight in tap water, then work with it still wet, you won't have those pesky skins sticking to your fingers, knives and countertop.

REFERENCES ————————————————————————————————————

Alix Kenagy, chef/owner of Partners Morningside Cafe and Indigo Coastal Grill in Atlanta, as reported in *The Atlanta Journal/Constitution*, March 25, 1993.

Hubert Keller, chef/co-owner of Fleur de Lys in San Francisco, as reported in *The Atlanta Journal/Constitution*, Feb. 25, 1993.

Joyce Goldstein, owner of Square One, and Barbara Tropp, chef/owner of China Moon Cafe, both in San Francisco, as reported in *The Atlanta Journal/Constitution*, Feb. 25, 1993.

Andrew D'Amico, chef at Sign of the Dove in New York City, as reported in *The Atlanta Journal/Constitution*, Feb. 25, 1993.

Security and safer living

20 ways to crimeproof your home

When it comes to making your home crimeproof, you really don't want to learn by experience. Here are some suggestions from law enforcement experts who deal with breaking and enterings every day.

Outside:

- ○ Trim trees and shrubs so that your windows are visible; police and neighbors should be able to see any access to your house.

- ○ Be sure trellises do not provide a burglar easy entry to second-story windows.

- ○ Put in lights at porches and entryways. Motion-sensitive floodlights are the best.

Doors:

- ○ Entry doors should be solid wood, at least 1 3/4 inches thick, or metal.

- ○ Doors and frames should fit snugly, with no more than 1/8-inch gap; special strips may be purchased to cover bigger spaces.

- ○ Glass panels on doors should be covered with a metal grille or a break-resistant plastic panel.

- ○ Avoid construction that places hinges on the outside where they can be unscrewed.

- ○ Fit sliding doors with special locks, or place a broom handle in the track to prevent opening.

Marking your possessions:

- ○ Most police departments have an electric engraving pen available to mark your valuable belongings with a special ID number or your social security number. Ask them about it. Engraving may actually stop a theft because a burglar knows marked goods will be harder to fence. In any case, it will certainly expedite recovery.

Vacation tips:

○ Turn telephone sound down or off so a ringing phone cannot be heard from outside.

○ Pack your car in the garage or behind the house if you can. A car with doors and trunk open, while family members haul bags and camping gear out to it, is an advertisement that you will be gone for a while.

○ Double-check locks on doors and windows; leave shades and curtains in normal positions; use timers to turn lights off and on, preferably in a random pattern.

○ Ask neighbors to pick up your mail and your newspapers.

○ In winter, ask neighbors to walk up your steps, or shovel your walk, to give the house a lived-in appearance.

○ Notify the local police department that you will be away.

Special cautions:

○ If your home contains a lot of valuables or is in an isolated area, consider installing an alarm system.

○ Don't let strangers use your telephone; offer to call for them if you want to be helpful and remain safe.

○ Be suspicious of telephone surveys and repeated wrong numbers. Is a burglar "casing" your home?

○ Have a friend "baby-sit" your home while you attend the funeral of a family member. Your name, after all, appeared in the paper along with the date and time the funeral would take you away from home.

○ If you return home and it appears someone has entered illegally, do not go inside. Call the police from another location.

REFERENCES ———————————————————————————————

How to Crimeproof Your Home published by The U.S. Dept. of Justice and prepared by the Law Enforcement Assistance Administration, 1989.
Safe and Alive by Terry Dobson and Judith Shepherd-Chow, J.P. Tarcher Inc., Los Angeles, 1981.

Surprising burglary facts

The typical burglary takes place on a sunny summer day, not in the dark of night as one might expect. In warm weather, people tend to leave windows open while they are away at work, at the beach or on vacation.

Most burglars are between the ages of 14 and 21 years. They're looking for the fastest, easiest way into your home. One out of four enters his targeted location through unlocked doors or windows. Locking every window and door is the most effective defense against burglars.

When asked what they would do to make their own homes more secure against their colleagues, a group of convicted burglars answered, "Get a dog." Give him the run of the house, if possible.

Police sources felt that the most effective protection is a monitored burglar alarm. Even if you don't install an alarm system, decals indicating that a system is in place are easily available. Burglars say they'd probably not take a chance on their being phony.

And don't flaunt valuables. Keep computers and TV sets away from windows where they can easily be seen by someone "casing" your house from outside.

A burglary takes place in the United States every 10 seconds.

REFERENCES ———————————————————————————————

Consumer Reports, February 1990.
How to Avoid Burglary, Housebreaking and Other Crimes by Ulrich Kaufmann, Crown Publishers Inc., New York, 1967.

The safest locks

The lock probably has not been made that will absolutely keep out the most determined burglar. In Consumers Union tests, even the most rugged-looking locks could be overcome by one or two swift kicks unless reinforcement was added. No locks tested by CU in 1990 could take six blows without yielding.

But since most burglars are looking for the quickest, easiest way in, a well-designed lock is still your best defense against most intruders.

○ The most effective locks are surface-mounted deadbolts or cylinder deadbolts. Rim-mounted locks are easily attached but hard to jimmy.

○ A deadbolt door lock should have a strike plate attached with 3-inch screws.

○ Mortised locks actually weaken the doors they are set in.

○ A metal bar bracketed against the door works well on rear and basement entrances.

○ Padlocks, typically used on sheds, workshops and garages, must be sturdy. The hasp should be bolted, not screwed in place.

○ On windows: Don't rely on the usual thumb-turn lock on windows. Install special key locks, or drill through the sashes and slip an eye bolt 5/16 inches in diameter into the hole.

○ Concerning keys: Never carry identification tags on your keys, and have your locks rekeyed when moving into a new house or condo. Don't hide keys outside — burglars know where to look.

REFERENCES
Consumer Reports, February 1990.
How to Crimeproof Your Home published by The U.S. Department of Justice, prepared by the Law Enforcement Assistance Administration, 1989.

Apartment dweller's self-protection tips

○ Coming home late, don't attract attention to yourself by running; you'll be off-balance in case of attack. Walk near the curb, avoiding shadowy corners. If parked cars provide hiding places along the curb, walk in the middle of the street. Never cut corners, and try to stay in the light.

○ Something suspicious about your own building? Keep walking, and come back only when it seems safe to do so. Still doesn't look right? Go to a telephone and either call someone at home or the police to escort you in.

○ If there is someone in the elevator with whom you'd prefer not to ride alone, find an excuse not to board: Check the mail or go back outside as though you've forgotten something. If you can't avoid getting into the elevator, stand next to the alarm button. In an emergency, keep pushing it even though you hear nothing — you may be activating a device out of your own hearing.

○ Consider ringing your own doorbell from the lobby — some experts feel this gives an intruder an opportunity to escape, thus avoiding possible violence. Never rush into dark rooms without caution; turn on lights and look around before locking the door behind you.

○ To give yourself a warning that someone has been in while you were out, stick a toothpick between door and doorjamb as you leave, then break off the protruding piece. Although it is conceivable an intruder could notice and replace it, he can't do so from the inside, and you will know someone is still there. (Don't use too much force, or it may remain stuck in place, defeating your purpose.)

REFERENCE —————————————————————————————
How to Avoid Burglary, Housebreaking and Other Crimes by Ulrich Kaufmann, Crown Publishers Inc., New York, 1967.

The best smoke detectors and fire extinguishers

Fire is a silent killer. Most fire victims never see, hear or feel the fire. Toxic gases suffocate victims long before fire gets to them. Contrary to what most people believe, they will not be awakened by the smell of smoke, but will die first.

Smoke detectors save lives — but only if they are in place and working. Install several in your home, placing at least one near bedrooms, in hallways, in the kitchen and in the garage. Buy a small portable unit to hang on hotel doors when you travel.

Choose detectors that are powered by house current with a battery backup, or by batteries alone. Use daylight-saving time as a reminder: Check smoke alarms when you reset your clocks.

Put several fire extinguishers in your home in areas where they are most likely to be needed, such as the kitchen, the garage or a workshop. Make sure they are accessible: A fire extinguisher mounted above the clothes dryer won't be much help if you can't get near enough to reach it.

Although fire extinguishers are available in styles specific to certain materials (A-type for ordinary combustibles, B for flammable liquids, C for electric equipment), don't trust yourself to have the presence of mind in an emergency to remember in which category a grease fire belongs.

The little extra you'll pay for extinguishers with combined ABC ratings may be the best fire insurance buy you can make. Check fire extinguishers periodically to be sure they are holding pressure.

REFERENCE ———————————————————————————
Home Sense by Mike McClintock, Charles Scribner's Sons, New York, 1986.

When you should get out
of bed lying down: basic fire escape techniques

Plan at least two fire escape routes from every room in the house, and practice using them regularly. A second floor escape plan might require the use of a portable safety ladder. Make sure everyone in your household is clear on basic fire escape techniques:

- Stay low from the moment you wake up — sitting up in bed could be deadly.

- Crawl to safety.

- Never open a closed door without feeling it first for heat.

- Never go back into a burning room or building.

- Meet at a predetermined location outside so everyone can be accounted for.

REFERENCES ———————————————————————————————————

Home Sense by Mike McClintock, Charles Scribner's Sons, New York, 1986.
Smoke Signals, 2nd edition, The International Society of Fire Service Instructors, Ashland, Mass., 1986.

Stop, drop and roll

The "stop, drop and roll" technique will save your life if your clothes catch fire.

Although the natural reaction is to run away from flame, motion fans the flames and makes your clothes burn faster. Your greatest danger is breathing in heat and toxic gases, which are worse when you're standing than when you're near the ground.

Smother the blaze by rolling yourself or the victim on the ground. Wrap a heavy coat, blanket or rug around yourself or the victim and, if possible, drench with water.

As long as they come off easily, pull burning clothing away from the body. Fabric that has melted against the skin, however, should not be removed. Cool water — not ice — applied to the burned area will relieve pain and help prevent additional injury.

Get medical assistance immediately. Burns often do not look as serious as they later turn out to be. Only a physician can assess the degree of damage.

REFERENCES ———————————————————————————————————

Smoke Signals, 2nd edition, The International Society of Fire Service Instructors, Ashland, Mass., 1986.
The Family Handyman Magazine's Home Emergencies and Repairs, Harper & Row, New York, 1971.

Natural fire extinguishers you have in your kitchen

Sometimes the most effective safety devices are the simplest. Use a large lid to smother a grease fire quickly. But if you have to reach into a cabinet to find one, you'll waste precious moments. Keep it close by whenever frying with fat or oil.

Another effective kitchen fire extinguisher is a box of ordinary baking soda. Sprinkled on flaming grease, it is far safer to use than water. Water splatters grease dangerously and can actually spread the fire.

REFERENCE ————————————————————————————————————

Smoke Signals, 2nd edition, The International Society of Fire Service Instructors, Ashland, Mass., 1986.

Preventing chimney fires

On the first really cool evening of every fall, the folks at your neighborhood fire department don't plan to have an uninterrupted dinner. As soon as homeowners get in from work, they're going to light the first fire of the season. And right after that comes the first chimney fire call of the season.

- Prevent chimney fires by having the chimney cleaned professionally every year or two — depending on how often you use the fireplace and whether you burn pine or other highly resinous woods. Keep fires to a manageable size, and never leave them alone.

- The first signs of a chimney fire are a loud roar, sucking sounds and shaking pipes.

- If a chimney fire does begin, shut air intake vents to cut off the fire's air supply and close the damper. Leave the house at once and call the fire department from a neighbor's phone.

- The danger may not be over when the fire appears to be out. Heat may have started wood smoldering between the walls, which may ignite after you and your family have gone to bed. Always have the fire department come and check the chimney, even if you are sure the fire is out.

- Dispose of ashes outside in metal containers. "Dead" ashes have relit days after their removal from a fireplace, and ashes left in paper bags have started fires on porches.

REFERENCE ————————————————————————————————————

Smoke Signals, 2nd edition, The International Society of Fire Service Instructors, Ashland, Mass., 1986.

Safety checklist for space heaters

The space heater that supplements your home heating system can be a killer. Check this safety list:

○ Use only the kind of space heater that turns off automatically if tipped over.

○ Replace heater or cord when cord is frayed or worn. Just taping over a worn spot is not enough to prevent a fire.

○ Use only a heavy-duty extension cord, if you must use one; too lightweight a cord will overheat.

○ Keep space heaters at least three feet from any flammable material and out of halls or doorways where they could block your escape in case of fire.

○ Turn them off when you leave or go to bed; be extra-vigilant when there are children or pets in the house.

○ Use only clear 1K kerosene with kerosene heaters. Kerosene that is yellow or contaminated can explode. Never substitute gasoline or other fuel in a kerosene heater.

○ Fill heaters outside, and always crack a window in the room where one is in use. Check local laws — some states ban the use of kerosene heaters because of the risks associated with them.

REFERENCE ————————————————————————————

Smoke Signals, 2nd edition, The International Society of Fire Service Instructors, Ashland, Mass., 1986.

Think before you 'light up'

Of all industrialized nations, the United States consistently has the worst record for fire deaths. More than a third of all home fire deaths start with cigarettes and take place at night.

A hot cigarette, ashes or match dropped into bedding, upholstery, clothing or carpeting can smolder for hours before flaming up. And even before fire or smoke appears, the fumes given off by burning fabrics can be deadly.

The basic rules:

- Never smoke in bed or while reclining in comfortable furniture.
- Check seat cushions before going to bed.
- Provide deep ashtrays for smokers, and don't balance them on the arms of furniture.
- Install extra smoke detectors in the bedrooms of smokers.
- Never empty ashtrays into wastebaskets. It's better to cover them securely and set them outside until morning.

REFERENCE ————————————————————————

Smoke Signals, 2nd edition, The International Society of Fire Service Instructors, Ashland, Mass., 1986.

You wouldn't keep a bomb in your house ...

So why do you store gasoline in the basement?

A single gallon of gasoline has the same explosive force as ten sticks of dynamite.

- Don't use gasoline as a cleaning fluid.
- Never spray lighter fluid on a barbecue grill that already has even a single glowing coal; it can explode before you can react.
- Store paint thinner or gasoline only in approved metal containers, and use only in well-ventilated areas.
- Put out that cigarette before using hair spray, nail polish, nail polish remover or glue. These liquids don't merely burn — they explode, often with deadly force.

REFERENCE ————————————————————————

Smoke Signals, 2nd edition, The International Society of Fire Service Instructors, Ashland, Mass., 1986.

Getting out of hot water

According to fire officials, household hot water is the biggest cause of scalds, especially among children and older people.

Many residential water heaters are set as high as 150 degrees Fahrenheit. An adult's skin can suffer third-degree burns at that temperature in only two seconds.

Test water temperature in your home by holding a candy or meat thermometer under hot water running from the faucet. If it reads above 125 degrees, turn your hot water down. Modern detergents are fully effective at 120 degrees or less.

Temperature regulators are available at hardware stores.

Teach children always to turn on the cold water first, and turn off the hot water first.

REFERENCE

Smoke Signals, 2nd edition, The International Society of Fire Service Instructors, Ashland, Mass., 1986.

Three life-saving gadgets

Whether caused by ice and snow in winter or by severe storms in summer, a power failure makes any emergency situation worse. And, especially with young children around, candles and oil lamps are simply not good options for light.

A couple of rechargeable flashlights in strategically located electrical outlets can make power failures less stressful. When the lights go out, the flashlight comes on automatically. You can see where it is (unlike a regular flashlight that never seems to be in the same place twice), and it will provide up to an hour of light.

Sanyo and Black & Decker offer good quality rechargeable lights — ask at your favorite hardware store.

Another warning gadget that could prove to be your best friend: a water alarm like one sold by Brookstone. Pipes can leak silently, or sump pumps can fail without warning.

The water alarm is battery-powered and is left standing on the floor. As little as .01 inches of water will set off its warning sound.

If you have a fireplace or wood stove, add a Chimfex to your arsenal of smoke alarms and fire extinguishers.

When a fireplace or wood stove fire gets out of control, you toss the Chimfex into the fire on the way out of the room. The Chimfex contents will follow the fire into the flue to reach hot spots and put them out.

REFERENCE

Home Sense by Mike McClintock, Charles Scribner's Sons, New York, 1986.

Remote house sitter

Worried about security at your out-of-town vacation home? What if there is a power, sump pump or furnace failure?

Consider a computerized monitor that connects you by telephone with your weekend home. Program in upper and lower temperature levels, electrical power status and interior noise levels (for fire or burglar alarms). Remote sensors report changes in water levels or temperature near the furnace.

When you call, a computer-synthesized voice reports on the status of things. You can also set your monitor to call up to four telephone numbers (your home, office, etc.) until it gets an answer when problems develop.

Peace of mind is worth far more than the relatively modest cost of such a remote control security alarm.

REFERENCE

Home Sense by Mike McClintock, Charles Scribner's Sons, New York, 1986.

Living through Mother Nature's rampages

Snow and ice:

○ If trapped in a car by a blizzard, stay there and wait for help. Before snow gets too deep, clear a space around the tailpipe to allow carbon monoxide to escape when you run the heater. Also get emergency equipment out of the trunk and into the passenger compartment: a jack handle to clear an air passage, extra blankets and large candles for heat.

○ Always crack open a window on the side away from drifts whenever you run the engine for heat — never for more than ten minutes every hour.

○ Try to stay awake and warm. If others are nearby, pack into one car for added warmth and boosted morale.

○ At home, clear sidewalks as soon as possible after a snowfall; homeowners may be held liable for injuries caused by slippery walkways.

○ Rock salt or calcium chloride will melt ice and packed snow except in extremely cold conditions. Salt-based materials damage plants, however, and should be kept off lawns. Flush concrete with water after the weather warms up to prevent damage to the surface.

○ Sprinkle walkways liberally with sand, ashes, or cat litter — before the storm begins to keep snow from sticking to sidewalk or driveway and afterwards to form a nonskid surface.

○ Falling icicles can kill. Knock them down with a garden rake if they dangle above walkways.

Floods:

○ If you live in a flood-susceptible area, be prepared with a supply of materials like sandbags, plastic sheeting, lumber and plywood. Always keep a few days' supply of food that doesn't require cooking or refrigeration, and be sure emergency lights and radios are working. (Don't forget a manual can opener!)

○ Clean bathtubs and sinks with household bleach, and use them to store fresh water. Fill all available jugs and bottles, too.

○ If there's enough time, carry valuables and furniture to higher floors. Cut off electrical power. Open doors and windows to allow water to flow through so fast-rising water cannot lift your house from its foundation.

○ Don't take chances: Get out and move to higher ground.

○ Afterwards, use extreme care in moving about flooded areas in case downed power lines are still live. Avoid carrying open flames into buildings where gas could have pocketed. Throw out any food that has come in contact with floodwater; boil all drinking and cooking water at least 10 minutes.

○ Never try to drive across a stream of fast-running water. If you stall in deep water, experts say the risk of staying in your car and being swept away is greater than the risk of leaving to get to higher ground.

Earthquakes:

○ Keep immunizations current for all family members.

○ Have emergency lights and a battery-powered radio ready at all times.

○ If indoors, stay away from windows, tall furniture and chimneys. A stairway, desk or strong table may protect you from falling debris or household furnishing.

○ If outdoors, avoid walls, power lines and high buildings. Move into an open area if you can, and if driving, stop in an open area.

○ As in a flood, use caution. Cut off utilities, don't use an open flame, and boil water before drinking it or cooking with it. Do not flush toilets until it is certain the sewer lines are intact.

○ Assess damage cautiously. Beware of structural instability and leaking gas when entering buildings. Wear shoes and work gloves for protection.

Tornadoes:

○ Tornadoes can and do occur in every state and in every month of the year. But they occur most frequently in the continental plains, and the season peaks in May.

○ A tornado watch means conditions are favorable for a tornado to develop.

No action is required except to remain alert to weather reports.

○ A warning means a tornado has actually been seen or tracked on radar. Take shelter in a basement or an interior room under a sturdy desk or table. Leave some windows open, but stay away from them.

Hurricanes:

○ Much of the above information applies to hurricanes as well. Be prepared for a possibly prolonged duration without utilities, fresh water, convenient food or medications.

○ Secure outdoor furniture, garden tools, signs, garbage cans.

○ Tape or board up windows.

○ Leave if ordered to evacuate, taking important papers such as birth certificates and insurance policies. Shelters cannot accept pets; leave them behind with food and water.

○ If permitted to stay home, remain indoors, but pay close attention to Weather Bureau advisories. Remember, there is often a temporary period of total calm when the eye of the storm passes — don't wander far from safety.

○ Flooding often causes more damage than wind. Beware of sudden surges through low-lying areas.

○ Drive cautiously afterwards. Roads may appear safe but collapse under the weight of a car.

REFERENCES ————————————————————————
The Family Handyman Magazine's Home Emergencies and Repairs, Harper & Row, New York, 1971.
Reader's Digest Practical Problem Solver, The Reader's Digest Association Inc., Pleasantville, N.Y., 1991.

Summertime risks

Hazards lurk in even the most harmless summer activities. A few common-sense precautions will keep a fun vacation from becoming a tragedy.

○ Gasoline — its invisible vapors are deadly. Have passengers wait on the dock while you refuel your boat. Run bilge fans briefly to clear fumes before starting the engine. Never smoke while refueling anything, from lawn mower to mini-bike.

○ Handle fireworks only with utmost care.

○ Watch out for lightning. At a pool or the beach, get out of the water. Take cover indoors. Lightning goes for the tallest object in an open area, especially metal. If you are caught away from shelter, lie down flat. Better to get wet than fried.

○ Camping? Keep flames (including cigarettes) out of tents, and ventilate campers adequately when cooking or heating. Look around your site, and avoid low areas prone to flash floods. Be prepared to move to safety in case of sudden emergency. A working flashlight can be a lifesaver in an unfamiliar location.

REFERENCE
Smoke Signals, 2nd edition, The International Society of Fire Service Instructors, Ashland, Mass., 1986.

Don't look like a victim

An appearance of self-confidence, a brisk business-like stride and a sense of purpose impart more protection than most people imagine. Some people just look like victims.

How not to look the part:

○ Appear to know where you're going. Get clear directions beforehand, but if you are lost and need directions, approach a police officer, store clerk or service station attendant.

○ Walk with a companion whenever possible. Experts say you can reduce your chances of being attacked by 70 percent by walking with one other person, and by 90 percent if you are in a group of three.

○ When at a meeting or convention for which name tags are issued, take yours off when you leave the meeting. Such a tag labels you a visitor to the area and hence a potential victim.

○ Look purposeful, as though you have something to accomplish and plan to be on your way. If one or more persons block your path, focus your eyes beyond them and make it clear you do not have time to stop.

○ Be conscious of what is going on around you. But understand that odd behavior in public may be a diversionary tactic to direct attention away from a pickpocket or mugger. Hold your belongings more securely and move away from the commotion, not toward it.

○ When entering a shop or office — especially a liquor store or bank — size up what is going on inside before letting the door close behind you. You wouldn't be the first person to walk innocently into a robbery in progress and become one of its victims.

○ Learn to get along without a purse, or use it only to carry a brush and makeup, not cash or credit cards. Wear clothes with pockets and carry money in any form in separate places.

○ Keep some quarters on your person. A telephone booth can be a temporary refuge if you sit on the floor with your feet against the door while awaiting police.

○ Pause to let your eyes adjust to light or darkness when you go from one to the other. An attacker will try to take advantage of this period of transition.

○ Sudden loud noise is remarkably effective in scaring off an attacker. Carry a shriek alarm in your hand when walking in unsafe areas. Scream with all your might or speak loudly, using direct orders like "Leave me alone!" and "Get out of here!" rather than weak questions like "What do you think you're doing?" You reinforce your authority in this way.

REFERENCE

Safe and Alive by Terry Dobson and Judith Shepherd-Chow, J.P. Tarcher Inc., Los Angeles, 1981.

Riding the subway

When traveling by subway, don't sit right next to the door. Thieves have become experts at the timing needed to dash aboard, grab a purse or package, and be gone just as the doors close you in and them out.

Take an aisle seat whenever possible so you can get up easily and get away if the person next to you bothers you. Stay awake if you can, but if you must sleep, keep your belongings close to you so you will be awakened if anyone tampers with them.

If you must carry a handbag or briefcase, hold it on your lap or wedge it between your feet.

Most cabbies are honest, but protect yourself against the exceptions. Be sure the identification taxi drivers are required to post matches the driver in your cab. Note the driver's name at the beginning of the trip.

If you have a cab pick you up at home to take you to the train station or airport, imply that you will not be gone long and allude to persons occupying your home while you are gone.

REFERENCE

Safe and Alive by Terry Dobson and Judith Shepherd-Chow, J.P. Tarcher Inc., Los Angeles, 1981.

Foiling the pickpocket

Here are some tips to keep a pickpocket from separating you from your money.

Men:

- Carry your wallet in a front pants pocket rather than in a back pocket or a jacket pocket. Get in the habit of stuffing your hand in on top of it when in a dense crowd.

- Thieves don't usually ask for a money belt (except in places like Las Vegas where they are common). Consider wearing one under your clothes.

- A wallet with a fabric exterior is harder to slip out of a pocket than a slick leather one.

○ Carry cash and credit cards separately.

Women:

○ Carry a wallet with important identification and credit cards in a pocket separately from a handbag.

○ Choose a handbag with a long strap worn across the body.

REFERENCE————————————————————————————

1,001 Helpful Tips, Facts & Hints from Consumer Reports, Consumers Union, Mount Vernon, N.Y., 1989.

How to act at gunpoint

Daily newscasts bring stories to our living rooms about violent crime involving guns. No one is immune today from this possibility. A bit of forethought may avert panic and provide you with just the right response to save your own life.

○ If someone is threatening you with a visible weapon, take him seriously. If he says, "Don't move," assume he means just that. If he starts shooting anyway, either at you or someone else, then move! Escape or duck for cover.

○ Your best reaction to the sound of gunfire is to drop to the ground or floor. Then get under or behind cover as soon as you can.

○ Faced with a weapon, watch the person, not the weapon. Staring at the muzzle of a gun pointed straight at you can freeze your own reaction. Try to make and keep eye contact with the assailant, and speak calmly and reassuringly.

○ There is no one right answer to the question of whether to comply with an armed attacker's demands. If he wants to force you to leave a public place and accompany him to a secluded place, you must rely on your own judgment of the situation. One expert, however, believes it may be wiser to refuse and take your chances where help is closer by.

REFERENCE ─────────────────────────────────

Safe and Alive by Terry Dobson and Judith Shepherd-Chow, J.P. Tarcher Inc., Los Angeles, 1981.

Safe telephone tactics

Intruders can get into your home by means of the telephone, too. If you live alone, you should be aware of several methods of stopping their unwanted attentions.

Check out what features the telephone company offers in your community, such as a device that displays the number of an incoming call before you answer or a code that calls back anyone who calls you.

Get an answering machine:

○ It can be used to screen calls before you pick up the phone.

○ Be cautious about your out-going message. Of course, you won't say "We are not home," but "We can't come to the phone."

○ Use plural pronouns rather than singular, to imply that you do not live alone.

Consider the following tactics for your phone book listing:

○ List your last name with first and middle initials only.

○ List name but not address.

○ Add the name of an imaginary roommate or husband to the listing.

○ Don't even list your name and number. (A note of caution: If you are being harassed and change to an unlisted number, psychiatrists say eliminating telephone access may actually push the caller into more drastic behavior.)

To deal with unwanted calls:

○ Simply cut off caller with, "I'm not interested," and hang up. The law now says certain solicitors are required to remove your name from their call list if you ask them to do so when they call.

○ Don't be fooled by disarming techniques like, "Steve gave me your number," unless you really believe it to be true. Even then, this may just be the prelude of an obscene call.

○ If you are the least bit suspicious about a call, pretend you are talking to a male companion: "Excuse me — honey, will you please turn down the television."

○ Hang up at once on obscene calls or the ones that deliver only silence. Don't keep asking, "Who is this?" Your uneasiness may be giving the caller exactly the thrill he is after.

○ The loud whistle into the mouthpiece still works.

○ Never give information to strangers. If you wish to participate in the caller's survey, get her name, the name of the company she represents and the phone number, and then return the call. If she balks, don't worry about it — hang up.

○ Call the telephone business office if you are harassed repeatedly. The people there are usually very supportive of their customers in situations like this, and they will tell you what to do. If it becomes necessary to call for police intervention, you will be able to demonstrate that you have already taken appropriate measures.

REFERENCE ───

Safe and Alive by Terry Dobson and Judith Shepherd-Chow, J.P. Tarcher Inc., Los Angeles, 1981.

Positive thinking

Getting life under control

Does the weather get you down? Do some people make you mad? Do you ever think, "That's just the way I am"?

If you can answer yes to any of these questions, remember—you can control your emotions and your environment instead of being controlled by them. You can choose how you will respond to events and people. Here are three tips to help you make things happen instead of just having things happen to you:

○ For one day, listen to yourself and those around you. How often do you use and hear phrases like "If only," "I can't," or "I have to"? These are the words of a person who is not taking control of what happens to him.

○ When you hear yourself say these words, decide to take control. Is it true that you *can't* do something or do you *choose* not to do it? Remind yourself that you have a choice about how to respond.

○ Determine whether or not you can solve a problem that is frustrating you. Work on things you can do something about. Don't worry about things beyond your control. You can't solve the national debt, you can't control other people, the weather or the past.

As far as *you* are concerned, there's a lot that you can control. Work on getting rid of your "shoulds" and "can'ts" and statements like "he made me mad."

REFERENCE

The 7 Habits of Highly Effective People by Stephen R. Covey, Simon & Schuster, New York, 1989.

How to make people like you

○ People will like you if you like them first. Be truly interested in other people's lives. Listen to their problems, remember their concerns, and show that you genuinely care.

Think how much people love their dogs who greet them at the door after work and stay by their feet all night. These animals don't impress people, tell witty stories or lead fascinating lives. They just show love and interest.

○ Brighten others' lives with a smile. Put a smile on your face, and people will be attracted to you. Smiles say, "I like you. You make me happy." Don't feel like smiling? Hum a tune to yourself, think happy thoughts or just force yourself to smile. You won't be able to help feeling better.

○ Use a person's name. If you want a bigger sandwich at the deli, look at the name tag on the shirt of the person working the counter. Smile and say, "Hello, Patty," before you order. A person's name is music to his ears.

Ask someone to repeat his name if you didn't catch it when you were introduced, then repeat it several times while you're talking. Try to associate names with faces.

○ Encourage others to talk about themselves. Determine to learn something from every conversation partner. People will think you're a brilliant conversationalist if you simply are fascinated by what they tell you.

○ If you want someone to be interested in you, find out what interests the other person and center your conversation around it. This works in job interviews, too. Tell a company president that you can make money for him, and you have his undivided attention.

○ Make other people feel important with sincere flattery and appreciation and with good manners. If you're waiting in line with a stranger who has beautiful hair, comment on it. He'll be on Cloud Nine all day.

When a waiter brings you the wrong order, say, "I'm sorry to bother you, but I ordered french fries, not potatoes." Your correct order will be brought out as quickly as possible, perhaps with extra fries to boot.

Thank an employee for a job well done in front of his fellow workers, and you'll get a more loyal and hardworking employee.

Your main goal in being nice to others is not to make them like you or to get something out of them, but these sure are pleasant benefits. Be cheery, friendly and genuinely interested in others, and you'll "win friends and influence people."

REFERENCE

How to Win Friends & Influence People, Revised Edition by Dale Carnegie, Simon & Schuster, New York, 1981.

How to win an argument

The only way to win an argument is to avoid it. What good do arguments do anyway? Almost every time, the two opponents end up more firmly convinced than ever that they are right.

Here are some helpful hints on keeping a disagreement from becoming an argument:

- Welcome the disagreement. Be glad everyone doesn't always agree with you — life would be boring.

- Don't react immediately. The natural reaction to a disagreeable statement is to be defensive. Your first reaction will probably show you at your worst. Stay calm.

- Control your temper.

- Let the other person finish talking. If you resist, defend yourself or start debating, you'll just build barriers between you.

- Talk first about the points you agree on.

- Admit your errors and apologize for your mistakes.

- Promise to think about your opponent's ideas, and do so!

- Thank the other person for his ideas.

- Don't do anything right away. Set up a meeting for later that day or next week.

If you can swallow your pride and follow this advice, you'll get the best of the situation every time.

REFERENCE ─────────────────────────────

How to Win Friends & Influence People, Revised Edition by Dale Carnegie, Simon & Schuster, New York, 1981.

Adjust attitude and live longer

Don't worry, be happy and live forever. It's a fact that angry and cynical people are five times as likely to die before they reach age 50 than calm and trusting people.

The troubles and hassles an angry cynic always manages to get into increase his blood pressure and damage his heart.

REFERENCE ─────────────────────────────

Dr. Redford B. Williams, *Family Happiness is Homemade.*

Five-minute stress reliever

These exercises are perfect for relieving stress during a hectic day at the office. After a tense meeting with the company president, a run-in with a co-worker or a rush to meet a deadline, take five:

Stress reliever No. 1:

1) Sit in a comfortable position and close your eyes (unless it makes you nervous to close your eyes at work).

2) Point your toes back towards your face and tighten your shins. Hold for five to 10 seconds. Release and relax for 20 to 30 seconds.

3) Point your toes downward and tighten your calves, thighs and buttocks. Hold for five to 10 seconds, then release and relax for 20 to 30 seconds.

4) Take a deep breath, arch your back slightly and push your stomach out. Hold for five to 10 seconds, then relax for 20 to 30 seconds.

5) Hunch your shoulders forward and up to your ears. Wrinkle your face up like an old, dried apple. Hold for five to 10 seconds, then relax.

After each step, note the difference between body tension and relaxation. You should feel your muscles relaxing in waves throughout your body.

Stress reliever No. 2:

1) Raise your right arm out to your side and over your head while breathing in. Breathe out. Breathe in and stretch your right arm up to the ceiling. Breathe out.

2) Repeat with left arm.

3) Let your arms come down slowly while you breathe out. Continue to breathe deeply for about 20 seconds.

4) Place your feet shoulder-width apart. Slowly let your head hang forward until your chin touches your chest.

5) Start to curl forward and bend over very slowly. Breathe deeply. Let your arms dangle and hang down as far as you can comfortably. Don't strain or bounce. Sway gently from side to side.

6) Now, on each inhale, raise back up a little. On each exhale, relax. In this way, slowly roll your body up until your spine and head are straight.

Your body should feel looser and more relaxed.

REFERENCE ————————————————————————

Less Stress in 30 Days by Peggy Roggenbuck Gillespie and Lynn Bechtel, New American Library, New York, 1986.

How a first lady lets off steam

If the pressures of the workday have been getting to you lately, take a tip from Nancy Reagan. (She may not have had a regular 9 to 5 job, but she spent many 12-hour days in her First Lady role.)

Nancy Reagan would come home and take a long, hot bath. She wasn't soothed so much by the hot water as by the conversations she would carry on in the bathtub.

She would debate, argue and have it out with all the enemies and irritating politicians she had encountered during the day.

You could use her technique even if you aren't into hot baths. You can scream in the car, write an angry memo that you throw away instead of send or mutter under your breath while jogging.

You can get all your anger out this way without taking it out on the people you live with.

REFERENCE ——
The Art of Self-Renewal by Barbara Mackoff, Lowell House, Los Angeles, 1992.

Shaking the blues

Everybody hopes that the older they get, the happier and more content they will become.

After all, you've made it past adolescent hormones, the instability of your '20s, the mid-life crisis and menopause. But often, older people seem more depressed than anyone.

Here are some reasons why:

○ Psychosocial stresses — Living alone, giving up a job, losing a loved one or worrying about money can cause depression.

○ Lack of exercise — The more a person rests, the worse he feels, and the less energy he has.

○ Nutrition — Eating properly is more difficult when one is alone. And if a person has digestive troubles or little money for food, he can easily fall into poor eating habits.

○ Alcohol abuse — Since older people are more sensitive to drugs, alcohol can become a problem. It can also foster poor nutrition habits.

○ Hidden disease — Illnesses like diabetes or thyroid disorders, anemia, arthritis, ulcers or cardiovascular disease can make a person feel bad without specific symptoms.

○ Side effects of medicine — A normal dose of medicine for a younger adult might actually be toxic for an older person. Drug reactions can also make you feel bad.

Old age doesn't have to mean that you will feel bad, be unhappy or lose your mental sharpness. Take these steps to avoid depression, and you'll be sharper, happier and young at heart:

- Give yourself permission to admit when you are down or worried. Covering up sorrows can make them worse.

- Establish a buddy system. Regular contact with a friend will boost your spirits.

- Practice an exercise routine. Swimming-pool aerobic classes or mall-walking with friends can be easy and fun ways to get fit.

- Eat a sensible diet. Seniors need fruits, fruit juices, vegetables, whole grains and milk products. People who live alone can keep powdered skim milk on hand and freeze one-person portions of meat, poultry and fish in aluminum foil for ease in cooking and cleanup.

- Enjoy companionship with your meals. Join a lunch club or other organized program. Share a meal with a neighbor. Listen to the radio or read a newspaper while you eat.

- Practice relaxation. Learn to meditate or use music to help you relax.

- Find a new challenge. A hobby, volunteer work or a class might provide you with a welcome change from your routine.

- Seek out humor. Laughing exercises your cardiovascular system and makes you feel better.

- Treat yourself to something special. Whether your treat is eating a favorite fruit or using the good china, be good to yourself.

Keeping yourself happy and healthy has an added benefit, too: You may find that the loss of memory and concentration you were calling old age was just a case of the blues.

REFERENCES

Postgraduate Medicine, January 1992.
Senior Patient, July/August 1989 and July 1990.
Tufts University Diet and Nutrition Letter, April 1989.

Making the most of your time

Have you ever heard these facts of life? You do 80 percent of your work in 20 percent of your time. Work expands to fill whatever time you have available.

Tons of ink has been spilled to tell us how to avoid these unavoidable truths and be more efficient, productive and stress-free people. Most time-management sermons boil down to this:

- Draw up your "life plan," or a list of everything you want to accomplish in life. A life plan helps you avoid the time-wasters by keeping you focused on important issues.

- Make a "to-do" list for days, weeks, months and years. Write tomorrow's list before you leave the office.

- Set priorities with the ABC system. The A tasks are top priority, B tasks are less important, and C tasks can be postponed indefinitely. (Remember that there are two kinds of priorities—those you set and those others set for you.)

- Are you a morning or afternoon person? Figure out your biological highs and lows and schedule your tasks accordingly.

- Delegate.

- Schedule "Quiet" and "I'm Available" hours. Get an "Only if it's urgent" sign for your door.

- Use technology. Personal computers, dictation systems, even calculators save time.

- Never handle a piece of paper more than twice. Either throw it away or do something about it.

- Don't smoke or eat while you work. Take a short walk during lunch instead of depending on coffee, cigarettes and soda to keep you going.

- Cut down on the amount of business reading you do. Read a few things well.

○ Don't attend unimportant meetings. Leave meetings when they become irrelevant.

○ Do business during coffee breaks and lunch, but sometimes take breaks to forget it all. Getting stressed out over saving time is counterproductive.

REFERENCE ————————————————————————————————

The Working Woman Report by the editors of *Working Woman* with Gay Bryant, Simon & Schuster, New York, 1984.

Finding time in unexpected places

How much time do most business people waste trying to find items that have been misplaced, misfiled or mislabeled?

Executives spend about 4.3 hours a week trying to find things, a nationwide study found recently. That's almost six weeks a year.

Take this messy test to find out if your lack of organization is losing you time:

○ Do you have scribbled notes on torn-out bits of paper or Post-it notes stuck everywhere? Does it get harder every day to find the one that tells you where you're supposed to be at 11 a.m.?

○ Is your desk off-limits to others because you "know where everything is" and you don't want them to "mess up your system"? (You just *think* you have a system.)

○ Do you sit in the center of towering stacks of business magazines and trade journals you don't have time to read? Watch out! You'll be buried alive!

○ Do you spend part of almost every day searching for items you "saw just last week"?

○ Are some documents taking root in your "In" basket? Spend a slow Friday afternoon getting rid of those low-priority tasks.

○ Do you hoard papers instead of throwing them away because you "never know when this might come in handy"? Think about it — if you ever did need that report on the Indonesian swine market you'd never be able to find it anyway! Could you replace that report or paper fairly easily? Then throw it away.

○ Do your fellow workers think finding something you've filed is hopeless? Even worse — do you have to hunt for papers you've filed yourself?

○ Is your excuse for the state of your work area, "I don't have time to clean off my desk"? Actually, the few hours you spend organizing will save you whole weeks worth of time every year.

Take some steps to get yourself organized. You'll find the most extraordinary things in unexpected places — that report you lost, and almost an hour's worth of time every day.

REFERENCE ─────────────────────────────
Quality 1st, Dec. 28, 1992.

The gospel according to Fred Flintstone

Who would have thunk it? Amid all his arguments with Barney, his collisions with Dino and his encounters with The Great Gazoo, Fred Flintstone was teaching us something.

And while the Federal Communications Commission doesn't view Fred's lessons in values as educational programming, chances are you walked away from the cartoon with more than you thought you did.

Among the lessons we learned from the Modern Stone-Age Family:

○ Never underestimate the strength of a child.

○ Never bet more than you have.

○ Wealthy oil men drive big cars.

○ Pets make excellent companions.

○ Never put Super Glue in a bowling ball.

○ It is possible to have pollution-free cars.

○ Never leave a child unattended.

○ Household appliances have minds of their own.

○ Never put too many items on a drive-in tray.

○ Carpooling can work.

○ It's always a good idea to remember your anniversary.

○ The little guy can beat the system.

○ Good stone walls make good neighbors.

○ Expectant fathers do crazy things.

○ Friendship is important.

REFERENCE ——————————————————————
The New York Times, March 25, 1993.

Seven cures for the sluggish brain

Does your brain ever feel as though it's been numbed? As though you couldn't think of a creative idea or understand the wording of an insurance policy if your life depended on it?

Here are seven ways to increase your thinking power:

Exercise to boost your brain power. Everyone knows that the cure for a sluggish body is exercise and nutritious food, but people don't realize how much food and physical activity affect brain power.

For one thing, exercise releases chemicals that keep the brain in top form. You've heard of the "runner's high" that comes from peptides released during exercise. Numerous studies have shown that a program of regular exercise improves intelligence, speed of performance, learning and brain function.

Physical inactivity is mind-numbing. If you've ever been confined to the bed for a period of time, you know that it turns your brain to mush.

Feed your brain. Your brain is very susceptible to blood sugar ups and downs. The brain uses two-thirds of the body's glucose, but it can only store a very small amount. Therefore, it needs a steady supply.

To keep your brain going during the day, eat several small protein snacks rather than three big meals. Never skip breakfast. Your brain is hungriest at night during rapid-eye-movement sleep.

If you tend to get sleepy and lose your mental sharpness after lunch, eat a high-protein meal (meat, eggs, nuts and cheese) rather than a starchy and sweet meal (white bread, pasta, corn and potatoes). Save the starches for nighttime.

Hold your ears. The noise of everyday life jars our brains, adds to our mental stress and damages our thinking power. Office noise that slips over partitions and through hollow doors is damaging to concentration, attention span, work quality, memory and mood.

You can block out noise with earplugs, a fan, a radio set between stations, a mechanical "white noise" generator or soft music. Music can also help some people learn and absorb information.

If noise is really a problem for you, you can install a tight-fitting, solid-wood door, heavy glass in your windows, a second layer of drywall and a wood floor on top of the existing floor.

Let the sunlight in. Offices without windows can sap brain power. Researchers say that our bodies need to be exposed to full-spectrum light, not just what lamps give off. If you don't have windows, take occasional breaks to walk outside and eat lunch outside, too. (Office air, cooled or heated and shared with co-workers, is another brain-sapping culprit. Fresh air will do wonders for you.)

Work with your lighting system to find what is most inspiring for you. Fluorescent lights are a brain drain for some people. Try turning them off and bringing in a lamp or two from home instead.

Learn your body rhythms. The easiest way to throw your mind and your body off track is to sleep irregular hours. Everyone must maintain a regular bedtime, sleep soundly at night and sleep as much as their body needs. Most people need between six and nine hours a night.

For sounder sleeping, lay off caffeine, cigarettes and alcohol in the evening; snack on starchy or sweet foods at night (apples, cereal, corn, etc.); avoid loud TV and fast music before you go to bed; and exercise.

Most people have certain times of the day when their brain power is at its peak. You may be barely able to remember your name at 8 a.m., but you're sharp as a whip at 10 a.m. or 7 p.m. Save your most intellectual tasks for your peak hours. If you have a flexible boss, you may even want to adjust your work schedule.

Relax! Stress, or the "need to succeed," can sabotage your powers of memory and concentration. Have you ever bumbled around during a job interview, blanked on the name of the company president just as you were introducing him to your husband, or experienced stage fright or writer's block?

When you're trying to say, do or write the perfect thing, your mind rebels. A stressed-out mind that is thinking of ten things at once can't perform either.

Try relaxation techniques such as deep breathing, muscle-relaxing exercises, meditation, yoga, massage or prayer.

Cut out caffeine, alcohol and nicotine. These drugs, especially caffeine and nicotine, serve as quick pick-me-ups for many people, but the drop after the drug wears off is a lot further and longer than the lift they give. If you're addicted to caffeine or nicotine, you'll feel sluggish, anxious, headachy and even dizzy when you're forced to do without it.

REFERENCE ───────────────────────────────
How to Boost Your Brain Power by Roger B. Yepsen, Rodale Press, Emmaus, Pa., 1987.

How to organize your
thoughts and beat writer's block

Computer programmers and CPAs, skip this suggestion, but the rest of you can read on. For most people, thoughts and ideas are disorderly things, popping into the brain topsy-turvy. Whole sentences rarely come at once, much less whole letters, sales reports or budgets.

If you get writer's block when you sit down to compose your monthly sales report, try a new way of organizing your thoughts. It's called mind mapping.

Write your subject matter — monthly sales report — in the middle of a blank sheet of paper.

As your thoughts come to you, jot them down all around the central subject matter. Try to group them according to subject.

For instance, you might have a "purpose" section where you put all your thoughts about why company executives want to hear your sales report. Another group of thoughts may be about a new idea you have to improve sales.

After you've brainstormed, use colored pens or pencils to surround your major subject areas with different colors. Underline and shade key thoughts; draw lines connecting related thoughts.

There, you've created an outline, and it wasn't even that painful.

REFERENCE

Sonja Sakovich, president of HighGain, a San Francisco consulting firm, in *Fortune*, Nov. 16, 1992.

How to make better decisions

Hindsight is 20/20. Most of us spend much of our time muddling through bad situations, pondering this insight about hindsight and regretting decisions we made.

Are you tired of wishing you'd never hired that dud employee, begun that doomed project, or eaten that first half gallon of ice cream that started your weight problem?

Want to make a decision you can feel good about? Ask yourself these questions:

○ *Am I considering what I really need or just what I want?* Here are some examples to help you distinguish between a "need" and a "want."

You may want big, quick profits, but you need long-term investments and assets. You just want a fancy house, but you need a happy, loving home. You really want that project completed in one day, but realistically, you need a project done well in one week. And most people want ice cream when they really need carrots.

○ ***Am I looking at all the options?*** "I have no other choice" is rarely a true statement. Sometimes we don't see our options because we are subconsciously afraid of them, or we are too busy feeling sorry for ourselves to explore our options.

○ ***Am I thinking my decision through?*** Like a good chess player, we should think several moves ahead: "If I choose this option, what will happen? Then what?" Every decision affects another decision you'll have to make later, so thinking things through will save you lots of time in the long run.

○ ***Am I being honest with myself?*** Don't fool yourself about a situation. Telling yourself the truth sometimes seems painful, but you're really being nice to yourself when you do. A good way to find out if you are fooling yourself is to let go of your pride and ask the people who care about you.

○ ***Am I trusting my intuition?*** Your best decisions come when you trust your intuition, or your "gut feeling." Ask yourself: Does this decision make me feel confident or paralyzed, calm or anxious, drained or energized, peaceful or resentful?

○ ***Am I being nice to myself?*** We often know when we are making a poor decision. So many people, even though they may not act like it, have poor self-images. They secretly believe, for one reason or another, that they don't have the ability to make a better decision or live a better life. Don't sabotage yourself! Make a decision that says "I deserve better."

○ ***Are you afraid to start over?*** You may be suffering from the consequences of a bad decision right now. If you are, you have to be willing to take a risk, cut your losses and begin again, even if it means firing someone who is incapable of doing his job or losing hours of work on a project. Unfortunately, decision-making is a learning process — starting over will always be a part of it.

REFERENCE ———————————————————————————————————
"Yes" or "No": The Guide to Better Decisions by Spencer Johnson, HarperCollins Publishers Inc., New York, 1992.

How to feel good about losing your memory

Worried because your memory just ain't what it used to be? Or maybe you're worried because you're only 25 and you already tend to forget that you stuck your pencil behind your ear five minutes ago.

Well, just forget your worries and be proud of your poor or failing memory. Here are two good reasons why:

○ Nature may have meant for older people to be able to remember long-ago events more easily than yesterday's happenings. In a study done at Washington College in Maryland, a group of students listened to stories told by people of various ages. When asked to repeat what they remembered, the students could recall much more of the stories told by the older tale-spinners than by the younger story-tellers.

   The researchers theorized that as you get older, your speech patterns change and your story-telling skills increase. Therefore, nature meant for events from long-ago to dominate the memory of older people. That way they can pass down information to younger generations and contribute to the survival of the species.

○ If you're young and absentminded, just call it creativity. The two do seem to be related. Remember the example of Albert Einstein. Einstein was a genius, but once, while working at Princeton University, he had to call the switchboard because he forgot where he lived! He would have called home, but his number was unlisted and he had forgotten it, too!

REFERENCE ————————————————————————————————
   How to Boost Your Brain Power by Roger B. Yepsen, Rodale Press, Emmaus, Pa., 1987.

Three attitudes of the workplace loser

Bosses and fellow workers can spot "loser" attitudes a mile away. You may not be interested in career success, but if you are, try to avoid these common habits:

○ Seeing yourself as a "survivor." Surviving hardships is commendable, but if you would describe yourself as a "survivor," you probably have a poor self-image. See yourself as a winner in life and you'll have a whole new attitude.

Winners get calluses and survivors get scars, says Joseph Mancuso, president of the Center for Organizational Excellence in Fairfax, Virginia.

○ Failing to connect with a good role model. If you associate only with fellow workers who have no interest in getting ahead or being successful, you may lose interest yourself. Connect with career-oriented workers with productive habits — they're easy to spot.

○ Experiencing intense fear. According to Mancuso, the fears that can lead to failure are:

- fear of failure
- fear of success
- fear of rejection
- fear of authority figures
- fear of power
- insecurity

Overcoming fear is a difficult task. The first step is recognizing the fears that are holding you back. Do any of these ring a bell with you?

REFERENCE
Quality 1st, Feb. 22, 1993.

How to be comfortable with your success

To guarantee your own unhappiness, spend your life trying to make others happy. Don't choose your career by considering what you are good at and what fulfills you. Choose what would make your mom and dad proud. (The two choices don't have to be mutually exclusive, but they often are.)

Don't try to measure your success by the outside world's specifications rather than by your heart's true desires. If you are not sure whether you are succeeding for yourself or for someone else, here are some things to consider:

○ Are you happy? Do you like the work that you do and, above all, are you doing it with a clear conscience?

○ Do you have a purpose and a goal in life, and are you moving toward that goal?

○ When a certain amount of self-denial is needed to take the next step toward your goal, do you face it with courage? Do you feel proud and energized once you take that step?

○ Every day is not the same, and all successes must include moments of failure. Do you make it through failures without breaking down and losing your confidence?

○ Once you reach your goals, do you enjoy the feeling of success, knowing that others may not see what you have done as particularly special?

○ Spirituality is a basic element of success. Do you feel in tune with a higher power and feel a strong sense of harmony within?

If you can answer "yes" to these questions, you are on the road to happiness. Remember, you can't pour yourself into a mold called "Success." Success is as individual as our fingerprints and our personalities. All we need to be successful is the courage to realize for ourselves what success means to us.

REFERENCE
University of Success by Og Mandino, Bantam Books, New York, 1982.

How to overcome shyness

Shy people miss so much of life. They are often sensitive, intelligent, talented people, but they can be very unhappy. They are too fearful, too uncertain, too afraid of making a fool of themselves, too guilt-ridden and too self-centered to enjoy life and other people.

Shyness tends to be self-perpetuating, too. You are so worried about what other people think about you that you do stumble over your words, create awkward situations or come across as snobbish.

The first step in overcoming shyness is to get your mind off yourself and onto helping other people. It's helpful to remember that other people feel awkward and uneasy, too.

Going out to lunch with an acquaintance or a business partner? Do some research on her company and favorite hobbies so you can put her at ease with topics that interest her. If you're going out on a date, concentrate on complimenting your date on his looks and his choice of restaurant. Try to pick out music he might like, and tell him what a good time you're having.

To get over shyness, you have to reach out to others. It's hard at first, but it will get easier and easier. If a fellow worker has been out for several days, tell her you missed her. Make eye contact and smile when you say "Good morning." Keep track of people's birthdays and call or send a card. Seek out another shy person at a party and make him feel comfortable.

When shy people were growing up, they somehow missed acquiring a feeling of self-worth. They feel as though they can't do anything right.

Make a list of things you're good at and special talents you have. Work on developing those talents. You may need to take up a hobby you can excel in, like woodworking, sewing, tennis or gardening. Feel good about small accomplishments in your job and slowly work on bigger accomplishments.

Shy people are fearful people. To overcome your fears, gradually expose yourself to the feared object or situation. If you're afraid of flying, read articles about airplanes, visit the airport and talk to people who enjoy flying. Discuss your fears with others. It's nice to know you're not alone. Reassuring other people will make you less afraid yourself.

Shy people have often been deprived of love. To be loved, you have to give it. Be interested in your companion's life, listen to him, sympathize with his sorrows and share your own feelings.

These words of advice may seem impossible for a shy, withdrawn person to follow. But shyness is a handicap, and you have to work hard to overcome it. There's no one else to do it for you.

REFERENCE ————————————————————————————

Coping with Shyness by Paul J. Gelinas, The Rosen Publishing Group, New York, 1987.

Hushing the voices in your head

You may have never noticed, but you have a voice in your head that spends most of its time telling you what a horrible person you are. The voice expects you to be perfect, and when things go wrong, it tells you you're "stupid" or "awful" or a "quitter" or a "failure." That voice rarely lets you feel good about yourself.

The first step in getting control of the voice is just noticing it's there. The voice's favorite thing to do is to take a small event and blow it up. Since you couldn't learn to use the new phone system the first day it was installed, "You're dumb."

Usually the voice generalizes about your appearance, performance or intelligence.

The voice will also use positive labels to make you feel bad: After a hard day at work, a friend asks you to help him move some furniture down to his basement.

Normally you would, but today you just want to go home and crash. The voice says, "If you were a good friend, you'd help him." You end up helping and resenting your friend. The guilt trips, the "shoulds" and the "oughts" all come from the voice.

The voice also filters out the positive things that happen to you during the day. If compliments make you uncomfortable, you're probably filtering them out and brushing them off as not really true. The voice blocks out a day's pleasant moments so that you remember the whole day as horrible. The voice makes you remember your failures and forget the times you shined.

When you hear the voice in your head, never agree with it. Talk back to it, out loud if you can. Tell it you're not a loser because you made one mistake, and you're not stupid but inexperienced.

If you catch your voice filtering out the positive and pointing out your failures, stress your successes. Make a list of compliments people give you and a list of things you do well. Use the lists to talk back to the voice.

Your voice thinks it can read minds. It tells you all the time that other people think you're incompetent or silly or a klutz. Tell the voice that you can't know what other people are thinking until you ask, and that they probably aren't thinking those things anyway.

Just remember that the voice always lies, and no matter what it says, you're OK.

REFERENCE ───────────────────────────────

Coping through Self-Esteem by Rhoda McFarland, The Rosen Publishing Group Inc., New York, 1988.

Contribute to charity without spending a dime

The businessman's contribution to charity usually consists of writing a check. Getting personally involved, using talent and energy, is left to those with less money and more time.

But the particular talents of the businessman are sometimes needed more than anything else. You can help most by:

○ Serving as a financial advisor to organizations and schools.

○ Working as a liaison between an organization in financial trouble and banks or the government. If an organization is having difficulty paying taxes or paying off a loan, it may just need a knowledgeable businessman to talk to the IRS or to the bank to work out a payment plan.

○ Using the skills you've gained in motivating employees to motivate volunteers. Your creative touch may be just what the nonprofit organization needs.

○ Reading past the business pages in the local paper. In the human interest and news pages, you will learn about problems local organizations are having and particular needs of your community.

REFERENCE ───────────────────────────────

Forbes, Oct. 19, 1992.

Communication secrets

Getting to know you: making introductions gracefully

Introducing a friend to your boss or even a peer to a peer can be an uncomfortable experience. We usually aren't taught how to do it and formalities are difficult in an informal world.

Just remember one piece of protocol and you'll be set: Always introduce a person of no rank to someone with rank, a friend to an out-of-town visitor, your husband to your boss, a younger person to an older one, and, preferably, a man to a woman. For example:

"Mr. Rogers, this is my son Todd. Todd, this is Mr. Rogers, the owner of this store."

"Angela, may I present my husband, Walt Smith. Walt, this is Mrs. Angela Reid, my boss at VideoComp."

Of course, when you introduce a peer to a peer, it doesn't matter who is introduced to whom. Just make sure you use both first and last names. Also, include any other information that might help others launch into conversation: where they work, their hometown, how you know them, etc.

Always use the names that the newly introduced pair should use in speaking to one another. For example, "Mother, I'd like you to meet my roommate, Rhonda Roomy. Rhonda, this is my mother, Mrs. Brown." Rhonda Roomy should know by this introduction that she should address her roommate's mother as Mrs. Brown.

Don't presume to use someone's first name. Wait until that person gives you permission. For example, Rhonda Roomy should respond to the above introduction, "Hello Mrs. Brown. I've heard so much about you that I feel like I already know you." To which Mrs. Brown could smile and begin to chat or smile and say, "Please, call me Betty."

To introduce yourself, simply say, "Hello, my name is Cindy Parrott." When visiting another city, include your hometown: "Hello, I'm Cindy Parrott from Atlanta."

If introducing people makes you nervous, practice in front of a mirror a couple of times to limber up.

What a relief:

The most tiresome introductions to make can come when you are walking with a group and someone you know approaches from the opposite direction. But, the good news is, the rules of etiquette don't require that you make introductions. The group should continue to move on slowly until the two people who know each other have chatted briefly and then parted.

Similarly, if someone you know walks by your table while you are with a group, you need not make introductions. It is polite to step away from the table to talk.

REFERENCES

Emily Post's Etiquette by Elizabeth L. Post, Harper & Row, New York, 1984.

Letitia Baldridge's Complete Guide to a Great Social Life by Letitia Baldridge, Rawson Associates, New York, 1987.

The Concise Guide to Executive Etiquette by Linda and Wayne Phillips, Doubleday, New York, 1990.

Mr. Smith or Frank: which one should you use?

Have you ever tried to completely avoid using someone's name because you don't know what to call them?

How we address others and how we wish to be addressed seem like the easiest questions in the world until you get tangled in a thicket of protocol. Some of the more complicated tangles entail employer/employee relations, unequal employees and religious titles.

Naturally, you can always ask the person how he wishes to be addressed, but that is frequently awkward for both the asker and the askee.

In the case of employer/employee, you should address those who are further up in the company by their last names until expressly asked to do otherwise. You should, however, remain alert for the eccentricities that crop up from company to company and place to place.

For example, if everyone from the mailroom to the penthouse calls the boss by his first name, you should, too. To do otherwise makes you look stiff or even snooty.

But if you notice that the only people who call the boss by his first name are long-time employees or those who are just below him on the flow chart, you should stick with Mr., Mrs., Miss or Ms. until the boss suggests first names.

Suppose Widget & Gidget just hired another person to help you with your workload. On the flow chart, the two of you have equal status. But she is 30 years older than you. How should you address this person?

Generally, you should call this person by her last name until she asks you to do otherwise. You might note how the person is introduced to you by management/personnel as a clue, though frequently the boss will introduce the person by a first name because that's what the boss intends to call his new employee.

The new employee, however, may not be altogether comfortable with the first-name designation but may be reluctant to say anything at that point in the relationship. Again, you'll rarely stray too far if you start formally and wait to be asked before presuming that Wanda-Jo Smith wants to be called Wanda-Jo.

Religious titles can be extremely sticky, because they frequently involve people's beliefs. But if you mix large doses of common sense with the desire not to offend, you'll probably survive.

Grammatically, it is wrong to introduce a member of the clergy as Reverend Jones because the word "reverend" is an adjective and not a noun. It would be the same as introducing a judge as Honorable Jones. You would introduce him as the Rev. Mr. Jones or as the Rev. Sam Jones.

The problem is more apt to arise, of course, with your response to the introduction. To say, "I'm pleased to meet you, Rev. Jones" is incorrect. To say, "I'm pleased to meet you, Mr. Jones" is correct but could sometimes give the (offensive) impression that you do not recognize this person as a bona fide clergyman.

This would be particularly true in those parts of the country where the word reverend has slipped into regular usage. Use Mr. if bad grammar bothers you more than giving offense. Otherwise, use Reverend but only in those special situations where to do otherwise would be discomforting to everyone.

Some Protestant denominations don't use titles at all and are annoyed when those outside their denomination call their clergy Reverend, Pastor, Father or Brother. In those situations, Mr. is a relief to both clergy and laity.

Lutheran pastors are normally introduced and addressed as Pastor Jones.

Roman Catholic and Orthodox priests are introduced and addressed as Father Jones, while Episcopal priests may be called either Father Jones or Mr. Jones.

No matter how well you think you know a clergyman, do not presume to call him by his first name unless he specifically asks you to. Usually, the clergy prefer to be informally addressed as Father Bob (instead of Jones), Pastor Jim or Brother Sam.

REFERENCE

Emily Post's Etiquette, A Guide to Modern Manners by Elizabeth L. Post, Harper & Row, New York, 1984.

I know I should know you

Sometimes it is not possible to avoid the embarrassment of having forgotten the name of someone you are expected to know. The best way to deal with it: a straightforward statement — "I'm sorry, I simply cannot recall your name."

Reminding others of your name to save them exactly that discomfiture is an endearing courtesy, especially when you shouldn't expect a person to remember it. Former teachers or group leaders of one-time meetings are often expected to remember every student they ever taught or every group participant.

To remember names better, use the old trick of repeating the name of the person you have just met. If the name is uncommon or difficult, don't feel shy about asking its owner to pronounce it, or even to spell it, until you can repeat it correctly.

REFERENCE

The Concise Guide to Executive Etiquette by Linda and Wayne Phillips, Doubleday, New York, 1990.

Introductions for the businesswoman of the '90s

○ For all women who are never sure when to shake hands: It is appropriate to shake hands under almost any circumstances, and doing so creates a good business impression. Shake firmly, for three or four seconds, and look the other person in the eye, both upon meeting and upon saying good-bye. Confirm his good impression of you by repeating his name upon greeting and leave-taking.

○ When introducing yourself, or announcing yourself in a telephone call, use your first and last names, not a title or honorific. You are Mary Smart, not Dr. Smart or Mrs. Smart.

○ Women, just as men, should always rise to be introduced (unless there is a good medical reason not to).

REFERENCE
The Concise Guide to Executive Etiquette by Linda and Wayne Phillips, Doubleday, New York, 1990.

Two quick conversing tips

○ Flattery of others (in small doses) makes them feel good and can be a great icebreaker.

○ Obviously, you shouldn't put others down, but don't constantly put yourself down either. Repeated self-deprecation is boring.

REFERENCE
Letitia Baldridge's Complete Guide to a Great Social Life by Letitia Baldridge, Rawson Associates, New York, 1987.

Be a big hit with these small talk topics

You don't want to step on anyone's toes or pry into private matters, so what can you talk about at parties or over lunch? Here are some conversational topics that are sure to please:

○ A new, enjoyable book you've read, a hilarious movie you've seen or a promising restaurant that just opened

○ A mutual friend's latest success story: a promotion at work, a newly announced pregnancy, the friend's wonder child

○ An optimistic report from the Department of Labor

○ The amazing, new athlete on the local basketball/baseball/football team

○ The latest discovery in genetic engineering research, the new Nobel prize winners or a fascinating National Geographic article you've read

○ The new lottery winner

○ The architectural wonder of the new shopping mall

Reading your newspaper carefully is a good idea when you know you'll have to make small talk later. Cheering news and funny stories are always welcome, and taking wagers on jury verdicts and discussing a critic's review of a musical can be fun.

Also, feel free to talk about an exciting event that happened to you, or a hobby or interest you are passionate about. Just make sure you aren't monopolizing the conversation or boring your audience.

REFERENCE ————————————————————————————
Letitia Baldridge's Complete Guide to a Great Social Life by Letitia Baldridge, Rawson Associates, New York, 1987.

Audience grabbers

You're not safe from bored listeners and glazed-over eyes just because you never give speeches to audiences of hundreds. If you work, there will come a time when you have to make a presentation to a group of managers, to another department or to a meeting of fellow employees.

Here are some pointers on how to grab an audience, large or small:

○ Don't tell people much more than they want to know.

○ Be simple. Don't use technical jargon or terms only an industry insider would know.

○ Try a bit of story telling. Audiences will remember your anecdote long after they forget your technical jargon.

○ Use posters, slides, charts, actual products and other visuals. Ten minutes of straight speech is sure to make listeners restless.

○ Don't hide behind the lectern.

○ Smile and look happy. You will seem enthusiastic and energetic, and you may have a better time.

○ Shorter is usually better. Leave your audience wanting more.

REFERENCE ———————————————————————————————
Quality 1st, Feb. 22, 1993.

Questions you should never ask

Most of us know better than to ask "How old are you anyway?" and "What do you weigh these days?" But these aren't the only questions you should avoid on social occasions. Certain inquiries are likely to earn you a cold shoulder, physically or mentally, from your conversation partner:

○ What year did you graduate from college? (This question is a barely disguised version of "How old are you?")

○ Why did you leave your job? Or, Is it true that your company is up for sale? (Don't probe into confidential or touchy business matters.)

○ Have you had a facelift (a nose job, liposuction, breast augmentation)? Or, Are you wearing a wig (dentures)?

○ Do you have cancer? (Terminal illness is also a topic you should avoid with casual acquaintances.)

○ Are you seeing a therapist? Who is your therapist? (Don't ask, unless someone wants to talk about their psychological treatment.)

○ What was it like behind bars in '65? (Avoid inquiring about past prison experience.)

○ So, are you and your husband separated now? Or, Why isn't your wife here? (Don't poke into someone's marital status or extramarital activities. If someone's spouse isn't at a party, don't mention it.)

The wise conversationalist will also avoid controversial subjects that can lead to emotional battles. Social wars will probably be waged if you bring up abortion, problems with our welfare program, religion or politics, especially during a political campaign. If you are certain that your conversation partner holds similar religious beliefs or political convictions, then forge ahead.

You may think you are being clever, refreshingly open or funny by bringing up "taboo" topics at a social event. Or, you may be genuinely caring and concerned for another person. Unfortunately, others will probably see you as prying. Save private topics for private situations.

REFERENCE
Letitia Baldridge's Complete Guide to a Great Social Life by Letitia Baldridge, Rawson Associates, New York, 1987.

Keeping your communication secret

That top-secret deal may no longer be top secret if you discuss it on your cellular phone. Remember that people with certain kinds of radio scanners can overhear cellular calls. Avoid sensitive conversations on your car phone — Eavesdroppers are everywhere!

REFERENCE
The Wall Street Journal, Nov. 14, 1991.

Talking with people with disabilities

The Americans with Disabilities Act of 1992 has brought many people with impairments into mainstream America. Talking with people with disabilities can be uncomfortable for the able-bodied.

Here's how to make life smoother:

○ Try to lose terms like "crippled," "handicapped," "retarded," "deformed" and "confined to a wheelchair," and don't call them "victims" or "afflicted." Advocates for people with disabilities say these expressions foster discrimination. "People with disabilities" is the preferred term, emphasizing that they are, first of all, people.

○ For people who use wheelchairs: Try to get on the same eye level, but don't make contact with the chair unless asked. Offer to help — don't just grab.

○ For those with mobility impairments: walk alongside, not in front. Unless they tell you otherwise, make no assumptions about what a person with a physical disability can or cannot do, such as using stairs. Don't move someone's crutches, cane or walker without permission.

○ For the blind or visually impaired: Be generous in offering verbal cues; identify yourself and whoever else is present. A guide dog is a working animal — don't distract or pet him without the owner's permission.

○ For the hearing impaired: Speak plainly in full view of the other person, but don't shout. Use gestures and facial expressions to help convey meaning.

○ For people with epilepsy: Say someone has a "seizure disorder" or has epilepsy, but don't say she "has fits" or is epileptic.

○ For those with a speech impairment: Don't pretend to understand when you do not — ask them to repeat. Give your undivided attention, making eye contact, as you would with any speaker. Don't say "relax" or "slow down" if a person stutters.

○ For people with cerebral palsy: That's how you describe them, as people with cerebral palsy, not "spastic." Don't hesitate to ask them to repeat a statement if you were unable to understand.

○ For those with learning disabilities: Do not assume these people are illiterate, stupid or have an attitude problem.

○ For people with mental retardation: These people are not "retards." Use shorter sentences and understandable basic language.

○ For people who are HIV-positive or have AIDS: You need not fear infection from shaking hands. Respect an employee or job applicant with AIDS as you would any other person. It is illegal to ask if an employee or job applicant has AIDS or is HIV-positive.

REFERENCE ──────────────────────────────

Complying With the Americans With Disabilities Act by Peter W. Thomas and Don Fersh, Quorum Books, Westport, Conn., 1993.

What to say when tragedy strikes

How do you say, "I'm sorry this has happened to you" when tragedy strikes a friend. The death of a child, AIDS, miscarriage, cancer or a family member with drug addiction — these tragedies could happen to anyone. This realization literally paralyzes friends and business colleagues with fear, and the "right" words will not come.

At the very moment that they most need support, many people in a crisis feel themselves abandoned and avoided. And those who abandon and avoid feel guilty for doing so.

What can you do when you hear that someone you know is facing death, serious illness or tragedy? First, say the experts, have the courage to confront your own fears. Understand why you prefer not to speak or visit, and arm yourself with a few questions or statements that will help open the door to conversation.

Visit, call or send a note — it helps just knowing someone cares enough to make the effort. Avoidance makes people who are suffering feel stigmatized. Be willing to listen; sometimes that is the one thing that helps most.

Remarks like these are helpful:

> - "I'm so sorry. I just don't know what to say."
> - "I'm here for you; I care."
> - "Tell me what it was like for you."
> - "I wish it could be better for you."
> - "You are in our prayers."
> - "I know this is difficult for you."

Offer specific suggestions — "I'll take the kids off your hands for a while Tuesday evening" — rather than vague offers to help. And keep the support coming; don't lose interest when a hospital stay drags on and on.

Be careful about what you say to children who are seriously ill. Talk to the parent ahead of time so you know how much the child understands.

Sentences that begin with "I had a friend who ..." and end either with miracle cures or tragedy can be very cruel. Remarks like the following tend to hurt rather than help:

> * "I know just how you feel."
> * "It's God's will."
> * "You're young; you can have another baby."
> * "Don't cry. Be strong."
> * "She had a good life."
> * "He's better off."

REFERENCE

"What do you say?" by Martha Woodham, *The Atlanta Journal/Constitution*, April 13, 1993.

Frankly, my dear . . .

Everyone cringes when they hear the word "frankly" because it is almost never followed by good news.

If you feel the urge to "be frank," first think:

> * Will my blunt words do anybody any good?
> * Am I just blowing off steam?
> * Is there a more courteous way to get my point across?
> * Does my frankness make me feel morally superior?

The euphemisms and ceremonies of the business world often seem stupid and insincere, but "saying exactly what you mean" often adds unnecessary stress to the workday and alienates your listener.

REFERENCE

101 Ways to Protect Your Job by George deMare with Joanne Summerfield, 1984.

Thank-you notes when the answer was 'no'

Writing to say "thank you" for a signed contract comes easily, but a thank-you note following negative results will mark you as a professional indeed.

There are a number of practical reasons for the appreciative follow-up to a "no" answer, besides making you look like a good sport.

○ The person who said "no" could be with another company next year and able to use your offer in his new capacity.

○ The company's needs may change, or financing may become available. Your graceful note may keep you in the front running.

○ Your note will likely be kept on file, a tangible record of the interaction, and evidence of the qualities you want the recipient to remember about you.

○ When you are the one who has to say "no," you can sometimes soften the impact by saying "no" in a thank-you note. The would-be client has made an effort in her presentation, or she has spent time getting you information you needed to make a decision. An acknowledgment of her hard work is certainly in order.

REFERENCE
The Concise Guide to Executive Etiquette by Linda and Wayne Phillips, Doubleday, New York, 1990.

How to play the name game overseas

One's own name is the sweetest sound in any language, so say the sages, and that is as true in the international community as in America. Conversely, however, misuse or mispronunciation of a name can chill an otherwise warm encounter.

Especially in the East, where names carry social and family status, a mistake can be a serious insult.

Here are a few rules about names:

○ In China, the surname comes first, the given name last — hence, Lo Win Hao is addressed as Mr. Lo.

○ The Taiwanese, however, sometimes give a child a Christian name as a first name. Jimmy Ho Chin is Mr. Ho to business acquaintances, Jimmy Ho to his friends.

○ In Korea, one's position as first or second son determines which name is used with "Mr."

○ In Latin America, surnames are usually a hyphenated combination of the father's and mother's names. Edmundo Ortiz-Perez would be Mr. Ortiz in Spanish-speaking countries, but where Portuguese is spoken, his mother's name comes first.

Don't trust the rules, since Easterners sometimes reverse names when dealing with Westerners to try to make it easier for us.

Play it safe: Ask.

REFERENCE

Do's and Taboos Around the World edited by Roger E. Axtell, compiled by the Parker Pen Company, produced by The Benjamin Company Inc., Elmsford, N.Y., 1985.

Breaking down the language barrier

○ Remember that your listener may not understand what you are saying, but that doesn't mean he's deaf. Don't insult him by shouting at him. Simply speak as clearly and slowly as possible.

○ Avoid slang, jargon, and idiom at all costs. Would you, after all, know what an Italian meant if he used his country's equivalent of "catching the red eye to L.A." or, "His pitch was all smoke and mirrors"?

○ Even exaggeration may confuse. Your listener may understand enough literal English to wonder if you really meant to call your boss an idiot, or was lunch really a disaster just because the salad bar lacked chives.

○ Overpunctuate by your tone of voice.

○ Use visual aids as much as possible, and when using videotapes or slide presentations, be sure both languages appear.

○ Write out a summary of the meeting and distribute it as soon as possible, being especially sure numbers are correctly represented. In fact, numbers should be written out as you go, since in some languages their position is the reverse of English (as in German, where "22" is read as "two-and-twenty.")

○ Pace yourself to match your counterpart's comprehension, and ask frequently, "Am I making myself clear?" Make him feel that any misunderstandings were caused by your failure to communicate.

○ Avoid questions that elicit yes and no answers, and do not ask rhetorical questions.

REFERENCE

Do's and Taboos Around the World edited by Roger E. Axtell, compiled by the Parker Pen Company, produced by The Benjamin Company Inc., Elmsford, N.Y., 1985.

Getting your message across, by hook or by crook

In the United States, you can crook your finger to beckon someone. In the Far East, that's a major insult.

If someone doesn't speak your language, be wary of resorting to gestures or hand signals to get your message across. You may find out the hard way that hand signals are not universal in meaning.

Consider the almost reflexive "OK" signal so common among Americans, the thumb and forefinger touching to make a circle. To us, its meaning may range from "I agree" to "Congratulations" to "Go ahead." And in most of the rest of the world, the connotation is very much the same as here.

However:

○ To the Japanese, the gesture makes a circle, and a circle is a positive symbol. But in some situations, the "OK" sign signifies money.

○ In Brazil, the sign is regarded as insulting and vulgar.

○ In southern France, it means "worthless" or "zero."

○ In most of the countries of the former Soviet Union and in Greece, our

"OK" sign is regarded as impolite or obscene.

○ In Colombia, the same gesture placed over the nose signifies that the person being discussed is homosexual.

Here are some more gestures you need to know before you offend someone:

○ While Americans may crook the index finger to beckon anyone from a child to a taxi to a colleague, in other countries the effect may not be the same. To most Middle and Far Easterners, it is insulting to be beckoned with the fingers. Instead, turn palm down and wave the fingers or the whole hand. The same goes in Portugal, Spain and Latin America.

○ In Europe, crossed fingers most commonly mean "good luck" or "protection." In Paraguay, crossed fingers may be offensive.

○ Most Europeans and some Latin Americans take the same meaning for a finger making a circle around the ear: "He's crazy." However, in the Netherlands, the same gesture means someone has a phone call.

○ Almost everywhere in the world, the "thumbs up" sign indicates approval — except in Australia, where it is considered rude.

○ In Europe, signal "good-bye" by raising the hand and wagging the fingers in unison. Waving back and forth as we do in America means "no" in Europe, while in Peru it means, "Come here."

○ Waving the hand close to someone's face is a serious insult in Greece and Nigeria, and it should never be done to flag a waiter or cabdriver.

○ In Finland, arms folded indicate pride or arrogance. In Fiji, the same posture shows disrespect.

○ In Bulgaria, shaking the head means yes; a nod means no!

○ The "V for Victory" sign requires caution abroad. If you use it, be sure your palm is facing out. Palm toward you and the gesture is offensive.

○ Incidentally, in much of Europe, if you raise the index and middle fingers to indicate that you want two of something, you may get three instead. The thumb counts too, so an upraised thumb and forefinger means "two."

REFERENCES ──

Do's and Taboos Around the World edited by Roger E. Axtell, compiled by the Parker Pen Company, produced by The Benjamin Company Inc., Elmsford, N.Y., 1985.
How to Behave in Japan, Matsushita Electric Corporation, LTD, Overseas Training Center, Osaka, Japan.
Letitia Baldridge's Complete Guide to Executive Manners by Letitia Baldridge, Rawson Associates, New York, 1985.

Using an interpreter to your advantage

Unless you are very comfortable with the language of the country where you are doing business, or unless your foreign counterparts are fluent in English, you may find that the only way to communicate will be through an interpreter.

If possible, hire your own. It's just human nature to shade things in favor of your employer, and an interpreter whose allegiance belongs to her boss may inadvertently give him an edge. The risk in hiring your own, however, is not knowing whether she has a regional accent that will set your business associate's teeth on edge.

Here are some thoughts on preparing an interpreter, as well as some things to remember as the session proceeds:

Beforehand

○ Familiarize the interpreter as much as possible with the subject matter of the meeting. If a lot of technical lingo is involved, provide her with a word list, or at least go over terminology in detail.

○ Explain to the interpreter not only the material that will be communicated, but also your objectives and the atmosphere you are trying to create.

○ She should also be briefed on the formality or informality of the occasion to avoid the embarrassment of dressing inappropriately.

○ Place the interpreter unobtrusively between the two parties speaking, but without blocking their full view of each other.

○ Offer her something to eat and drink if the meeting takes place over a mealtime, although she may find it more convenient to eat before or after the assignment.

During

○ Carefully avoid using slang or jargon in your presentation. Even presuming your interpreter has perfect knowledge of both languages — a rare likelihood — you may be asking her to translate expressions that have no ready equivalent in the other tongue.

○ Keep your sentences short and as uncomplicated as possible, and pause frequently for interpretation to minimize inaccuracies or omissions.

○ Familiarize yourself, if possible, with some of the speech habits and patterns of the other language. It is helpful to know how long translation will take, proportionate to English. Japanese, for example, requires 30 percent more time than English to say the same thing, largely due to heavy embellishment in honorifics and digressions. Therefore, if the interpreter takes less time to repeat what was said than the speaker took to say it, she may have misunderstood or is only paraphrasing.

○ Never slip up and say something in English that you don't want someone else to hear, assuming that your business associates will not understand. Chances are they know a great deal more English than you suspect.

REFERENCES

How To Do Business with the Japanese by Mark A. Zimmerman, Random House, New York, 1983.

Letitia Baldridge's Complete Guide to Executive Manners by Letitia Baldridge, Rawson Associates, New York, 1985.

The Federal Express World Business Advisory and Calendar, Educational Extension Systems, Clarks Summit, Pa., 1992.

Do's and Taboos Around the World edited by Roger E. Axtell, compiled by the Parker Pen Company, produced by The Benjamin Company Inc., Elmsford, N.Y., 1985.

Career ladder

Moving up in your company: Are you on the track to the top?

"We were hired at the same time and now he's vice president of marketing. I haven't moved an inch." You may be thinking thoughts like these and wondering why your accomplishments seem to be overlooked while your peers are bounding to the upper ranks of company management.

Everyone knows that promotions are based on everything but how well you do your job, but it's always discouraging when you can't figure out what your bosses are looking for.

Researchers at the University of Maryland studied 55 Fortune 500 companies in an attempt to pinpoint the secrets of the successful employees — the ones who always get that promotion they want. What did the study reveal?

○ Employees in departments that are considered critical to the long-term success of the company will get promotions much more quickly than employees in departments that keep the company running profitably in the present.

In other words, employees who work to build market share or to create new products, even if they hurt short-term profits, are in the best position to be promoted. They are highly visible because they have to discuss their strategies and the risks they're taking with upper management.

And what if they don't meet their goals or get the job done? Management will most likely decide that the goals were too difficult to reach, not that the person did a bad job. If your job is to maximize profits and keep costs low, you may be left out in the cold at promotion time.

○ By the same token, employees in departments that spend a lot of the company money are the most likely to be promoted. Even if you only do an average job in a "high-resource-sharing" department, you are more visible and more likely to move up than employees in departments that don't spend much money.

○ Employees who are promoted every three years or so will continue to be promoted. Once you lose momentum, upper management will start to overlook you when promotions are available.

○ Lady Luck can't be denied. If the company decides to focus on cost control for the next three years instead of on new products or increased market share, the financial employees will get the promotions.

○ Employees who attended the same state college as most of the upper management move ahead quickest — even more quickly than your Ivy League executives.

○ Thirty-five or 40-year-old employees who haven't yet received a promotion are often considered "over the hill." Upper management considers them "behind schedule," and they may never receive a promotion.

Use these "success secrets" to get the promotion you want. If you haven't received a promotion in three years or so, speak up, and let your boss know you are interested in taking on more responsibility. If your department isn't very visible, consider making a lateral move to another department, even if you don't get a pay raise.

You can't change your alma mater, but you can try to emphasize the connections you may have with your bosses so you can break into the good-old-boy network that exists in every company. You can't change your luck, but you can help your chances of moving up to the top.

REFERENCE ——————————————————————————————
Investor's Business Daily, Feb. 13, 1992.

How *not* to make it to the top

No matter what you may have heard, you don't make it to the top of the business world by stepping on the people under you.

The Center for Creative Leadership in North Carolina did a study of 41 executives in Fortune 500 companies who were slated for the top. Twenty of these executives succeeded and 21 didn't.

The fatal flaws of those who failed are listed here in order of importance:

○ Insensitivity to others: abrasive, intimidating, bullying

○ Cold, aloof, arrogant

○ Betrayal of trust, breaking a promise

○ Overly ambitious, always thinking of the next job, playing office politics

○ Specific performance problems with the business

○ Overmanaging, unable to delegate or build a team

○ Unable to staff effectively

○ Unable to think strategically

○ Unable to adapt to boss with different style

○ Overdependent on advocate or mentor

REFERENCE ———————————————————————————————

101 Ways to Protect Your Job by George deMare with Joanne Summerfield, McGraw-Hill Book Co., New York, 1984.

Worst time for a job interview

Want to land your dream job? Don't go for the interview on Monday afternoon. It's irrational, illogical and most job interviewers will never admit it, but your chances of getting the job shrink when you interview late on Monday afternoon.

Why? There's no answer, but these are the facts:

○ Late afternoon is the worst time for an interview.

○ Monday is, by far, the worst day for an interview.

○ The last person interviewed for a job is hired about 55 percent of the time. The first person interviewed gets the job only about 17 percent of the time.

Be careful not to lose the interview by manipulating dates and times, but if you get to choose between a Monday, Tuesday or Thursday interview, choose Thursday. And choose the 11:00 interview over the 4:00.

REFERENCE ——————————————————————————————————————
How To Get A Better Job In This Crazy World by Robert Half, Crown Publisher Inc., New York, 1990.

Questions you need to ask in a job interview

So many job interviews end on a bad note because they end with that question we should expect, but we almost always answer poorly: "Do you have any questions for me?"

Most of us do prepare some questions to ask our interviewer, but they end up being addressed during the interview. Here are some good questions to ask if all yours are answered:

○ What do you believe are the major challenges of this job?

○ What major challenges and opportunities are facing this company?

○ What qualifications do you think a person needs for success in this job?

○ Is this a new position? If not, what is the status of the person who holds the job now?

○ Is the company undergoing any changes that will affect this position?

○ What problems does the company have that I could solve?

○ What do you think are the negative aspects of this job?

○ When do you want to have the position filled?

○ What opportunities for advancement does the person in this job have?

○ How would you describe the work atmosphere here?

Try to ask questions in an honest effort to learn more about the company and the job rather than just for the sake of asking questions. Your sincerity, or lack of it, will be obvious.

Asking questions throughout the interview instead of at the end is the best tactic. You can present yourself better when you know more about the company and its needs.

REFERENCE ——————————————————————————

The Business of Living by Stephen M. Pollan and Mark Levine, Simon & Schuster, New York, 1991.

Six sure ways to let your boss know you're looking for another job

Some people don't mind if their boss finds out they are job searching, but usually it's better to be discrete. Here are some signs of departure your boss is sure to pick up on:

- ○ Dressing much better than before. When you are dressed to the nines at your office and you don't usually take such pains with your appearance, "job interview" is probably the first thing that jumps to your employer's mind. Even if you dress better for several days in a row, it may seem as though you are prepared for interviews whenever they come up.

- ○ The long lunch hour. If you habitually take regular one hour lunches and you suddenly begin stretching your lunch hour, it looks suspicious. Also, if you're the "I never take a sick day" type, and you begin to call in sick, your employer will suspect job interviews.

- ○ The low profile. If you are a highly visible employee and you more or less disappear into the woodwork, a smart employer will know you're on your way out. For instance, you begin avoiding your boss's door instead of stopping in for your usual daily chat. Or you sit back in your chair at meetings and observe others when you are usually one of the most vocal participants.

- ○ Personal phone calls pouring in. If you suddenly begin taking an unusual amount of personal phone calls, your employer will wonder if you are talking to recruiters or prospective employers.

○ The vacation switch. If you always take a week of vacation at Christmas and one in June, and you suddenly take two weeks in February, you could be launching an intensive job search or trying to get a vacation in before you leave the company.

○ The personal belongings clue. If you start taking home the pictures of the wife and kids and the leather-bound dictionary your grandmother gave you, your boss would be slow if she didn't suspect that you may be leaving soon.

REFERENCE
How To Get A Better Job In This Crazy World by Robert Half, Crown Publisher Inc., New York, 1990.

Success strategies of top entrepreneurs

Thinking of starting your own business?

If you "don't know when to give up," and "quitting while you're ahead" never seems to enter your mind, you may have what it takes to be a successful entrepreneur.

Entrepreneurs who make it to the top are just not familiar with fear of failure. In a Forbes study of 50 of the top business founders, almost all of them said that if their business had gone under, they would have started another.

Since so many small businesses fail, you have to want to run your own business so badly that failing again and again only makes you want to try harder. Having a good idea is much less important than having the itch to be your own boss.

To make it on your own, you need to be:

○ Self-confident, and have the ability to inspire confidence in others

○ Persistent, wanting to keep on trying

○ Resilient, able to keep on trying

○ Daring, not afraid to take a risk

○ Independent, getting more satisfaction from being responsible to yourself than from getting supervisor's praise

○ Visionary, knowing where you want your company to go and how it should get there

The successful entrepreneur's patron saint is Robert the Bruce, a 14th-century Scottish king. Robert the Bruce was defeated and discouraged, hiding from his English pursuers on a remote island. One day he noticed a spider in the corner of the room, trying to attach her web to a wooden beam. The spider tried over and over to attach the web and failed every time. The spider never quit, and she finally succeeded.

Robert the Bruce's spirits were restored by the spider's determination. He left his hiding place, gathered together a small group of followers and, against great odds, rid Scotland of the English.

REFERENCE ──────────────────────────
Forbes, Nov. 9, 1992.

Resume myths

Not all conventional wisdom about creating a resume is useful in today's job market. Some of these old resume rules need to be reconsidered:

○ ***Always start your resume with a "Job Objective."*** Flexibility is the key these days when seeking job opportunities. When applying for a particular job, you may be taking yourself out of the running for other positions the company has open if you put a "Job Objective" on your resume. Discuss your qualifications for a specific job in your cover letter.

○ ***Resumes should only list the basic information: where and when you went to school; where and when you've worked.*** While you shouldn't fill your resume with endless details, you should always try to highlight at least one improvement or unique contribution you made at each company. You want to show that you were a valuable employee.

○ ***Resumes should never be over one page, especially if you're*** *young.* Resumes should be as long as they need to be to show your accomplishments and contributions fully. A very-experienced worker shouldn't list all her high-school and college jobs, but a working-world beginner needs to prove her experience and competence. You should never pack too much information on one page—your resume will look gray.

○ ***Inject a personal touch with a section devoted to your interests outside the workplace.*** Better advice is: Don't put anything on your resume that doesn't have a direct bearing on your job qualifications. This includes age, religion, marital status and health.

○ ***End your resume with "References available upon request."*** This line is unnecessary and distracting. You should, of course, have a list of references available, but any employer assumes there will be references to check.

REFERENCE ———————————————————————————————
How To Get A Better Job In This Crazy World by Robert Half, Crown Publishers Inc., New York, 1990.

Sharing the thanks

Appreciation helps oil the cogs of business. When others have helped you succeed, even if they have merely satisfied their job description, they should be included in the congratulations. A personal note of thanks may be displayed, shared, given to supervisors, kept and savored.

REFERENCE ———————————————————————————————
The Concise Guide to Executive Etiquette by Linda and Wayne Phillips, Doubleday, New York, 1990.

Losing your job without losing your shirt

If you lose your job through a company downsizing or corporate failure, it seems like the end of the world. But instead of crying over spilt milk, get aggressive and prepare to negotiate. You can't get your job back, but you can work to extend your benefits as long as possible and to get the best severance package for you.

The most obvious issue that you will confront is severance pay. Standard practice is to offer one week of pay for every year worked. You may not be able to negotiate how much you get paid, but you can negotiate how you get paid.

Usually, a lump sum is more desirable than a continuation of salary. But before asking for a lump sum, check to see if continuation of salary would ensure a continuation of your benefits.

Unemployment insurance is a stickier issue these days than it used to be. Many companies are challenging unemployment-insurance claims. So before you agree to resign in exchange for more severance pay, find out what you might lose in unemployment insurance.

Unemployment insurance typically pays a percentage of your salary for 26 weeks. Maximum benefits are usually less than $300 a week.

Your company may not tell you this, but it is required to offer you the right to buy your group health insurance coverage. You can typically extend your coverage for 18 months.

The coverage will be expensive, and you should shop around for other plans. However, most people will find that they can't do any better. If you have health problems, you should definitely stick with your old plan since getting a new plan that covers pre-existing conditions will be costly.

On the other hand, extending the life insurance you had with your company is not a good idea for most people. If your company allows you to purchase your life insurance, it is probable that you won't get adequate coverage, or you'll pay more than you need to.

Of course, if you have health problems that will make purchasing new insurance impossible, you should buy your old insurance.

Ask about other, more unconventional benefits, too. For instance, if you depend on the company car, you may be able to buy it. Many companies offer out-placement services that will help you find a new job.

In your search for a new job, you may find it helpful to have an office to work out of and to have access to copy machines, fax machines and computers. Struggling companies that won't be hiring as quickly as they are firing may allow you to use a space for a while.

Consider negotiating consultant work, too. Your boss may not know everything that you do. Let him know that you are willing to do some of your jobs on a consultant basis. The part-time work could keep you afloat for months or even years.

REFERENCE
The Wall Street Journal, Jan. 17, 1992.

Proving you weren't fired

Did you lose your job or leave it for greener pastures? Don't forget that you may have to prove you left on good terms.

When you leave your present employer for a new and better job, you should write a letter of resignation for the company files. First, tell your boss that you will be leaving for a new position, but then, write a formal letter.

A few years from now, your boss and the personnel director who accepted your resignation may no longer be at the company. You may be trying for yet another new job.

If the employer checks your references and can find no written record of your departure, he will have only your word that you left on positive terms.

REFERENCE
How To Get A Better Job In This Crazy World by Robert Half, Crown Publishers Inc., New York, 1990.

How to be less dependent on your job

Losing your job doesn't have to be a disaster. Many people slump into depression when they are fired or laid off or when their job changes beyond recognition due to a company reorganization. These people tend to rely solely on their jobs for money and fulfillment. You can control your life instead of letting your employer control it for you.

○ **Start looking for other jobs before you lose the one you have.** Always be on the lookout for a new and better job. Take a few minutes a day to scan the want ads. At the least, this will keep you up to date on current salaries in your field. Knowing how your salary compares with others will give you an upper hand at salary-negotiating time. You may see jobs you want to apply for. If you decide to go on an interview and they offer you the job, your company may surprise you with a counteroffer. You'll come out ahead either way.

○ **Find fulfillment outside of work.** Find hobbies and projects that interest and satisfy you, and you will be better able to cope if you lose your job. Are you good at writing, drawing, gardening, teaching, designing jewelry, making pottery or programming computers? Consider joining an organization you find interesting or doing volunteer work.

○ **Maintain a source of income outside of your job.** Turn your hobbies into a small business — you can sell items you make or do free-lance work. If you don't have a hobby that's a potential money-maker, go to your local library where you will find plenty of books listing small businesses you can start for a few hundred dollars or less.

○ **Some small business ideas:**
  * automobile washing, waxing
  * caring for ill or elderly people
  * day-care for young children
  * catering
  * lawn care
  * painting/wallpapering
  * real estate sales
  * tutoring
  * videotaping
  * woodworking
  * making/delivering office lunches

○ **Develop a social network outside of your coworkers.** When you socialize with your fellow workers, you tend to talk about the office. If coworkers are your only social outlet, your life centers more and more around your job, and you will be crushed if you lose it.

REFERENCE

If You Want Guarantees, Buy a Toaster by Robert M. Hochheiser, William Morrow and Co., New York, 1991.

Best careers for the '90s

What are the best careers for the '90s? Here are some sure bets and losers:

Fastest Growing	Percent Increase*
○ Medical Assistants	+70%
○ Home health aides	+68%
○ Radiologic technologists	+66%
○ Medical secretaries	+58%
○ Financial services salespeople	+55%
○ Travel agents	+54%
○ Computer systems analysts	+52%
○ Computer programmers	+48%
○ Human services workers	+45%
○ Corrections officers and jailers	+41%

Fastest Declining	Percent Decrease*
○ Precision electronic/electronic assemblers	-44%
○ Farmers	-23%
○ Stenographers	-23%
○ Telephone/Cable TV installers	-21%
○ Sewing machine operators	-14%
○ Mixing machine operators	-14%
○ Textile machine operators	-13%
○ Machine feeders and offbearers	-13%
○ Hand packers and packagers	-12%

* Anticipated percentage of growth in the number of positions in each field in the 1990s.

REFERENCE

U.S. Bureau of Labor Statistics.

Most claustrophobic jobs

Sweat beads on your forehead. Your tie feels like a noose. If you are assaulted by sensations like these in a slow-moving elevator or on a crowded plane, you probably suffer from claustrophobia.

Stressful, tense, competitive and cramped environments are not for you.

These are jobs you should avoid:

- Astronaut
- Surgeon
- Dancer
- Fashion model
- Psychiatrist
- Doctor of Osteopathy
- Photojournalist/Actor
- Wholesale sales rep./Auto salesperson
- Basketball player
- Attorney

REFERENCE
Jobs Rated Almanac.

Most stressful careers for the '90s

In the '90s, the most stressful fields to work in will be telecommunications, financial services and nonprofit groups, says a study by Human Synergistics, a job consultant group in Michigan.

The study says these fields will demand more and more of employees over the next decade, and workers won't be properly recognized for their achievements.

REFERENCE
The Wall Street Journal, Feb. 22, 1993.

Best public service jobs

Many of us would take a job helping others if we didn't feel like we'd be hurting ourselves. Serving your fellow man is hard work.

But these ten public service jobs rank high on the quality scale. Income, stress, physical demands, work environment, outlook and security are all considered.

- Urban/Regional Planner
- Federal Judge
- Postal Inspector
- Parole Officer
- Tax Examiner/Collector
- Commissioned Officer
- Protestant Minister
- Warrant Officer
- Rabbi
- Social Worker

REFERENCE
Jobs Rated Almanac.

Get an MBA while you commute

Whether your long bus commute puts you on edge or just puts you to sleep, there is an alternative: You can spend that wasted time getting an MBA.

Some managers hoping to get ahead at work or, these days, simply save their jobs are enrolling in on-line education programs. You just plug in your personal computer at home and send your assignments by modem to your professor at the university's business school. Motivated commuters can do their homework on laptop computers.

You don't even miss out on class discussions since students are required to "attend" school five days a week. You send in your contributions, and professors monitor written discussions which can last for several days.

The University of Phoenix has about 200 on-line MBA students who pay an average of $11,800 for the two and a half year course. This price is slightly more than the regular students pay. Purdue University also offers on-line MBAs.

REFERENCE ———————————————————————————
Fortune, Aug. 24, 1992.

How to keep your job and boot the commute

Are you one of the millions who drive over 40 miles to work every day? If you are a commuter and you know working at home is not an option your company will consider, here's another idea, straight from the Japanese, for you to propose: a "satellite" office.

The Japanese started opening satellite offices outside of Tokyo about five years ago, and now 20 or 30 exist in Japan.

Your company could either set up a small office on the outskirts of the city or go in with other companies with the same problem. For instance, employees from IBM, Xerox, Southern California Edison and four other companies work at a satellite office in Ontario, California, 62 miles east of Los Angeles. Certain workers can work there one to five days a week.

The workers get a lot done with few interruptions, have all the equipment they need, and the company doesn't worry so much about the home-office problem of lack of supervision. It's a commuter's dream come true and a solution to pollution.

REFERENCE ———————————————————————————
American Demographics, June 1992.

How not to rock your boat when you're transferred overseas

Nothing would spice up your business life like taking a job across the globe. Can't you just see yourself strolling through the historical, sprawling streets of London or ducking through doors in crowded Japan? But before you take that job far away, consider the complications.

- **Pets.** If you are a pet lover, find out the animal regulations in the new country before you decide to move. British law, for instance, requires that pets be quarantined for six months. Some pets couldn't withstand the quarantine and may have to be put to sleep or given away.

- **Renting.** If you choose to rent overseas instead of buy, you may find it's more complicated than in the United States. Some property owners may demand illegal fees or payment in U.S. dollars. You could be expelled or jailed if you go along with the deal.

- **Selling or renting your home.** Don't act too hastily, either selling your home for less than it's worth or renting to a deadbeat. Trying to extract rent payments when you're thousands of miles away is no picnic.

- **Paying the bills.** Make sure you let banks and other lenders know about your move at least six weeks in advance. Remember that the mail will probably be slower than you could have believed possible. You don't want to end up with a bad credit record because your mortgage payments arrived late.
  Arrange direct deposit for checks you expect to receive regularly, such as checks from renters. Give a few blank checks to a family member or a secretary for bills you forget to cover before leaving.

- **Working spouses.** If your spouse plans to work in the new country, check the job market before you leave. Unemployment is so bad in many countries that spouses are forbidden to work.

- **Visa regulations.** Check out restrictions your visa might carry. If you want to explore the new country, for instance, make sure your visa doesn't restrict you to business travel only.

- **Telephone bills.** Be prepared for big bills. In many countries, you can dial directly to an AT&T operator and call the United States at a fixed per-minute rate. That way you can avoid local company surcharges. To get the details on this service, call 1-800-874-4000.

You might want to invest in a fax machine, a computer with electronic mail or a camcorder so you can swap tapes with relatives and friends back home. Since television systems differ, tapes made on the U.S. system can't be played on systems in Africa and Europe. You can buy multisystem VCRs and TV sets — they will probably be cheaper in the United States than anywhere else.

- ○ **220-volt appliances.** Remember, your 110-volt toasters, micro-waves, food processors, stereos, vacuum cleaners, washing machines, etc., aren't going to work overseas. Home computers and printers will need large transformers, and you may need a device called an "uninterrupted power supply" if you are going to a country where power failures are common.

- ○ **Taxes.** Make sure you find out how the foreign country taxes resident aliens. You can exclude from U.S. taxes the first $70,000 earned from a foreign source.

- ○ **Salary.** After you settle on a salary, insist that you and your company can review it after six months. The raise you got for transferring may not look so good after all your unexpected expenses.

REFERENCE ——————————————————————
Business Week, Jan. 11, 1992.

Tips for staying 'in the know'

Never underestimate the power of the grapevine and never consider yourself too good to gossip.

Even when the grapevine isn't right (and it often is), it reflects the fears, the opinions, the hopes and the anxieties of a business organization. Power and influence come from being in the know.

Techniques for plugging into the grapevine:

- ○ *Get out of your office or workplace and move around.* You never hear anything when you're sitting in one place.

- ○ *Identify the opinion leaders and the gossips.* Opinion leaders are sensitive to events and are influential people. Gossips transmit the personal and more "interesting" information. Personal information doesn't have to be harmful.

○ ***Become trusted.*** To build trust, you must give sound information. Don't use the grapevine to start baseless rumors or no one will tell you anything.

○ ***Keep circulating and listen.*** Build friendships outside of the office and network.

REFERENCE —————————————————————————
101 Ways to Protect Your Job by George deMare with Joanne Summerfield, 1984.

When to use (and not use) your business card

We've all seen the movies where the ambulance chaser gives his business card to the mourning wife at her husband's funeral, and promptly gets thrown out on his ear. Obviously, there are times when it is not appropriate to hand out your business card.

Your business card is your calling card, and it should present the best possible impression of you and your company. A card case is a worthwhile investment to prevent your cards from becoming dirty and tattered.

Appropriate uses of business cards:

○ As a gift card, with personal note added, affixed to flowers or a small gift sent to express appreciation.

○ As a calling card, again with a brief note, when the person you have called on is not in.

○ Attached to corporate literature so the recipient feels that he has a personal contact within your company.

○ Business cards should not be presented during a meal, even an informal meal.

REFERENCE —————————————————————————
The Concise Guide to Executive Etiquette by Linda and Wayne Phillips, Doubleday, New York, 1990.

Business cards: your entree in a foreign land (if you know how to use them)

The exchange of business cards is especially important when unfamiliar language creates a barrier. Next to your passport, your business card may be the most significant document you carry abroad.

Americans are much more relaxed about position than most other nationals. Your business card may help establish your credentials more assertively than you are likely to do yourself.

Your name is easier to understand when it is written, and your rank, title or profession (never abbreviated) makes your position clear. And having your business card printed in the local language is a thoughtful touch.

In most of Southeast Asia, Africa and the Middle East (except Israel), never present your business card with your left hand.

The Japanese exchange cards very seriously and deliberately. Present your card to Japanese businessmen with both hands, the print facing the recipient. Don't carry your business cards in your back trouser pocket. Accept a card with two hands, and then read it. Don't write on a card presented to you, at least not in its owner's presence.

REFERENCES

Do's and Taboos Around the World edited by Roger E. Axtell, compiled by the Parker Pen Company, produced by The Benjamin Company Inc., Elmsford, N.Y., 1985.
The Concise Guide to Executive Etiquette by Linda and Wayne Phillips, Doubleday, New York.
Simply Japan, News from the Consulate General of Japan in Atlanta, Atlanta, Ga.

How to know when your job is on the line

Your boss isn't going to send you a telegram when he makes a change that may affect your job security a few months down the road. But, when the company changes or when business is poor, putting your job on the line, there are plenty of warning signs. These signs may not mean anything if they are isolated incidents. But, if you put several of them together, you've got trouble.

If you've noticed several of these warning signs at work, start looking for another job:

○ ***Changes in sales trends, especially in small orders.*** To find out if the product your company sells is still popular, talk to customers. To get them to open up, ask them how they think things look down the road for your company.

Or ask if they agree with a recent newspaper article on the state of your industry. The falloff of small orders is a sure sign of future negative changes in total sales. Another route: Ask the customer-service workers and the salespeople how customers are responding to products. Other employees in touch with customers' wants: switchboard operators, secretaries, shipping personnel, order entry clerks.

○ ***Relying on a few key customers.*** Some firms rely on a few large customers for their business or one market area. This is always a vulnerable situation. If the company loses one customer or an important market goes into a decline, look out!

○ ***Poor service to small customers.*** Watch to see how small customers are handled and how their orders are processed. If they are treated poorly, the company you work for won't last long.

○ ***New products.*** It's usually a good thing when new products are introduced, but it's still a sign of change you should keep an eye on. Is your boss trying to spruce up company business so it will look more attractive to a buyer? What if the buyer wants to clean house when he takes over?

○ ***Competition.*** If another company comes out with a product that's better than yours, change is in the works. (Consider sending your resume to the competitor.)

○ ***Unwarranted stock-price increases.*** If the price of company stock increases when sales are flat and no new products are coming through Research and Development, you can be sure that change is in the wind. For instance, the company president could be getting ready to retire and sell his stock. He may launch a media campaign about the company's prospects to drive up stock prices. When he retires, dumps his shares and stock prices plummet, what will happen to the company, and your job?

○ **Morale is low and office politics are high.** When no one has a good word to say about the company or his fellow workers, when no one will do anything unless the manager is there to see him, something will have to change. This environment often occurs when a shake-up causes people to panic.

○ **Company struggles to pay bills.** Suppliers and sales reps will tell you quickly when they are not getting paid. The people in the accounting office will know, too, and will be more likely to tell you than management.

○ **High employee turnover.** When the company can't keep good employees and key personnel, it's doomed. If the boss fires employees who do good work, the company isn't stable, either.

○ **The new boss.** If he doesn't bring his own people, he will at least bring his own management style.

○ **Important positions are not being filled.** When people leave and aren't replaced, the company is probably short on cash.

○ **Management starts pressuring employees to cut down costs.** Why? Has something happened?

○ **Fewer and fewer people have the authority to approve expenses.** Any increases in red tape are a sign of weakness.

○ **Management holds meetings away from the office.** Obviously, they don't want to be overheard.

○ **An increase in the number of strangers meeting with your boss.** Are they looking to buy the company or interviewing for jobs?

○ **You have nothing to do.** If things have been reorganized and you are just taking up space when you used to be busy, use the spare time to send out resumes and job-application letters — you'll probably be needing a new job soon.

○ **Other cutbacks.** Product line dropped, field offices closed, production shift eliminated.

○ *No clear goals or plans.* If the company doesn't know where it's heading and has no plans to get there, beware.

○ *Too many bosses or too many assistants.* If the company is running over with vice-presidents and lacking enough people to do the work, trouble's ahead. On the other hand, if the boss has tons of assistants whose job description is to do what the boss tells them to do, the company won't last long. No one can take risks on his own and no one can answer questions when the boss is gone.

○ *A focus on finding people to blame instead of solutions.* If the boss is spending no time or money looking for real problems, the company is vulnerable.

These warning signs are only a few of the hundreds you could look for when change is in the air. As long as you stay awake and are ready when change occurs, you won't become a victim of it.

REFERENCE ─────────────
If You Want Guarantees, Buy a Toaster by Robert M. Hochheiser, William Morrow and Co., New York, 1991.

Moonlighting — a solution to overwork

Feeling stressed and overworked? The solution: Work some more.

More and more managers and professionals are finding that the best cure for job burnout is taking on a night job.

If your day job is no longer satisfying and fulfilling, try to moonlight in a totally different field. The creative fields work the best — singing, gourmet cooking, playing a musical instrument, working with children or whatever you enjoy doing.

A night job that lets you express a different part of yourself than your day job will revitalize you and make you a better worker. Burnout comes from giving everything you've got to your company. (Moonlighting helps pay the bills, too.)

REFERENCE ─────────────
The Wall Street Journal, Dec. 22, 1992.

Smooth career moves at sporting events

Tickets to sporting events are among the premier perks of the business world. If you and your business associates will be attending a game and you're not familiar with the sport, try to learn the fundamentals before you go. You'll have a better time, and those around you won't have to engage in tedious explanations well into the next play.

It's also a smooth move to familiarize yourself with the parking and seating layouts of the stadium or track, especially if you are the host. When you are seated by an usher, tip her — a dollar per couple is customary.

And, as always, courtesy requires putting the feelings of others before your own. Don't jump up and block the view of those behind you, unless everyone is on his feet, and do show restraint in remarks and criticism, especially if fans of the other team are nearby.

Be extremely cautious in your use of alcohol. In the excitement of a game, it is easy to overindulge and then say or do things you would not dream of doing in a business setting — which this is.

REFERENCE

The Concise Guide to Executive Etiquette by Linda and Wayne Phillips, Doubleday, New York, 1990.

How to play sports and impress your boss at the same time

Your athletic skills or lack of them are much less important than your display of good sportsmanship. The way you behave on the playing field says a lot about your character as an executive.

Here are some tips:

- Let your teammates know your strengths and weaknesses before the game begins — honestly.

- Be on time, appropriately dressed and equipped.

- Don't cheat or display your temper, and keep your language clean.

- Behave in the dressing room and on the playing field as though you were a guest in another's home.

○ Shake hands with everyone at game's end, and thank them all for including you.

○ If tennis is the game, bring at least one unopened can of new tennis balls.

○ When invited to play golf, expect to pay your own green fee and caddie fee. If you are the host, pick up all other costs. If you are the guest, you should insist on paying both your caddie's fee and your host's.

○ Don't lord it over less-able participants.

○ Sportsmanship means winning and losing with equal grace, and bearing no grudges. You don't have to act as though you like losing; just don't let on how much you hate it.

REFERENCES —————————————————————————————————

Esquire Etiquette: The Modern Man's Guide to Good Form by Glen Waggoner and Kathleen Moloney, Macmillan Publishing Company, New York, 1987.
The Concise Guide to Executive Etiquette by Linda and Wayne Phillips, Doubleday, New York, 1990.

Telephone tips and turn-offs

Any time you call someone on the telephone, unless the call was prearranged, you may be sure you are interrupting whatever she was doing. Make life easier for both yourself and the person you are calling by taking these simple steps:

○ Identify yourself and the company you represent to whomever answers the phone.

○ When the person you are calling answers, identify yourself again, just in case your name was given incorrectly. As in all initial encounters, don't use first names until invited to do so.

○ Give the person you are calling an idea of how long your call will take.

Then ask if this is a good time, or would she prefer you to call at another time?

○ Try smiling while you speak, and speak clearly. Your voice will sound much more pleasant.

Answering the office phone

You have only one opportunity to make a first impression. Be sure you and your company give the desired first impression to telephone callers.

Those who call you are probably busy people and don't want to listen to an endless greeting replete with commercial, cheery wishes and offers to help:

"Smith, Jones, Williams and Associates law offices, San Francisco branch, ready to serve you in any legal capacity here on the West Coast and nationwide, good afternoon, this is Mr. Smith's executive assistant, Veronica Escanaba, and how may I help you today?"

Far more effective: "Good morning — Smith, Jones, Williams and Associates."

Putting callers on hold

As offensive as the too-long telephone greeting is a curt answer followed by, "Please hold," a click, then unwanted music — when all you wanted to say was, "Just tell Mr. Smith we'll have to reschedule; our building's on fire."

Far better: "May I ask you to hold for a moment?" followed by, "Thank you." Then, "Thank you for holding — may I help you?"

The person who answers your company's incoming calls should likewise be instructed to check frequently with the party who is holding. The short time this courtesy requires reduces anxiety and gives the caller the option of asking that you call him back.

How to politely screen calls

Don't take offense when you are asked to explain your call to an assistant who answers the phone. Screening calls is a common business practice, but it should not be used as a means of insulating the boss from people she wants to avoid.

Placing a caller on hold, then saying that the person being called is unavailable, sends a very unpleasant signal. As with placing calls, the best policy may be to answer them yourself, too. If this is not practical, instruct your assistant not to cross-examine a caller more than absolutely necessary.

'I'll have my assistant call ...'

While having a secretary place your calls for you may seem to telegraph your position and busyness, in fact, it can be quite an inconvenience. Unless the other party is indeed hard to reach, call him yourself. When the person receiving your call must wait for you to get on the line, the implication is that your time is more valuable than his.

Another hazard in having an assistant make calls for you: a possible error in communication, either in the message you want the other person to receive, or in his reply to you.

REFERENCES ————————————————————

The New York Public Library Desk Reference, Simon & Schuster Inc., New York, 1989.

The Concise Guide to Executive Etiquette by Linda and Wayne Phillips, Doubleday, New York, 1990.

Business management skills

Managing secrets you'll surely profit from

○ One way to pay more than lip service to employee participation is to call a vote on company policies once a year. Employees can vote on such issues as bonuses, tardiness penalties, choice of insurance and dress codes. After each vote, enter the decision in the employee handbook.

○ If you have problems with hourly, part-time employees not showing up for work, assign two people for each job. The buddy system is especially helpful for teen-agers or college students.
One person works the job Monday through Wednesday, the other Thursday through Sunday. If one worker can't cover his shift, he calls his buddy and asks him to switch shifts. People are willing to cover for each other because they know they'll need the favor returned someday.

○ How productive, enthusiastic and well-adjusted an employee will be is often determined the first few weeks on the job. Consider assigning a "sponsor" to each new recruit. The sponsor can spend 30 minutes a day for a couple of weeks teaching the newcomer how to use the electronic mail system, introducing the employee to others, and generally showing him the ropes.
Sponsors can volunteer for the assignments. That way you won't force any recluses you may have on staff to a task they might not like.

○ Throw away your suggestion box. You are an unusual manager if you actually read and act on the suggestions piled in your suggestion box. And an ignored suggestion is worse than none at all.
If you don't have the staff or the resources to keep up a year-round suggestion program, try a six-week program. Give a reward for the best idea each week and a grand prize at the end.

○ Hard work can be hard on families and friends as well as on the worker. During busy times when you require lots of overtime from your employees, you could help by sending flowers and dinner coupons to the employee's spouse or to a friend, along with a personal note.

REFERENCE ────────────────────────────────

301 Great Management Ideas from America's Most Innovative Small Companies edited by Sara P. Noble, published by *Inc.* magazine, 1991.

How to delegate without offending

No boss wants to be seen as a slave driver. That's one of the concerns that keeps a manager from delegating some of his work.

Other concerns that may have run through your mind are: "Nobody can do this work like I can," "What will happen if an employee does this work better than I could?" and "I don't have time to teach an employee how to do this job."

You've got to get over your delegating fears. Otherwise, you'll be so bogged down with day-to-day, low-priority work that you won't have time for your top-priority jobs.

Here are some tips on how to get the help you need quickly and still stay the boss everyone likes:

- Don't demand help — ask for it.

- If a job seems trivial or boring, stress that it's necessary and be extra grateful for the help.

- When you give someone a job to do, take the time to talk through it and give a clear picture of what you want. Never assume your employee understood you — encourage questions.

- Don't assign a task that you aren't familiar with or that you're not certain the employee can handle.

- Don't withhold any information or material that a person will need to complete a project.

- Set a realistic deadline! Make sure your employee agrees he can accomplish the task in that time.

○ Allow plenty of room for the employee to contribute his imagination and initiative to the project.

○ Don't bow out on a project completely once you've delegated it. Be available for questions and assistance, and check on your employee's progress occasionally. Remember to put the project's deadline along with the employee's initials on your calendar.

REFERENCE ————————————————————

If you haven't got the time to do it right, when will you find the time to do it over? by Jeffrey J. Mayer, Simon & Schuster, New York, 1990.

Managing Japanese-style

Japanese factories are mushrooming in the United States, giving Americans a new choice: Should we work for the foreign firms or stick with our native U.S. companies?

If you are aggressive, ambitious, independent, used to making decisions on your own and used to individual attention, you will probably feel out of place in a Japanese firm.

The Japanese share decision making. Their consensus approach means that seven or eight people typically review an idea before reaching a decision.

Perks and privileges of rank don't exist in Japanese firms. Forget about reserved parking, special bonuses, stock options and executive dining rooms. Presidents sit at the same metal desks as secretaries, often in large open areas instead of offices.

American managers complain that the Japanese have not yet learned to trust them. They claim that they are passed over for promotion and that Japanese-only meetings sometimes follow the joint Japanese-American meetings.

For managers who like to be in the know, fax machines that transmit messages in Japanese can be very frustrating.

Another sore point between Japanese and American managers is the Japanese attention to detail. Japanese managers see dropped screws on the factory floor as a serious discipline problem, indicating defects in the quality of the products being made. This pickiness tends to irritate American supervisors.

For factory workers, a job with the Japanese seems like a good deal, even though the Japanese expect hard work and plenty of overtime.

Factory workers are called "team members" or "associates." They do morning exercises, wearing company uniforms. Since one Japanese company made morning warm-up exercises mandatory two years ago, its 140 employees haven't had a single serious back or wrist injury.

In this same company, workers rotate jobs every two hours and move through all 18 assembly jobs in a few days. Workers are less bored, and they work together better since they know how each job works.

Factory workers in Japanese companies have more job security than their counterparts in American companies. Most factories try not to lay off employees during recessions and periods of slack demand. Managers are expected to find odd jobs to keep employees busy.

One company educated its employees during the seven weeks the plant was shut down. The workers were trained in various analytical and statistical procedures.

The education paid off: When the factory was up and running again, plant productivity rose 50 percent and costs dropped 55 percent.

Japanese companies also offer excellent child-care facilities. One company keeps their facility open 24 hours a day to accommodate the night-shift workers, too.

REFERENCE
The Wall Street Journal, Nov. 27, 1991.

Catching applicants who lie

Have you been burned on a company hire? If that person who looked so great on paper turned out to be your worst employee yet, consider using an employee-screening company next time. Their services are usually fast and cheap, with an average background check costing about $100.

"Eighty percent of the time someone has fudged on their job application. We get a criminal record hit almost every single day," claims the owner of a small reference-checking firm in Atlanta, Ga. And, she has also found that people are most prone to lie about their education.

A lot of employee-screening firms are out there (listed in the yellow pages under "management consultants") so do some checking of your own to find the right one. Here are a few questions to ask:

○ What services do you offer? You don't have to pay for every service they have available. Depending on your budget, you can have a potential employee's education, employment, professional references, criminal history, credit history, motor vehicle reports and drug tests checked, among other things.

○ How do you get your information? The screener should have researchers, or people power, as well as databases. The company should be able to explain how the various states store information and what information can be legally obtained in each state.

○ What's your background? Experience and a degree in personnel, criminal justice or industrial psychology are helpful.

○ Will you run a background check on me? This is an excellent way to discover the quality of their services.

○ Do you use your own services? The correct answer is yes.

Finally, don't forget the old standards of checking out a company when you want to use their services. Ask for references and actually call some of their clients. Ask your state's Department of Consumer Affairs if the company is licensed. Call your Better Business Bureau or chamber of commerce to see if any complaints have been lodged against the company.

REFERENCES ————————————————————————————

Inc., August 1992.
Jean Fitzgerald, co-owner, Vericon Resources Inc.

Assigning homework to job applicants

After interviewing several job applicants, you may have the feeling that you know who you'd like to work with, but you have no idea who would do the best job.

Solution: Give the job candidate a "take-home exam." Assign a job-related task or ask for ideas on a new program you are implementing.

The right person for the job will be the one who asks questions to get a clear idea of the project, scores well on your exam and sends it in as soon as possible.

REFERENCE ────────────────────────────────

135 Great Management Ideas, supplement to *Inc.*, January 1990.

How not to waste time at meetings

Some (notice the word some) business meetings are necessary, but almost every meeting lasts way too long. They waste your time, sap your energy and throw your entire day off schedule.

Here's how to have productive meetings and to get time-wasters under control:

○ Never have a "routine meeting" — the meeting you hold every week just because you always hold a meeting every week.

○ Never hold an impromptu meeting, unless there's a crisis. Everyone has to drop what they're doing to run to the meeting. When they get back to their desk, they find they can't get back into the project they were working on or they need to start over, and the rest of the day is wasted.

○ Avoid Monday morning meetings. They start the week off with a whimper instead of a bang. No morning is good for meetings. If the meeting ends around 11:00 a.m., workers tend to waste time until lunch. People are generally at their most productive in the mornings, and they could be getting a lot of work done or preparing for a later meeting. Try afternoon meetings instead.

○ Never meet on Friday afternoons. Who can concentrate?

○ Don't think your presence is necessary? Ask if someone could go in your place. But if you're going to grill them when they get back, wasting both your time and theirs, just attend the meeting yourself.

○ See if a few phone calls or an informal conversation would work instead of a meeting.

○ Always prepare an agenda for any meeting and give it to your employees before the meeting starts.

○ Begin and end meetings on time. Don't wait for latecomers. Make the last person to arrive take minutes.

○ Set time limits for discussions on each topic and ask people to stand when they speak. They'll speed up.

○ Does your meeting have to run a few minutes long? When the scheduled time for the meeting's end arrives, go ahead and announce it.

○ For meetings away from the office, confirm them before you leave and call if you're running late.

REFERENCE ———————————————————————————

If you haven't got the time to do it right, when will you find the time to do it over? by Jeffrey J. Mayer, Simon & Schuster, New York, 1990.

How to make sure your employees aren't stealing from you

When you've got workers like these, who needs shoplifters?

Studies show that employee theft accounts for 38 percent of inventory loss in the retail business while shoplifting accounts for 25 percent. How can you know who you can trust?

Many small-business owners and managers are too trusting and don't take some obvious steps that would help stop employee theft. Here are some suggestions made by theft-prevention consultants:

○ Tell job candidates that they are subject to drug testing. The threat alone will weed out many bad characters.

○ Do background checks on potential employees, especially those that will be in sensitive positions. A few hundred dollars spent now could save thousands later.

○ Learn to ask the right questions in the right way in interviews. One company has developed an oral test of 125 rapid-fire questions and estimates that it has cut employee theft by 12 percent. Many people will even admit to stealing from a former employer. They think that everybody steals a little so they will look as though they are lying if they deny stealing.

○ Keep valuable property under lock and key.

○ Let employees know that they are expected to be honest. If you don't define clear rules of right and wrong, some employees will take advantage of you: "They never said these supplies weren't for personal use." Develop a written policy on ethical behavior for employees to sign. There are software programs available to help write such policies.

○ Simply keep a closer eye on employees.

○ Order an inexpensive guide to money-saving business methods, such as the one put out by the Small Business Administration. The SBA guide suggests testing employees by occasionally putting temptation in their way.

REFERENCE
The Wall Street Journal, Oct. 5, 1992.

Catching the time thieves

Managers, are you stopping employee theft? You may be certain that no embezzlement is going on in your department. No one even uses the copy machine for personal use without letting you know first.

But what about the theft of company time? Many employees are time thieves without being aware of it, contributing to the hundreds of billions of dollars worth of employee time stolen every year in American companies.

Do your workers:

○ make long and unnecessary personal calls while at work?

○ linger over the coffee pot chatting with co-workers?

⊃ deliberately drag their feet on projects?

You could begin solving the problem of time theft by making your employees aware of it.

REFERENCE ————————————————————————————

How To Get A Better Job In This Crazy World by Robert Half, Crown Publishers Inc., New York, 1990.

Calming first-day jitters

Remember what your first day on the job was like?

Many managers have been working so long that they've forgotten, or they seem to have. New employees need to know the basic company rules and benefits, and you can't expect newcomers to get their information from other employees.

Some suggestions for Day One:

⊃ Documentation: payroll, income tax, pension, health insurance, personal records, union membership.

⊃ Hours of work, breaks, lunch.

⊃ Policy on tardiness and missing work.

⊃ Policy on allowed time off, such as sick days, personal days, holidays, leaves of absence.

⊃ Information on dress rules, parking privileges, smoking policies and telephone use. Can you use your phone for long-distance calls?

⊃ Job duties and responsibilities, even if you think you covered it in the interview.

⊃ Performance appraisal — when and how the supervisor will conduct it.

⊃ Introduction to supervisor, to fellow employees, to workplace.

⊃ Training — on and off the job.

○   Overtime.

○   Grievances — how to deal with them.

REFERENCE

Successful People Management: How to Get and Keep Good Employees by R.E. Smith, Financial Post Books, Toronto, 1982.

Business overseas

Germany

Always be the gentleman in Germany: social rules you need to know

Germans practice the kind of courtesy most Americans were taught early in the 20th century: men rising when women enter or leave the room, walking to the lady's left, shaking hands upon meeting and departing, careful use of titles and speaking in modulated voices.

In short, formality is normality among business associates in Germany. Even long-time friends may not use first names, so a new acquaintance never does. Germans love to talk about Germany and, although usually quite well-informed, are much less interested in the sports, culture or geography of other nations.

Social rules you need to know:

○ Business contacts are not commonly invited to German executives' homes. Respond to such an invitation as the honor that it is.

○ Take flowers, unwrapped, if invited to a private home, but avoid red roses — they imply romance.

○ Many Germans are very proud of their wine cellar; don't bring wine.

○ Answer the telephone by stating your last name. If answering in someone else's home, say, "Bei (their name)," to indicate you are not the resident.

○ Don't bring up sensitive subjects, such as the role of the military. Common sense suggests topics better left alone.

REFERENCE

Do's and Taboos Around the World edited by Roger E. Axtell, compiled by the Parker Pen Company, produced by The Benjamin Company Inc., Elmsford, N.Y., 1985.

Escalators, the
Autobahn and public transportation

○ Germans tend to be very conscientious about rules and regulations — how else would a virtually honor-system transportation plan work?

○ If you are going to stand still on an escalator, keep to the right; if you're going to walk, move to the left. You keep your feet on the floor, not propped on another seat in the train. And you exit through the ausgang and enter at the eingang — to go against the flow is considered bad form.

○ Do not be startled to see dogs in restaurants, public transportation, even grocery stores. They are invariably well-behaved and are allowed there.

○ True, there is no speed limit on the Autobahn (at least not as of press time), but slow traffic is expected to stay to the right — and does. Germans never pass on the right, only on the left. It works.

○ It is considered extremely rude to blow one's car horn except in extreme emergency, or to flash lights as a signal to pass.

REFERENCE
The Federal Express World Business Advisory and Calendar, Educational Extension Systems, Clarks Summit, Pa., 1992.

Don't be caught short

○ In Germany, plan ahead or do without. Nearly all stores close at 6:00 p.m. or 6:30 p.m. weekdays (exceptions: shops in railroad stations) and at noon on Saturdays. Discount stores and all-night supermarkets are virtually nonexistent.

○ Between "bank holidays" and religious holy days, there are a lot of off-days in Germany. Don't be caught short of cash or supplies.

○ The tip (15 percent) is figured into the bill at most restaurants. One is expected, however, to "round up" one's check to the next full deutsche mark, or beyond, if service is exceptional.

○ Punctuality is, of course, de rigueur. And don't for a moment doubt that this also applies to transportation. If the schedule says the train leaves at 7:29, it leaves at 7:29, not 7:28 or 7:30.

REFERENCE ────────────────────────────────

The Federal Express World Business Advisory and Calendar, Educational Extension Systems, Clarks Summit, Pa., 1992.

France

Will they appreciate my high-school French?

Language is something of a no-win impediment in France. If you trot out your high-school French, your listener is apt to respond in excellent English, thus signaling that he'd rather not hear his beloved language butchered. Yet offense sometimes seems to be taken if we make no effort at all to speak the native tongue.

By and large, however, the reputed rudeness of Parisians toward Americans appears to have faded in recent years. Travelers now report an air of cordiality from the Frenchman on the street, and they are finding service personnel downright engaging.

As is so often the case, pleasant surprises await Americans who leave their preconceptions at home.

It may help to know:

○ Food and food service are taken seriously in France — there is virtually no such thing as a casual lunch.

○ Chrysanthemums represent mourning, and for that reason would not go over well as a hostess gift. Avoid even numbers of flowers, or 13 blossoms — bad luck.

○ Tipping is similar to American practice, although "servis compris" on a menu means 15 percent has been added for service. Go ahead and add a bit more anyhow, especially if service was very good. "Servis non compris" means no gratuity has been added. Leave 8 to 12 percent.

○ Let your host order the wine. The French pride themselves on their knowledge of the grape, so defer to their recommendation.

REFERENCES

The Federal Express World Business Advisory and Calendar, Educational Extension Systems, Clarks Summit, Pa., 1992.

Do's and Taboos Around the World edited by Roger E. Axtell, compiled by the Parker Pen Company, produced by The Benjamin Company Inc., Elmsford, N.Y., 1985.

Great Britain

Clothes you shouldn't wear and subjects you shouldn't discuss

Americans have so much in common with the Brits that it's almost impossible to imagine either side taking offense. We like them; they like us.

But even within families, strained relationships can occur, and this is true even with the nation we think of as a sort of parent.

To keep the British happy:

○ Call them "British" or "Brits," not "English."

○ "Scotch" is a drink. The people are "Scots" or "Scotsmen," and the language and the adjective are "Scottish."

○ Avoid striped ties. If yours happens to be a copy of a British regimental, your wearing it will look pretentious — one does not wear an old-school tie unless one has attended the old school.

○ One subject to avoid is criticism of the royal family. Politics and religion are touchy subjects.

○ Similarly, to begin a conversation with "What do you do?" is considered rather personal.

○ Business talk is usually left in the office at close of day. Social time is for socializing.

○ Don't be surprised if the Brits answer your "Thank you" with a "Thank you" of their own, instead of "You're welcome."

○ Honorary titles are widely used. To be sure of the preferred form of address, pay attention to what others use.

REFERENCE ————————

The Federal Express World Business Advisory and Calendar, Educational Extension Systems, Clarks Summit, Pa., 1992.

Scandinavia

Timing and tipping

○ Danes, Icelanders, Finns, Norwegians and Swedes cherish their long-awaited summer months. Don't expect to do much business then.

○ Punctuality is important in most of the Nordic countries, with Iceland the exception. Make appointments well in advance.

○ Generally, a tip has been added to a restaurant or hotel bill. If not, add 10 to 15 percent. No tipping in taxis.

○ Iceland is also the exception to the rule "Use last names until invited to do otherwise." In that island nation, first names are commonly used, although a foreigner will be excused if he stays with established protocol.

Don't touch that drink!

○ Guests do not touch their drinks until the toast begins — an important point to remember if you are the host.

○ In Denmark and Sweden, rules concerning the toast are somewhat more formal than in the other Scandinavian countries. The host offers the first toast, and you should not toast him or another guest until your host has raised his glass to you.

○ Lift your glass to eye-level, look directly at the recipient of the toast, say "Skoal!" and drink, then make a wave of the glass toward your host before bringing it back down to the table.

○ Alcohol is consumed in large quantities in Scandinavia, but drunk driving laws are strictly enforced. Choose a designated driver.

○ The Danes' aquavit (a clear liquor) is potent, and they like to surprise guests with it.

REFERENCES ────────────────────────────────

Do's and Taboos Around the World edited by Roger E. Axtell, compiled by the Parker Pen Company, produced by The Benjamin Company Inc., Elmsford, N.Y., 1985. *Letitia Baldridge's Complete Guide to Executive Manners*, Rawson Associates, New York, 1985.

The Mediterranean

Tips on drinking water and kissing cheeks

In general, those countries that share a hot, humid climate tend to be a bit more relaxed in matters of protocol than their northern neighbors. Punctuality is not a priority, nor are appointments always required or honored. In Spain, however, you do take seriously the start of the bullfight.

○ Mealtimes are perhaps the most difficult adjustment for Americans. Lunch is usually the main meal of the day, and it may last for several hours.

○ Offices and stores close in Spain from about 1 p.m. to 4:30 p.m., after which business resumes until around 8 p.m. Dinner does not begin in earnest until after 9 p.m., and may continue until 11 p.m.

○ In Italy, handshaking has been called the national pastime, and gesturing is an art form.

○ Greetings are more affectionate than in the northern countries. Men often embrace, and even kiss each other's cheeks.

○ An upward nod of the head means "no" in Greece, not "yes," and tilting the head to one side means "yes."

○ Leave a 10-percent tip in a Greek restaurant; the staff will share it. In Italy, 15 percent has already been added to the bill in most hotels and restaurants, but it is customary to add a bit to that. Tip about 10 percent in taxis.

○ In Greece, tap water is safe to drink. In Spain and Portugal, water quality is variable, but usually safe in the cities.

○ Coffee is the traditional social drink in most Latin countries. Accept a cup even if you don't really want it, or your host, to be polite, won't drink his.

REFERENCES

The Federal Express World Business Advisory and Calendar, Educational Extension Systems, Clarks Summit, Pa., 1992.
Do's and Taboos Around the World edited by Roger E. Axtell, compiled by the Parker Pen Company, produced by The Benjamin Company Inc., Elmsford, N.Y., 1992.

Japan

Understanding the Japanese

Books have been written about understanding the Japanese behavior patterns, but a brief summary of the four chief character traits follows:

○ *Nintai* - Patience, a difficult concept for the result-oriented Westerner. This is the kind of patience that means having the endurance to consider every possible detail of the business at hand, plus any factors, no matter how minute. The Japanese are quickly put off by displays of impatience, regarding them as signs of weakness. On the other hand, they appreciate the efforts of outsiders to match their slow, deliberate decision-making process.

○ *Kao* - Face, the most precious commodity a Japanese has, his badge of respectability within society. Criticism must be couched in layers of praise, and then delivered vaguely and indirectly.

If you must disagree, do so in the most discreet and subtle way possible, so that the Japanese businessman knows you do not disapprove of him or his company.

⊃   *On, Giri*- Obligations and duties, twin concepts for the indebtedness that every Japanese feels simply for existing. Understanding this sense of responsibility, to both forebears and contemporaries, helps Westerners see why the Japanese cannot grasp the American attitude that we don't owe anybody anything. *On* is the obligation incurred by the granting of major favors such as assuming responsibility for another's education; *giri* is the duty or loyalty one owes to the world.

REFERENCE ————————————————————————

How To Do Business with the Japanese by Mark A. Zimmerman, Random House, New York, 1983.

When a handshake should give way to a bow

Most Japanese businesspersons are sophisticated in the ways of the international community. They travel much in the West and have frequent contact with Westerners.

Therefore, they are not usually offended by handshaking Americans who ignore the protocols of greeting and departure so carefully observed by the Japanese.

Nevertheless, it is flattering and a sign of good will when we at least attempt to emulate the ways of others, whether on their "turf" or on our own.

Contrary to American thinking, bowing is not a sign of submissiveness. The Japanese do not care much for casual body touching, and feel more comfortable greeting business contacts with a bow than with a handshake. To the Japanese, the bow indicates respect for wisdom or experience.

Here's how: Bow straight from the waist, with hands at sides or sliding down your legs, and eyes turned away. Your hands should never be clasped behind your back or thrust into pockets.

Allow business inferiors to bow longer and lower than you do. Match bows with an equal, although a little extra bow gives you a slight edge of respect, a good move if you want his business. When meeting someone who clearly outranks you, be sure you bow lower and longer than he does.

REFERENCES

Do's and Taboos Around the World edited by Roger E. Axtell, compiled by the Parker Pen Company, produced by The Benjamin Company Inc., Elmsford, N.Y., 1985. *How to Behave in Japan*, Matsushita Electric Corporation, LTD, Overseas Training Center, Osaka, Japan.

Taboo behavior in Japan

○ Crossing legs while seated: Don't. To sit with your legs crossed is a breach of the formality expected by the Japanese in a meeting or interview, especially when a higher-ranking person is present.

○ Hands in your pockets while talking or greeting someone — the Japanese consider this very discourteous.

○ A Japanese may also regard a too-direct look in the eyes as an affront; take only an occasional brief glance into the other person's face, especially while conversing.

○ No one but family and very close friends use the first name. You're safe if you add "san" to end of the last name, thus forming the equivalent of our "Mister (last name)."

○ The Japanese do not eat or chew gum while walking in public — they consider it very unsightly.

○ Blowing your nose at the table or in public is taboo.

○ Lateness — especially for business meetings, but also for social events — will not earn you points in Japan. Be punctual.

REFERENCES

Do's and Taboos Around the World, edited by Roger E. Axtell, compiled by the Parker Pen Company, produced by The Benjamin Company Inc., Elmsford, N.Y., 1985. *How to Behave in Japan*, Matsushita Electric Corporation, LTD, Overseas Training Center, Osaka, Japan.

Tipping

In a chart on tipping compiled for business travelers, Japan stood out for the repetition of the word "no" in every possible tipping situation: not in restaurants, hotels, taxis, barbershops or toilets. To offer a Japanese a tip is to imply that he has to be bribed to do what is simply expected of him — his best work.

REFERENCE
The Concise Guide to Executive Etiquette by Linda and Wayne Phillips, Doubleday, New York, 1990.

Visiting in a private home

If your host extends to you the honor of an invitation to his home, there are a few things you should know to feel more confident:

- Take off your shoes as you enter a Japanese home, and line them up with the others, toes pointing away from the house. Usually a pair of house slippers is given to you for use in the house. You will probably receive another pair for use in the toilet, too.

- Remove your coat when visiting, even if you plan to stay only a minute.

- When you enter a tatami room, or a room with a carpet, take off the slippers and leave them at the door.

- If you are invited to dinner in a Japanese home, do not be surprised if your host's wife remains in the kitchen or just serves the meal. This is her traditional role in Japan, and you should not insist on her joining you.

- Resist the temptation to visit her in the kitchen as you might do with an American hostess. The kitchen is considered off-limits to guests.

- As you presumably would straighten your bed in a Western home, put your quilted futon back in order after you get up in the morning.

REFERENCES
How to Behave in Japan, Matsushita Electric Corporation, LTD, Overseas Training Center, Osaka, Japan.
Simply Japan, News from the Consulate General of Japan in Atlanta, January 1992.

The Japanese bath: it isn't for washing

In Japan, the bath is a social event, and a little knowledge may mean the difference between embarrassment and enjoyment.

Washing takes place before you enter the bath. You may be offered the use of a shower or a bowl to dip water from the bath. In either case, your host expects you to rinse, soap, and rinse again completely before entering the bath. This is because the same very hot water will be used by everyone — so don't pull the plug when you get out!

Enter slowly to become accustomed to the heat of the water — you'll soon enjoy the hot water's relaxing effects.

REFERENCE
How to Behave in Japan, Matsushita Electric Corporation, LTD, Overseas Training Center, Osaka, Japan.

Giving gifts in Japan

○ Presenting a gift: Red flowers are for weddings and white are for funerals. Don't take a potted plant to someone who is ill, because the Japanese believe it will cause the illness to take firmer root. Make every effort to exchange gifts of equal value, even though the polite Japanese will say, "Here is something completely worthless," to show his humility in presenting a gift. To save face, in case of discrepancy, he will not open the gift in your presence. Only good friends open gifts immediately. If you are giving a collection of items, remember that the Japanese consider an odd number more beautiful and artistic. Avoid four and nine; these numbers symbolize death and suffering.

○ Accepting gifts: While a Westerner may view lavish gift-giving with some suspicion, he would do well to understand that the bestowing of gifts is an honorable tradition among the Japanese. Refusal to accept a gift constitutes an insult second only to a deliberate attack on the Japanese self-esteem, or "face."

○ The gift of a compliment: The Japanese believe that the efforts of the group, rather than the individual, should be praised. Nonetheless, express praise with reservation — too much is considered insincere. If a compliment you give is received in silence or with denial, understand that modesty through self-deprecation is a desirable trait among the Japanese.

REFERENCES

Simply Japan, News from the Consulate General of Japan in Atlanta, January 1992.
How To Do Business with the Japanese by Mark A. Zimmerman, Random House, New York, 1983.

You and the law

How to get free legal advice

Need a little legal advice but don't have money to pay for it? You do have some places to turn:

○ The Legal Aid Society. This group of lawyers offers free legal advice to people whose income is below poverty level. Many firms require lawyers to do a certain amount of "pro bono" work, free work for the public good, and other lawyers just participate on their own.

○ Your local bar association. Many bar associations offer a legal referral service that can set up a consultation with a lawyer for $10 or so.

○ Low-cost legal clinics. Look in your telephone directory under "Legal Services" for these clinics.

○ The American Civil Liberties Union, the Women's Law Project or other similar organizations. Many organizations offer free legal advice on issues that are in their realm of concern. Labor unions often provide counsel on job-related and personal matters. Lawyers who will work on a "contingency-fee" basis. Some lawyers are willing to work for a percentage of your award if they win the case for you. They receive nothing if you lose.

○ Government agencies. There are federal, state and local agencies that deal with everything from housing to taxes. Check in the government pages of the telephone directory for agencies that might handle the kind of problem you have. Attorneys employed by the agency can answer your questions for free. For instance, call the "United States Government — Internal Revenue Service" if you have a question about your federal income tax return.

REFERENCE ————————————————————————————————

The Family Legal Companion by Thomas Hauser, McGraw-Hill Book Co., New York, 1985.

How much can a lawyer charge?

The good news: In some cases, lawyers are limited by law on how much they can charge their clients for personal injury cases.

The bad news: That legal limit is pretty high.

Lawyers usually charge an hourly fee, a set amount for the whole case, or a percentage of your winnings. Lawyers who charge on a contingency basis, or a percentage of your winnings, usually ask for about a third of what you get.

You can easily find out from your local bar association what the legal limit is for your area. In some New York counties, for instance, lawyers can choose to charge either a third of the amount you recover after payment of court expenses, or a sliding scale: 50 percent of the first $1,000 recovered, 40 percent of the next $2,000, 35 percent of the next $22,000, and 25 percent of anything over $25,000.

Some lawyers will give you a better deal than others. Get several names from the local bar association and shop around for the best price.

REFERENCE

The Family Legal Companion by Thomas Hauser, McGraw-Hill Book Co., New York, 1985.

How to defend yourself in small claims court

Ever been taken to small claims court by someone who claims you owe him money?

When a person you owe (a creditor) files a suit against you, you will be served with a summons issued by the court. The summons will give you a date and time you need to appear in court.

You'll also get a copy of the document the creditor filed with the court in which he explains why he thinks he's entitled to money from you.

Even if you think the creditor is crazy, never fail to respond to the summons or appear in court. The court may enter a "default judgment" against you. The judge simply grants the creditor's request and writes a judgment requiring you to pay. The judgment can accrue interest until you pay up.

You can defend yourself against your creditor's demand for payment in small claims court. Here are some possible legal defenses you may have. Any of these, if true, will keep a case from proceeding in court.

○ You've already paid your debt.

○ The creditor never performed the service he is demanding payment for.

○ You're not the person responsible for payment of the debt. (Your employer or your spouse could be responsible.)

○ You were not properly served with summons.

○ The creditor didn't file suit against you soon enough. There is a "Statute of Limitations" on how much time can pass before someone files suit to collect a debt. The time a creditor has to file suit ranges from two to 15 years, depending on the state you live in and the kind of contract between you and the creditor.

○ The creditor's actions were "unscrupulous." You were taken advantage of by the creditor, or he forced you in some outrageous way to promise to pay. For this defense to work, you need to have notified the creditor very soon after your agreement that you weren't going to pay and why.
It also helps if you never made any payments to the creditor. If the creditor performed a service for you, your best defense is if you asked him to stop his work once you realized he was not trustworthy.

○ You received faulty or damaged goods from the creditor, or the product you received did not do what the creditor claimed it would do.

○ The creditor breached its warranty. The creditor must meet the conditions set out in the warranty, or you don't have to pay.

○ If you're being sued for failing to pay child support — you lost your job and you request a reduction in your payment amounts.

REFERENCE ————————————————————————————
Debtors' Rights, A Legal Self Help Guide by Gudrun M. Nickel, Sphinx Publishing, Clearwater, Fla., 1992.

How to defend yourself in traffic court

Most people at one time or another have paid for a speeding ticket they thought was unfair. People just assume that trying to fight a speeding ticket is a useless battle.

Actually, you can win in traffic court. It's up to the state to prove that you broke the law. If you can create any doubt in the judge's mind about the validity of your ticket, you can win your case.

Possible ways to defend yourself against a speeding ticket:

○ The police officer did not identify the correct vehicle. Particularly in heavy traffic, a person operating a radar gun can't be sure which vehicle the radar picked up as speeding. Cross-examine the radar operator in court to see if he could have been mistaken in selecting you as the speeder.

○ The evidence from the radar unit or the speedometer is not reliable and cannot be used in court. The state must prove that the radar unit or speedometer was tested for accuracy and regularly inspected and that the radar operator was properly trained. If the state cannot show proof, the speed measurements may not be allowed as evidence. (If they are allowed, you can at least argue that they shouldn't be taken too seriously.)

○ The speed limit signs were not adequately posted. If your ticket is for doing 55 in a 35 miles-per-hour zone, your argument could be that you passed no 35 mph signs or only one sign that you could barely see.

○ You had no control over your speeding. Example: A part of your car broke (like the spring that closes the throttle plate) and caused your car to speed.

○ You were speeding out of self-defense. Example: You're a single woman and were driving alone. A car was following you very closely on a dark, deserted street and blinding you with its headlights. You sped to get away from potential danger. You had no idea it was a police car.

○ You sped to avoid an emergency. Example: You sped in order to pass and avoid colliding with a car that was rapidly slowing in front of you.

○ You are speeding to get away from a life-threatening situation. If someone has threatened to harm or kill you, and you believe they're serious, you can speed if it's the only way to get away.

○ You broke the speed limit "legally." In about one-fourth of the states, it's not necessarily against the law to speed! These states have *prima facie* speed statutes instead of "fixed" speed laws. So, in some states, you could defend yourself by saying that driving over the speed limit was reasonable because the weather was perfect, very little traffic was on the road and the road was straight.

REFERENCE ——

How to Win in Traffic Court by Phil Bello, Major Market Books, Gibbsboro, N.J., 1990.

Should you be in jail?

Chances are you've committed a crime in the last few months.

No need to turn yourself in, though. Unfortunately, virtually everybody breaks the law on a fairly regular basis.

Did you speed on the way to work this morning? That could cost you up to $200 in fines. Bet in the office pool? You could spend up to six months in jail and pay a $1,000 fine.

Take a pen or legal pad home from work? You're off to the slammer for 12 months and $1,000 poorer.

Though you'll probably never be prosecuted for it, it's a safe (though illegal) bet that some aspect of your life breaks the letter of the law. But all that will ever come of it is a feeling of guilt.

Among the common offenses:

○ Taking office supplies home.

○ Evading taxes.

○ Gambling illegally.

○ Committing computer crimes (such as illegally copying software).

○ Drinking in public. (This includes parks and beaches.)

○ Shoplifting.

○ Stealing TV signals (with an illegal cable hookup, descrambler or satellite dish, for example).

○ Speeding.

○ Parking illegally.

○ Fishing illegally.

○ Smoking in public where an ordinance prohibits it.

○ Failing to recycle where an ordinance requires it.

○ Lying to customs agents to avoid duties.

○ Importing prohibited products (like Cuban cigars and tortoise-shell jewelry).

○ Lying on an application where the form states false statements are punishable (such as for a government job).

○ Disregarding a jury summons.

○ Knowingly buying stolen goods.

○ Selling tickets without authorization for above the listed price.

REFERENCE ———————————————————————————
The Wall Street Journal, March 12, 1993.

When neighbor noise is driving you crazy

Are your peaceful, quiet evening hours often destroyed by rock music blasting from your neighbor's basement or electric drills screaming from your neighbor's workshop?

Loud noise of any kind can be a very serious matter, even a legal matter, when it disrupts your home life. With a little knowledge of your local laws, you may find that you can do something about that neighborhood noise.

Almost every community has a noise ordinance that prohibits excessive, unnecessary and unreasonable noise. Your local ordinance is your most effective weapon in maintaining your peace and quiet.

Some noises that are considered necessary or acceptable at certain times of the day are considered unreasonable at 2 a.m. A neighbor hammering on a wood project that he is building or playing his stereo loud enough to keep you awake are examples of unnecessary noise.

A dog that barks if someone comes into the yard is not considered a nuisance, but one that barks incessantly most of the night probably would be.

Most cities have special rules governing particularly bothersome sounds. For instance, some cities prohibit the honking of auto horns except as a warning of danger.

So when the carpoolers that come for your neighbor every day honk across the street to signal their arrival, they are violating the law.

Even if you are the only neighbor on the block that is bothered by your neighbor's noise, you may be able to sue him for creating a private nuisance. You can ask a court for money damages and to have the noise stopped, and you just might win.

Your neighbor may not know about the noise ordinances, so just talking it over with him may do the trick. It would be the neighborly thing to do.

REFERENCE ─────────────────────────────────
Neighbor Law: fences, trees, boundaries and noise by Cora Jordan, Nolo Press, Berkeley, Calif., 1991.

What you can do
about your neighbor's messy yard

Does your neighbor's untidy property keep you from enjoying the view out the windows of your home? Would you enjoy grilling out on your back deck if the garbage from next door were not so offensive?

Do you work hard to keep your lawn neatly mowed, your shrubbery trimmed, your house painted and repaired and your driveway clean?

If you take pride in your home and your neighborhood it can be pretty disheartening to be bordered by a neighbor's overgrown weeds and rubbish, broken fences and property that just looks messy and in need of repair.

Blighted property can be the breeding ground for rats and insects, and can greatly diminish the value of the property in the neighborhood.

There is hope. Most towns have ordinances that prohibit property that has become an eyesore or a health hazard.

You need to first find out what your local ordinances cover. You can usually find this information at the local library or county courthouse. Make a copy of the ordinance and show it to your neighbor.

He may not even realize he is breaking the law. But once you point it out to him, that may be all that is necessary to get things cleaned up.

If he ignores your confrontation or refuses to clean up his act, you may then report his violation to the authorities. They may give him another warning.

If he still doesn't respond, he may be fined, or the city may fix the problem for him and send him the bill. If he wants to fight this in court, he may do so. But if he loses the battle, he may be fined again, and in some cases may even get a jail sentence.

REFERENCE ————————————————————————————————

Neighbor Law: fences, trees, boundaries and noise by Cora Jordan, Nolo Press, Berkeley, Calif., 1991.

What collection
agencies don't want you to know

Collection agencies don't want you to know that there is little they can do legally to get you to pay a debt. In fact, if most people knew how little they can do, collection agencies would have a hard time staying in business.

Collection agencies will do almost anything to get money from you because they're only paid on the amounts they collect. Sometimes what they do is illegal.

If a collector violates the Fair Debt Collection Practices Act, you can sue the collection agency for damages, and you can use the violation in your defense if the agency takes legal action against you.

The agency can take legal action against you if your creditor has "sold" your account to the collection agency at a discount. If the collection agency is just receiving a percentage of whatever they collect from you, the agency doesn't own your account and can take no legal action against you.

The worst it can do is report you to a credit reporting service, if it is a member of one. If you never pay your debt, it will be on your credit report for seven years.

(Important note: When you apply for a loan over $50,000 or for a job with a salary over $20,000, the "seven years" rule doesn't apply. Information such as debts, arrests, tax liens, etc., can stay on your credit report forever.)

Your collection agency rights:

○ When a collector makes his first call to you, within five days he must send you in writing:

- The amount of the debt he claims you owe

- The name of the person or business you owe

- A statement that the debt will be assumed to be correct unless you dispute it within 30 days

○ If you write to the collector within 30 days of his phone call and state that you don't owe part or any of the money, he has to mail to you proof of your debt. He also has to give you the name of your original creditor if your debt has switched hands.

○ Once you dispute your debt, the collector has to stop trying to collect money from you until he proves your debt. He must notify anyone he has told about your debt (like a credit reporting service) that you've disputed it.

○ By law, a collection agency must stop harassing you even if you simply write a letter to the agency requesting that they not contact you anymore. (Remember, laws that apply to collection agencies don't necessarily apply to the creditor to whom you owe the debt.)

○ A collection agency representative shouldn't try to appear to be a law enforcement official, an attorney or a representative of any government agency. He can't try to mislead you with a document that looks like a court order, judgment or a subpoena. He shouldn't imply that you've committed a crime or any misconduct.

○ A debt collector should never call you before 8 a.m. or after 9 p.m., and should never call you at work if you tell him not to.

○ A collector cannot try to force you to pay by embarrassing you. He can't threaten to publish your name, sell your account or send you letters in embarrassing envelopes.

If you do owe money and the debt collector doesn't violate any laws when it contacts you, you'll probably be able to work with the collector to clear up debts. You may be able to negotiate to reduce the amount of your debt.

Collection agencies want to get your money as quickly as possible. They would probably rather have a reduced lump-sum payment than small payments extending over a long period of time.

REFERENCE

Debtors' Rights, A Legal Self Help Guide by Gudrun M. Nickel, Sphinx Publishing, Clearwater, Fla., 1992.

Things detectives don't want to tell you

Looking for a missing person? Got your own trench coat and fedora? Who needs a detective? Finding someone who has faded into obscurity is a challenge, but not an impossible one. All you really need to know is the person you're looking for.

Was the missing person a sports fanatic? If so, he may subscribe to one of the special interest magazines some sports enthusiasts swear by. If not, what about his favorite sport's fan club?

Both magazines and fan clubs keep records and are generally willing to share (for a price) as long as you don't mention your reasons. Remember, whatever new identity a person assumes, they can't give up what they truly enjoy — their hobbies.

Does the missing person like to fish or hunt game? Most states require registration and licenses to do so. And that information is most often stored in a database at the state's Department of Natural Resources.

The state department should have names, addresses, social security numbers and dates of birth on file. The information is usually up-to-date, too, since the license is mailed to the applicant.

People with boats might have run afoul of the Coast Guard or other harbor patrols. Check out registration lists from state boating registrars and the Coast Guard. However, boaters only have to register once a year.

Avid bowlers can be particularly easy to track, believe it or not. The American Bowling Congress (located in Paramus, New Jersey) can tell you the town where your missing person's league record is being kept. Just tell them you're looking for your old partner.

Also, sports fanatics tend to be season ticket holders. If college sports are their passion, ask their favorite school's alumni association or athletic department where the team is playing that week. It might be worth a trip.

If it's speed the missing person likes, be it racing cars, boats, hot rods, etc., he very likely belongs to a national organization in order to get a rating in that sport. Not only do these organizations keep track of current addresses, they also chart where people are racing. You might even be able to beat someone to their next stop.

REFERENCE ────────────────────────────────

Check It Out! by Edmund J. Pankau, Contemporary Books, Chicago, 1992.

Can't anybody have any privacy around here?

You may think you have a private life, but think again! Just about everything you do — from renting videos to applying for a pilot's license or buying a toaster oven — can become part of records that may fall into the hands (or computers) of, well, you may be surprised.

One of the first things we all get when we are born is a set of nine digits — your Social Security number. It's not like the lottery, where you or your parents can pick your favorite numbers. Once they are assigned to you by the Social Security Administration, they are yours and yours alone, forever.

Your Social Security number becomes a part of you and goes wherever you go for the rest of your life. Since it is such an important and reliable identifier, you are required to disclose this number many, many times in order to receive certain benefits and privileges.

While some agencies and companies insist upon obtaining your Social Security number, others may compromise if you are persistent in not giving it. In many cases, you must sacrifice services if you are not willing to tell your private number.

Most of us are aware that the Internal Revenue Service keeps tabs on exactly where our income comes from and what we do with it. But as much as the IRS knows about your finances, the Social Security Administration may know even more.

The Social Security Administration, through your Social Security number, has a record of your entire employment history. They also know about your debts and your living arrangements, as well as your marital status and medical history.

If you have ever worked for the federal government, been in the military or sought a security clearance, the Federal Bureau of Investigation has a file on you. They also may have a file on you if you subscribe to certain publications, contribute to certain political or social causes, or join certain organizations — usually those that lean politically left-of-center.

If you ever served in the Armed Forces, the Veterans' Administration has a record of where you've lived and worked, your education and your medical history.

The VA keeps track of you after you are discharged or retire, for the purpose of determining eligibility of benefits such as medical care, educational assistance and real estate loans.

School days, school days. Those dear old golden rule days may still be on record if you attended school in the United States. In addition to your academic achievement, you may find information about your family, health and discipline during your school years.

Who has access to your records?

Many government agencies may share information that may be pertinent to their needs. While access is usually restricted to federal or state agencies, it may sometimes be obtained by others through a court order.

You may be able to obtain a copy of your own records by writing to the agency or organization involved. You will need to give them your name and address (both past and current), and dates relating to the information you are asking for. A small fee is usually charged for this information, and it may take weeks to actually receive it. So be prepared to wait.

As for your school records, besides your parents and yourself if you are over 18, school officials, government agencies and colleges are allowed access to your records.

Private organizations (no pun intended) also keep records on you. There are many organizations who are in the business of finding out what your hobbies and interests are. They make money by giving other organizations names of people like you, who may be interested in their products or services.

National Demographics and Lifestyles is one large company of this kind. If they know that you like photography, for example, your mailbox may soon be filled with catalogs on camera equipment.

How do the private organizations find out about you? Well, have you ever bought an appliance and filled out a warranty card? Chances are, you were also asked for information about your lifestyle, or more specifically, what activities you enjoy on a regular basis. It's all innocent enough, but are you starting to get the picture?

If you don't mind sharing this information, go ahead. But just remember, it goes a lot further than just "the warranty department."

And your warranty is still good even if you don't care to share.

Don't forget the credit bureaus. Have you ever had a credit card, rented a home, married, divorced or been arrested? Credit bureaus know all this and more.

They sell this information to prospective creditors, landlords, employers and insurance companies.

Banks and other financial institutions get extremely personal, too. They have records not only of your deposits and withdrawals, but also of whom you write your checks to.

Only a few states prohibit banks from giving this information to anyone other than a government agency, account holder or person named in a court order.

And if you list your bank as a credit reference, you can expect the bank to give this information freely to others who are considering granting credit to you.

Just keep in mind that whatever you do these days goes down in history. And since your personal files can work to your benefit or to your detriment, you may want to check them yourself for accuracy.

If you find that information on record is incorrect, you have a right to dispute it and have it corrected.

Be careful. Anything you say or do can, and may, be held on record.

REFERENCE ───────────────────────────────────
Nolo News, Spring 1993.

Your job and the law

Overtime. Did you know that for many jobs in the United States, your boss has to pay you overtime if you work more than 40 hours a week? Unless you have an "executive," "professional," or "administrative" job, the Fair Labor Standards Act requires your employer to pay you one-and-a-half times your regular pay for any extra hours worked.

Your employer can't average the hours you work over two or more weeks, either. So if you work 30 hours one week and 50 hours the next, you must receive overtime pay of 10 hours for the second week, even though the two weeks average out to 40 hours.

If you're not sure if you qualify for overtime pay, check with the nearest office of the Wage and Hour Division of the United States Department of Labor. They will even file a suit on your behalf for payment of back wages if they find that your employer has violated the law.

Personnel file. Has an employer ever prevented you from looking at your personnel files? They may be violating the law.

All employees of the federal government have access to their personnel files. You have the right to see your file if you're a member of a union that has negotiated a contract allowing workers to see their files.

And most states have laws requiring employers to give workers access to their employment records. The laws differ from state to state on how much of your records you can see. For instance, you usually can't see letters of reference and any records that relate to an investigation for a criminal offense.

Call the state Department of Labor to find out the laws on personnel files in your state.

Overpayment. It doesn't happen often, but occasionally you get a paycheck that's larger than it should be. If your accounting department makes a mathematical error and overpays you on payday, you have to report it. It's the law.

If your company discovers the error, it can take action against you for "unjust enrichment."

No payment. Children and teen-agers sometimes take on a job, like painting a house or assisting in landscaping a yard, without signing a written contract first. It's a bad idea, but it happens.

You and your child do have legal recourse if the employer claims he's not satisfied and refuses to pay for the work.

First send a letter to the employer asking for payment or for a written statement explaining why he isn't satisfied. Then, if necessary, file suit in small claims court for breach of an oral contract. You don't need a lawyer, but witnesses and photographs of the finished job are very helpful.

In the future, unless the employer is a neighbor you absolutely trust, encourage your child to draw up a contract detailing the exact work to be done, the materials he'll need to do the job, the dates the work will be done, and the date and the amount he'll be paid.

REFERENCE ——————————————————————————
The Family Legal Companion by Thomas Hauser, McGraw-Hill Book Co., New York, 1985.

How to lower your child support payments when you just can't keep up

You may be like many other divorced parents these days who are struggling to keep up with child support payments. The amounts awarded for child support are skyrocketing, and more and more paying parents are going deeper into debt every day.

The amount of child support you pay isn't chiseled in stone. When circumstances change, you can change the amount you pay.

How is the amount determined in the first place? If both parents can agree on an amount, judges usually OK it. If you can't reach an agreement, judges will award a "reasonable" amount based, for the most part, on the paying parent's income. But the income of the receiving parent may also be a determining factor.

There are circumstances that may justify having the amount you have been ordered to pay lowered. Here are some of them:

○ The paying parent loses his job, is demoted, is forced by his employer to take a pay cut, or becomes disabled and earns less.

○ The paying parent has a new child for which he is also responsible.

○ The receiving parent remarries, gets a new job or a pay raise.

○ The medical or educational needs of the children decrease significantly.

The amount of child support may also be raised if circumstances warrant. Some common reasons for increases are:

○ The paying parent's income increases significantly.

○ The receiving parent's income decreases significantly.

○ New and necessary medical or education expenses are incurred by the receiving parent or the children.

○ The children's needs change due to age or other reasons.

○ The law changes after a child support order is issued.

If you want or need to have your child support payments changed, it's your responsibility to get it done.

First, try to reach an agreement with the other parent. Then simply ask the judge to modify the existing order based on your agreement.

If you cannot reach an agreement with the other parent, you may ask the court to order a change.

Even then, you don't necessarily need a lawyer. While the procedures differ from state to state, you will usually have to file several documents that ask the court to grant a modification in the child support order. Be prepared to justify the changes you are asking for.

Self-help books are available in most states, and many states also have special programs for people representing themselves. You may also ask the American Bar Association to assist you in preparing the necessary court papers.

It's up to the mothers and fathers to act quickly when circumstances change to modify an existing child support order. If they don't, children can lose support they deserve, and paying parents can pile up debts they may never be able to pay off. Child support debts cannot be wiped out by bankruptcy or set aside by a court.

REFERENCE ————————————————————————————————
Nolo News, Spring 1993.

What can happen to you if you send a chain letter

Chain letters promising you big payoffs if you participate are illegal. Most ask you to send $5 to the top few names on a list, add your name to the bottom, and wait for the cash to come flowing in.

These letters are considered an illegal lottery because they aren't a chain, they're a pyramid, and somebody is going to lose money in the end.

If you get involved in a chain letter, nothing is likely to happen. You're not likely to earn any money, either.

But what could happen to you?

○ You could be fined up to $1,000.

○ You could be sentenced to two years in jail.

○ The postal service can direct the postmaster to inspect your mail and return to the sender any money you might receive.

Your best bet: Don't get involved.

REFERENCE ————————————————————————————————
The Family Legal Companion by Thomas Hauser, McGraw-Hill Book Co., New York, 1985.

Index

Vinegar
  as a cleaner 52
  for pet urine 290
Vitamin A
  cataract risk reduced by 417
Vitamin C
  cataract risk reduced by 417
  colon cancer risk lowered by 411
Vitamins
  immune system improved by 370
Voluntary-separation packages 217

W

W-4 form 196
Walking 252
  with a partner 255
Warranties 27
Washing machine 17
Waste disposer 49
Water
  in European countries 233
  reducing water bills 39
  testing bath temperature 433
  testing for hardness 49
Water alarm 433
WD-40
  for car batteries 82
  for drying out engine 76
  for frozen door locks 76
  to keep clocks running 47
  to prevent light bulbs from
    sticking 47
  to remove road tar 82
Weddings 323–334
  boss/co-workers 331
  bringing children 332
  cutting costs 333
  divorced parents 327
  invitations 332
  photographs 334
  second weddings 326
  stepparents 328
  thank-you notes 334
  what to wear 323
  who pays 329
Weight lifting 245
Weight-loss program 372
Wills 203
  dying intestate 203
  for a second marriage 205
  overruling 206
  probate court 207
Writer's block 456

Y

Yogurt mask 358